Bloom's Shakespeare Through the Ages

Bloom's Shakespeare Through the Ages

JULIUS CAESAR

Edited and with an introduction by
Harold Bloom
Sterling Professor of the Humanities
Yale University

Volume Editor
Pamela Loos

BLOOM'S
LITERARY CRITICISM
An imprint of Infobase Publishing

Bloom's Shakespeare Through the Ages: Julius Caesar

Copyright ©2008 by Infobase Publishing

Introduction ©2008 by Harold Bloom

Bloom's Literary Criticism
An imprint of Infobase Publishing
132 West 31st Street
New York NY 10001

Library of Congress Cataloging-in-Publication Data
Julius Caesar / edited and with an introduction by Harold Bloom ; volume editor, Pamela Loos.
    p. cm. — (Bloom's Shakespeare through the ages)
  Includes bibliographical references and index.
  ISBN-13: 978-0-7910-9593-5 (acid-free paper)
  ISBN-10: 0-7910-9593-2 (acid-free paper) 1. Shakespeare, William, 1564-1616. Julius Caesar. I. Bloom, Harold. II. Loos, Pamela. III. Shakespeare, William, 1564–1616. Julius Caesar.
  PR2808.A2B57 2007
  822.3'3—dc22   2007026814

Series design by Erika K. Arroyo
Cover design by Ben Peterson
Cover photo © The Granger Collection, New York

Printed in the United States of America

Bang EJB 10 9 8 7 6 5 4 3 2 1

This book is printed on acid-free paper.

CONTENTS

❧

SERIES INTRODUCTION

Shakespeare Through the Ages presents not the most current of Shakespeare criticism, but the best of Shakespeare criticism, from the seventeenth century to today. In the process, each volume also charts the flow over time of critical discussion of a particular play. Other useful and fascinating collections of historical Shakespearean criticism exist, but no collection that we know of contains such a range of commentary on each of Shakespeare's greatest plays and at the same time emphasizes the greatest critics in our literary tradition: from John Dryden in the seventeenth century, to Samuel Johnson in the eighteenth century, to William Hazlitt and Samuel Coleridge in the nineteenth century, to A.C. Bradley and William Empson in the twentieth century, to the most perceptive critics of our own day. This canon of Shakespearean criticism emphasizes aesthetic rather than political or social analysis.

Some of the pieces included here are full-length essays; others are excerpts designed to present a key point. Much (but not all) of the earliest criticism consists only of brief mentions of specific plays. In addition to the classics of criticism, some pieces of mainly historical importance have been included, often to provide background for important reactions from future critics.

These volumes are intended for students, particularly those just beginning their explorations of Shakespeare. We have therefore also included basic materials designed to provide a solid grounding in each play: a biography of Shakespeare, a synopsis of the play, a list of characters, and an explication of key passages. In addition, each selection of the criticism of a particular century begins with an introductory essay discussing the general nature of that century's commentary and the particular issues and controversies addressed by critics presented in the volume.

Shakespeare was "not of an age, but for all time," but much Shakespeare criticism is decidedly for its own age, of lasting importance only to the scholar who wrote it. Students today read the criticism most readily available to them, which means essays printed in recent books and journals, especially those journals made available on the Internet. Older criticism is too often buried in out-of-print books on forgotten shelves of libraries or in defunct periodicals. Therefore, many students, particularly younger students, have no way of knowing that some of the most profound criticism of Shakespeare's plays was written decades or centuries ago. We hope this series remedies that problem, and more importantly, we hope it infuses students with the enthusiasm of the critics in these volumes for the beauty and power of Shakespeare's plays.

INTRODUCTION BY HAROLD BLOOM

ᘒ

James Joyce, asked the question of which writer's works he would take with him to a desert island, replied that he would like to select Dante but would have to take Shakespeare, because he is *richer*. That extraordinary wealth of the creation of personalities by Shakespeare can blind the reader-playgoer to the most fascinating (for me) quality of Shakespearean art: the elliptical or leaving-out element. Why do we not see Antony and Cleopatra alone on stage together? How is it that Lear and Edmund never address a word to one another? Is the marriage of Othello and Desdemona consummated? What happens to Lear's Fool? Why does Shakespeare have Macbeth slain off-stage? What do we make of an undergraduate Hamlet in Act I, and a thirty-year old in Act V, a few weeks later? There are many other leavings-out, but these will suffice.

Shakespeare's source for *Julius Caesar* was North's translation of Plutarch's *Lives*. Plutarch tells us that Marcus Brutus was Caesar's illegitimate son, as was recognized by all in Rome, Brutus and Caesar included. Many in the audience had read Plutarch, or learned this fascinating gossip from one another. Shakespeare seems to ignore this in the play. Why? It certainly makes a difference. Hamlet does not know when the sexual relationship of Gertrude and Claudius began, nor do we. The Prince rarely says what he means or means what he says, but is that another cause for his delay in revenge? *Contra* Freud, there is no Oedipal aspect to this drama unless Hamlet fears that Claudius indeed may be his phallic father. There certainly is an Oedipal struggle in *Julius Caesar* even though Shakespeare allows it to be implicit.

Angus Fletcher, a great literary critic of my generation, remarks that what matters most in *Hamlet* is what doesn't happen. I would expand that observation to all of Shakespeare, even to *King Lear*. In *Julius Caesar* what does not happen is any confrontation between Brutus and his likely father. Only once do they share the stage alone together, in an amazingly banal exchange, which is subtly deliberate. Caesar asks Brutus the time of day, Brutus obliges, and is gravely thanked for his courtesy.

Surveying the criticism represented in this volume, from Ben Jonson through Dr. Samuel Johnson and on to Goethe, Hazlitt, Coleridge, Nietzsche, Wilson

Knight, Kenneth Burke, Frank Kermode and other distinguished hands, I find no realization among them of this ellipsis. And yet there are hints scattered throughout *Julius Caesar*, as I note in my book *Shakespeare: The Invention of the Human*. So sly was William Shakespeare that he allows his best auditors and readers the labor of assimilating the irony of what may constitute the deepest ambivalences and ambiguities in Brutus's motivations.

Admirable as everyone in the play finds Brutus to be (including Brutus) he is at least as flawed as great Caesar himself, who now is in decline. But Caesar's attitude towards danger is another extraordinary ellipsis in the play. Why are their no guards to protect Caesar? He is vainglorious, yet still a great realist, and he knows Cassius and some of the others are his enemies. I wonder if Shakespeare, endlessly subtle in his ironies, does not give us a Julius Caesar who courts assassination as a step towards becoming a god?

Dr. Johnson found this to be a *cold* play, missing the passions. Even the Grand Cham's misses are any other critic's palpable hits. Something is repressed throughout *Julius Caesar* and it could be one of several evasions. Brutus' desperate pride in his anti-tyrannical family heritage is overstressed by him because he cannot be certain as to whose family he belongs. Cassius, who keeps yielding to Brutus' wrong-headed tactics, loses because his own political and military skill is countermanded by Brutus' blunders. Brutus has inherited Caesar's pride but not the would-be monarch's brilliance at seeing that politics and war are the same enterprise. There are intimations that Cassius, allied to Brutus through Portia, is helpless to govern Brutus because of a homoerotic attachment to him, never expressed as such.

By tradition, this epitome of the "well-made" play is the tragedy of Brutus, and not of Caesar. As always, Shakespeare writes no genre, and therefore Johnson was not wholly off the track; this is too cold to be tragedy. Like *Coriolanus* and *Antony and Cleopatra*, this is no tragedy but a history-play, like the tetralogy *Richard II*, *Henry IV*, Parts I and II, *Henry V* which scholars call *The Henriad*. I myself prefer to title *Henry IV*'s two parts as *The Falstaffiad* since I join William Hazlitt and A.C. Bradley in judging Prince Hal/Henry V to be a Machiavelli, and a dark one at that. A.D. Nuttall whitewashes Hal/King Henry, but he remains what Hazlitt charmingly called "an amiable monster."

Nuttall is refreshingly free of the New Historicist delusion that Michel Foucault was more intelligent than William Shakespeare. There is no Falstaff to heat up *Julius Caesar* but Brutus seems to me closer to Henry V than he is to Hamlet. Shakespeare hardly wrote a major tragedy in Brutus' blunders, and yet I doubt if "tragedy" was Shakespeare's true mode, though here again I part from most Shakespearean scholarship. We never will catch up with Shakespeare, and that is his glory, or part of it.

BIOGRAPHY OF
WILLIAM SHAKESPEARE

WILLIAM SHAKESPEARE was born in Stratford-on-Avon in April 1564 into a family of some prominence. His father, John Shakespeare, was a glover and merchant of leather goods who earned enough to marry Mary Arden, the daughter of his father's landlord, in 1557. John Shakespeare was a prominent citizen in Stratford, and at one point, he served as an alderman and bailiff.

Shakespeare presumably attended the Stratford grammar school, where he would have received an education in Latin, but he did not go on to either Oxford or Cambridge universities. Little is recorded about Shakespeare's early life; indeed, the first record of his life after his christening is of his marriage to Anne Hathaway in 1582 in the church at Temple Grafton, near Stratford. He would have been required to obtain a special license from the bishop as security that there was no impediment to the marriage. Peter Alexander states in his book *Shakespeare's Life and Art* that marriage at this time in England required neither a church nor a priest or, for that matter, even a document—only a declaration of the contracting parties in the presence of witnesses. Thus, it was customary, though not mandatory, to follow the marriage with a church ceremony.

Little is known about William and Anne Shakespeare's marriage. Their first child, Susanna, was born in May 1583 and twins, Hamnet and Judith, in 1585. Later on, Susanna married Dr. John Hall, but the younger daughter, Judith, remained unmarried. When Hamnet died in Stratford in 1596, the boy was only 11 years old.

We have no record of Shakespeare's activities for the seven years after the birth of his twins, but by 1592 he was in London working as an actor. He was also apparently well known as a playwright, for reference is made of him by his contemporary Robert Greene in *A Groatsworth of Wit*, as "an upstart crow."

Several companies of actors were in London at this time. Shakespeare may have had connection with one or more of them before 1592, but we have no record that tells us definitely. However, we do know of his long association with the most famous and successful troupe, the Lord Chamberlain's Men. (When James I came to the throne in 1603, after Elizabeth's death, the troupe's name changed to the King's Men.) In 1599 the Lord Chamberlain's Men provided the financial backing for the construction of their own theater, the Globe.

The Globe was begun by a carpenter named James Burbage and finished by his two sons, Cuthbert and Robert. To escape the jurisdiction of the Corporation of London, which was composed of conservative Puritans who opposed the theater's "licentiousness," James Burbage built the Globe just outside London, in the Liberty of Holywell, beside Finsbury Fields. This also meant that the Globe was safer from the threats that lurked in London's crowded streets, like plague and other diseases, as well as rioting mobs. When James Burbage died in 1597, his sons completed the Globe's construction. Shakespeare played a vital role, financially and otherwise, in the construction of the theater, which was finally occupied sometime before May 16, 1599.

Shakespeare not only acted with the Globe's company of actors; he was also a shareholder and eventually became the troupe's most important playwright. The company included London's most famous actors, who inspired the creation of some of Shakespeare's best-known characters, such as Hamlet and Lear, as well as his clowns and fools.

In his early years, however, Shakespeare did not confine himself to the theater. He also composed some mythological-erotic poetry, such as *Venus and Adonis* and *The Rape of Lucrece*, both of which were dedicated to the earl of Southampton. Shakespeare was successful enough that in 1597 he was able to purchase his own home in Stratford, which he called New Place. He could even call himself a gentleman, for his father had been granted a coat of arms.

By 1598 Shakespeare had written some of his most famous works, *Romeo and Juliet, The Comedy of Errors, A Midsummer Night's Dream, The Merchant of Venice, Two Gentlemen of Verona,* and *Love's Labour's Lost,* as well as his historical plays *Richard II, Richard III, Henry IV,* and *King John.* Somewhere around the turn of the century, Shakespeare wrote his romantic comedies *As You Like It, Twelfth Night,* and *Much Ado About Nothing,* as well as *Henry V,* the last of his history plays in the Prince Hal series. During the next 10 years he wrote his great tragedies, *Hamlet, Macbeth, Othello, King Lear,* and *Antony and Cleopatra.*

At this time, the theater was burgeoning in London; the public took an avid interest in drama, the audiences were large, the plays demonstrated an enormous range of subjects, and playwrights competed for approval. By 1613, however, the rising tide of Puritanism had changed the theater. With the desertion of the theaters by the middle classes, the acting companies were compelled to depend more on the aristocracy, which also meant that they now had to cater to a more sophisticated audience.

Perhaps this change in London's artistic atmosphere contributed to Shakespeare's reasons for leaving London after 1612. His retirement from the theater is sometimes thought to be evidence that his artistic skills were waning. During this time, however, he wrote *The Tempest* and *Henry VIII.* He also wrote the "tragicomedies," *Pericles, Cymbeline*, and *The Winter's Tale*. These were thought to be inspired by Shakespeare's personal problems and have sometimes been considered proof of his greatly diminished abilities.

However, so far as biographical facts indicate, the circumstances of his life at this time do not imply any personal problems. He was in good health and financially secure, and he enjoyed an excellent reputation. Indeed, although he was settled in Stratford at this time, he made frequent visits to London, enjoying and participating in events at the royal court, directing rehearsals, and attending to other business matters.

In addition to his brilliant and enormous contributions to the theater, Shakespeare remained a poetic genius throughout the years, publishing a renowned and critically acclaimed sonnet cycle in 1609 (most of the sonnets were written many years earlier). Shakespeare's contribution to this popular poetic genre are all the more amazing in his break with contemporary notions of subject matter. Shakespeare idealized the beauty of man as an object of praise and devotion (rather than the Petrarchan tradition of the idealized, unattainable woman). In the same spirit of breaking with tradition, Shakespeare also treated themes previously considered off limits—the dark, sexual side of a woman as opposed to the Petrarchan ideal of a chaste and remote love object. He also expanded the sonnet's emotional range, including such emotions as delight, pride, shame, disgust, sadness, and fear.

When Shakespeare died in 1616, no collected edition of his works had ever been published, although some of his plays had been printed in separate unauthorized editions. (Some of these were taken from his manuscripts, some from the actors' prompt books, and others were reconstructed from memory by actors or spectators.) In 1623 two members of the King's Men, John Hemings and Henry Condell, published a collection of all the plays they considered to be authentic, the First Folio.

Included in the First Folio is a poem by Shakespeare's contemporary Ben Jonson, an outstanding playwright and critic in his own right. Jonson paid tribute to Shakespeare's genius, proclaiming his superiority to what previously had been held as the models for literary excellence—the Greek and Latin writers. "Triumph, my Britain, thou hast one to show / To whom all scenes of Europe homage owe. / He was not of an age, but for all time!"

Jonson was the first to state what has been said so many times since. Having captured what is permanent and universal to all human beings at all times, Shakespeare's genius continues to inspire us—and the critical debate about his works never ceases.

Summary of
Julius Caesar

❧

Act I

Act I opens with Flavius and Marullus, both tribunes (elected officials that represent the people in the Roman republic), on the streets of Rome, where commoners (working tradesmen) have gathered. The tribunes ask two tradesmen what is going on and why they are out in their best attire, rather than working. The men reward the tribunes' condescension with indirect answers, especially the cobbler, whose answers contain some puns that annoy the tribunes even more.

Eventually Flavius and Marullus learn that the men are out to pay tribute to Caesar, who has had a recent victory. They chastise the tradesmen for their quick reversal of loyalties: It was not so long ago that they cheered for Pompey's victory, but now they are ready to cheer Caesar's victory over Pompey's own sons. The tribunes then rebuke the men, saying that instead of encouraging Caesar they should be weeping in shame over their own faulty behavior. Flavius and Marullus advise them to leave, which they do, seemingly feeling guilty.

Flavius tells Marullus that they must take down any ornaments they see. Marullus questions this plan, since it also happens to be the Feast of Lupercal, a celebration of fertility. But Flavius is adamant and further insists that they disperse any other men they see assembling to praise Caesar. Doing both, he says, will keep Caesar from seeing himself as too extraordinary and will check his ability to "keep all in servile fearfulness."

Scene 1 is important for a number of reasons. It reveals, for instance, that there is a strong force, even within the government, that is against Caesar and afraid of his becoming too powerful. It gives the first glimpse of the commoners, who will play such a major role after Caesar's death. It also shows how readily changeable they are: Not only do they easily switch their allegiances from Pompey to Caesar, but when berated by the tribunes they appear to switch their allegiances yet again. At the same time, these malleable commoners are a great force, a fact the tribunes recognize. Finally, scene 1 demonstrates that the tribunes, while determined to avoid being controlled by a tyrant, are themselves willing to push around the populace.

In scene 2 Caesar appears on stage for the first time, surrounded by many others, en route to a race that is part of the holiday celebration. Antony is the only one of the group to be in the race, an early sign of his competitiveness and his view of himself as a winner. The first word comes from Caesar, who instructs his wife to stand in Antony's path during the race, so that he may touch her, which, as the elders teach, will rid her of her barrenness. The action points to a few things: Antony's strong physicality is contrasted with Calphurnia and Caesar's malfunctioning bodies (unable to have a baby); Caesar's power is immediately clear, for he tells others what to do and others speak as if they are his servants; and Caesar is superstitious. Superstition is again at the forefront when a man from the crowd cries out to Caesar, "Beware the ides of March" (March 15). Caesar makes a point of summoning this soothsayer, yet then dismisses him and his warning. The warning, of course, sets an ominous tone for the play.

All continue onward to watch the race, leaving Brutus and Cassius. Though ready to go to the event as well, Cassius stays behind when his close friend Brutus says he is not in the right spirit to go. Cassius says he has wondered what has been wrong with Brutus, who has not been his usual loving self but instead has kept his distance. Brutus assures him his behavior has nothing to do with his feelings for his friends but with an internal battle. Brutus sees that something is on Cassius's mind as well. Before Cassius can explain, the men hear trumpets and shouting and Brutus says he fears Caesar has been made king.

Cassius makes the most of this comment, launching into his reasoning on how Caesar has unjustly become a powerful figure. Cassius begins with stories of Caesar's physical weakness. He relates how the man nearly drowned and Cassius saved him and describes how sickly Caesar was when struck with illness. Again the men hear a commotion. Cassius then questions how Caesar has any more right to greatness than Brutus or Cassius; in Rome's history, he says, no man has had such power. Further invoking history, Cassius recalls another Brutus, who helped found the republic of Rome expressly to ensure that no single man became too powerful.

Brutus says he will think about Cassius's words. Again he is distracted when he sees Caesar and his men coming near them; based on their looks, Brutus says, he knows something bad must have happened. The audience is held in suspense here: Instead of an explanation of what has happened, the next exchange is a conversation between Antony and Caesar in which Caesar tells Antony why Cassius should be feared. (See commentary on these lines in the section of this book called "Key Passages in *Julius Caesar*.")

The audience does not get to hear how Antony responds to Caesar's comments. Rather, the focus returns to Brutus and Cassius, who have asked Casca to tell them what made Caesar and the others look so troubled. With a good amount of questioning, Brutus and Cassius finally learn that Caesar was offered the crown three times, that each time he seemed more reluctant to let it go, and that the crowd finally rejoiced in his refusal, causing Caesar to faint. They also hear that Marullus and Flavius were "put to silence" because they removed the ornamentation from Caesar's images—meaning they either lost their posts, were exiled, or were killed. Again, the uncertainty is ominous. What really happened to the tribunes? And who ordered the action against Marullus and Flavius? If it was Caesar, this demonstrates his power. The question is whether he is as dangerous as Cassius, Marullus, and Flavius have warned.

The scene ends with Cassius arranging to meet again with Brutus and Casca. Then Cassius, alone on stage, remarks how easily Brutus can be swayed. Cassius knows he needs Brutus to be involved in the murder of Caesar because of the public's love and respect for Brutus. As a result, Cassius plans to play on Brutus's sense of public duty and to flatter him by reminding him of the people's admiration for him.

Scene 3 opens with thunder and lightning. Casca, breathless and shaken, meets Cicero in the street and tells him of strange and horrific recent events: Fire has fallen from the sky; a man's hand burned and yet was left unharmed; and women say they saw men on fire. Casca believes these occurrences are portents that either the gods are fighting among themselves or they are angry at how men on earth are behaving. Cicero agrees that the events are strange, but he remarks that men decide how to read such things and do not always read them properly. Casca does not absorb this apparent warning.

Cicero bids Casca good night, adding that they should not be out in this weather. Cassius appears, and Casca again mentions the storm. Cassius, in contrast to Cicero, describes the weather as something to be confronted. Not only has he been walking in it, he says, but he has left his doublet open while doing so. Casca declares this a mistake: Men should fear the gods at this point. But Cassius suggests that all these strange occurrences are a warning against a man that has become too powerful and ominous. Guessing that Cassius is speaking of Caesar, Casca reports the rumor that the senators will make Caesar king on the following day. Despite Cicero's warning, Casca accepts Cassius's reading of the strange occurrences.

Cassius says that Caesar has become a tyrant only because he believes the Romans are weak—that the Romans have put themselves in these straits. Casca agrees to help Cassius fix matters, and only then does Cassius tell him he has already spoken with some of "the noblest-minded Romans" to rectify the situation, albeit in a "most bloody, fiery, and most terrible" way. Cinna enters and tells Cassius the other conspirators are waiting for him. He implores Cassius to convince "the noble Brutus" to take part in the plan. Of course, Cassius already realizes the importance of Brutus's involvement. Cassius sends Cinna off to plant fake letters where Brutus will find them. The letters appear to be written by a number of concerned citizens, and Brutus will read them, be flattered, and feel he must answer the will of the people and set Rome right. Even though Casca has not appeared very intelligent, he, too, voices the necessity of Brutus's involvement in the conspiracy. If Brutus is involved, says Casca, a most horrible deed "will change to virtue and to worthiness."

Act II

Brutus enters his garden, calling for his servant Lucius, as Act II opens. The soundly sleeping servant finally awakens and finds that his master wants him to light a candle. When the servant goes off, Brutus speaks to himself of the advantages and disadvantages of killing Caesar. First saying Caesar must be killed, Brutus admits he knows no personal reason to be against him. The question, he believes, is how Caesar might be changed if he gains the crown. Brutus continues to debate with himself and reflects that most people scorn the underlings they leave behind when they gain power. He finally decides that Caesar will do this too and that, therefore, he must be killed before he ever reaches his full, dangerous potential.

Lucius enters again and tells Brutus he has found some notes inside Brutus's study, near the window. Brutus turns his attention to these notes, which he does not know Cassius has had planted there. As Brutus opens the letters, he comments that he does not even need the candle to read them because it is so bright from the meteors flying through the night sky—yet another sign that nature is in an abnormal state.

The letters push Brutus to a decision: He must help save Rome. Again Lucius appears, at a critical moment. The two hear a knock at the door, and the audience knows that at this very late hour, it must have something to do with the conspiracy or some other grave matter. As Lucius goes to the door, Brutus talks of the internal struggle that has plagued him ever since Cassius first spoke to him against Caesar. He feels like he is in a horrific dream as he awaits the killing, which he refers to as "a dreadful thing."

Lucius returns and tells Brutus that Cassius is at the door with other men, whom he does not recognize since their faces are covered. Brutus tells Lucius to let them in. In his short moment alone, Brutus reflects that the conspirators must feel ashamed that even at night they keep themselves covered. Cassius enters with the men and introduces them; Brutus gives each one a personal welcome and then Cassius speaks to Brutus privately. The fellow conspirators wait for the two men to return to the group, as does the audience. As they wait, the men make small talk about the sunrise. But each believes the sun is rising in a different place, a circumstance showing their disconnect with the natural world. Already many unusual and disturbing events have occurred. While in those instances nature was wreaking havoc, apparently as a sign of warning against the murder that is yet to come, in this case nature is just acting naturally, and again the conspirators are not in sync with it.

Brutus and Cassius return to the group. Brutus asks for each of the conspirators' hands, but when Cassius says they should make an oath, Brutus objects in a long speech arguing that they do not need an oath because they are Romans and are doing what is needed. The men do not verbally respond to Brutus's words, but they do not take an oath. They then turn to practical matters. Cassius says they should have Cicero join the conspiracy; others agree, but when Brutus disagrees because he believes Cicero will pose problems, the others give in. Next they consider whether Antony should be killed as well as Caesar. Cassius argues in favor of this; Brutus is against it, believing such an act would make the conspirators look worse and that Antony will not create trouble if left alive. In this case, Cassius attempts to convince Brutus that Antony must go, but Brutus cuts him off and another conspirator agrees with Brutus. The idea of killing Antony is dropped.

Two more points are brought up. First, there is concern that Caesar may not even go to the Capitol, but Cassius says they will all go to his home to make sure he leaves it. Another conspirator, Metellus, asks if they should enlist Caius Ligarius in their cause. Brutus says this is a good idea and tells Metellus to summon him so Brutus can convince him to join. This shows Brutus's decision to be a conspirator is indeed definite; now the previously undecided Brutus is the one who will be convincing another to join in their plan. First Cassius and then Brutus say good-bye to the men, reminding them to be "true Romans."

After the men are gone, Portia appears. She asks what is bothering Brutus, saying he has not been himself for some time. She rejects his excuse that he is ill; that answer does not make sense, she says. Down on her knees, Portia asks Brutus to tell her the truth about what is wrong. She asks, too, who the men were that came to their home with their faces hidden. She reminds him that while she is only a woman she is the daughter of an important man and so is stronger than most. She reveals that she has even gone so far as to harm herself to show how strong she is. Brutus's distress is interrupted by someone knocking. He tells Portia he will let her know everything, but first he will find out who it is at the door.

The visitor is Caius Ligarius, whom Brutus said he would convince to join the conspirators. Caius considers Brutus so honorable, he says, that he will do anything to help Brutus. The two go off, with thunder sounding.

Thunder and lightning continue in scene 2, at Caesar's house. Caesar appears in his night attire, saying he heard his wife cry out three times that Caesar is being murdered. He sends his servant to the priests for their predictions of what is to happen. When Calphurnia enters she tells Caesar he must not leave the house that day, he says he will. Calphurnia tells him the frightening omens the night watchmen have observed, but they do not discourage Caesar: These signs, he says, need not mean something bad is going to happen to him. At this his wife reminds him that nothing out of the ordinary happens when a beggar dies, only when someone significant does. Caesar counters that he does not fear death, a necessary part of life.

The servant returns and tells husband and wife that the priests say Caesar should not leave the house. Caesar stubbornly insists he will not be a coward. Now dropping to her knees, Calphurnia begs him to heed her, just as Portia had done in the earlier scene. As in that scene, here the husband gives in to his wife. He says he will stay home after all.

Decius Brutus arrives to escort Caesar to the senate. When he hears that Caesar has decided not to go because of Calphurnia's dream, which Caesar relates to him, Brutus reinterprets the dream. Decius explains how the dream is actually quite positive and says that Caesar must go, because the senate has decided to crown him; they must not hear he is staying home because of foolish fears. Convinced, Caesar calls for his day clothes. The other conspirators arrive, and Caesar speaks kindly to them all. Brutus, in an aside, remarks on the sad fact that the very men who seem like Caesar's friends are actually enemies.

Scene 3 occurs near the capitol. Artemidorus, in the street, reads a letter he plans to give to Caesar as he passes by. It warns Caesar of all the conspirators.

Scene 4 takes place in another part of the street. Portia is here, panicky, with the servant Lucius. She is so distraught she cannot even clearly tell the servant what she wants him to do. It becomes apparent that Brutus has told her his secret. A soothsayer comes near and Portia asks him if he has news for Caesar. He will try to talk with him as he comes by, the soothsayer says, since he fears Caesar may be harmed today. Portia is extremely upset and feels faint. She sends the boy off to Brutus to see how he is.

Act III

Caesar, the conspirators, and Antony make their way to the capitol building as Act III opens. Along the way, Caesar sees the soothsayer and with some bravado tells him it is the ides of March, implying that the soothsayer's warning had no merit since nothing bad has happened. The soothsayer responds that the day is not over yet. Artemidorus, intent on warning Caesar of danger, also addresses him in the street. Caesar must read his scroll before addressing any other matters, Artemidorus says, because it is of more concern to Caesar. Believing he is acting nobly, Caesar responds that his concerns should not be addressed before those of others. Artemidorus is insistent, but Caesar and others push him away. Tension builds as the audience sees that the two influences that could have thwarted the murder now appear powerless to stop it.

But an unexpected event suddenly suggests the plot will go awry: Popilius approaches Cassius and says he hopes his plan goes well, then walks away. Cassius immediately is concerned and tells Brutus what happened. As they watch Popilius approach Caesar, Cassius asks Brutus what they should do, because Popilius may very well be telling Caesar about the plot. Brutus tells him to stay calm; he sees that Caesar does not look upset by what Popilius has said, so Popilius must not have revealed anything about the plot after all.

Now the plan moves along smoothly, as various conspirators perform their parts leading up to the murder. An ironic and unnerving question then sounds: Caesar asks if all are ready. Caesar is referring to senate business; the same question, however, could easily have been posed by one of the lead conspirators in reference to the killing.

Metellus approaches Caesar, kneeling before him to make a request. Before Metellus even voices his request, however, Caesar says he will not be swayed by Metellus's fawning. Caesar reminds him that long-established rules must be followed and insists that he is not like other weak men who are easily changeable. Despite the strong words, Metellus asks if any others will help him plead for his brother's release from exile. Brutus and Cassius do so. Caesar is surprised Brutus has gotten involved, but still he will not give in. Caesar compares himself to the North Star because of his fixedness; he says he is the only man who remains so constant. The conspirators clamor about Caesar, calling for him to reconsider. He dismisses their entreaties, remarking that he rejected even Brutus's plea on the matter.

Casca then stabs Caesar, and the other conspirators stab him as well. Caesar sees that even Brutus has been in on the murder, and, just before he dies, utters his now-famous reproach, "Et tu, Brute?" ("You too, Brutus?") While the conspirators are elated that Caesar is dead, believing they are now liberated from a tyrant, the senators and other witnesses are afraid. Two conspirators advise Brutus and Cassius to speak to the crowd. It appears that the conspirators had not planned what to do after the murder.

Thoughtfully, Brutus asks where Publius is. Publius is an old senator who cannot readily flee, and he may believe the conspirators will harm him. Brutus assures Publius that they will not. Yet Brutus remains unconcerned about what may happen next, whereas Metellus and Cassius both realize the conspirators are in danger. The scope of the chaos becomes clear when Trebonius says Antony has run off and that "Men, wives, and children stare, cry out and run, / As it were doomsday." Now Brutus recognizes that the conspirators could be killed. Still certain they have done the right thing, he tells the others they must cover their arms and swords in Caesar's blood, go out to the crowds, and cry out "Peace, freedom, and liberty!" Cassius, too, becomes enamored with the idea and speaks of their action as a historic reclamation of liberty.

Before the audience can see how the crowds will react to such further bloody spectacle, Antony's servant appears, drops to his knees as his master has ordered, and gives Antony's message to the conspirators: that Antony loves Brutus, that he loved Caesar, and that he wants to speak with the conspirators in safety, to find out why they took such a drastic measure against Caesar. Upon learning this, the servant says, Antony will remain faithful to Brutus.

Brutus appears grateful and tells the servant to bring Antony. Cassius, however, warns Brutus that Antony should not be trusted. Before Brutus can respond, Antony enters and immediately cries out over Caesar's body, saying all the glory has been reduced to this. He turns to the conspirators and says if they are to kill him, now is the time he would be most ready.

Brutus assures Antony they do not want to kill him, explains why they killed Caesar, and welcomes him. Antony shakes the hand of each conspirator but says he now is in the awkward position of being either a coward or a flatterer. He speaks to the spirit of Caesar, believing the dead man must be upset to see Antony with his killers. When he praises Caesar, too, Cassius bluntly asks if he will be on their side or not. Antony repeats his need for an explanation of why the murder was necessary and then asks to speak to the people with Caesar's body at his side. Brutus readily assents. Cassius draws him aside and warns him this is dangerous, but Brutus disagrees. He says Antony's speech will do them more good than harm because Brutus will speak to the crowd first and let them know the conspirators gave Antony permission to speak. Though Cassius still protests, Brutus tells Antony he can speak but that in his oration he is not to blame the conspirators for their action, only to say good things about Caesar.

The conspirators exit, leaving Antony alone with the dead man. Again he speaks to Caesar's body, apologizing for his cordial behavior to the conspirators and laying out his true perspective. He plans not only to get the most horrific revenge but also to raise complete chaos, and he is confident that Caesar's spirit will join in the mission.

Octavius Caesar's servant enters and cries out when he sees Caesar's body; Antony, too, is again stricken with sorrow. He tells the servant to stay and see what happens when he addresses the masses. It is evident that Antony, knowing the power of the common people, is looking to manipulate them.

Scene 2 opens in the forum, as Brutus and Cassius each move to different pulpits to explain to the crowd why they killed Caesar. The crowds yell that they demand an explanation and grow quiet when they see Brutus, whom someone calls "noble Brutus," ascend the pulpit. Brutus says that he had great love for Caesar but an even greater love for Rome and for keeping it free. He uses rhetorical questions to get the people to understand his perspective and to make the conspirators look favorable. For instance, Brutus asks, "Had you rather Caesar were living, and die all slaves, than that Caesar were dead, to live all free men?"

The assembled people believe Brutus was right in his decision. Before he leaves the people, Brutus assures them that if circumstances ever reached the point where his country would be better off without him, he would be ready to die for it. They admire Brutus even more than they did before. They propose erecting a statue of him, carrying him home like a hero, and—most ironically—crowning him. It is thus evident that they do not really understand Brutus's view that no one person should have control over the people. Brutus quiets the crowd and tells them they must listen to all that Antony has to say.

Throughout his speech Antony refers to Brutus and the conspirators as honorable men but also describes what made Caesar so good. He says that Caesar, through his victories against enemies, amassed much money for the treasury; he cried when the poor suffered; and he turned down the crown when it was offered to him three times. How, Antony asks, was this ambition? Then he says he must turn away from the crowd because he is so overcome with emotion. The assembled people respond with mixed reactions, unsure whether to go along with Antony's reasoning.

Antony starts to speak again. He tells the people he has found Caesar's will and if they knew what it said they would realize how great Caesar truly was. The crowd, of course, calls for Antony to read the will, but Antony says he will not read it: It will only madden them to know they are his heirs. Again the crowd calls for Antony to read the will, and again he stalls. The people begin to yell that the conspirators are far from honorable but rather are "villains, murderers!" There is more shouting for Antony to read the will; still he stalls.

Riling the crowd more, Antony steps down from the pulpit and draws everyone's attention to Caesar's corpse. Antony warns them, "If you have tears, prepare to shed them now." He looks at each gash in the corpse and speaks of the men who put the gashes there, leaving for last Brutus, the man that he says Caesar loved and who therefore "burst his [Caesar's] mighty heart" when he saw that Brutus was one of the conspirators. Antony calls the murder treason, a blow not only to Caesar but to all. The people are now completely in his grip, yelling out against the conspirators and for revenge: "Burn! Fire! Kill! Slay! Let not a traitor live!"

Antony's listeners are ready to cause massive destruction, but he stops them. Again saying the conspirators are honorable, he credits Brutus as such a better speaker than he that if Antony and Brutus were to trade places, Brutus would have indeed inspired the people to mutiny. This statement only whips the crowd into even greater frenzy—as Antony intends. The people agree that mutiny is what is needed and are ready to run off when Antony stops them again, reminding them that they still have not heard the will. They cry out for him to read it, and he does. He reads that Caesar has left money to each citizen and also has left them parks, gardens, arbors, and other places of recreation. At this, the crowd rings with shouts, and the people set off to cause great destruction. Antony takes pleasure in this manipulation.

Octavius's servant enters and tells Antony that Octavius is already in Rome with Lepidus. He says that Brutus and Cassius have fled.

In scene 3 Cinna, a poet, is in the street, recalling to himself a dream he had the night before. In the dream Cinna was feasting with Caesar; he feels uneasy in light of Caesar's murder. Several members of the crowd accost

Cinna, demanding to know where he is going, where he lives, and the like. He says he is going to Caesar's funeral, as a friend. But when he says his name, a man in the crowd yells that Cinna was one of the conspirators. Cinna says he has the same name as a conspirator but that he is Cinna the poet. The men do not care, however; they attack him and then head off to burn the conspirators' homes.

Act IV

Scene 1 opens to a meeting of Antony, Octavius Caesar, and Lepidus. The end of the previous act had shown the evil of the crowd being unleashed; here evil continues as the three men deliberate over whom they must kill. As each name is brought up, the men consent to that person's murder, despite the fact that some of those named are actually the men's kin.

Antony asks Lepidus to get Caesar's will so that they can alter it to direct less money to the people, as Caesar had earmarked, and more for their own use. While Lepidus is gone, Antony declares him unworthy of becoming one of the new rulers alongside himself and Octavius. Octavius wonders, then, why Antony had the man join in the decisions of whom to kill. Antony replies that Lepidus is like a dumb animal: He will work and be useful but can offer little more, and they should be rid of him when the work is done. Antony observes that Brutus and Cassius have already gathered their troops, and he says they must do likewise and make their own war plans. Octavius agrees and says they are already in danger, because it is unclear who truly is on their side.

In scene 2, loyalties are again questioned, but this time the subject is the loyalty between Brutus and Cassius. Brutus, accompanied by Lucilius and Lucius, is at a camp near Sardis with his troops. Cassius's servant arrives to announce that Cassius is coming to meet Brutus. Brutus talks to Lucilius; Brutus is disturbed at how Cassius has been acting and asks Lucilius what happened when he last saw him. Lucilius says meeting was cordial, not as warm as usual, and from that Brutus assumes something is wrong. Cassius arrives and his first words are an accusation against Brutus. Brutus says Cassius must be calm and that they should talk inside Brutus's tent rather than let their armies see that there is a problem between the men.

In scene 3, inside the tent, Cassius immediately says Brutus has wronged him: Brutus has condemned a man for taking bribes even though Cassius had asked him not to. Cassius's logic is that some flaws must be overlooked during these difficult times. But Brutus disagrees. Moreover, he points out Cassius's own flaw of being mercenary. This only makes Cassius angrier, but Brutus is quick to remind him of the noble reasons they had for destroying Caesar; morality, he says, must not now be compromised. Their argument intensifies, with Cassius making threats and protesting his poor treatment and Brutus declaring he should not have to put up with Cassius's quick temper.

Brutus also faults Cassius for denying Brutus's request for money to pay his men. Cassius says Brutus was given the wrong message, since Cassius never said he would not give the money. The arguing continues. Cassius, in abject frustration, offers Brutus his dagger to slash through Cassius's chest, just as Brutus slashed Caesar; even when Brutus felt the worst toward Caesar, Cassius says, Brutus must have loved him more than he ever loved Cassius. Brutus tells him to put the dagger away and concedes that he shall accept Cassius's anger as part of his disposition. Cassius admits he is in poor spirits, and Brutus acknowledges he is as well. Cassius recognizes that his temperament is much to endure, but Brutus says he can bear it. The two are interrupted by a poet who tells them they must stay good friends. Cassius takes the interruption in stride; Brutus is antagonized. The man leaves.

Cassius says he did not think Brutus could get so angry, and Brutus says he is "sick of many griefs." He tells Cassius that Portia has killed herself. Cassius is shocked and also surprised that Brutus is not in a worse state. Brutus says Portia could not stand his absence and killed herself in a most horrific manner; she "swallowed fire." When he learned of her death, Brutus says, he also learned of the great forces Octavius and Antony were amassing against Cassius and him. Cassius is very upset over the news of Portia; Brutus says they should stop talking of Portia. He takes his wine and dismisses his argument with Cassius, saying, "In this I bury all unkindness, Cassius."

Titinius and Messala enter to speak of their news and the upcoming war. Brutus compares his notes with theirs and finds they too have word that Antony and Octavius are coming to them with a great army. They also have heard that Antony, Lepidus, and Octavius have put senators to death. Messala reports that 100 senators have died and Brutus says he has heard 70 have died; whichever is correct, this act of pure brutality has occurred in a short period of time.

Messala also asks Brutus if he has heard news of Portia. (Some scholars have said that the conversation that occurs here about Portia was originally the only conversation about Portia's death in the play. They say that Shakespeare later changed the play so that the conversation between Brutus and Cassius, wherein Brutus is less stoic than he is with Messala, was the only one about Portia's death but that the printer of the text included both versions by mistake.) Messala does not want to tell the news of Portia's death but Brutus forces him to. When Brutus hears it, he hardly responds and says he has thought about her dying before and that this gives him the ability to handle it now. Messala and especially Cassius say they expect him to be more emotional. He responds that since they are living they must focus on the task at hand, which is the upcoming war.

Brutus asks the men if they should march to meet Antony and Octavius's men at Philippi. Cassius says he thinks they should not, that it is better to make the enemy travel to them and wear themselves out along the way. Brutus sees matters differently, noting that the people between themselves and Philippi are on the side of Antony and Octavius, which means the enemy's army would pick up new recruits and greater momentum as they advanced. Cassius begins to repeat his dissent, but Brutus argues that the time is ripe for them to act; they should move their men to Philippi. Cassius then agrees, and the men say good night.

Brutus asks Lucius to play some music for him. Brutus sees how tired Lucius is and calls Varro and Claudius into his tent, telling them to sleep there in case he must send them off to Cassius with a message during the night. The men propose to stay awake with Brutus, but he tells them they must sleep because he may not need to send them off anyway. They settle in, and Brutus finds in his pocket a book he had been looking for. Brutus and Lucius comment that since Brutus has not been himself, it is not surprising that he had forgotten where he had put it. Brutus cannot sleep and again asks Lucius to play some music. Brutus realizes his servant is tired but says he will not keep him long and adds, "If I do live, I will be good to thee." This remark reveals why Brutus is restless and distracted: He is concerned that the war may go poorly for him and his men.

Lucius succumbs to sleep in the middle of playing, and Brutus decides he will let him sleep while he just reads. He sees someone and addresses the figure, calling it a "monstrous apparition." The figure says it is "thy evil spirit" and that Brutus will see it again at Philippi. It disappears. Brutus is frightened and wakes everyone in the tent. He asks each servant why he cried out and what he saw, but they all report that they did not cry out and that they saw nothing. Brutus sends Varro and Claudius off to tell Cassius that he and his men should start advancing early and that Brutus and his men will follow.

Act V

Octavius and Antony at are Philippi with their army as scene 1 opens. They know now that Brutus and Cassius are headed toward them with their army. Octavius sees this as an advantage, since it means Brutus and Cassius no longer are on higher ground. This battle planning scene contrasts with the earlier one, where Brutus considered moving in a favorable plan, while Cassius did not but gave in. Here Octavius and Antony both see Brutus and Cassius's move as positive to them, although Antony had not anticipated it. Antony says Brutus and Cassius's move is one of pretended bravery.

A messenger comes to tell Octavius and Antony that they must do something, since the army is approaching. They seem to have no fear of the battle. One slight disagreement over tactics arises. Antony asks why Octavius would go against him at this very moment of crisis, a sign that Antony may not be as confident as he had appeared. But Octavius gives in to Antony's plan and the two move forward. In fact, a few lines later Octavius asks Antony what they should do, seeming to show that he is ready to follow Antony.

Antony, Octavius, Brutus, and Cassius meet in the field and exchange insults. Antony says how despicable he finds his enemies because of their villainy against Caesar; they pretended to be subservient to Caesar and in the next moment unleashed their violence upon him. Cassius yells back at Antony. He also reminds Brutus that Antony would now be dead and their current circumstances much more favorable if Cassius had had his way. Indeed, killing Antony along with Caesar was only one of several recommendations that Cassius made and Brutus rejected, with disastrous consequences.

Octavius draws his sword and says they should get to the business of avenging Caesar's death. Though he may die fighting the conspirators, he will not give up the fight. Octavius and Brutus exhibit their exalted self-images when Octavius says he was not destined to be killed by Brutus and Brutus replies that it would be the most honorable death. Cassius goes back to spewing out names at his enemies, and Octavius says they will let Brutus and Cassius decide if, in fact, they want to fight this day. Octavius, Antony, and their army leave.

Cassius tells Messala that while he generally is not superstitious, he has noticed that the two great eagles that were flying along with the men have left and scavenger birds have taken their place. He sees this as a sign of doom, an indication that their men will soon be dead.

Brutus enters the conversation. Cassius speaks positively of the task ahead of them but then asks Brutus what he will do if they lose. Brutus responds that he will not commit suicide because he considers it cowardly. Cassius presses, then, and asks what Brutus will do if their enemies try to take him prisoner. Brutus's strong self-image is clear here as he says he will never be a prisoner; however, he still does not explain what he will do if the enemies attempt to make him a prisoner. There is a sense of impending doom. Both men say good-bye as if for the last time.

Scene 2 is only a brief moment on the battlefield. Brutus gives Messala orders to take to Cassius. Cassius is to move in on Octavius, since Brutus sees Octavius's wing of his army weakening.

Scene 3 takes place on another part of the battlefield. Cassius and Titinius are talking about the sorry state of affairs for their army. Some men have deserted, and Brutus has left Cassius's men to fend for themselves against Antony's men, while Brutus's men are looting after having overpowered Octavius's men.

Pindarus arrives and tells the men that Antony is coming closer. The men believe they see fire by Cassius's tents. Cassius dispatches Titinius to find out what is happening and sends Pindarus up a hill to watch. As Pindarus moves into position, Cassius thinks aloud that this day, his birthday, may very well be his last. Interrupting Cassius's thoughts, Pindarus reports what he sees: Titinius is surrounded, he says; he is captured and the men who have taken him shout for joy. Cassius is crushed that his best friend is gone. He summons Pindarus down from the hill. Cassius recalls the day he took Pindarus prisoner and saved his life, when Pindarus had sworn to be Cassius's servant and do whatever he asked. Cassius now asks Pindarus to take his sword, the very one Cassius used on Caesar, and kill him. He tells Pindarus that then he will be a free man. Pindarus agrees, Cassius dies, and Pindarus runs before he can be captured.

Titinius and Messala arrive. Titinius says he knows Cassius will be happy to hear of Brutus's victory over Octavius. They look for Cassius and Pindarus and see Cassius dead on the ground. Titinius mourns Cassius; he says they are now in great danger and that Cassius died because he felt that Titinius could not carry out his orders. Messala says he must tell Brutus and leaves to do so. Titinius speaks to himself, revealing to the audience what really happened when he went off to Cassius's tents. It was not Antony's men that were there, but Brutus's. They enthusiastically surrounded Titinius, gave him a victory wreath to take back to Cassius, and cheered over their win. Now Titinius places the wreath on Cassius. He then kills himself with Cassius's sword.

Brutus, having heard of Cassius's death, arrives with some of his men. He sees Cassius and also Titinius lying dead, and he shouts to Julius Caesar, whose spirit, he says, has caused these deaths. Brutus pays tribute to the two men, says he will have to shed his tears later; they must return to the battlefield.

Scene 4 takes place in the midst of battle. Lucilius tells the enemy that he is Brutus, and young Cato is killed. An enemy is ready to kill Lucilius, who continues to act as Brutus. The soldier, believing he is Brutus, decides it is best to take him prisoner. Antony arrives and sees that the prisoner is not Brutus but is still a good man that they should keep as a prisoner. Antony sends his men to look for Brutus and goes off to Octavius's tent.

In scene 5 Brutus is with some of his men on the battlefield. Brutus privately asks first one, then another of his men to help him put himself to death. Each refuses. Brutus then asks the same of Volumnius, an old school friend of his; Brutus explains that Caesar has appeared to him twice and he knows it is time for his death, but Volumnius wants no part of it. Clitus arrives and says the men must leave immediately.

Brutus bids good-bye to all, even to Strato, who has been asleep. Brutus says his end is near but that he still shall have more glory than Octavius and Mark Antony will have by winning against those who prevented tyranny. Clitus again calls for all to flee. Brutus tells them to go, saying he will follow. He asks his servant Strato to stay with him, and the others exit. Brutus requests that Strato hold Brutus's sword while he runs on it. Strato first asks for Brutus's hand and says good-bye, treating Brutus nobly to the end. Brutus pushes himself on the sword, saying Caesar can now be at rest. He dies.

Antony, Octavius, their army, Messala, and Lucilius enter. They see Strato and he explains that Brutus has killed himself so that no one else should have the honor of taking his life. Octavius says he will take into service those men who had been with Brutus. Antony describes Brutus as "the noblest Roman of them all," different from the others since he actually killed Caesar because he believed it was for the good of all. He calls Brutus a great man. Octavius has the last word. He says Brutus's body will lie in Octavius's tent and be treated with the greatest honor. Octavius appears more practical and businesslike whereas Antony appears more emotional. Octavius says the men must all rest; what will happen next now that the noblest has died and the ruthless are in charge is unclear.

KEY PASSAGES
IN *JULIUS CAESAR*

૪๑

Act I, ii, 192–214

Caesar: Let me have men about me that are fat,
Sleek-headed men, and such as sleep a-nights.
Yond Cassius has a lean and hungry look;
He thinks too much: such men are dangerous.

Antony: Fear him not, Caesar, he's not dangerous.
He is a noble Roman, and well given.

Caesar: Would he were fatter! But I fear him not.
Yet if my name were liable to fear,
I do not know the man I should avoid
So soon as that spare Cassius. He reads much,
He is a great observer, and he looks
Quite through the deeds of men. He loves no plays,
As thou dost, Antony; he hears no music;
Seldom he smiles, and smiles in such a sort
As if he mocked himself, and scorned his spirit
That could be moved to smile at anything.
Such men as he be never at heart's ease
Whiles they behold a greater than themselves,
And therefore are they very dangerous.
I rather tell thee what is to be feared
Than what I fear; for always I am Caesar.
Come on my right hand, for this ear is deaf,
And tell me truly what thou think'st of him.

Caesar and Antony exchange these words soon after a series of dramatic events, in which Caesar was offered the crown, turned it down, offered to let himself be killed if that was what the crowd truly desired, and then fell in a faint. In short, Caesar has just undergone an intense exchange with the people and has seen that they are not ready to give him any more power. As Caesar is leaving the people, he passes Cassius and Brutus. Cassius has just been trying to convince Brutus that Caesar is too ambitious and must be put to death. It is as if Caesar has a keen sixth sense; he is very conscious of Cassius being dangerous and voices his mistrust of Cassius to Antony, his confidant. Perhaps because Caesar had not anticipated the crowd's negative response, he now is very conscious of just who else may be against him.

In this passage, Caesar voices his apprehension about Cassius, but Antony quickly dismisses his concern. Caesar then gives a longer explanation about why he thinks Cassius is dangerous, and after that asks Antony what he thinks. Apparently Caesar thinks Antony may now be convinced of his perspective; at the very least, Caesar wants Antony to think about Cassius more. The audience does not get to hear, though, how Antony responds. Antony's later actions—specifically, manipulating Brutus into letting him speak to the crowd and manipulating the crowd against the conspirators—show his keen understanding of people, so it is somewhat surprising that Antony has no suspicions about Cassius. Perhaps after Caesar prompts him further, Antony does reveal some.

Just what disturbs Caesar about Cassius? Caesar says Cassius is dangerous because he is "lean" and "hungry"; that is, Caesar believes Cassius has great desires. He considers Cassius in some way ambitious, like Caesar himself. Caesar says Cassius's discontentedness comes from seeing others who are "greater than" himself. In other words Caesar, with his inflated ego, considers Cassius a threat not to just anyone, but only to someone like himself.

Another complaint Caesar voices is that Cassius "is a great observer" who sees the hidden motives of men's actions. Given that, at this moment in the play, Caesar is carefully observing Cassius and his motives, it appears that Caesar considers Cassius too like himself for comfort. Caesar also charges that Cassius "thinks too much" and "reads much," rather than enjoying plays and music like other men. These comments suggest that Caesar prefers to be surrounded by people who are less serious and less studious. This may indicate that Caesar can be intimidated and is not as confident about himself as circumstances might suggest.

Caesar's desire to always appear invincible is apparent here, too. Even as he explains why Cassius is dangerous, he makes a point of saying that he does not fear Cassius, since Caesar fears nothing; even to a confidant, Caesar tries to project invulnerability. He nonetheless appears physically vulnerable by the end of his speech, when he tells Antony to move to his other side, away from his deaf ear. This physical failing makes Caesar unable to hear certain things. But it is also metaphorically suggestive: Caesar's personality may be filtering what he hears.

Act I, ii, 234–250

Casca: I can as well be hanged as tell the manner of it: It was mere
foolery; I did not mark it. I saw Mark Antony offer him a crown—yet
'twas not a crown neither, 'twas one of these coronets—and as I told
you, he put it by once; but for all that, to my thinking, he would fain
have had it. Then he offered it to him again; then he put it by again;
but to my thinking, he was very loath to lay his fingers off it. And then
he offered it the third time. He put it the third time by; and still as he
refused it, the rabblement hooted, and clapped their chopt hands, and
threw up their sweaty nightcaps, and uttered such a deal of stinking
breath because Caesar refused the crown, that it had, almost, choked
Caesar; for he swounded and fell down at it. And for mine own part, I
durst not laugh, for fear of opening my lips and receiving the bad air.

Brutus had said he was not in the mood for celebrating, so he and Cassius did
not witness what happened between Caesar and the crowd. As a result, they
must rely on someone else's account of what has happened, and they ask Casca
to tell them. In this speech, Casca explains that in front of the crowd, Antony
offered Caesar a small crown three times and that each time Caesar pushed it
away. Each time Caesar declined the crown the throng cheered.

Of course, Casca describes the events from his own perspective. He says, for
example, that he could not take the situation seriously; he observed that each
time Caesar pushed the crown away, Caesar actually wanted to take it, and with
each offer he seemed to want it even more. Casca describes those in the crowd
in a contemptuous manner, as a group of common, ragged, working men with
"stinking breath."

Casca does not tell the story in a completely chronological manner, and this
adds some surprise to the event. Only in Casca's later lines does he explain that
the crowd was definitely happy that Caesar refused the crown and that Caesar,
having hoped they would respond in exactly the opposite way, became dramatic,
offering to let his throat be cut.

The exchange between Caesar and the crowd should be compared with two
major events that occur later in the play: Brutus's speech to the angered mob
after Caesar's murder, and Antony's speech that immediately follows Brutus's.
Both of these speeches are given onstage, unlike Caesar's interaction with the
crowd, which occurs offstage and is later described indirectly by a third party.
When Brutus and Antony speak, the crowds are completely swayed to agree
with the speakers, whereas when Caesar turns down the crown in front of the
citizens they encourage his refusal—which is exactly opposite the reaction he
wants. Additionally, the crowds that press Caesar to turn down the crown are
described in a derogatory way and those who listen to Brutus and then to Antony

are not, although the latter are easily influenced by these two men and end up being a much more dangerous force.

After Caesar's crushing dismissal by the crowd, one wonders why Brutus joins the conspiracy. Since the people do not want Caesar to be king, it would seem not so difficult to keep Caesar in check; murdering him might not be the only answer after all. Yet Brutus, though described as honorable, is not necessarily a great thinker. He sees the events surrounding Caesar and the crown as a precursor of more attempts to gain power. Additionally, the momentum of the plot against Caesar is itself a significant force.

Act II, i, 10–34

Brutus. It must be by his death; and for my part,
I know no personal cause to spurn at him,
But for the general. He would be crowned.
How that might change his nature, there's the question.
It is the bright day that brings forth the adder,
And that craves wary walking. Crown him that,
And then I grant we put a sting in him
That at his will he may do danger with.
Th' abuse of greatness is when it disjoins
Remorse from power; and, to speak truth of Caesar,
I have not known when his affections swayed
More than his reason. But 'tis a common proof
That lowliness is young ambition's ladder,
Whereto the climber upward turns his face;
But when he once attains the upmost round,
He then unto the ladder turns his back,
Looks in the clouds, scorning the base degrees
By which he did ascend. So Caesar may;
Then lest he may, prevent. And, since the quarrel
Will bear no color for the thing he is,
Fashion it thus: that what he is, augmented,
Would run to these and these extremities;
And therefore think him as a serpent's egg
Which hatched, would as his kind grow mischievous,
And kill him in the shell.

This soliloquy shows the indecisive Brutus. His words here are contemplative as he tries to determine why Caesar should be killed; he wants an answer that is just, noble, and therefore appropriate to his true self. The soliloquy begins startlingly strong: "It must be by his death." It is as if Brutus believes that the powerful statement will overrule his undecided self. Much of the rest of his speech, however, is laden with the hesitating words "might" and "may."

Brutus considers whether Caesar would be an uncontrollable tyrant if crowned king, even though he realizes that this is pure speculation. He compares Caesar at the beginning and the very end of the speech to a venomous snake waiting to hatch from its egg, posing no threat and easy to kill before it is born. Brutus says that he personally has nothing against Caesar, but that this man's death will be for the good of the people. His reasoning is more palatable to himself when he pushes aside his personal view of the man and instead sees the execution as acting in the name of Rome.

Brutus speaks of great leaders overall whose drive for power consumes them and their own good sense. He then admits that he has never observed such behavior in Caesar. Brutus goes on, however, to note that the common wisdom that those who have humble beginnings turn their backs on their people; when they reach the peak of power, they have nothing but scorn for those left far below them. Caesar's death would prevent this from happening, Brutus rationalizes. But he repeats that there is no case against Caesar for who he is today. Brutus's only arguments against Caesar are based on pure speculation. Yet he closes his speech with the image of Caesar as the ugly, deadly serpent still inside its shell, and this shows that Brutus is willing to base his decision on what might be.

It seems curious that, having convinced himself that he must act on behalf of Rome, Brutus does not even contemplate any method for keeping Caesar in check other than killing him. Likewise, his concern for Rome seems incomplete: While he has decided it is best that Caesar die, he makes no plans for helping Rome in the immediate aftermath of Caesar's death.

⚬⚬⚬ ⚬⚬⚬ ⚬⚬⚬

Act III, ii, 12–35

Brutus: Be patient till the last. Romans, countrymen, and lovers, hear me for my cause, and be silent, that you may hear. Believe me for mine honor, and have respect to mine honor, that you may believe. Censure me in your wisdom, and awake your senses, that you may the better judge. If there be any in this assembly, any dear friend of Caesar's, to him I say that Brutus' love to Caesar was no less than his. If then that friend demand why Brutus rose against Caesar, this is my answer: Not that I loved Caesar less, but that I loved Rome more. Had you rather Caesar were living, and die all slaves, than that Caesar were dead, to live all free men? As Caesar loved me, I weep for him; as he was fortunate, I rejoice at it; as he was valiant, I honor him; but, as he was ambitious,

I slew him. There is tears, for his love; joy, for his fortune; honor, for his valor; and death, for his ambition. Who is here so base that would be a bondman? If any, speak; for him have I offended. Who is here so rude, that would not be a Roman? If any, speak; for him have I offended. Who is here so vile, that will not love his country? If any, speak; for him have I offended. I pause for a reply.

Caesar has just been killed, and the public response is chaos and fear. In this passage, Brutus plans to restore the peace. The gathered crowd is quite distressed, and Brutus asks them to hear him out. He reminds them that he is reputable and tells them he will explain what has happened; they can be the judges.

Brutus makes the bold move of first addressing those in the crowd who loved Caesar. Here is a very different Brutus from the one who earlier was so distressed about whether Caesar should be killed; now he appears so confident that killing Caesar was the right thing to do that he feels he can convince even the dead man's close friends of its necessity. Brutus tells Caesar's dear friends that he loved Caesar, just as they did. He then explains why he nonetheless killed him: Brutus loved Caesar, but he loved Rome even more. He asks the crowd a question that seems to have only one logical answer: Would they rather have Caesar alive and all be his slaves, or dead and remain free? Brutus offers the people nothing in between. He believes the people will accept his vision that they would be slaves under Caesar even though, as Brutus himself had contemplated, what might have happened if Caesar had been crowned remains pure speculation.

Brutus also feels confident enough in his decision to speak not only of the man's flaws, but of his admirable qualities. Caesar was a loving friend and a fortunate and valiant man, Brutus says, and these things need to be recognized. Yet because he was also ambitious, Brutus says, he had to be killed. Again he asks the crowd rhetorical questions, knowing what the answers will be: No one, of course, would say he wants to be a slave, is content to be a bad Roman, or does not love his country.

Now so certain both that Caesar had to be killed and that the people will understand this, Brutus pauses to let them respond. They all are on his side.

Act III, ii, 74–108

Antony. Friends, Romans, countrymen, lend me your ears;
I come to bury Caesar, not to praise him.
The evil that men do lives after them,
The good is oft interrèd with their bones;
So let it be with Caesar. The noble Brutus
Hath told you Caesar was ambitious.

If it were so, it was a grievous fault,
And grievously hath Caesar answered it.
Here, under leave of Brutus and the rest
(For Brutus is an honorable man,
So are they all, all honorable men),
Come I to speak in Caesar's funeral.
He was my friend, faithful and just to me;
But Brutus says he was ambitious,
And Brutus is an honorable man.
He hath brought many captives home to Rome,
Whose ransoms did the general coffers fill;
Did this in Caesar seem ambitious?
When that the poor have cried, Caesar hath wept;
Ambition should be made of sterner stuff.
Yet Brutus says he was ambitious;
And Brutus is an honorable man.
You all did see that on the Lupercal
I thrice presented him a kingly crown,
Which he did thrice refuse. Was this ambition?
Yet Brutus says he was ambitious;
And sure he is an honorable man.
I speak not to disprove what Brutus spoke,
But here I am to speak what I do know.
You all did love him once, not without cause;
What cause withholds you then to mourn for him?
O judgment, thou art fled to brutish beasts,
And men have lost their reason! Bear with me;
My heart is in the coffin there with Caesar,
And I must pause till it come back to me.

Antony gives this speech directly after Brutus has spoken to the crowd and convinced them that Caesar needed to be killed. Before Brutus was even done speaking, Antony arrived with Caesar's bloody body. The body itself is a sign of the brutality of the murder and helps Antony as he makes his case against the conspirators.

Antony explains to the crowd that he is not there speaking to them because he needs to enumerate Caesar's good points; rather, he is only there to be a part of Caesar's funeral. This explanation implies that Antony is only there to do his duty, not to advocate for or against what has happened. He agrees with Brutus's comment that ambition is a great fault, and he remarks on how noble Brutus and his cohorts are. They were even good enough to allow him to speak to the crowd, Antony says.

Then he speaks of Caesar, starting on a personal note. Antony explains that he and Caesar were friends and that Caesar always showed himself to be "faithful and just." These two adjectives are suggestive. A "faithful" person is loyal; such a person would not turn on others, as Brutus suggested Caesar would do if he had the crown. A "just" person, as Antony describes Caesar, would never turn citizens into slaves, as Brutus had led the crowd to believe Caesar would do. Antony's word choices directly contrast with Brutus's description of Caesar and indirectly call into question the honesty of the conspirators.

Immediately after describing Caesar as faithful and just, Antony contrasts his experience with Brutus's judgment: "But Brutus says he was ambitious, / And Brutus is an honorable man." Antony uses these or very similar words throughout his speech to the crowd. Initially this description suggests that Antony is polite and respects Brutus and the fellow conspirators, just as a good Roman would. With repetition, however, it emphasizes Antony's view that Brutus and his cohorts have gone against the facts. Antony then repeats that his goal is not to "disprove what Brutus spoke" but to "speak what I do know." Antony is claiming that though he does not set out to speak against the conspirators, he will nonetheless tell the citizens the truth.

Antony continues to highlight Caesar's virtues in his speech to the citizens of Rome. He emphasizes what would appeal to them most—that Caesar's victories brought much money to Rome, and that Caesar had great compassion for the poor. Antony also reminds the crowd that he repeatedly offered the crown to Caesar, but that each time Caesar turned it down. This certainly does not indicate ambition, Antony says.

Then Antony appeals to shame: He points out the people's fickleness toward Caesar. After all, they were his greatest supporters; their judgment has left them, he says. Antony concludes his tribute to Caesar with a touch of drama. He says he is so choked up he must stop speaking. Unlike Brutus, who only told the crowd how much he and Caesar loved each other, Antony has *shown* how much love he and Caesar had for each other. In the few moments that Antony is silent, the crowd starts to turn against Brutus, just as Antony wishes.

Act V, v, 68–81

Antony. This was the noblest Roman of them all.
All the conspirators save only he
Did that they did in envy of great Caesar;
He, only in a general honest thought
And common good to all, made one of them.
His life was gentle, and the elements

So mixed in him that Nature might stand up
And say to all the world, "This was a man!"

Octavius. According to his virtue, let us use him
With all respect and rites of burial.
Within my tent his bones tonight shall lie,
Most like a soldier ordered honorably.
So call the field to rest, and let's away
To part the glories of this happy day.

These words from Antony and Octavius are the last lines in the play. The two leaders, as well as Messala, Lucilius, and the army, have come upon Brutus's body, watched over by Strato. They learn that Brutus has run on his sword to kill himself while Strato held the sword. Octavius says he will take into his service all the men that served Brutus. Perhaps because he respects Brutus, Octavius believes Brutus's men will be helpful to him. He does not appear concerned that any of them will turn against him.

Antony does not participate in Octavius's decision to take on Brutus's men. In fact, as the others speak, Antony says nothing. The others are concerned about what happens now, whereas Antony is preoccupied with Brutus and who he was. Although Antony had tricked Brutus into letting him speak at Caesar's funeral, had stoked the crowd into violence against Brutus and the other conspirators, and had fought Brutus's army on the battlefield, Antony now gives tribute to Brutus. As stated earlier, Antony has proven to be a keen observer of people; for example, recognizing the strengths and weaknesses of others allowed him to manipulate Brutus and the crowd. It is apparent here that he recognized Brutus not just as a target that could be manipulated, but as an outstanding person.

Antony speaks only of what made Brutus great. He comments on Brutus's noble nature, and he shows how well he understood Brutus when he brings up Brutus's motivation for killing Caesar—that he felt it was for the good of his country. In this Brutus was different from the others, who, according to Antony, killed Caesar out of selfish motivation. Antony praises Brutus for being gentle and for having the best mix of qualities. He pronounces Brutus outstanding in the broad context of the world.

When Octavius speaks, he remarks on what should be done next rather than reminiscing or admiring Brutus as Antony has just done. In light of Brutus's great stature, Octavius says, his body will be given proper respect and laid out in Octavius's own tent. Octavius seems to realize that even though he, Antony, and Lepidus have won, those from the other side must be treated properly. After all, it was not so long ago that the conspirators turned against Caesar and the citizens turned against the conspirators; Brutus and Cassius's men could still cause trouble if they wanted to, if not immediately, perhaps later.

Octavius does not seem especially concerned about Brutus and Cassius's men, however. In his last lines he observes that they all must rest and refers to "the glories of this happy day," seeming not to care that those on the losing side would hardly call this day happy. Indeed, the audience already knows that Antony and Octavius are heartless killers, meaning Rome's future may not see happy days for long.

LIST OF CHARACTERS
IN *JULIUS CAESAR*

Julius Caesar is the Romans' successful military leader who has an inflated opinion of himself. The conspirators believe they must do whatever is necessary to keep him from being crowned.

Octavius Caesar, the young relative of Julius Caesar, is outside Rome when Julius Caesar is killed but is quick to align himself with Antony and Lepidus against the conspirators. While Octavius does not appear as emotional and manipulative as Antony and does not have his experience, Octavius nevertheless is ruthlessly ready to kill to gain control.

When **Marcus Antonius (Antony)** first appears, he is ready to run a race, an early sign of his vigor and vitality (especially since no other main characters are in the race), although he has a reputation for being a lover of wild parties. He is most loyal to Julius Caesar, who confides in him, and quite upset at Caesar's death. He proves himself a masterful manipulator as well as a heartless killer.

Lepidus joins with Octavius and Antony to be part of the triumvirate that will rule the Roman Empire after Julius Caesar's death. Like Octavius and Antony, he is ruthless, yet Antony believes he is useful only for menial tasks and that he and Octavius should discard him when he is no longer needed.

A senator of the Roman Republic, **Cicero** is respected and older than the conspirators, who consider asking him to join in their plot against Caesar.

Publius is an elderly senator whom Brutus looks out for when chaos erupts after Caesar's death.

Popilius Lena is a senator who somehow has learned of the conspiracy and whom Brutus and Cassius fear may alert Caesar about it.

A judicial magistrate of Rome, **Marcus Brutus** is highly respected, and therefore the conspirators feel he must join them to lend credence to their killing of Caesar. Brutus is the one conspirator who struggles with whether to be a part of the murder. He is determined to do what is right, yet his naiveté causes him to make mistakes and be manipulated.

Cassius is Brutus's brother-in-law. While he considers himself a great friend as well, in his zeal to have Brutus join the conspiracy he uses tricks on Brutus. Until Brutus joins, Cassius is the clear leader of the conspiracy. He has an understanding of how events and people work, yet he gives in to Brutus on key decisions, which proves harmful.

Casca relates to Cassius and Brutus the tumultuous circumstances in which Caesar is offered the crown. Cassius sees that Casca could be a help to the conspirators and gets him to join them.

Trebonius, one of the conspirators, agrees with Brutus that Antony should not be killed along with Caesar. Trebonius is responsible for luring Antony away just prior to the killing.

Caius Ligarius is said to have a grudge against Caesar, who berated him for speaking positively of Pompey. He readily joins the conspiracy.

Decius Brutus is the conspirator who questions whether they should kill others aside from Caesar. He skillfully convinces Caesar to go to the senate on the day he is to be murdered, even though Caesar previously decided it was best not to go.

Metellus Cimber gets down on his knees to beg Caesar to call off his brother's banishment. While Caesar harshly rebukes him, he remains steadfast, and the other conspirators close in on Caesar for the stabbing.

One of the conspirators who very much wants Brutus to join them is **Cinna**. At Cassius's request, he plants at Brutus's home a collection of fake letters that are designed to convince Brutus that the citizens want Caesar to be stopped.

Flavius is a tribune who is upset to see the crowds gathering to support Caesar in his latest victory. Disturbed that Caesar could become too powerful, he instructs Marullus that they should take down the ornaments celebrating Caesar's win.

Marullus is a tribune. Along with Flavius he is angry that people have gathered to cheer for Caesar, and he turns them against Caesar.

Artemidorus is a teacher of rhetoric. He plans to warn Caesar of the conspirators' plan against him.

The **soothsayer** (one who attempts to predict the future) twice warns Caesar that he is in grave danger.

Cinna is a poet. He has the same name as one of the conspirators, a fact that stirs up the crowd, which Antony has already pushed to frenzy and violence.

Another **poet** interrupts the arguing Brutus and Cassius; he fears what they may do while left alone and angry at each other.

On the battlefield in the midst of fighting, **Lucilius,** a man in the army of Brutus and Cassius, tells the enemy that he is Brutus. He speaks with bravado to Antony, who then tells his men to treat Lucilius well.

Titinius is a part of the army of Brutus and Cassius; he is given the task of being a guard as well as a scout and is greatly disturbed when he finds Cassius dead.

Messala is a man in Brutus and Cassius's army. He reports to his leaders information about their enemy, as well as about Brutus's wife. Cassius reveals his anxiety to him about the army's fate.

Young Cato is the brother of Brutus's wife and the son of Marcus Porcius Cato, who was a highly respected statesman that fought with Pompey against Caesar. Young Cato is in Brutus and Cassius's army and tries to inspire their men.

Volumnius is an old friend of Brutus's from school and a member of Brutus and Cassius's army. He will not help Brutus kill himself.

Varro is a servant of Brutus who stays in his tent at Sardis but does not see or hear Caesar's ghost.

Clitus is a servant of Brutus who refuses to help him kill himself.

Claudius is a servant of Brutus who stays in his tent at Sardis but does not see or hear Caesar's ghost.

Strato is a servant of Brutus who helps Brutus kill himself.

Lucius is a servant of Brutus who helps him in his home and later near Sardis.

Dardanius is a servant of Brutus who refuses to help him kill himself.

Pindarus is a servant of Cassius who agrees to help Cassius kill himself.

Calphurnia is Julius Caesar's wife. She is superstitious and fearful for her husband's safety, and she temporarily convinces him to stay home from the senate on the ides of March.

Portia is Brutus's wife and the daughter of Marcus Porcius Cato. She appears strong and is insistent that her husband tell her why he has been so disturbed. She is highly concerned about him.

The **citizens** of Rome are fickle, easily manipulated, and dangerous.

CRITICISM
THROUGH THE AGES

❧

Julius Caesar
in the Seventeenth Century

ॐ

The first known performance of *Julius Caesar* took place at the very end of the sixteenth century, in 1599. Prior to this performance there were other plays that had been written about Julius Caesar, who apparently was an appealing subject to writers and the public alike. Shakespeare's *Julius Caesar* became quite well known. Even though no printed copy of it appeared until Shakespeare's First Folio was published in 1623, by then there must have been numerous productions of the play, since dramatists often referred to lines from the play in their own works and poetry of the time also referred to the play. The quarrel scene between Brutus and Cassius seemed to be a particular favorite. In 1601, John Weever, an English poet, wrote about the funeral scene in the play, noting that the crowd believes Brutus's comments about Caesar's ambition but also believes Antony when he speaks. According to Weever, this demonstrates that people are too easily swayed.

Another English poet who was also a famous playwright, Ben Jonson, admired Shakespeare intensely but believed that he should have edited himself more closely. Jonson pointed in particular to a "ridiculous" line in *Julius Caesar* that he said Shakespeare should have corrected: "Caesar never did wrong but with just cause." Interestingly, that line apparently was indeed altered after the play's initial production, since the First Folio edition of Shakespeare's works contains a slightly different version of it.

The play's popularity could perhaps be attributed to the similarities between its dramatic situation and the state of the English in the seventeenth century. The English had experienced years of peace and prosperity under the rule of Elizabeth I, yet by 1599 Elizabeth was aged and without heirs. People feared that a civil war might ensue as a means of determining the new ruler. Already there had been turmoil. No matter how control ultimately would be gained, the English people were anxious about whether the new ruler would be able to maintain a prosperous and peaceful land.

Indeed, some of their fears were well founded. In the mid-seventeenth century, the English Civil War (1642–1651) divided the country and ousted the king. Under the rule of Oliver Cromwell and the Puritans, the theaters were closed, but by 1660, the English monarchy was restored. The new king, Charles II, was was a patron of the arts who had the theaters reopened.

A few years later, in a verse prologue to *Julius Caesar*, the famous Augustan poet John Dryden remarked on Shakespeare's willingness to take risks, comparing him in particular to Ben Jonson. Shakespeare made mistakes, Dryden wrote, but ultimately excelled further and had a natural wit. He compared Shakespeare to a country beauty; both, he said, win admiration though they may not understand their own charm. Alluding specifically to *Julius Caesar*, Dryden praised Antony's eloquence in the funeral scene.

The critic Thomas Rymer, however, was severely critical of Shakespeare; Rymer did not see Shakespeare as naturally talented and could not understand Shakespeare's methods. In his view, Caesar and Brutus were truly noble Romans and should have been treated with dignity. Instead, in Shakespeare's play, even the senators are no wiser than others and everyone looks foolish. Rymer admitted that Shakespeare was a genius in comedy and humor, but he claimed that in tragedy Shakespeare rambled and was incoherent. Rymer chose some parts of the play to examine, such as the argument between Cassius and Brutus, which he considered an embarrassing spectacle of swaggering. He highlighted what he considered inconsistencies in the character of Brutus as well, pointing out that at one moment Brutus says the conspirators cannot kill Antony when they kill Caesar, because it would look too bloody, but at another, shortly after Caesar's death, Brutus encourages all the conspirators to bathe their arms in Caesar's blood.

1601—John Weever.
From *The Mirror of Martyrs*

John Weever was an English poet. He published poetry as well as a book on his travels in his country.

___

The many-headed multitude were drawne
By *Brutus* speech, that *Caesar* was ambitious,
When eloquent *Mark Antonie* had showne
His vertues, who but *Brutus* then was vicious?
Mans memorie, with new, forgets the old,
One tale is good, untill another's told.

1641—Ben Jonson. "De Shakespeare nostrat[i]," from *Timber, or Discoveries Made Upon Men and Matter*

Ben Jonson was an English playwright and poet. He died in 1637, but for almost a century after that his effect on English drama was as significant as Shakespeare's. Some of his plays are *Every Man in His Humour*, *Volpone*, and *The Alchemist*.

I remember the players have often mentioned it as an honor to Shakespeare, that in his writing, whatsoever he penned, he never blotted out a line. My answer hath been, "Would he had blotted a thousand," which they thought a malevolent speech. I had not told posterity this but for their ignorance, who chose that circumstance to commend their friend by wherein he most faulted; and to justify mine own candor, for I loved the man, and do honor his memory on this side idolatry as much as any. He was, indeed, honest, and of an open and free nature; had an excellent fancy, brave notions, and gentle expressions, wherein he flowed with that facility that sometime it was necessary he should be stopped. "*Sufflaminandus erat*," as Augustus said of Haterius. His wit was in his own power; would the rule of it had been so too. Many times he fell into those things, could not escape laughter, as when he said in the person of Caesar, one speaking to him: "Caesar, thou dost me wrong." He replied: "Caesar did never wrong but with just cause;" and such like, which were ridiculous. But he redeemed his vices with his virtues. There was ever more in him to be praised than to be pardoned.

1672—John Dryden. "Prologue to *Julius Caesar*"

John Dryden was a poet, literary critic, translator, and playwright. Named poet laureate, he was perhaps best known for his Restoration comedies.

In Country Beauties as we often see,
Something that takes in their simplicity;
Yet while they charm, they know not they are fair,
And take without the spreading of the snare;
Such Artless beauty lies in *Shakespears* wit,
'Twas well in spight of him what ere he writ.
His Excellencies came and were not sought,

His words like casual Atoms made a thought:
Drew up themselves in Rank and File, and writ,
He wondring how the Devil it was such wit.
Thus like the drunken Tinker, in his Play,
He grew a Prince, and never knew which way.
He did not know what trope or Figure meant,
But to perswade is to be eloquent,
So in this *Caesar* which to day you see,
Tully ne'r spoke as he makes *Anthony.*
Those then that tax his Learning are to blame,
He knew the thing, but did not know the Name:
Great *Johnson* did that Ignorance adore,
And though he envi'd much, admir'd him more;
The faultless *Johnson* equally writ well,
Shakespear made faults; but then did more excel.
One close at Guard like some old Fencer lay,
T'other more open, but he shew'd more play.
In Imitation *Johnsons* wit was shown,
Heaven made his men; but *Shakespear* made his own.
Wise *Johnson's* talent in observing lay,
But others follies still made up his play.
He drew the life in each elaborate line,
But *Shakespear* like a Master did design.
Johnson with skill dissected humane kind,
And show'd their faults that they their faults might find:
But then as all Anatomists must do,
He to the meanest of mankind did go,
And took from Gibbets such as he would show.
Both are so great that he must boldly dare,
Who both of 'em does judge and both compare.
If amongst Poets one more bold there be,
The man that dare attempt in either way, is he.

1693—Thomas Rymer. From *A Short View of Tragedy*

Thomas Rymer was a critic and translator. He was appointed historiographer royal in 1692.

In *(Othello)*, our Poet might be the bolder, the persons being all his own Creatures, and meer fiction. But here he sins not against Nature and Philosophy only, but against the most known History, and the memory of the Noblest Romans, that ought to be sacred to all Posterity. He might be familiar with *Othello* and *Jago*, as his own natural acquaintance: but *Caesar* and *Brutus* were above his conversation: To put them in Fools Coats, and make them Jack-puddens in the *Shakespear* dress, is a *Sacriledge*, beyond any thing in *Spelman*. The Truth is, this authors head was full of villainous, unnatural images, and history has only furnish'd him with great names, thereby to recommend them to the World; by writing over them, *This is* Brutus; *this is* Cicero; *this is* Caesar. But generally his History flies in his Face; And comes in flat contradiction to the Poets imagination. As for example: of *Brutus* says *Antony*, his Enemy.

> *Ant.:* His life was gentle, and the Elements
> So mixt in him, that Nature might stand up,
> And say to all the World, this was a Man.

And when every body jug'd it necessary to kill *Antony*, our Author in his *Laconical* way, makes *Brutus* speak thus:

> *Bru.:* Our Course will seem too bloody, *Caius Cassius,*
> To cut the Head off, and then hack the Limbs,
> Like wrath in death, and envy afterwards;
> For Antony is but a Limb of *Caesar.*
> Let's be Sacrificers, but not Butchers, Caius,
> We all stand up against the Spirit of *Caesar,*
> And in the Spirit of man there is no blood;
> O that we then cou'd come by *Caesars* Spirit,
> And not dismember *Caesar,* but, alas!
> *Caesar* must bleed for it. And gentle friends,
> Let's kill him boldly, but not wrathfully;
> Let's carve him, as a dish fit for the Gods,
> Not hew him, as a Carkass fit for Hounds.
> And let our Hearts, as subtle Masters do,
> Stir up their Servants to an act of rage,
> And after seem to chide 'em. This shall make
> Our purpose necessary, and not envious:
> Which so appearing to the common eyes,
> We shall be call'd Purgers, not murderers.
> And for *Mark Antony* think not of him:

For he can do no more than *Caesars* arm,
When Caesars head is off.

In these two speeches we have the true character of Brutus, according to History. But when *Shakespear's* own blundering Maggot of self contradiction works, then must *Brutus* cry out.

Bru.: Stoop, *Romans,* stoop,
And let us bath our hands in *Caesars* blood
Up to the Elbows—

. . . For, indeed, that Language which *Shakespear* puts in the Mouth of *Brutus* wou'd not suit, or be convenient, unless from some son of the Shambles, or some natural offspring of the Butchery. But never any Poet so boldly and so barefac'd, flounced along from contradiction to contradiction. A little preparation and forecast might do well now and then. For his *Desdemona's* Marriage, He might have helped out the probability by feigning how that some way, or other, a Black-amoor Woman had been her Nurse, and suckl'd her: Or that once, upon a time, some *Virtuoso* had transfus'd into her Veins the Blood of a black Sheep: after which she might never be at quiet till she is, as the Poet will have it, *Tupt with an old black ram.*

But to match this pithy discourse of *Brutus;* see the weighty argumentative oration, whereby *Cassius* draws him into the Conspiracy.

Cas.: Brutus, and *Caesar:* what shou'd be in that
Caesar?
Why shou'd that name be sounded more than yours?
Write them together: yours is as fair a name:
Sound them, it doth become the mouth as well.
Weigh them, it is as heavy: conjure with them,
Brutus will start a Spirit as soon as *Caesar.*
Now, in the names of all the Gods at once,
Upon what meat doth this our *Caesar* feed,
That he is grown so great? Age, thou art sham'd;
Rome thou hast lost the breed of noble bloods.
When went there by an Age since the great flood,
But it was fam'd with more, than with one man?
When could they say (till now) that talk'd of *Rome,*
That her wide Walls encompass'd but one man?
Now it is *Rome* indeed, and room enough
When there is in it but one only Man—

One may Note that all our Authors Senators, and his Orators had their learning and education at the same school, be they Venetians, Black-amoors, Ottamites, or noble Romans. *Brutus* and *Cassius* here, may *cap sentences,* with *Brabantio,* and the *Doge* of *Venice,* or any *Magnifico* of them all. We saw how the Venetian Senate spent their time, when, amidst their alarms, call'd to Counsel at midnight. Here the Roman Senators, the midnight before Caesar's death (met in the Garden of *Brutus,* to settle the matter of their Conspiracy) are gazing up to the Stars, and have no more in their heads than to wrangle about which is the East and West.

Decius: Here lies the East, doth not the day break here?
Caska: No.
Cinna: O, pardon, Sir, it doth, and yon grey lines,
That fret the Clouds, are Messengers of Day.
Caska: You shall confess, that you are both deceiv'd:
Here as I point my Sword, the Sun arises,
Which is a great way growing on the South,
Weighing the youthful season of the year,
Some two months hence, up higher toward the North,
He first presents his fire, and the high East
Stands as the Capitol directly here.

This is directly, as *Bays* tells us, to *shew the World a Pattern here, how men shou'd talk of Business.* But it wou'd be a wrong to the Poet, not to inform the reader, that on the Stage, the Spectators see *Brutus* and *Cassius* all this while at *Whisper* together. That is the importance, that deserves all the attention. But the *grand question* wou'd be: does the *Audience hear 'em Whisper?*

Ush.: Why, truly I can't tell: there's much to be said
upon the word Whisper

Another Poet wou'd have allow'd the noble *Brutus* a Watch-Candle in his Chamber this important night, rather than have puzzel'd his man *Lucius* to grope in the dark for a Flint and Tinderbox, to get the Taper lighted. It wou'd have been no great charge to the Poet, however. Afterwards, another night, the Fiddle is in danger to be broken by this sleepy Boy.

Bru.: If thou dost nod thou break'st thy Instrument.

But pass we to the famous Scene, where *Brutus* and *Cassius* are by the Poet represented acting the parts of *Mimicks:* from the Nobility and Buskins, they are made the *Planipedes;* are brought to daunce *barefoot,* for a Spectacle to the people, Two Philosophers, two generals, *(imperatores* was their title) the *ultimi Romanorum,* are to play the Bullies and Buffoon, to shew their Legerdemain, their *activity* of face, and divarication of Muscles. They are to play a prize, a tryal of skill in huffing and swaggering, like two drunken Hectors, for a two-penny reckoning.

When the Roman Mettle was somewhat more allaid, and their Stomach not so very fierce, in Augustus's time; *Laberius,* who was excellent at that sport, was forced once by the Emperor to shew his Talent upon the Stage: in his Prologue, he complains that

> Necessity has no law.
> It was the will of *Caesar* brought me hither,
> What was imagin'd for me to deny
> This *Caesar;* when the Gods deny him nothing?

But says he,

> Twice thirty years I liv'd without blemish;
> From home I came a Roman Gentleman,
> But back shall go a *Mimick.* This one day
> Is one day longer than I shou'd have liv'd.

This may shew with what indignity our Poet treats the noblest Romans. But there is no other cloth in his Wardrobe. Every one must be content to wear a Fools Coat, who comes to be dressed by him. Nor is he more civil to the Ladies. *Portia,* in good manners, might have challeng'd more respect: she that shines, a glory of the first magnitude in the Gallery of Heroick Dames, is with our Poet, scarce one remove from a Natural: She is the own Cousin German, of one piece, the very same impertinent silly flesh and blood with *Desdemona. Shakespears* genius lay for Comedy and Humour. In Tragedy he appears quite out of his Element; his Brains are turn'd, he raves and rambles, without any coherence, any spark of reason, or any rule to controul him, or set bounds to his phrenzy. His imagination was still running after his Masters, the Coblers, and Parish Clerks, and *Old Testament Stroulers.* So he might make bold with *Portia,* as they had done with the Virgin Mary. Who, in a Church Acting their Play call'd *The Incarnation,* had usually the *Ave Mary* mumbl'd over to a stradling wench (for the blessed Virgin) straw-hatted, blew-apron'd, big-bellied, with her Immaculate Conception up to her chin.

The Italian Painters are noted for drawing the *Madonna's* by their own Wives or Mistresses; one might wonder what sort of *Betty Mackerel, Shakespear* found in his days, to sit for his *Portia,* and *Desdemona;* and Ladies of a rank, and dignity, for their place in Tragedy. But to him a Tragedy in *Burlesk*, a merry Tragedy was no Monster, no absurdity, nor at all preposterous: all colours are the same to a Blind man. The Thunder and Lightning, the Shouting and Battel, and alarms every where in this play, may well keep the Audience awake; otherwise no Sermon wou'd be so strong an Opiate. But since the memorable action by the *Putney Pikes*, the *Hammersmith Brigade*, and the *Chelsey Cuirassiers:* one might think, in a modest Nation, no Battel wou'd ever presume to shew upon the Stage agen, unless it were at *Perin* in *Comwal*, where the story goes that, some time before the year 88. the *Spaniards* once were landing to burn the Town, just at the nick when a Company of *Stroulers* with their Drums and their shouting were setting *Sampson* upon the *Philistines*, which so scar'd Mr. Spaniard, that they Scampered back to their Galions, as apprehending our whole *Tilbury* Camp had lain in Ambush, and were coming souse upon them.

At *Athens* (they tell us) the Tragedies of *Æschylus, Sophocles, and Euripides* were enroll'd with their Laws, and made part of their Statue-Book.

We want a law for Acting the *Rehearsal* once a week, to keep us in our senses, and secure us against the Noise and Nonsence, the Farce and Fustian which, in the name of Tragedy, have so long invaded, and usurp our Theater.

Tully defines an Orator to be, *Vir bonus dicendique peritus.* Why must he be a *good Man*, as if a bad Man might not be a good Speaker? But what avails it to Speak well, unless a man is well heard? To gain attention *Aristotle* told us, it was necessary that an Orator be a *good Man;* therefore he that writes Tragedy should be careful that the persons of his *Drama*, be of consideration and importance, that the Audience may readily lend an Ear, and give attention to what they say, and act. Who would thrust into a crowd to hear what Mr. *Jago, Roderigo*, or *Cassio*, is like to say? From a Venetian Senate, or a Roman Senate one might expect great matters: But their Poet was out of sorts; he had it not for them; the Senators must be no wiser than other folk.

Ben. Johnson, knew to distinguish men and manners, at an other rate. In *Catiline* we find our selves in *Europe*, we are no longer in the *Land of Savages*, amongst Blackamoors, Barbarians, and Monsters.

The Scene is Rome and first on the Stage appears *Sylla's* Ghost.

Dost thou not feel me, Rome? Not yet?

One would, in reason, imagine the Ghost is in some publick open place, upon some Eminence, where Rome is all within his view: But it is a surprising thing to find that this ratling Rodomontado speech is in a dark, close, private sleeping hole of *Catiline's*.

Yet the *Chorus*, is of all wonders the strangest. The *Chorus* is always present on the Stage, privy to, and interested in all that passes, and thereupon make their Reflections to Conclude the several *Acts*.

Sylla's Ghost, tho' never so big, might slide in at the Keyhole; but how comes the *Chorus* into *Catilins* Cabinet?

Aurelia is soon after with him too, but the Poet had perhaps provided her some Truckle-bed in a dark Closet by him.

In short, it is strange that *Ben,* who understood the turn of Comedy so well; and had found the success, should thus grope in the dark, and jumble things together without head or tail, without any rule or proportion, without any reason or design. Might not the *Acts of the Apostles,* or a Life in *Plutarch,* be as well Acted, and as properly called a Tragedy, as any History of a Conspiracy?

Corneille tells us, in the *Examen* of his *Melite,* that when first he began to write, he thought there had been no Rules: So had no guide but a little *Common sence,* with the Example of Mr. *Hardy,* and some others, not more regular than he. This *Common sence* (says he) *which was all my rule, brought me to find out the unity of Action to imbroyl four Lovers by one and the same intreague.* *Ben. Johnson,* besides his Common sence to tell him that the *Unity of Action* was necessary; had stumbl'd. (I know not how) on a *Chorus;* which is not to be drawn through a Key-hole, to be lugg'd about, or juggl'd with an *hocus pocus* hither and thither; nor stow'd in a garret, nor put into quarters with the *Brentford* Army, so must of necessity keep the Poet to *unity of place;* And also to some Conscionable *time,* for the representation: Because the *Chorus* is not to be trusted out of sight, is not to eat or drink till they have given up their Verdict, and the *Plaudite* is over.

One would not talk of rules, or what is regular with *Shakespear,* or any followers, in the Gang of the *Strouling* Fraternity; but it is lamentable that *Ben. Johnson,* his Stone and his Tymber, however otherwise of value, must lye a miserable heap of ruins, for want of Architecture, or some Son of *Vitruvius,* to joyn them together. He had red *Horace,* had Translated that to the *Pisones:*

> Nec verbum verbo curabis reddere, fidus interpres.
> *Ben:* Being a Poet, thou may'st feign, create,
>   Not care, as thou wouldst faithfully translate,
>   To render word for word

And this other precept.

> Nec circa vilem, patulumque moraberis Orbem.
> *Ben:* The vile, broad-trodden ring forsake.

What is there material in this *Catiline,* either in the *Manners,* in the *Thoughts,* or in the *Expression,* (three parts of Tragedy) which is not word for word translation? In the *Fable,* or Plot (which is the first, and principal part) what see we, but the *vile broad trodden ring?* *Vile, Horace* calls it, as a thing below, and too mean for any man of wit to busie his head withal. *Patulum*, he calls it, because it is obvious, and easie for any body to do as much as that comes to. 'Tis but to plodd along, step by step in the same tract: 'Tis drudgery only for the blind Horse in a Mill. No Creature sound of Wind and Limb, but wou'd chuse a nobler Field, and a more generous Career.

Homer, we find, slips sometime into a *Tract* of *Scripture*, but his *Pegasus* is not stabl'd there, presently up he springs, mounts aloft, is on the wing, no earthly bounds, or barriers to confine him.

For *Ben*, to sin thus against the clearest light and conviction, argues a strange stupidity: It was bad enough in him, against his Judgement and Conscience, to interlard so much fiddle faddle, Comedy, and *Apocryphal* matters in the History: Because, forsooth,

> his nam plebecula gaudet.

Where the Poet has chosen a subject of importance sufficient and proper for Tragedy, there is no room for this petty interlude and diversion. Had some Princes come express from *Salankemen* (remote as it is) to give an account of the battel, whilst the story was hot and new, and made a relation accurate, and distinctly, with all the pomp, and advantage of the Theatre, wou'd the Audience have suffer'd a Tumbler or Baboon, a Bear, or Rope dancer to have withdrawn their attention; or to have interrupted the Narrative; tho' it had held as long as a Dramatick Representation. Nor at that time wou'd they thank a body for his quibbles, or wit out of season: This mans Feather, or that Captains Embroidered Coat might not be touched upon but in a very short *Parenthesis*.

It is meerly by the ill-chosen Subject, or the ill-adjusting it, that the Audience runs a gadding after what is forreign, and from the business. And when some senceless trifling tale, as that of *Othello;* or some mangl'd, abus'd, undigested, interlarded History on our Stage impiously assumes the sacred name of Tragedy, it is no wonder if the Theatre grow corrupt and scandalous, and Poetry from its Ancient Reputation and Dignity, is sunk to the utmost Contempt and Derision.

JULIUS CAESAR
IN THE EIGHTEENTH CENTURY
❧

Julius Caesar continued to be a popular subject of commentary in the eighteenth century. In his memoir, published in the middle of the century, the playwright and actor Colley Cibber praised Shakespeare's works. He commented in particular on the success of the late-seventeenth-century actor Betterton in many of Shakespeare's roles, including Brutus. To Cibber's mind, Betterton understood the subtleties of Brutus and other characters of Shakespeare. That is, he knew that Brutus still had to maintain dignity during his fight with Cassius; Brutus's anger was clear but not "fierce and flashing" like that of other characters of Shakespeare that he portrayed.

The editor and critic John Upton also wrote about the characters of Shakespeare and described his own rules that the dramatic playwright should follow in creating his characters. One of these rules was that characters modeled after real people should be true to those people. Upton believed that Shakespeare followed this rule but when he did break with it he did so in an artful way. Another rule that Upton discussed in relation to *Julius Caesar* was that characters must behave consistently, and when they act in a way that at first may seem inconsistent there must be a good reason. Upton saw Brutus's behavior as consistent and explained his perspective about this character. Interestingly, he discussed the same scene Thomas Rymer had analyzed earlier ("Let's carve him, as a dish fit for the Gods . . . ") but arrived at a much different conclusion.

The famous French philosopher and writer Voltaire created his own version of the play. Ironically, while Voltaire was a critic of Shakespeare's, he also translated Shakespeare's *Julius Caesar* into French and was ultimately responsible for increasing French awareness of the playwright's work. Voltaire was scornful of *Julius Caesar*, writing that it abounded with "barbarous irregularities." He believed Shakespeare lived at a time of ignorance and was appalled that Shakespeare himself did not understand Latin. Nevertheless, Voltaire saw that Shakespeare had genius. He focused his commentary on the funeral speeches in the play.

The venerable English critic Samuel Johnson also had some complaints about the play. He acknowledged Shakespeare's skill but found the work "somewhat cold and unaffecting" compared with his other plays. Johnson disagreed with Upton about the value of historical accuracy; he believed that what weakened the play was that Shakespeare followed a historical story and portrayed Roman manners too closely.

Elizabeth Montagu, who hosted what might be called a literary salon in London, wrote a book on Shakespeare that responded to some of Voltaire's criticism. She believed that since Shakespeare was "possessed of all the magic of poetical powers" he should not have restricted himself to the historical story of Caesar's death. She believed, however, that he knew that his play would attract more attention by being true to history, since its audience would want to know about this great event. Montagu also wrote that the quarrel scene between Cassius and Brutus was exactly fitting for Shakespeare's purpose of showing us a certain side of Brutus, the good, sensitive man. She remarked on how Shakespeare purposely put small touches into the play to show Brutus in this way. For instance, she mentioned Brutus's concern for his servant as the servant falls asleep.

Later in the eighteenth century, Shakespeare also gained attention outside of England and France. In Germany, for example, his work became greatly admired. In the American colonies, too, there was finally recognition, despite obstacles. For instance, when settlers first arrived in America, actors were prohibited from traveling to the new world. Quakers, Puritans, and others opposed theater and prevented its establishment. Virginia was the first colony where plays were performed, beginning in 1716, and by the mid-1700s theater had been introduced more broadly. The first known Shakespearean play performed in America was *Richard III,* which records show was staged in New York in 1750. The first known colonial production of *Julius Caesar* took place either in 1770 or 1774.

1739—Colley Cibber. Chapter IV,
from *An Apology for the Life of Mr. Colley Cibber*

Colley Cibber was an English actor and playwright who also managed his own acting company. Additionally, he was poet laureate, though many of his contemporaries had little regard for his talent.

. . . *Betterton* was an Actor, as *Shakespear* was an Author, both without Competitors! form'd for the mutual Assistance and Illustration of each others Genius! How *Shakespear* wrote, all Men who have a Taste for Nature may read and know—but with what higher Rapture would he still be *read* could they conceive how *Betterton play'd* him! Then might they know the one was born alone to speak what the other only knew to write! Pity it is that the momentary Beauties flowing from an harmonious Elocution cannot, like those of Poetry, be their own Record! That the animated Graces of the Player can live no longer than the instant Breath and Motion that presents them, or at best can but faintly glimmer through the Memory or imperfect Attestation of a few surviving Spectators. Could how *Betterton* spoke be as easily known as *what* he spoke, then might you see the Muse of *Shakespear* in her Triumph, with all her Beauties in their best Array rising into real Life and charming her Beholders. But alas! since all this is so far out of the reach of Description, how shall I shew you *Betterton*? Should I therefore tell you that all the *Othellos, Hamlets, Hotspurs, Mackbeths,* and *Brutus*'s whom you may have seen since his Time, have fallen far short of him; this still would give you no Idea of his particular Excellence. Let us see then what a particular Comparison may do! whether that may yet draw him nearer to you?

You have seen a *Hamlet* perhaps, who, on the first Appearance of his Father's Spirit, has thrown himself into all the straining Vociferation requisite to express Rage and Fury, and the House has thunder'd with Applause; tho' the misguided Actor was all the while (as *Shakespear* terms it) tearing a Passion into Rags[1]—I am the more bold to offer you this particular Instance, because the late Mr. *Addison*, while I sate by him to see this Scene acted, made the same Observation, asking me, with some Surprize, if I thought *Hamlet* should be in so violent a Passion with the Ghost, which, tho' it might have astonish'd, it had not provok'd him? for you may observe that in this beautiful Speech the Passion never rises beyond an almost breathless Astonishment, or an Impatience, limited by filial Reverence, to enquire into the suspected Wrongs that may have rais'd him from his peaceful Tomb! and a Desire to know what a Spirit so seemingly distrest might wish or enjoin a sorrowful Son to execute towards his future Quiet in the Grave? This was the Light into which *Betterton* threw this Scene; which he open'd with a Pause of mute Amazement! then rising slowly to a solemn, trembling Voice, he made the Ghost equally terrible to the Spectator as to himself![2] and in the descriptive Part of the natural Emotions which the ghastly Vision gave him, the boldness of his Expostulation was still govern'd by Decency, manly, but not braving; his Voice never rising into that seeming Outrage or wild Defiance of what he naturally rever'd.[3] But alas! to preserve this medium, between mouthing and meaning too little, to keep the Attention more pleasingly awake by a temper'd Spirit than by meer Vehemence of Voice, is of all the Master-strokes of an Actor the most difficult to reach. In this none yet have equall'd *Betterton*. But I am unwilling to shew his Superiority only by recounting the Errors of those who now cannot answer to them, let their farther Failings therefore be forgotten! or rather, shall I in some measure excuse them? For I am not yet sure that they might not be as much owing to the false judgment of the Spectator as the Actor. While the Million are so apt to be transported when the Drum of their Ear is so roundly rattled; while they take the Life of Elocution to lie in the Strength of the Lungs, it is no wonder the Actor, whose end is Applause, should be also tempted at this easy rate to excite it. Shall I go a little farther? and allow that this Extreme is more pardonable than its opposite Error? I mean that dangerous Affectation of the Monotone, or solemn Sameness of Pronounciation, which, to my Ear, is insupportable; for of all Faults that so frequently pass upon the Vulgar, that of Flatness will have the fewest Admirers. That this is an Error of ancient standing seems evident by what Hamlet says, in his Instructions to the Players, *viz.*

Be not too tame, neither, &c.

The Actor, doubtless, is as strongly ty'd down to the Rules of *Horace* as the Writer.

Si vis me flere, dolendum est
Primum ipsi tibi—[4]

He that feels not himself the Passion he would raise, will talk to a sleeping Audience: But this never was the Fault of *Betterton*; and it has often amaz'd me to see those who soon came after him throw out, in some Parts of a Character, a just and graceful Spirit which *Betterton* himself could not but have applauded. And yet in the equally shining Passages of the same Character have heavily dragg'd the Sentiment along like a dead Weight, with a long-ton'd Voice and absent Eye, as if they had fairly forgot what they were about: If you have never made this Observation, I am contented you should not know where to apply it.[5]

   A farther Excellence in *Betterton* was, that he could vary his Spirit to the different Characters he acted. Those wild impatient Starts, that fierce and flashing Fire, which he threw into *Hotspur*, never came from the unruffled Temper of his *Brutus* (for I have more than once seen a *Brutus* as warm as *Hotspur*): when the *Betterton Brutus* was provok'd in his Dispute with *Cassius*, his Spirit flew only to his Eye; his steady Look alone supply'd that Terror which he disdain'd an Intemperance in his Voice should rise to. Thus, with a settled Dignity of Contempt, like an unheeding Rock he repelled upon himself the Foam of *Cassius*. Perhaps the very Words of *Shakespear* will better let you into my Meaning:

Must I give way and room to your rash Choler?
Shall I be frighted when a Madman stares?

And a little after,

There is no Terror, *Cassius*, in your Looks! &c.

Not but in some part of this Scene, where he reproaches *Cassius*, his Temper is not under this Suppression, but opens into that Warmth which becomes a Man of Virtue; yet this is that *Hasty Spark* of Anger which *Brutus* himself endeavours to excuse.

NOTES [by Robert W. Lowe, editor, 1889]

1. The actor pointed at is, no doubt, Wilks. In the last chapter of this work Cibber, in giving the theatrical character of Wilks, says of his Hamlet: "I own the Half of what he spoke was as painful to my Ear, as every Line that came from Betterton was charming."

2. Barton Booth, who was probably as great in the part of the Ghost as Betterton was in Hamlet, said, "When I acted the Ghost with Betterton, instead of my awing him, he terrified me. But divinity hung round that man!"—"Dram. Misc.," iii. 32.

3. "The Laureat" repeats the eulogium of a gentleman who had seen Betterton play Hamlet, and adds: "And yet, the same Gentleman assured me, he has seen Mr. *Betterton*, more than once, play this Character to an Audience of twenty Pounds, or under" (p. 32).

4. *Ars Poetica*, 102. This is the much discussed question of Diderot's "Paradoxe sur le Comédien," which has recently been revived by Mr. Henry Irving and M. Coquelin, and has formed the subject of some interesting studies by Mr. William Archer.

5. This is doubtless directed at Booth, who was naturally of an indolent disposition, and seems to have been, on occasions, apt to drag through a part.

1748—John Upton. Section X, from
Critical Observations on Shakespeare

John Upton was an Oxford graduate and clergyman, as well as a literary critic. Besides his work on Shakespeare, he produced an edition of Edmund Spenser's *The Fairie Queene* and a critical work on Ben Jonson.

. . . To consider in this view some of the characters in *Julius Caesar* M. Junius Brutus was a Stoic Philosopher; the Stoics were of all sects the most human and mild, and all professedly commonwealthmen. They made everything submit to honesty, but that they submitted to nothing. 'Twas therefore the tyrant Caesar, the subverter of his country and of his countrymen, that Brutus killed, not the friendly Caesar. . . .

C. Cassius was more of an Epicurean by name, than principle. He was of an imperious temper, could not brook the thoughts of a matter, and was beside of a severe life, and manners . . .

The characters of the conspirators were in after ages all abused, when historians and poets turn'd court-flatterers. And even the proscriptions of those three successful villains, the false and cruel Octavius, the wild and profligate Antony, the stupid Lepidus, were either palliated or excused. The cruelty of Octavius is particularly mention'd by Suetonius . . . But with these and other vices he still preserved great dignity and what we moderns call good-breeding; a sort of mock-virtues of a very low class. And this character of Octavius Shakespeare has very justly preserved in his play.

. . . The philosophical character of Brutus bids you expect consistency and steadiness from his behaviour: he thought the killing of Antony, when Caesar's assassination was resolved on, would appear too bloody and unjust:

Let us be sacrificers, but not butchers:
Let's carve him as a dish fit for the Gods.

The hero therefore, full of this idea of sacrificing Caesar to his injured country, after stabbing him in the Senate, tells the Romans to stoop, and besmear their hands and their swords in the blood of the sacrifice. This was agreeable to an ancient and religious custom. So in Aeschylus we read, that the seven captains, who came against Thebes, sacrificed a bull, and dipped their hands in the gore, invoking, at the same time, the gods of war, and binding themselves with an oath to revenge the cause of Eteocles . . . By this solemn action Brutus gives the assassination of Caesar a religious air and turn; and history too informs us, that he marched out of the senate house, with his bloody hands, proclaiming liberty.

⎯⏦⎯ ⎯⏦⎯ ⎯⏦⎯

1761—Voltaire. "Essay on Tragedy," from *Critical Essays on Dramatic Poetry*

Francois Marie Arouet (pen name Voltaire) was a philosopher and writer of books, plays, and other works. Among his writings are the tragedy *Brutus*, as well as the more famous *Candide* and *Letters Concerning the English Nation*.

. . . With how much pleasure I saw in London your tragedy of Julius Caesar, which has been the delight of your nation for a century and a half past! I do not indeed pretend to approve the barbarous irregularities with which it abounds. It is only surprising that there are not still greater defects in a work, written in an age of ignorance, by a man who did not even understand Latin, and whose only master was his genius. But amidst so many gross faults, with what ecstacy did I see Brutus still holding the poynard stained with the blood of Cæsar, and having assembled the Roman people, addressing himself to them in the following manner: "Romans, countrymen, and friends! hear for my cause; and be silent, that you may hear . . ."

. . . After this scene, Mark Antony comes to raise the compassion of these very Romans, in whom Brutus had just inspired all his sternness and inhumanity. Anthony, by an artful oration, brings back insensibly these proud minds; and when they are softened into pity, then he discovers to them the body of Cæsar; and by a display of the most pathetic expressions, and most moving complaints, he stirs them up to mutiny and revenge.

Perhaps the French would not suffer upon the stage a chorus composed of Roman plebeians and artizans; or the bloody corpse of Cæsar exposed to the eyes of the multitude; and, that multitude provoked to revenge from the rostrum. It is custom alone, the governor of the world, that can change the taste of nations, and turn into entertainment what was before the object of their antipathy.

The Greeks have hazarded spectacles which would not be less agreeable to us. . . .

1768—Samuel Johnson. "Julius Caesar," from *General Observations on Shakspeare's Plays*

Samuel Johnson was one of the greatest critics in English history. He wrote many essays in periodicals of the time and served as editor of an edition of Shakespeare's plays. He also published a collection of essays on famous poets, *The Lives of the English Poets*, and produced a *Dictionary of the English Language* nearly completely on his own.

Of this tragedy many particular passages deserve regard, and the contention and reconcilement of Brutus and Cassius is universally celebrated; but I have never been strongly agitated in perusing it, and think it somewhat cold and unaffecting compared with some other of Shakspeare's plays; his adherence to the real story, and to Roman manners, seems to have impeded the natural vigour of his genius.

1769—Elizabeth Montagu. "Upon the Death of Julius Caesar," from *An Essay on the Writings and Genius of Shakespear*

Elizabeth Montagu was an intellectual hostess in London who established "conversation parties," during which literature was usually a topic.

The tragedies of Cinna, and Julius Caesar, are each of them the representation of a conspiracy; but it cannot be denied, that our countryman has been by far more judicious in his choice of the story. An abortive scheme, in which some people of obscure fame were engaged, and ever in whom, as they are represented, the attempt was pardoned, more from contempt of their abilities and power, than the clemency of the emperor, makes a poor figure in contrast with that conspiracy, which, formed by the first characters in Rome, effected the destruction of the greatest man the world ever produced, and was succeeded by the most memorable consequences. History furnishes various examples of base and treacherous natures, of dissolute manners, ruined fortunes, and lost reputations; uniting in horrid association to destroy their prince. Ambition often cuts itself a bloody way to greatness. Exasperated misery sometimes plunges its desperate dagger in the breast of the oppressor. The cabal of a court, the mutiny of a camp, the wild zeal of fanatics, have often produced events of that nature. But this conspiracy was formed of very different elements. It was the genius of Rome, the rights of her constitution, the spirit of her laws, that rose against the ambition of Caesar; they steeled the heart, and whetted the dagger of the mild, the virtuous, the gentle Brutus, to give the mortal wound, not to a tyrant, who had fastened fetters on his fellow-citizens, but to the conqueror, who had made the world wear their chains. one empire only remained unsubjected to them, and that he was preparing to subdue.

Can there be a subject more worthy of the tragic muse, than the imitation of an action so important in its consequences, and unparalleled in all its circumstances? How is our curiosity excited to discover what could engage the man of virtue in an enterprize of such a terrible kind; and why, after its accomplishment, instead of being stigmatized with the name of conspirator and assassin, the decrees of an august senate, the voice of Rome, unite to place him one of the first on the roll of patriots; and the successor of the murdered Caesar, who devoted to destruction the most illustrious men of Rome, durst not offer violation to the statue of Brutus!

To obtain, from the English spectator, the same reverence for him, it was necessary we should be made to imbibe those doctrines, and to adopt the opinion by which he himself was actuated. We must be in the very capitol of Rome; stand at the base of Pompey's statue, surrounded by the effigies of their patriots; we must be taught to adore the images of Junius Brutus, the Horatii, Decii, Fabii, and all who had offered dear and bloody sacrifice to the liberty of their country, to see this action in the point of view to which it offered itself to the deliberation of Brutus, and by which it was beheld by those who judged of it when done. To the very scene, to the very time, therefore, does our poet transport us: at Rome, we become Romans; we are affected by their manners; we are caught by their enthusiasm. But what a variety of imitations were there to be made by the artist to effect this! and who but Shakespear was capable of such a tack? A poet of ordinary genius would have endeavoured to interest us for Brutus, by the means of some imagined fond mother, or fonder mistress. But can a few female tears wipe out the stains of assassination? A base conspirator, a vile assassin, like the wretched Cinna of Corneille, would Brutus have appeared to us, if only the same feeble arts had been exerted for him. It is for the genuine son of ancient Rome, the lover of the liberty of his country, we are interested. A concern raised for him, from compassion to any other person, would only have excited some painful emotions in the spectator, arising from discordant sentiments. Indeed, the common aim of tragedy writers seems to be merely to make us uneasy, for some reason or other, during the drama. They take any thing to be a tragedy in which there are great persons, and much lamentation; but our poet never represents an action of one sort, and raises emotions and passions of another sort. He excites the sympathies, and the concern, proper to the story. The passion of love, or maternal affection, may give good subjects for a tragedy. In the fables of Phaedra and Merope those sentiments belong to the action; but they had no share in the resolution taken to kill Caesar; and, if they are made to interfere, they adulterate the imitation; if to predominate, they spoil it. Our author disdains the legerdemain trick of substituting one passion for another. He is the great magician that can call forth passions of any sort. If they are such as time has destroyed, or custom extinguished, he summons from the dead those souls in which they once existed.

(. . .)

The quarrel between Brutus and Cassius does not by any means deserve the ridicule thrown upon it by the French critic. The characters of the men are

well sustained: it is natural, it is interesting; but it rather retards than brings
forward the catastrophe, and is useful only in setting Brutus in a good light.
A sublime genius, in all its operations, sacrifices little things to great, and
parts to the whole. Modern criticism dwells on minute articles. The principal
object of our poet was to interest the spectator for Brutus; to do this he was
to shew, that his temper was the furthest imaginable from any thing ferocious
or sanguinary, and by his behaviour to his wife, his friends, his servants,
to demonstrate, that out of respect to public liberty, he made as difficult a
conquest over his natural disposition, as his great predecessor had done for
the like cause over natural affection. Clemency and humanity add lustre to
the greatest hero; but here these sentiments determine the whole character of
the man, and the colour of his deed. The victories of Alexander, Caesar, and
Hannibal, whether their wars were just or unjust, must obtain for them the
laurel wreath, which is the ambition of conquerors: but the act of Brutus in
killing Caesar, was of such an ambiguous kind, as to receive its denomination
from the motive by which it was suggested; it is that which must fix upon him
the name of patriot or assassin. Our author, therefore, shews great judgment
in taking various opportunities to display the softness and gentleness of
Brutus: the little circumstance of his forbearing to awaken the servant who
was playing to him on the lute, is very beautiful; for one cannot conceive, that
he whose tender humanity respected the slumber of his boy Lucilius, would
from malice or cruelty, have cut short the important and illustrious course of
Caesar's life.

Shakespear seems to have aimed at giving an exact representation on the
stage, of all the events and characters comprehended in Plutarch's life of
Marcus Brutus; and he has wonderfully executed his plan. One may perhaps
wish, that a writer, possessed of all the magic of poetical powers, had not so
scrupulously confined himself within the limits of true history. The regions of
imagination, in which the poet is allowed an arbitrary sway, seem his proper
dominion. There he reigns like Pluto over shadows huge and terrible, of
mighty and august appearance, but yielding and unresisting. The terra firma of
real life, and the open day-light of truth, forbid many pleasing delusions, and
produce difficulties too stubborn to yield to his art. On this solid foundation
however our author knew he could always establish a strong interest for his
piece. Great knowledge of the human heart had informed him, how easy it is
to excite a sympathy with things believed real. He knew too, that curiosity is a
strong appetite, and that every incident connected with a great event, and every
particularity belonging to a great character, engages the spectator. He wrote to
please an untaught people, guided wholly by their feelings, and to those feelings
he applied, and they are often touched by circumstances that have not dignity
and splendor enough to please the eye accustomed to the specious miracles of

ostentatious art, and the nice selection of refined judgment. If we blame his making the tragic muse too subservient to the historical, we must at least allow it to be much less hurtful to the effect of his representation upon the passions, than the liberties taken by many poets to represent well-known characters and events in lights so absolutely different from whatsoever universal fame, and the testimony of ages, had taught us to believe of them, that the mind resists the new impression attempted to be made upon it. Shakespear, perhaps not injudiciously, thought that it was more the business of the dramatic writer to excite sympathy than admiration; and that to acquire an empire over the passions, it was well worth while to relinquish some pretensions to excellencies of less efficiency on the stage.

JULIUS CAESAR
IN THE NINETEENTH CENTURY

⁂

In the 1800s a number of critics examined the characters in *Julius Caesar*, with Caesar himself becoming a prime subject of analysis. William Hazlitt, one of the great critics of his time, lauded Shakespeare for his skill in understanding character, yet found fault with his Caesar, who Hazlitt felt was an imperfect representation of the man. Hazlitt also faulted Shakespeare for creating a plot where Caesar has nothing to do. Much later in the century, George Bernard Shaw, who often criticized Shakespeare, expressed his revulsion at the Caesar Shakespeare created, a "silly braggart" (Shaw preferred Shakespeare's characterization of Antony). The German critic August Wilhelm Schlegel, too, felt that the portrayal of Caesar was inappropriate and that his pomposity was exaggerated. The critic H.N. Hudson found the character "perplexing."

Other German critics, such as Georg Gottfried Gervinus, also examined the play and its characters from a historical point of view. Gervinus wrote that Shakespeare followed Plutarch's description of Caesar. Plutarch saw Caesar's character as declining before his death, and Shakespeare also portrayed Caesar in this way—negatively affected by his victory and power. According to Gervinus, Caesar's pride and defiance of danger are ultimately what bring his downfall. Like Pompey, his death came about because of civil war, and as a result of his death more war occurs. In this way, Caesar plays an important role in the action. The great German writer Johann Wolfgang von Goethe, focusing on Shakespeare's overall method, categorized the playwright as thoroughly modern and as having the ability to fuse the old and the new.

The scholars Oscar Fay Adams and F.A. Marshall agreed with Gervinus's view that Shakespeare followed Plutarch's characterization of Caesar as a man who had become too ambitious at a key point in his career. They, too, saw the character of Caesar as the center of the play, and they saw his ghost as what connects the first part of the play (about Caesar's death) to the second part (about the retribution for the death).

Other critics concentrated on the design of the play. Some, such as Schlegel, felt that the last two acts did not live up to the first three. Schlegel praised the reaction of the characters to Caesar and also the portrayal of the conspiracy. Another critic, Richard G. Moulton, said the play has the simplest of plots, and he examined how Shakespeare guides the audience's emotion. The beginning of the play centers on providing the justification for the conspirators' plan to kill Caesar. Sympathy for this justification grows until the assassination, after which Shakespeare is able to shift the audience's sympathies against the conspirators. Through all stages, Shakespeare deftly uses techniques such as suspense and supernatural events to accomplish this emotional progression.

Hermann Ulrici focused not so much on Shakespeare's skill as on the reason the events surrounding Caesar's death took place. Like others who looked at Caesar in the play in terms of how true the character was to the historical figure, Ulrici examined events in historical terms. His view was that history has its own course and that no human, even if he is as powerful as Caesar or as moral as Brutus, can affect its path. Therefore, Brutus and Cassius have to die because they do not understand the historical problems that need to be resolved: They are a part of a dying republic, a land where the flow of history is tending toward monarchy and change. Even the oligarchy that occurred after Caesar's death was only temporary. According to Ulrici, Caesar's ghost is the disturbed spirit of history itself. It appears briefly, but the audience feels its presence powerfully.

Nineteenth-century critics also looked closely at the play's other major character, Brutus. Hazlitt, for example, commented on the sensitive side of Brutus, pointing out how sympathetically he responds when Lucius falls asleep. While most critics praised the character, some found less to admire. To Shaw, Brutus was a "familiar type of English suburban preacher." The great Romantic poet Samuel Taylor Coleridge found Brutus inconsistent and criticized the speech in which Brutus is struggling with whether to join the conspirators; Coleridge considered this passage strange, since Brutus neglects to consider Caesar's obviously objectionable qualities. Adams and Marshall, however, wrote that Brutus's inconsistencies are exactly consistent with his character. In their view, Brutus is the idealist but his noble ideas are not practical.

The German philosopher Friedrich Nietzsche praised Shakespeare for believing in Brutus and his "virtue"—"independence of soul." According to Nietzsche, *Julius Caesar* was Shakespeare's best tragedy, though "called by the wrong name." (It apparently should have been called *Brutus;* in the following century, Harold Bloom would agree with this assessment.) In Brutus's mind, the love of freedom overpowers all, so that even one's dearest friend can be sacrificed for freedom's sake. Nietzsche also remarked on Shakespeare's contempt for poets in the play, which was a kind of self-contempt. Similarly, the French critic Paul Stapfer also cited the "inglorious" death of the writer Cicero in the play.

Critical analysis extended to other characters as well. Adams and Marshall drew comparisons between Brutus and his wife Portia, both of whom they saw as noble and self-disciplined as well as very sensitive. Paul Stapfer likewise examined Portia, but he declared Plutarch's Portia better than Shakespeare's. Stapfer also recorded how women were viewed and treated at various points in history, showing how striking it was for a woman like Portia to appear in antiquity.

1809—August Wilhelm Schlegel.
From *Lectures on Dramatic Art and Literature*

August Wilhelm Schlegel was a scholar, critic, poet, and professor at the University of Bonn. He was one of the most influential disseminators of the ideas of the German Romantic movement, and his translations of Shakespeare into German are highly regarded.

...The piece of *Julius Caesar*, to complete the action, requires to be continued to the fall of Brutus and Cassius. Caesar is not the hero of the piece, but Brutus. The amiable beauty of this character, his feeling and patriotic heroism, are portrayed with peculiar care. Yet the poet has pointed out with great nicety the superiority of Cassius over Brutus in independent volition and discernment in judging of human affairs; that the latter from the purity of his mind and his conscientious love of justice, is unfit to be the head of a party in a state entirely corrupted; and that these very faults give an unfortunate turn to the cause of the conspirators. In the part of Caesar several ostentatious speeches have been censured as unsuitable. But as he never appears in action, we have no other measure of his greatness than the impression which he makes upon the rest of the characters, and his peculiar confidence in himself. In this Caesar was by no means deficient, as we learn from history and his own writings; but he displayed it more in the easy ridicule of his enemies than in pompous discourses. The theatrical effect of this play is injured by a partial falling off of the last two acts compared with the preceding in external splendour and rapidity. The first appearance of Caesar in festal robes, when the music stops, and all are silent whenever he opens his mouth, and when the few words which he utters are received as oracles, is truly magnificent; the conspiracy is a true conspiracy, which in stolen interviews and in the dead of night prepares the blow which is to be struck in open day, and which is to change the constitution of the world;—the confused thronging before the murder of Caesar, the general agitation even of the perpetrators after the deed, are all portrayed with most masterly skill; with the funeral procession and the speech of Antony the effect reaches its utmost height. Caesar's shade is more powerful to avenge his fall than he himself was to guard against it. After the overthrow of the external splendour and greatness of the conqueror and ruler of the world, the intrinsic grandeur of character of Brutus and Cassius is all that remain to fill the stage and occupy the minds of the spectators: suitably to their name, as the last of the Romans, they stand there, in some degree alone; and forming a great and hazardous determination is more powerfully calculated to excite our expectation, than supporting the consequences of the deed with heroic firmness.

━◦/◦/◦━ ━◦/◦/◦━ ━◦/◦/◦━

1813–1816—Johann Wolfgang von Goethe. "Shakespeare Compared with the Ancients and the Moderns," from *Shakespeare Ad Infinitum*

Johann Wolfgang von Goethe was a novelist, poet, playwright, translator, and scientist. His greatest work is the dramatic poem *Faust*.

The interests which vitalize Shakespeare's great genius are interests which centre in this world. For if prophecy and madness, dreams, omens, portents, fairies and gnomes, ghosts, imps, and conjurers introduce a magical element which so beautifully pervades his poems, yet these figures are in no way the basic elements of his works, but rest on a broad basis of the truth and fidelity of life, so that everything that comes from his pen seems to us genuine and sound. It has already been suggested that he belongs not so much to the poets of the modern era, which has been called "romantic," but much more to the "naturalistic" school, since his work is permeated with the reality of the present, and scarcely touches the emotions of unsatisfied desire, except at his highest points.

Disregarding this, however, he is, from a closer point of view, a decidedly modern poet, separated from the ancients by an enormous gulf, not perhaps with regard to his outer form, which is here beside our point, but with regard to his inner and most profound spirit.

Here let me say that it is not my idea to use the following terminology as exhaustive or exclusive; it is an attempt not so much to add another new antithesis to those already recognized, as to indicate that it is already contained in these. These are the antitheses:—

Ancient	Modern
Natural	Sentimental
Pagan	Christian
Classic	Romantic
Realistic	Idealistic
Necessity	Freedom
Duty (*sollen*)	Will (*wollen*)

The greatest ills to which men are exposed, as well as the most numerous, arise from a certain inner conflict between duty and will, as well as between duty and its accomplishment, and desire and its accomplishment; and it is these conflicts which bring us so often into trouble in the course of our lives. Little difficulties, springing from a slight error which, though taking us by surprise, can be solved easily, give the clue to situations of comedy. The great difficulties, on the other hand, unresolved and unresolvable, give us tragedy.

Predominating in the old poems is the conflict between duty and performance, in the new between desire and accomplishment. Let us put this decided divergency among the other antitheses and see if it does not prove suggestive. In both epochs, I have said, there predominates now this side, now that; but since duty and desire are not radically separated in men's characters, both will be found together, even if one prevails and the other is subordinate. Duty is imposed upon men; "must" is a bitter pill. The Will man imposes upon himself; man's will is his kingdom of heaven. A long-continued obligation is burdensome, the inability to perform it even terrible; but a constant will is pleasurable, and with a firm will men can console themselves for their inability to accomplish their desire.

Let us consider a game of cards as a kind of poem; it consists of both those elements. The form of the game, bound up with chance, plays here the role of necessity, just as the ancients knew it under the form of Fate; the will, bound up with the skill of the player, works in the other direction. In this sense I might call whist "classic." The form of play limits the operation of chance, and even of the will itself. I have to play, in company with definite partners and opponents, with the cards which come into my hand, make the best of a long series of chance plays, without being able to control or parry them. In Ombre and similar games, the contrary is the case. Here are many openings left for skill and daring. I can disavow the cards that fall to my hand, make them count in different ways, half or completely discard them, get help by luck, and in the play get the best advantage out of the worst cards. Thus this kind of game resembles perfectly the modern mode of thought and literature.

Ancient tragedy was based on unescapable necessity, which was only sharpened and accelerated by an opposing will. Here is the seat of all that is fearful in the oracles, the region in which Oedipus lords it over all. Less tragic appears necessity in the guise of duty in the "Antigone"; and in how many forms does it not appear! But all necessity is despotic, whether it belong to the realm of Reason, like custom and civil law, or to Nature, like the laws of Becoming, and Growing and Passing-away, of Life and of Death. Before all these we tremble, without realizing that it is the good of the *whole* that is aimed at. The will, on the contrary, is free, appears free, and is advantageous to the *individual*. Thus the will is a flatterer, and takes possession of men as soon as they learn to recognize it. It is the god of the modern world. Dedicated to it, we are afraid of opposing doctrines, and here lies the crux of that eternal division which separates our art and thought from the ancients. Through the motive of Necessity, tragedy became mighty and strong; through the motive of Will, weak and feeble. Out of the latter arose the so-called Drama, in which dread Necessity is overcome and dissolved through the Will. But just because this comes to the aid of our weakness we feel moved when, after painful tension, we are at last a little encouraged and consoled.

As I turn now, after these preliminaries, to Shakespeare, I must express the hope that the reader himself will make the proper comparisons and applications. It is Shakespeare's unique distinction that he has combined in such remarkable fashion the old and the new. In his plays Will and Necessity struggle to maintain an equilibrium; both contend powerfully, yet always so that Will remains at a disadvantage.

No one has shown perhaps better than he the connection between Necessity and Will in the individual character. The person, considered as a character, is under a certain necessity; he is constrained, appointed to a certain particular line of action; but as a human being he has a will, which is unconfined and universal in its demands. Thus arises an inner conflict, and Shakespeare is superior to all other writers in the significance with which he endows this. But now an outer conflict may arise, and the individual through it may become so aroused that an insufficient will is raised through circumstance to the level of irremissible necessity. These motives I have referred to earlier in the case of Hamlet; but the motive is repeated constantly in Shakespeare,—Hamlet through the agency of the ghost; Macbeth through the witches, Hecate, and his wife; Brutus through his friends gets into a dilemma and situation to which they were not equal; even in Coriolanus the same motive is found. This Will, which reaches beyond the power of the individual, is decidedly modern. But since in Shakespeare it does not spring from within, but is developed through eternal circumstance, it becomes a sort of Necessity, and approaches the classical motive. For all the heroes of ancient poetry willed only what was possible to men, and from this arose that beautiful balance between Necessity, Will, and Accomplishment. Still their Necessity is a little too severe for it really to be able to please us, even though we may wonder at and admire it. A Necessity which more or less, or even completely, excludes human freedom does not chime with our views any longer. It is true that Shakespeare in his own way has approximated this, but in making this Necessity a moral necessity he has, to our pleasure and astonishment, united the spirit of the ancient and the modern worlds. If we are to learn anything from him, here is the point where we must study in his school. Instead of singing the praises of our Romanticism so exclusively, and sticking to it so uncritically,—our Romanticism, which need not be chidden or rejected,—and thus mistaking and obscuring its strong, solid practical aspect, we should rather attempt to make this great fusion between the old and the new, even though it does seem inconsistent and paradoxical; and all the more should we make the attempt, because a great and unique master, whom we value most highly, and, often without knowing why, give homage to above all others, has already most effectively accomplished this miracle. To be sure, he had the advantage of living in a true time of harvest, and of working in a vigorous Protestant country, where the madness of bigotry was silent for a time, so that freedom was given to a true child of nature, such as Shakespeare was, to develop religiously his own pure inner nature, without reference to any established religion.

1817—William Hazlitt. "Julius Caesar," from *Characters of Shakespear's Plays*

William Hazlitt was an English essayist and one of the finest critics of his time. He examined the work of poets, dramatists, essayists, and novelists. Other volumes of his include *English Poets*, *English Comic Writers*, and *A View of the English Stage*.

JULIUS CAESAR was one of three principal plays by different authors, pitched upon by the celebrated Earl of Hallifax to be brought out in a splendid manner by subscription, in the year 1707. The other two were the *King and No King* of Fletcher, and Dryden's *Maiden Queen*. There perhaps might be political reasons for this selection, as far as regards our author. Otherwise, Shakespear's JULIUS CAESAR is not equal as a whole, to either of his other plays taken from the Roman history. It is inferior in interest to *Coriolanus*, and both in interest and power to *Antony and Cleopatra*. It however abounds in admirable and affecting passages, and is remarkable for the profound knowledge of character, in which Shakespear could scarcely fail. If there is any exception to this remark, it is in the hero of the piece himself. We do not much admire the representation here given of Julius Caesar, nor do we think it answers to the portrait given of him in his Commentaries. He makes several vapouring and rather pedantic speeches, and does nothing. Indeed, he has nothing to do. So far, the fault of the character is the fault of the plot.

The spirit with which the poet has entered at once into the manners of the common people, and the jealousies and heart-burnings of the different factions, is shewn in the first scene, where Flavius and Marullus, tribunes of the people, and some citizens of Rome, appear upon the stage.

'*Flavius.* Thou art a cobler, art thou?

Cobler. Truly, Sir, *all* that I live by, is the *awl*: I meddle with no tradesman's matters, nor woman's matters, but *with-al*, I am indeed, Sir, a surgeon to old shoes; when they are in great danger, I recover them.

Flavius. But wherefore art not in thy shop to-day? Why dost thou lead these men about the streets?

Cobler. Truly, Sir, to wear out their shoes, to get myself into more work. But indeed, Sir, we make holiday to see Caesar, and rejoice in his triumph.'

To this specimen of quaint low humour immediately follows that unexpected and animated burst of indignant eloquence, put into the mouth of one of the angry tribunes.

'*Marullus.* Wherefore rejoice!—What conquest brings he home?
What tributaries follow him to Rome,
To grace in captive-bonds his chariot-wheels?
Oh you hard hearts, you cruel men of Rome!
Knew you not Pompey? Many a time and oft
Have you climb'd up to walls and battlements,
To towers and windows, yea, to chimney-tops,
Your infants in your arms, and there have sat
The live-long day with patient expectation,
To see great Pompey pass the streets of Rome:
And when you saw his chariot but appear,
Have you not made an universal shout,
That Tyber trembled underneath his banks
To hear the replication of your sounds,
Made in his concave shores?
And do you now put on your best attire?
And do you now cull out an holiday?
And do you now strew flowers in his way
That comes in triumph over Pompey's blood?
Begone—
Run to your houses, fall upon your knees,
Pray to the Gods to intermit the plague,
That needs must light on this ingratitude.'

The well-known dialogue between Brutus and Cassius, in which the latter breaks the design of the conspiracy to the former, and partly gains him over to it, is a noble piece of high-minded declamation. Cassius's insisting on the pretended effeminacy of Caesar's character, and his description of their swimming across the Tiber together, "once upon a raw and gusty day," are among the finest strokes in it. But perhaps the whole is not equal to the short scene which follows, when Caesar enters with his train:—

> '*Brutus.* The games are done, and Caesar is returning.
> *Cassius.* As they pass by, pluck Casca by the sleeve,
> And he will, after his sour fashion, tell you
> What has proceeded worthy note to-day.
> *Brutus.* I will do so; but look you, Cassius—
> The angry spot doth glow on Caesar's brow,
> And all the rest look like a chidden train.
> Calphurnia's cheek is pale; and Cicero
> Looks with such ferret and such fiery eyes,
> As we have seen him in the Capitol,
> Being crost in conference by some senators.
> *Cassius.* Casca will tell us what the matter is.
> *Caesar.* Antonius—
> *Antony.* Caesar?
> *Caesar.* Let me have men about me that are fat,
> Sleek-headed men, and such as sleep a-nights:
> Yon Cassius has a lean and hungry look,
> He thinks too much; such men are dangerous.
> *Antony.* Fear him not, Caesar, he's not dangerous:
> He is a noble Roman, and well given.
> *Caesar.* Would he were fatter; but I fear him not:
> Yet if my name were liable to fear,
> I do not know the man I should avoid
> So soon as that spare Cassius. He reads much;
> He is a great observer; and he looks
> Quite through the deeds of men. He loves no plays,
> As thou dost, Antony; he hears no music:
> Seldom he smiles, and smiles in such a sort,
> As if he mock'd himself, and scorn'd his spirit,
> That could be mov'd to smile at any thing.
> Such men as he be never at heart's ease,
> Whilst they behold a greater than themselves;
> And therefore are they very dangerous.
> I rather tell thee what is to be fear'd
> Than what I fear; for always I am Caesar.
> Come on my right hand, for this ear is deaf,
> And tell me truly what thou think'st of him.'

We know hardly any passage more expressive of the genius of Shakespear than this. It is as if he had been actually present, had known the different characters and what they thought of one another, and had taken down what he heard and saw, their looks, words, and gestures, just as they happened.

The character of Mark Antony is farther speculated upon where the conspirators deliberate whether he shall fall with Caesar. Brutus is against it—

> 'And for Mark Antony, think not of him:
> For he can do no more than Caesar's arm,
> When Caesar's head is off.
>   *Cassius.* Yet I do fear him:
> For in th' ingrafted love he bears to Caesar—
>   *Brutus.* Alas, good Cassius, do not think of him:
> If he love Caesar, all that he can do
> Is to himself, take thought, and die for Caesar:
> And that were much, he should; for he is giv'n
> To sports, to wildness, and much company.
>   *Trebonius.* There is no fear in him; let him not die:
> For he will live, and laugh at this hereafter.'

They were in the wrong; and Cassius was right.

The honest manliness of Brutus is however sufficient to find out the unfitness of Cicero to be included in their enterprize, from his affected egotism and literary vanity.

> 'O, name him not: let us not break with him;
> For he will never follow any thing,
> That other men begin.'

His scepticism as to prodigies and his moralising on the weather—'This disturbed sky is not to walk in'—are in the same spirit of refined imbecility.

Shakespear has in this play and elsewhere shewn the same penetration into political character and the springs of public events as into those of every-day life. For instance, the whole design of the conspirators to liberate their country fails from the generous temper and over-weening confidence of Brutus in the goodness of their cause and the assistance of others. Thus it has always been. Those who mean well themselves think well of others, and fall a prey to their security. That humanity and honesty which dispose men to resist injustice and tyranny render them unfit to cope with the cunning and power of those who are opposed to them. The friends of liberty trust to the professions of others, because they are themselves sincere, and endeavour to reconcile the public good with the least possible hurt to its enemies, who have no regard to any thing but their own unprincipled ends, and stick at nothing to accomplish them. Cassius was better cut out for a conspirator. His heart prompted his head. His watchful jealousy made him fear the worst that might happen, and his irritability of temper added to his inveteracy of purpose, and sharpened his patriotism. The mixed nature of his motives made him fitter to contend with bad men. The vices are never so well employed as in combating one another. Tyranny and servility are to be dealt with after their own fashion: otherwise, they will triumph over those who spare them, and finally pronounce their funeral panegyric, as Antony did that of Brutus.

'All the conspirators, save only he,
Did that they did in envy of great Caesar:
He only in a general honest thought
And common good to all, made one of them.'

The quarrel between Brutus and Cassius is managed in a masterly way. The dramatic fluctuation of passion, the calmness of Brutus, the heat of Cassius, are admirably described; and the exclamation of Cassius on hearing of the death of Portia, which he does not learn till after their reconciliation, "How 'scaped I killing when I crost you so?" gives double force to all that has gone before. The scene between Brutus and Portia, where she endeavours to extort the secret of the conspiracy from him, is conceived in the most heroical spirit, and the burst of tenderness in Brutus—

'You are my true and honourable wife;
As dear to me as are the ruddy drops
That visit my sad heart'—

is justified by her whole behaviour. Portia's breathless impatience to learn the event of the conspiracy, in the dialogue with Lucius, is full of passion. The interest which Portia takes in Brutus and that which Calphurnia takes in the fate of Caesar are discriminated with the nicest precision. Mark Antony's speech over the dead body of Caesar has been justly admired for the mixture of pathos and artifice in it: that of Brutus certainly is not so good.

The entrance of the conspirators to the house of Brutus at midnight is rendered very impressive. In the midst of this scene, we meet with one of those careless and natural digressions which occur so frequently and beautifully in Shakespear. After Cassius has introduced his friends one by one, Brutus says—

'They are all welcome.
What watchful cares do interpose themselves
Betwixt your eyes and night?

> *Cassius.* Shall I entreat a word? (*They whisper.*)
> *Decius.* Here lies the east: doth not the day break here?
> *Casca.* No.
> *Cinna.* O pardon, Sir, it doth; and yon grey lines,
> That fret the clouds, are messengers of day.
> 　　*Casca.* You shall confess, that you are both deceiv'd:
> Here, as I point my sword, the sun arises,
> Which is a great way growing on the south,
> Weighing the youthful season of the year.
> Some two months hence, up higher toward the north
> He first presents his fire, and the high east
> Stands as the Capitol, directly here.'

We cannot help thinking this graceful familiarity better than all the fustian in the world.—The truth of history in Julius Caesar is very ably worked up with dramatic effect. The councils of generals, the doubtful turns of battles, are represented to the life. The death of Brutus is worthy of him—it has the dignity of the Roman senator with the firmness of the Stoic philosopher. But what is perhaps better than either, is the little incident of his boy, Lucius, falling asleep over his instrument, as he is playing to his master in his tent, the night before the battle. Nature had played him the same forgetful trick once before on the night of the conspiracy. The humanity of Brutus is the same on both occasions.

> 　　　　—'It is no matter:
> Enjoy the honey-heavy dew of slumber.
> Thou hast no figures nor no fantasies,
> Which busy care draws in the brains of men.
> Therefore thou sleep'st so sound.'

1818—Samuel Taylor Coleridge. "Julius Caesar," from *Lectures and Notes on Shakspere and Other English Poets*

Samuel Taylor Coleridge was an English poet, philosopher, and critic. In collaboration with his good friend William Wordsworth, he published *Lyrical Ballads*, which among other pieces contained his enduring poem "The Rime of the Ancient Mariner." His best-known critical work is *Biographia Literaria*.

Act ii. sc. 1. Speech of Brutus:—

> "It must be by his death; and, for my part,
> I know no personal cause to spurn at him,
> But for the general. He would be crown'd:—
> How that might change his nature, there's the question.
> 　　　　　— And, to speak truth of Caesar,
> I have not known when his affections sway'd
> More than his reason.
> 　　　　　— So Caesar may;
> Then, lest he may, prevent.

This speech is singular;—at least, I do not at present see into Shakspere's motive, his *rationale*, or in what point of view he meant Brutus' character to appear. For surely—(this I mean is what I say to myself, with my present *quantum* of insight, only modified by my experience in how many instances I have ripened into a perception of beauties, where I had before descried faults;) surely, nothing can seem more discordant with our historical preconceptions of Brutus, or more lowering to the intellect of the Stoico-Platonic tyrannicide, than the tenets here attributed to him—to him, the stern Roman republican; namely,—that he would have no objection to a king, or to Caesar, a monarch in Rome, would Caesar but be as good a monarch as he now seems disposed to be! How, too, could Brutus say that he found no personal cause—none in Caesar's past conduct as a man? Had he not passed the Rubicon? Had he not entered Rome as a conqueror? Had he not placed his Gauls in the Senate?—Shakspere, it may be said, has not brought these things forward.—True;—and this is just the ground of my perplexity. What character did Shakspere mean his Brutus to be?

(...)

Act iv. sc. 3. Speech of Brutus:—

> "—What, shall one of us,
> That struck the foremost man of all this world,
> But for *supporting robbers*."

This seemingly strange assertion of Brutus is unhappily verified in the present day. What is an immense army, in which the lust of plunder has quenched all the duties of the citizen, other than a horde of robbers, or differenced only as fiends are from ordinarily reprobate men? Caesar supported, and was supported by, such as these;—and even so Buonaparte in our days.

I know no part of Shakspere that more impresses on me the belief of his genius being superhuman, than this scene between Brutus and Cassius. In the Gnostic heresy, it might have been credited with less absurdity than most of their dogmas, that the Supreme had employed him to create, previously to his function of representing, characters.

1846— Hermann Ulrici. From *Shakespeare's Dramatic Art, and His Relation to Calderon and Goethe*

Hermann Ulrici was a German philosopher who taught at the University of Halle. He wrote works of literary criticism as well as books that severely criticized Hegel's ideas. Later he wrote on the relationship of philosophy to science and to the thought of his time.

In the historical drama the interest—if it is to be historical—must, above all things, be truly historical, then it will be truly poetic as well. History, however, in a certain sense does not trouble itself about persons; its chief interest is in historical facts and their meaning. Now in *Jul. Caes.* we have absolutely only one point of interest, a true, but variously jointed unity. One and the same thought is reflected in the fall of Caesar, in the deaths of Brutus and Cassius, and in the victory of Antony and Octavius. No man, even though he were as mighty as Caesar and as noble as Brutus, is sufficiently great to guide history according to his own will; every one, according to his vocation, may contribute his stone to the building of the grand whole, but let no one presume to think that he can, with impunity, experiment with it. The great Caesar, however, merely experimented when he allowed the royal crown to be offered to him, and then rejected it thrice against his own will. He could not curb his ambition—this history might perhaps have pardoned—but he did not understand her, and attempted that which he, at the time at least, did not yet wish. The consequence of this error which was entirely his own, the consequence of this arrogant presumption which the still active republican spirit, the old Roman love and pride of freedom, stirred up against him, proved his downfall. But Brutus and Cassius erred also by imagining that Rome could be kept in its glory and preserved from its threatening ruin simply by the restoration of the republic; as if the happiness, the power, and the greatness of a state depended upon its form, and as if a single man could repair a nation's demoralization by a mere word of command. And as Caesar had thought life unendurable without the outward dignity of the royal throne, so they imagined life not worth having without the honour of outward freedom, for they confounded outward with inward moral freedom, or, at all events, omitted to consider that the former can exist only as the result and expression of the latter. They, too, experimented with history; Cassius trusted that his ambitious and selfish will, and Brutus, that his noble and self-sacrificing will, would be strong enough to direct the course of history. For both felt that the moral spirit of the Roman nation had sunk too deep to be able in future to govern itself as a Republic; Cassius knew, Brutus suspected, that the time of the Republic was coming to an end. But in their republican pride and feeling that republican honour hurt, they thought themselves called upon to make an attempt to save it, they trusted to their power to be able, as it were, to take it upon their shoulders and so keep its head above water. This was the arrogance which was added to the error, and which spurred them on not only to unreasonable undertaking, but to commit a criminal act, and, therefore, they doubly deserved the punishment which befell then. Antony, on the other hand, with Octavius and Lepidus—the talented voluptuary, the clever actor and the good-natured simpleton—although not half so powerful and noble as their opponents, come off victorious, because, in fact, they but followed the course of history, and knew how to make use of it. Thus in all the principal parts we have the same leading thought, the same unity in the (historical) interest, except that it is reflected in various ways. But it also shines forth in the secondary parts in Portia's death, as well as in the fall of Cato, Cicero, and the other conspirator; Portia and Cato perish with the noble but erring Brutus, who desires only what is good; the other with the selfish Cassius, who thinks only of himself. All perish because they do not understand, but endeavoured arbitrarily to make history or, as arbitrarily, went round the problem which bad to be solved in its own time and 'spoke Greek.' Thus history appears represented from one of its main aspects, in its inner autocratic, active, and formative power, by which, although externally formal by individual men, it nevertheless controls and marches over the heads of the greatest of them.

This is the general, ideal point of view from which history appears here to be conceived, and also to determine the fate of the dramatic characters. The special historical condition upon which the whole is founded is again one of the transition stages in political life, one of the most interesting points of history, both in a poetical and historical respect. As *Coriolanus* forms the transition from the aristocratic to the democratic form of government, here it is the transition from the republican to the monarchial, the latter being demanded by the historical circumstances as their stimulating and formative principle. This transition, according to its idea and the position of things, required an intermediate stage between the republican and the monarchical form, the oligarchical form which had been aimed at ever since the days of Sulla, but had hitherto not been able to obtain a legal existence. Regarded from this point of view, Caesar's death was the necessary consequence of his anti-historical attempt to leap over his intermediate stage. Caesar was, in reality, right; monarchy had become a necessity, an historical right. But history will not tolerate any bounds, and where such are made with violence, they are again corrected by retrogressions, so-called reactions. It was, accordingly, the oligarchical principle. represented by Octavius, Antony, and Lepidus, that in reality gained the victory over Caesar—the representative of the monarchy which was still a thing of the future—as well as over Brutus and Cassius, the representative of the Republic which was already a thing of the past. It conquered because it had the right of the immediate present on its side.

But it may be asked, What is the meaning of the introduction of spirits into an historical drama? Does it not, in the present case, appear a mere dramatic *bonne marche* for the multitude? Shakspeare found the ghosts in Plutarch, and retained them in accordance with his principle of following the historical tradition as faithfully as possible, but assuredly not merely out of regard for the historical subject-matter, but doubtless also because it appeared to him to be an important symbol, a significant reference to the actual motive and leading thought in the historical events, and because it, at the same tune, seemed to indicate the point where the historico-political cause meets the ethical and moral cause. This is why Shakspeare makes the ghost—which according to Plutarch appears to Brutus 'as his evil genius'—assume the likeness of Caesar: this is why—as in Plutarch—he makes it appear to Brutus and not to Cassius. Brutus is of a peaceful and tranquil disposition, truly noble in mind, devoted to the ethical principles of stoicism, desiring only the good and the welfare of his country, a worthy and faithful husband to his high-minded wife, a patriot ready for any sacrifice, but little inclined for energetic action and still less for political activity. Yet he nevertheless allows himself to be so far deluded by Cassius's seductive artificer and well-calculated eloquence, by the republican fame of his own race—which he thinks it his duty to maintain—and by his own pride in his duty as a man—which will not bow to any single individual, not even to a Caesar—that not only does he not see or ignores the evident signs of the times, but determines (even though after great inward struggles) to commit a deed the worth of which, in a political respect, is extremely doubtful, became extremely doubtful in its consequences, and which, from a moral point of view, is undoubtedly equal to a crime. For, apart from the fact that every delicate sense of moral feeling must revolt with horror from a treacherous murder (even though politically justifiable), Brutus, like Coriolanus, tramples upon the most natural and the noblest emotions of the human heart—the duty of gratitude, of esteem, and loyalty to Caesar—for the sake of the phantom honor of free citizenship. He murders a man who is not only politically great, but who, as a man, had always proved himself great and noble, and who had more especially overwhelmed him with kindness, with proofs of his affection and high esteem. On the other hand, Brutus was the soul of the conspiracy; if his mind became confused, his courage unnerved, the whole enterprise must inevitably collapse. And it did collapse because it was as much opposed to the moral law as to the will of history.

Accordingly, Shakspeare allows the ghost to play a part in the drama in order to point out this twofold crime. It appears but once and utters a few, pregnant words; but we continually feel that it is hovering in the background, like a dark thundercloud; it is, so to say, the offended spirit of history itself, which, in fact, not only avenges political crimes, but visits ethical transgressions with equal severity. This spirit, so it were, perpetually holds up before our view the moral wrong in the murder of Caesar, as well as the political right which he had on his side owing to the necessity of the monarchy, and points to the fact that even the triumph of the oligarchical principle is but transitory, oligarchy itself but a transition stage. A similar intention induced Shakspeare to introduce the spectral apparitions in his *Richard III*, for both of these dramas occupy the same historical stage, both represent turning points in history, the end of an old and the beginning of a new state of things; they also exhibit a certain affinity from an ethical point of view.

1849–1850—Georg Gottfried Gervinus. "Character of Caesar," from *Shakespeare Commentaries*

Georg Gottfried Gervinus was a literary and political historian. He was a professor of history and literature at Göttingen and later an honorary professor in Heidelberg.

The character of Caesar in our play has been much blamed. He is declared to be unlike the idea conceived of him from his *Commentaries*; it is said that he does nothing, and only utters a few pompous, thrasonical, grandiloquent words, and it has been asked whether this be the Caesar that "did awe the world?" The poet, if he intended to make the attempt of the republicans his main theme, could not have ventured to create too great an interest in Caesar; it was necessary to keep him in the background, and to present that view of him which gave a reason for the conspiracy. According even to Plutarch, whose biography of Caesar is acknowledged to be very imperfect, Caesar's character altered much for the worse shortly before his death, and Shakespeare has represented him according to this suggestion. With what reverence Shakespeare viewed his character as a whole we learn from several passages of his works, and even in this play from the way in which he allows his memory to be respected as soon as he is dead. In the descriptions of Cassius we look back upon the time when the great man was natural, simple, undissembling, popular, and on an equal footing with others. Now he is spoiled by victory, success, power, and by the republican courtiers who surround him. He stands close on the borders between usurpation and discretion;

he is master in reality, and is on the point of assuming the name and the right; he desires heirs to the throne; he hesitates to accept the crown which he would gladly possess; he is ambitious, and fears he may have betrayed this in his paroxysms of epilepsy; he exclaims against flatterers and cringers, and yet both please him. All around him treat him as a master, his wife as a prince; the senate allow themselves to be called his senate; he assumes the appearance of a king even in his house; even with his wife he uses the language of a man who knows himself secure of power; and he maintains everywhere the proud, strict bearing of a soldier, which is represented even in his statues. If one of the changes at which Plutarch hints lay in this pride, this haughtiness, another lay in his superstition. In the suspicion and apprehension before the final step, he was seized, contrary to his usual nature and habit, with misgivings and superstitious fears, which affected likewise the hitherto free-minded Calphurnia. These conflicting feelings divide him, his forebodings excite him, his pride and his defiance of danger struggle against them, and restore his former confidence, which was natural to him, and which causes his ruin; just as a like confidence, springing from another source, ruined Brutus. The actor must make his high-sounding language appear as the result of this discord of feeling. Sometimes they are only incidental words intended to characterize the hero in the shortest way. Generally they appear in the cases where Caesar has to combat with his superstition, where he uses effort to take a higher stand in his words than at the moment he actually feels. He speaks so much of having no fear, that by this very thing he betrays his fear. Even in the places where his words sound most boastful, where he compares himself with the north star, there is more arrogance and ill-concealed pride at work than real boastfulness. It is intended there with a few words to show him at that point when his behaviour could most excite those free spirits against him. It was fully intended that he should take but a small part in the action: we must not, therefore, say with Scottowe that he was merely brought on the stage to be killed. The poet has handled this historical piece like his English historical plays. He had in his eye the whole context of the Roman civil wars for this single drama, not as yet thinking of its continuation in *Antony and Cleopatra*. He casts a glance back upon the fall of Pompey and makes it evident that Caesar falls for the same reason as that for which he had made Pompey fall. In the triumph over him, men's minds rise up at first against Caesar, the conspirators assemble in Pompey's porch, and Caesar is slain in front of his statue. As his death arose out of the civil war, so civil war recommences at his death, and just as Antony predicts:—

> Caesar's spirit, ranging for revenge,
> With Até by his side, come hot from hell,
> Shall in these confines, with a monarch's voice,
> Cry Havock, and let slip the dogs of war.

In this symbolic sense Caesar, after his death, has a share in the action of the play, which does not bear his name without a reason. That curse of Antony's, too, falls back upon himself in *Antony and Cleopatra* because he had destroyed those who had spared him and offered him friendship, and even there the manes of Pompey interfere with continuous power, giving this history also the background of remoter histories, to which this drama is but an episode.

1872—H.N. Hudson.
From *Shakespeare: His Life, Art, and Characters*

Henry Norman Hudson (1814–1886) was an American essayist and Shakespearean scholar. According to *The Cambridge History of English and American Literature*, his criticism was "popular rather than scholarly" and of the Romantic tradition of Coleridge, in that it "endeavours to set forth Shakespeare's inwardness, and pays comparatively little attention to his outwardness."

The characterization of this drama [*Julius Caesar*] in some of the parts is, I confess, not a little perplexing to me. I do not feel quite sure as to the temper of mind in which the Poet conceived some of the persons, or why he should have given them the aspect they wear in the play. For instance, Caesar is far from being himself in these scenes; hardly one of the speeches put into his mouth can be regarded as historically characteristic; taken all together, they are little short of a downright caricature. As here represented, he is indeed little better than a grand, strutting piece of puff-paste; and when he speaks, it is very much in the style of a glorious vapourer and braggart, full of lofty airs and mock-thunder; than which nothing could be further from the truth of the man, whose character, even in his faults, was as compact and solid as adamant, and at the same time as limber and ductile as the finest gold. Certain critics have seized and worked upon this, as proving that Shakespeare must have been very green in classical study, or else very careless in the use of his authorities. To my thinking it proves neither the one nor the other.

It is true, Caesar's ambition was indeed gigantic, but none too much so, I suspect, for the mind it dwelt in; for his character in all its features was gigantic. And no man ever framed his ambition more in sympathy with the great forces of Nature, or built it upon a deeper foundation of political wisdom and insight. Now this "last infirmity of noble minds" is the only part of him that the play really sets before us; and even this we do not see as it was, because it is here severed from the constitutional peerage of his gifts and virtues; all those transcendent qualities

which placed him at the summit of Roman intellect and manhood being either
withheld from the scene, or thrown so far into the background, that the proper
effect of them is mainly lost.

Yet we have ample proof that Shakespeare understood Caesar thoroughly;
and that he regarded him as "the noblest man that ever lived in the tide of times."
For example, in *Hamlet*, he makes Horatio, who is one of his calmest and most
right-thinking characters, speak of him as "the mightiest Julius." In *Antony and
Cleopatra*, again, the heroine is made to describe him as "broad-fronted Caesar."
And in *King Richard the Third*, the young Prince utters these lines

> That Julius Caesar was a famous man;
> With what his valour did enrich his wit,
> His wit set down to make his valour live:
> Death makes no conquest of this conqueror.

In fact, we need not go beyond Shakespeare to gather that Julius Caesar's was
the deepest, the most versatile, and most multitudinous head that ever figured in
the political affairs of mankind.

Indeed, it is clear from this play itself that the Poet's course did not proceed
at all from ignorance or misconception of the man. For it is remarkable that,
though Caesar delivers himself so out of character, yet others, both foes and
friends, deliver him much nearer the truth; so that, while we see almost nothing
of him directly, we nevertheless get, upon the whole, a pretty just reflection of
him. Especially, in the marvellous speeches of Antony and in the later events of
the drama, both his inward greatness and his right of mastership over the Roman
world are fully vindicated. For, in the play as in the history, Caesar's blood just
hastens and cements the empire which the conspirators thought to prevent. They
soon find that in the popular sympathies, and even in their own dumb remorses,
he has "left behind powers that will work for him." He proves indeed far mightier
in death than in life; as if his spirit were become at once the guardian angel of
his cause and an avenging angel to his foes.

And so it was in fact. For nothing did so much to set the people in love
with royalty, both name and thing, as the reflection that their beloved Caesar,
the greatest of their national heroes, the crown and consummation of Roman
genius and character, had been murdered for aspiring to it. Thus their hereditary
aversion to kingship was all subdued by the remembrance of how and why their
Caesar fell; and they who, before, would have plucked out his heart rather than
he should wear a crown, would now have plucked out their own, to set a crown
upon his head. Such is the natural result when the intensities of admiration and
compassion meet together in the human breast.

From all which it may well be thought that Caesar was too great for the hero
of a drama, since his greatness, if brought forward in full measure, would leave

no room for any thing else, at least would preclude any proper dramatic balance and equipoise. It was only as a sort of underlying potency or a force withdrawn into the background, that his presence was compatible with that harmony and reciprocity of several characters which a well-ordered drama requires. At all events, it is pretty clear that, where he was, such figures as Brutus and Cassius could never be very considerable, save as his assassins. They would not have been heard of in after-times, if they had not "struck the foremost man of all this world"; in other words, the great sun of Rome had to be shorn of his beams, else so ineffectual a fire as Brutus could nowise catch the eye.

<hr />

1875—Edward Dowden.
From *Shakspere: A Critical Study of His Mind and Art*

Edward Dowden (1843-1913) was an Irish critic, university lecturer, and poet.

In Shakspere's rendering of the character of Caesar, which has considerably bewildered his critics, one thought of the poet would seem to be this—that unless a man continually keeps himself in relation with facts, and with his present person and character, he may become to himself legendary and mythical. The real man Caesar disappears for himself under the greatness of the Caesar myth. He forgets himself as he actually is, and knows only the vast legendary power named Caesar. He is a *numen* to himself, speaking of Caesar in the third person, as if of some power above and behind his consciousness. And at this very moment—so ironical is the time-spirit—Cassius is cruelly insisting to Brutus upon all those infirmities which prove this god no more than a pitiful mortal.

Julius Caesar appears in only three scenes of the play. In the first scene of the third act he dies. Where he does appear, the poet seems anxious to insist upon the weakness rather than the strength of Caesar. He swoons when the crown is offered to him, and upon his recovery enacts a piece of stagy heroism; he suffers from the falling-sickness; he is deaf; his body does not retain its early vigor. He is subject to the vain hopes and vain alarms of superstition. His manner of speech is pompous and arrogant; he accepts flattery as a right; he vacillates, while professing unalterable constancy; he has lost in part his gift of perceiving facts, and of dealing efficiently with men and with events. Why is this? And why is the play, not withstanding, *Julius Caesar*? Why did Shakspere decide to represent in such a light the chief man of the Roman world? Passages in other plays prove that Shakspere had not really misconceived "the mightiest Julius," "broad-fronted Caesar," the conqueror over whom "death makes no conquest." The poet," writes Gervinus, "if he intended to make the attempt of the republicans his main theme, could not have ventured to create too great an interest in Caesar; it was necessary to keep him in the background, and to *present that view of him which gave a reason for the conspiracy*. According even to Plutarch, ... Caesar's character altered much for the worse shortly before his death, and Shakspere has represented him according to this suggestion." Mr. Hudson offers a somewhat similar explanation: "I have sometimes thought, that the policy of the drama may have been to represent Caesar not as he was indeed, but as he must have appeared to the conspirators; to make us see him as they saw him, in order that they, too, might have fair and equal judgment at our hands. For Caesar was literally too great to be seen by them, save as children often see bugbears by moonlight, when their inexperienced eyes are mocked with air." And Mr. Hudson believes that he can detect a "refined and subtle irony" diffusing itself through the texture of the play; that Brutus, a shallow idealist, should outshine the greatest practical genius the world ever saw, can have no other than an ironical significance.

Neither Gervinus nor Mr. Hudson has solved the difficulty. Julius Caesar is indeed protagonist of the tragedy; but it is not the Caesar whose bodily presence is weak, whose mind is declining in strength and sure-footed energy, the Caesar who stands exposed to all the accidents of fortune. This bodily presence of Caesar is but of secondary importance, and may be supplied when it actually passes away, by Octavius as its substitute. It is the spirit of Caesar which is the dominant power of the tragedy; against this—the spirit of Caesar—Brutus fought; but Brutus, who forever errs in practical politics, succeeded only in striking down Caesar's body; he who had been weak now rises as pure spirit, strong and terrible, and avenges himself upon the conspirators. The contrast between the weakness of Caesar's bodily presence in the first half of the play, and the might of his spiritual presence in the latter half of the play, is emphasized, and perhaps over-emphasized, by Shakspere. It was the error of Brutus that he failed to perceive wherein lay the true Caesarean power, and acted with short-sighted eagerness and violence. Mark Antony, over the dead body of his lord, announces what is to follow:

> Over thy wounds now do I prophesy—
> . . . .
> A curse shall light upon the limbs of men;
> Domestic fury and fierce civil strife
> Shall cumber all the parts of Italy;
> . . . .
> And Caesar's spirit, ranging for revenge,
> With Ate by his side come hot from hell,

Shall in these confines with a monarch's voice
Cry "Havoc," and let slip the dogs of war.

The ghost of Caesar (designated by Plutarch only the "evil spirit" of Brutus), which appears on the night before the battle of Philippi, serves as a kind of visible symbol of the vast posthumous power of the dictator. Cassius dies with the words:

> Caesar, thou art revenged,
> Even with the sword that killed thee.

Brutus, when he looks upon the dead face of his brother, exclaims,

> O Julius Caesar, thou art mighty yet!
> Thy spirit walks abroad, and turns our swords
> In our own proper entrails.

Finally, the little effort of the aristocrat republicans sinks to the ground, foiled and crushed by the force which they had hoped to abolish with one violent blow. Brutus dies:

> Caesar, now be still
> I killed not thee with half so good a will.

Brutus dies; and Octavius lives to reap the fruit whose seed had been sown by his great predecessor. With strict propriety, therefore, the play bears the name of *Julius Caesar*.

1879—Paul Stapfer. "*Julius Caesar* (continued). Casca. Cicero. Portia," from *Shakespeare and Classical Antiquity: Greek and Latin Antiquity as Presented in Shakespeare's Plays*

Paul Stapfer was a French literary critic and professor at the Faculté des Lettres of Grenoble and later at Bordeaux. He also wrote *Moliére and Shakespeare* (1887). This chapter from *Shakespeare and Classical Antiquity* illuminates minor characters in *Julius Caesar*; other chapters examine Caesar, Brutus, and Cassius in depth.

CASCA.

If it were not a somewhat hazardous conjecture when applied to the most impartial of dramatic poets, one would be inclined to suspect that the type of character to which Casca belongs was a peculiar favourite of Shakespeare's. In the first place, he is a humourist, he has a strong sense of the comedy of human life, and of the nothingness of the things of this world. It is he that relates in a tone of transcendent mockery, to Brutus and Cassius who are not at all in a mood to laugh with him, the great event of the feast of Lupercal, and describes how Antony offered the crown to Caesar. Brutus is shocked at his levity of tone, and when Casca leaves them, he expresses his disapprobation with all the weighty injustice of a stern moralist, who takes everything seriously and who as a matter of course is invariably wrong in his judgments of men. Cassius, who has no obtuseness of this sort, answers that what shocks Brutus in him is only put on, and that he may be safely counted on for any bold or noble enterprise. Casca, when enrolled amongst the conspirators, soon justifies this opinion of him, and is the one to strike the first blow. This mingled good-humour and practical energy, this strength and solidity of character underlying all his merry jests and laughter, cannot but represent not only one of Shakespeare's favourite types, but the special type of his predilection, if we admit, with his most learned commentators, that Henry V., in whom these characteristics are most strongly marked, was his ideal.

Casca is moreover an aristocrat in true disdainful English fashion. He expresses the most elegant contempt, which is all the more cutting because he speaks without any bitterness, and with a smile on his lips, for the folly of the crowd, and for their dirty hands and sweaty night-caps and stinking breath: "It had almost choked Caesar; for he swooned, and fell down at it: and for mine own part, I durst not laugh, for fear of opening my lips and receiving the bad air."

One of the rare expressions to be met with in Shakespeare, which would seem to indicate a personal sentiment, occurs in this narrative of Casca's: "If the tag-rag people did not clap him, and hiss him, according as he pleased and displeased them, as they used to do the players in the theatre, I am no true man."

M. Guizot, after describing the populace which composed the pit in English theatres in the sixteenth century, and which contemporary writers designated by the name of *stinkards*, adds:—

> "In the lot of actors, working for the amusement of such a
> public, there must have been much that was unpleasant, and to what
> he suffered in this way we may be allowed to attribute the aversion
> for popular assemblies which Shakespeare shows so strongly in
> his plays."

To what extent Shakespeare shared in Casca's aristocratic disdain, and how far personal antipathy caused him to depart in his portrayal of the people, from the poetic impartiality which is one of his highest titles to glory, is a curious question, but one which it would be premature to attempt to answer before we come to examine the play of "Coriolanus," in which the people play an important part.

One last thing to be noticed concerning Casca is the wonderful effect that the prodigies foretelling the death of Caesar have upon him; they work a complete revolution in his nature, and give a suddenly meditative turn to his usual airiness of tone: his irony is in reality only a thin and superficial covering, which falls at the first serious occasion and lets the true nature of the man be seen.

CICERO.

Cicero only makes his appearance in the tragedy as listening to Casca's account of the marvellous sights of the night he had been witnessing; he answers his religious terror with a philosophical commonplace:—

"Indeed, Indeed, it is a strange-disposèd time
But men may construe things, after their fashion,
Clean from the purpose of the things themselves."

There is nothing highly original or daring in this remark, but its very insignificance seems to belong to Shakespeare's conception of the character; besides which, though the Roman orator may say nothing very important himself, he is twice mentioned in the play in terms sufficiently explicit to make his faults and failings known. When Casca describes the scene at the offering of the crown to Caesar, Cassius inquires—

"Did Cicero say anything?
Casca. Ay, he spoke Greek.
Cas. To what effect?
Casca. Nay, an I tell you that I'll ne'er look you i' the face again; but those that understood him smiled at one another, and shook their heads: but, for mine own part, it was Greek to me."

It has been thought ridiculous in Shakespeare to make Cicero speak Greek, but this is to overlook the possibility of a characteristic touch being intended by it. To speak at a time like that in Greek, in a language not to be understood by the common people, and in a manner that made those who did understand smile meaningly at each other, implies a skilfulness and a regard for prudence quite at one with the traditional, and more or less historically true, representation of the friend of Atticus.[1]

The conspirators did not dare, Plutarch tells us, to acquaint Cicero with their conspiracy,—

> "for they were afraid that he, being a coward by nature, and age also having increased his fear, he would turn and alter all their purpose, and quench the heat of their enterprise, seeking by persuasion to bring all things to such safety, as there should be no peril."

But such an endeavour is absolutely fatal to a spirit of enterprise, and to action of every kind: Hamlet did nothing, because he sought "by persuasion to bring all things to such safety, as there should be no peril."

Cassius, for once making a mistake and failing in his usual penetration—though the mistake, after all, might be on the part of the poet,—is inclined at first starting to enroll Cicero among the conspirators, but Brutus objects:—

> "For he will never follow anything
> That other men begin."

In this instance, Brutus was enabled by the natural antipathy which he felt towards Cicero, in spite of his friendly relations with him, to estimate him more accurately than even Cassius did, the close observer of men. Pure men of letters like Cicero, who are chiefly concerned with the improvement of their mental faculties, are looked upon askance by stoics like Brutus, whose whole aim is moral perfection.

> "Cicero's friendship with Brutus," says M. Boissier, "was a very disturbed and stormy one; and violent discussions broke out more than once between them, although they held many opinions in common. These dissensions naturally arose from the diversity of their characters: never did two friends less resemble each other; Cicero was pre-eminently fitted for society, possessing all the necessary qualities for social success, great flexibility of opinion, a wide tolerance for others, and sufficiently easy terms for himself, besides a talent of steering safely between all parties, and a naturally indulgent, easy-going disposition which made him understand everything and accept almost everything. Though he wrote very indifferent verses, he was of a poetic temperament, strangely versatile in his impressions, and irritably sensitive; his mind was swift and supple and far-reaching, quick to conceive, but equally quick to abandon his ideas, and passing with a bound from one extreme to the other. He never formed a serious resolution without repenting of it the next day. Whenever he took a side in any matter, he was warm and decided at the beginning, and then gradually grew colder and colder."

Cicero is accordingly left out of the conspiracy for the reason given by Brutus:—

"For he will never follow anything
That other men begin."

But neither would he begin anything himself; he would rather remain inactive, which in the time of civil troubles, when calm wisdom is only a form of selfishness, and when men should be able to range themselves unreservedly on the side that is least wrong, is always a culpable mode of conduct. His fate, however, was to die by the sword, like those who live by the sword, but with this difference—that theirs is an honourable death, while his was inglorious. Such is the moral lesson taught by Cicero's death, in Shakespeare's tragedy.

PORTIA.

Portia as she appears in Plutarch is, I think, an even finer and more interesting character to study than she is in Shakespeare. The poet has undoubtedly endued the historian's account with the more vivid life of the drama, and has given more force to her words, more distinctness to her actions, but he could add no further feature of any importance to her character. History furnishes a complete and finished portrait of Portia, to which poetry may give a warmer glow and richer colouring, but which in its essential lines it can never improve. It is only fair that this should be openly and clearly stated, that Plutarch may have the full credit of his victories in a most unequal combat, in which it would seem that his highest success could only consist in not being entirely beaten. But not only does the poet's rendering not surpass his model, but it seems to me to fall a little short of it, and to leave out some of its beauties, which apparently belong peculiarly to the form of narrative and refuse to be transplanted into dramatic regions. It requires all the wooden inflexibility of a systematic admiration not to regret the absence, in Shakespeare's tragedy, of the beautiful scene in which Brutus and Portia take leave of each other at Elea:—

"There Porcia, being ready to depart from her husband, Brutus, and
to return to Rome, did what she could to dissemble the grief and sorrow
she felt at her heart: but a certain painted table[2] bewrayed her in the
end, although until that time she showed always a constant and patient
mind. The device of the table was taken out of the Greek stories, how
Andromache accompanied her husband Hector when he went out of the
city of Troy to go to the wars, and how Hector delivered her his little
son, and how her eyes were never off him. Porcia, seeing this picture, and
likening herself to be in the same case, she fell a-weeping: and coming
thither oftentimes in a day to see it, she wept still. Acilius, one of Brutus'

friends, perceiving that, rehearsed the verses Andromache speaketh to this purpose in Homer:—

'Thou, Hector, art my father, and my mother, and my brother,
And husband eke, and all in all: I mind not any other.'

Then Brutus, smiling, answered again: 'But yet,' said he, 'I cannot for my part, say unto Porcia, as Hector answered Andromache—

Tush, meddle thou with duly weighing out
Thy maids their task, and pricking on a clout.

For, indeed, the weak constitution of her body doth not suffer her to perform in show the valiant acts that we are able to do: but for courage and constant mind, she showed herself as stout in the defence of her country as any of us.'"

The Portia of Plutarch, in the way in which she understood and exhibited married love, certainly represents the most beautiful type of a wife easily conceivable, and yet she belongs to the ancient world. Before the publication of various important works, among which that of M. Havet,[3] on the origin of Christianity, and that of M. Boissier, on the religion of Rome,[4] must be specially mentioned, had begun to spread abroad more exact notions on the subject, there existed in commonly received opinion an abyss between the condition of women in ancient and their condition in modern times; and it was ordinarily believed that women were looked down upon by classical antiquity, and that respect for them was due to Christian and Germanic influences.

Apparent proofs were not wanting in support of this prejudice. If we consult the laws of Greece and Rome, we shall see women everywhere kept in what one is inclined to call a barbarous state of legal inferiority, and never considered free to act alone and to dispose of themselves.

In marriage, as understood by the ancients," writes M. Lallier, the author of an interesting essay on "La Condition de la Femme dans la Famille Atédnienne au Ve. et au VIe. Siècle," "the wife counted as nothing. Her feelings were never consulted, nor was she chosen for her own sake, but simply accepted as a necessary instrument for the continuation of the family and of the city; nothing further seems to have been expected of her, nor was she supposed to have any other virtue: her duty was fulfilled when she had given birth to her sons. . . . There was no question of mutual inclination or motives of affection; the married couple did not come together to share each other's thoughts and feelings, or to be mutual helps in the trials of life, but were simply acquitting themselves of a patriotic and religious obligation, in providing future citizens for the state, who would take

their fathers' places, and in their turn offer domestic sacrifices. . . .
But from the moment that marriage is degraded into a civic duty, and
becomes nothing but an obligation which it is impossible to evade
without sinning against religion and against the State, the charm of
domestic life is done away with, and at the same time the influence
of the wife is greatly lessened. The Athenian lent himself to marriage
in much the same spirit as that in which one pays a debt,—slowly
and reluctantly. The interest of the Republic required the introduction
of a wife into his household, and so far he obeyed its behests, but he
strictly measured the share she would have in his life, and when these
limits were once settled he troubled himself no further with the cares
of his family."

At Rome, the Censor Metellus, in the time of the Gracchi, preached
matrimony to his fellow-citizens in these terms, as quoted by Montesquieu, and
often repeated since:—

"Citizens, if we could live without having wives, we should all avail
ourselves of the possibility, *ea molestia careremus*, but since Nature has
chosen to make it as impossible to do without them as it is disagreeable
to live with them, let us sacrifice the pleasures of our short life to the
interests of the Republic, which endures for ever."

If we turn from legislators to philosophers, we shall find many contemptuous
passages in their writings, in which wives are slightingly spoken of and the idea
of marriage reduced to a very low level indeed. Socrates says to one of his friends,
as though it were quite a matter of course, "Is there anybody that you talk less
to than to your wife?" When Plato wishes to describe a democratic society, over
which the magistrates, like awkward cupbearers, have spilt the wine of liberty so
that it has become intoxicated with it, and utterly lost its reason, he represents
the slave refusing to obey his master, and the wife alleging her equality with
her husband, as the climax of disorder. And Aristotle is still more impertinent:
"There certainly may be some honest women and slaves," he says, "but it may be
said in general that women are an inferior species, and that the slave is altogether
bad." The Roman philosophers express themselves in their speculative writings in
the same strain as the Greeks.[5]

And when after having read these impertinent remarks, we enter with
Tacitus into the new world of Germany, with all its veneration for women
and its deep sense of the majesty of marriage, the contrast certainly appears
complete. Later on, the Germanic idea received the fullest consecration from
Christianity, so much so that the supreme expression of respect for women
may be found in the incident related in the biography of a mystic German in
mediaeval times:—

"One day he met a woman in the dirtiest street of the town, and immediately stepped into the mud to let her pass in the only part that was dry. She, seeing this act of humility, said to him, 'My father, what are you doing? You are a priest and a monk. Why do you give up the path tome, who am only a weak woman?' Brother Henry answered, 'My sister, it is my custom to honour and venerate all women, because they remind my heart of the powerful Queen of Heaven, the Mother of my God.'"[6]

But to mix up all the different periods of classical antiquity together, and then to say of it, as a whole, that it despised women, and showed itself incapable of conceiving an elevated ideal of marriage, would be to make a great mistake; many distinctions and reservations have to be made before arriving at a conclusion on this matter,—the distinction between law and custom, between the paradoxes of philosophers and the general feeling of the community, between the heroic age of Greece and the succeeding periods of its history, and finally the distinction between Athens and Rome.

In studying closely the life of ancient societies, we find that the laws were often considerably at variance with the prevailing custom, the consideration claimed for women by manners and habits going far beyond their legal rights; in which conflict it was custom that invariably carried the day. In our own times, as M. Lallier ingenuously remarks

"A very erroneous notion would be entertained of the important part played by women in French society, if we were to judge simply by the articles of the civil code which define the respective rights and duties of husband and wife."

And France is probably not the only country to which the remark applies. In point of fact, the paradoxes of philosophers signify nothing. Witticisms of a commonplace kind on the good and bad qualities of women are as frequent now as they were in former days, all resolving themselves in their final analysis into the sentence pronounced by Hesiod, which is weighty and full of wisdom as any maxim of the seven sages of Greece: "There is nothing in the world better than a good woman, or worse than a bad one." And even Aristotle, in spite of his depreciatory remarks already cited, speaks of the tenderness between man and wife, and of the harmony of soul necessary for happiness; while Pythagoras dwells with great eloquence upon the love with which a man should regard the woman who has left her father's house for his sake, and who loves him even more dearly than her parents, the authors of her existence.

No women were more surrounded with respect than those of Homer's heroic world; but later on, a grave alteration took place in this respect in the manners of the Greeks, so that the most important distinction to be made in speaking of the condition of women in antiquity comes to be that between Athens and Rome.

In Rome, women were treated with far greater consideration than in Athens. The Athenians shut their women up in the apartments specially reserved for them, and esteemed it their highest honour to have nothing said of them, good or bad. Rome knew nothing of the institution of the gynecium, and frankly associated women with the life of men, and in the atrium, the centre of a Roman house, used as a general sitting-room for the family, and as a reception-room for either friends or strangers, the married woman—the Matron, as the Romans reverently called her—took her place beside her husband. The Romans always had a very high ideal of marriage, which they regarded as the blending of two lives into one, and it is to their legal writers that we owe the well-known definition: "Marriage is a union for the pursuit of things human and divine—*juris humani et divini communicatio . . . uxor socia humanoe rei atque divinoe.*"

The personal importance of women continually increased in Roman society: the time at which they played the greatest part in history was towards the close of the Republic and the beginning of the Empire:—

> "We see them," wrote M. Saint-Mart Girardin,[7] "taking part in conspiracies and civil wars, as for instance Servilia in Sallust's 'War of Catalina,' and Fulvia in the proscriptions. They also took part in the court-intrigues under Augustus and the other Caesars, as is seen in Livia and Agrippina. Their new-found independence was used by some to subserve their love of pleasure; by others, their ambition; and by others again, to contribute to the dignity of married life: take, for example, Pauline ready to die with Seneca, or Arria who, to encourage her husband to kill. himself, stabbed herself with a sword and then, drawing it covered with blood from her breast, gave it to her husband, saying, 'Take it, Poetus; there is nothing painful in it.'"

To this heroic race belonged Portia; but what adds a peculiar attraction to the grandeur of her character is that in her case, as in that of Brutus, heroism extinguished none of the gentler feelings of humanity: nothing could be less theatrical than her stoicism, and her whole nature was intensely sensitive—it was this, indeed, that killed her. How acute her feelings were may be seen in her deadly anguish on the morning of the Ides of March, and in the tearful farewell she took of Brutus when leaving Elea; we know, too, that she died, as Brutus himself says, of grief, causing her own death in the madness of despair.

Plutarch tells us of her heroism in giving herself a wound in the thigh to make sure that no pain or grief could overcome her; and in Shakespeare the scene is given with all the perfection of dramatic language (Act II., Sc. 1):—

> "*Por.* Upon my knees
> I charm you, by my once commended beauty,
> By all your vows of love, and that great vow
> Which did incorporate and make us one,
> That you unfold to me, yourself, your half,
> Why you are heavy. . . .
> *Bru.* You are my true and honourable wife;
> As dear to me as are the ruddy drops
> That visit my sad heart.
> *Por.* If this were true, then should I know this secret.
> I grant I am a woman; but, withal,
> A woman that lord Brutus took to wife
> I grant I am a woman; but, withal,
> A woman well reputed,—Cato's daughter.
> Think you I am no stronger than my sex,
> Being so father'd and so husbanded?
> Tell me your counsels, I will not disclose them:
> I have made strong proof of my constancy,
> Giving myself a voluntary wound
> Here, in the thigh: can I bear that with patience,
> And not my husband's secrets?
> *Bru.* O ye Gods,
> Render me worthy of this noble wife!"

In this splendid metamorphosis of a simple narrative into a dramatic scene, the poet naturally accentuates every point of Portia's character, and especially her sense of the dignity of marriage and of what is owing to her as a wife.

> "Shakespeare's Portia," says M. Saint-Marc Girardin, "ventures further than the Portia of Plutarch in claiming her share in her husband's perils; and, in fact, in her notions of her rights and of her duties, there is much of the Christian and even of the English wife."

That Shakespeare's Portia is a Christian and an Englishwoman may be true— I have no wish to dispute it, but between her and her prototype I see no essential difference, but one in degree only. And, as I have said before, what strikes me as even more marvellous than Shakespeare's poetry is the existence and portrayal of such a character in the heart of pagan antiquity. Ever since ancient times there have been those who did honour to marriage, even as there have been some—and, in point of fact, many—in modern days who have not entirely reached Plutarch's ideal in his treatise on love, in which he protests against any lower and meaner doctrine of marriage than that of its being the union of two hearts.

If we wish to see a case presenting the most complete and amusing contrast to the relations between Brutus and Portia, we can also find it in that collection of all possible characters, Shakespeare's plays. We have only to turn to "Henry IV." (Act II., Sc. 3), where Hotspur abruptly tells his wife he is about to start in two hours' time, without telling her why he leaves or where he is going. A man of rash and hasty disposition, with none of the refinements of thought and culture, without any need or wish for an ideal love, he is not likely to have such a wife as Brutus had, or to be capable of such veneration as Brutus was; and accordingly he treats his wife more as a child than as a woman:—

> "Come, wilt thou see me ride?
> And when I am a horseback, I will swear
> I love thee infinitely. But hark you, Kate;
> I must not have you henceforth question me
> Whither I go, nor reason whereabout
> Whither I must, I must; and, to conclude,
> This evening must I leave you, gentle Kate.
> I know you wise; but yet no further wise
> Than Harry Percy's wife: constant you are,
> But yet a woman: and for secrecy,
> No lady closer; for I will believe
> Thou wilt not utter what thou lost not know;
> And so far will I trust thee, gentle Kate!
>   *Lady.* How! so far?
>   *Hot.* Not an inch further."

Hotspur thought with Racine that a woman is "a body which is all tongues," and would have said with La Fontaine, "Nothing weighs more heavily than a secret, to carry it far is difficult for ladies." But here I stop, for if I were to quote French authors, beginning with the greatest, I should find more satirical hits at women in one single period, than in the whole of antiquity, Greek or Roman; and what is worse, I should also find a constant tendency, which neither England, nor Rome, nor even light and gay Athens ever exhibited, to turn the sacred institution of marriage into ridicule.

NOTES

1. Voltaire had no higher idea of Cicero than Shakespeare had: see the lines in his tragedy of "Brutus":—

> "Cicéron qui d'un traitre a puni l'insolence,
> Ne sert le liberté que par son eloquence

Hardi dans le sénat, faible dans le danger,
Fait pour haranguer Rome et non pour la venger,
Laissons à l'orateur qui charme sa patrie
Le soin de nous louer quand nous l'aurons servie."

2. Picture.
3. "Le Christianisme et ses Origines," Paris, Michel Lévy, 1871.
4. "La Religion Romaine d'Auguste aux Antonins," Hachette, Paris, 1874.
5. Gaston Boissier.
6. Heinrich, "History of German Literature."
7. "Cours de littérature dramatique," Vol. IV., p. 262.

1882—Friedrich Nietzsche. "In Honour of Shakespeare," from *The Complete Works of Friedrich Nietzsche*

Friedrich Nietzsche was one of the most important philosophers of the nineteenth century. A professor of classical philology at the University of Basel, he wrote critiques in many areas. His works include *The Birth of Tragedy* and *Beyond Good and Evil.*

The best thing I could say in honour of Shakespeare, *the man*, is that he believed in Brutus, and cast not a shadow of suspicion on the kind of virtue which Brutus represents! It is to him that Shakespeare consecrated his best tragedy—it is at present still called by a wrong name,—to him, and to the most terrible essence of lofty morality. Independence of soul!—that is the question at issue! No sacrifice can be too great there: one must be able to sacrifice to it even one's dearest friend, although he be the grandest of men, the ornament of the world, the genius without peer,—if one really loves freedom as the freedom of great souls, and if *this* freedom be threatened by him:—it is thus that Shakespeare must have felt! The elevation in which he places Caesar is the most exquisite honour he could confer upon Brutus; it is thus only that he lifts into vastness the inner problem of his hero, and similarly the strength of soul which could cut *this knot!*—And was it actually political freedom that impelled the poet to sympathy with Brutus,—and made him the accomplice of Brutus? Or was political freedom merely a symbol for something inexpressible? Do we perhaps stand before some sombre event or adventure of the poet's own soul, which has remained unknown, and of which he only cared to speak symbolically? What is all Hamlet-melancholy in comparison with the melancholy of Brutus!—and perhaps Shakespeare also knew this, as he knew the other, by experience! Perhaps he also had his dark hour and his bad angel, just as Brutus had them!—But whatever similarities and secret relationships of that kind there may have been, Shakespeare cast himself on the ground and felt unworthy and alien in presence of the aspect and virtue of Brutus:—he has inscribed the testimony thereof in the tragedy itself. He has twice brought in a poet in it, and twice heaped upon him such an impatient and extreme contempt, that it sounds like a cry,—like the cry of self-contempt. Brutus, even Brutus loses patience when the poet appears, self-important, pathetic and obtrusive, as poets usually are,—persons who seem to abound in the possibilities of greatness, even moral greatness, and nevertheless rarely attain even to ordinary uprightness in the philosophy of practice and of life. "He may know the times, but I *know his temper*,—away with the jigging fool!"—shouts Brutus. We may translate this back into the soul of the poet that composed it.

⧧ ⧧ ⧧

1893—Richard G. Moulton. "How the Play of *Julius Caesar* Works to a Climax at the Centre: A Study in Passion and Movement," from *Shakespeare as a Dramatic Artist: A Popular Illustration of the Principles of Scientific Criticism*

Richard G. Moulton was professor of English at the University of Chicago. He wrote *The Moral System of Shakespeare* and *The Literary Study of the Bible*, among other books.

The preceding chapters have been confined to two of the main elements in dramatic effect, Character and Plot: the third remains to be illustrated. Amongst other devices of public amusement the experiment has been tried of arranging a game of chess to be played by living pieces on a monster board; if we suppose that in the midst of such a game the real combative instincts of the living pieces should be suddenly aroused, that the knight should in grim earnest plunge his spear into his nearest opponent, and that missiles should actually be discharged from the castles, then the shock produced in the feelings of the bystanders by such a change would serve to bring out with emphasis the distinction between Plot and the third element of dramatic effect, Passion. Plot is an interest of a purely intellectual kind, it traces laws, principles, order, and design in the incidents of life. Passion, on the other hand, depends on the human character of the personages involved; it consists in the effects produced on the spectator's emotional nature as his sympathy follows the characters through the incidents of the plot; it is War as distinguished from *Kriegspiel*. Effects of such Passion are numerous and various: the present study is concerned with its *Movement*. This Movement comprehends a class of dramatic effects differing in one obvious particular from the effects considered so far. Character-Interpretation and Plot are both analytical in their nature; the play has to be taken to pieces and details selected from various parts have to be put together to give the idea of a complete character, or to make up some single thread of design. Movement, on the contrary, follows the actual order of the events as they take place in the play itself. The emotional effects produced by such events as they succeed one another will not be uniform and monotonous; the skill of the dramatist will lie in concentrating effect at some points and relieving it at others; and to watch such play of passion through the progress of the action will be a leading dramatic interest. Now we have already had occasion to notice the prominence which Shakespeare in his dramatic construction gives to the central point of a play; symmetry more than sensation is the effect which has an attraction for his genius, and the finale to which the action is to lead is not more important to him than the balancing of the whole drama about a turning-point in the middle. Accordingly it is not surprising to find that in the Passion-Movement of his dramas a similar plan of construction is often followed; that all other variations are subordinated to one great Climax of Passion at the centre. To repeat an illustration already applied to Plot: the movement of the passion seems to follow the form of a regular arch, commencing in calmness, rising through emotional strain to a summit of agitation at the centre, then through the rest of the play declining into a calmness of a different kind. It is the purpose of this and the next studies to illustrate this kind of movement in two very different plays. *Julius Caesar* has the simplest of plots; our attention is engaged with a train of emotion which is made to rise gradually to a climax at the centre, and then equally gradually to decline. *Lear*, on the contrary, is amongst the most intricate of Shakespeare's plays; nevertheless the dramatist contrives to keep the same simple form of emotional effect, and its complex passions unite in producing a concentration of emotional agitation in a few central scenes.

The passion in the play of *Julius Caesar* gathers around the conspirators, and follows them through the mutations of their fortunes. If however we are to catch the different parts of the action in their proper proportions we must remember the character of these conspirators, and especially of their leaders Brutus and Cassius. These are actuated in what they do not by personal motives but by devotion to the public good and the idea of republican liberty; accordingly in following their career we must not look too exclusively at their personal success and failure. The exact key to the movement of the drama will be given by fixing attention upon the *justification of the conspirators' cause* in the minds of the audience; and it is this which is found to rise gradually to its height in the centre of the play, and from that point to decline to the end. I have pointed out in the preceding study how the issue at stake in *Julius Caesar* amounts to a conflict between the outer and inner life, between devotion to a public enterprise and such sympathy with the claims of individual humanity as is specially fostered by the cultivation of the inner nature. The issue is reflected in words of Brutus already quoted:

The abuse of greatness is, when it disjoins
Remorse from power.

Brutus applies this as a test to Caesar's action, and is forced to acquit him: but is not Brutus here laying down the very principle of which his own error in the play is the violation? The assassin's dagger puts Brutus and the conspirators in the position of power; while 'remorse'—the word in Shakespearean English means human sympathy—is the due of their victim Caesar, whose rights to justice as a man, and to more than justice as the friend of Brutus, the conspirators have the responsibility of balancing against the claims of a political cause. These claims of justice and humanity are deliberately ignored by the stoicism of Brutus, while the rest of the conspirators are blinded to them by the mists of political enthusiasm; this outraged human sympathy asserts itself after Caesar's death in a monstrous form in the passions of the mob, which are guided by the skill of Antony to the destruction of the assassins. Of course both the original violation of the balance between the two lives and the subsequent reaction are equally corrupt. The stoicism of Brutus, with its suppression of the inner sympathies, arrives practically at the principle—destined in the future history of the world to be the basis of a yet greater crime—that it is expedient that one man should die rather than that a whole people should perish. On the other hand, Antony trades upon the fickle violence of the populace, and uses it as much for personal ends as for vengeance. This demoralisation of both the sides of character is the result of their divorce. Such is the essence of this play if its action be looked at as a whole; but it belongs to the movement of dramatic passion that we see the action only in its separate parts at different times. Through the first half of the play, while the justification of the conspirators' cause is rising, the other side of the question is carefully hidden from us; from the point of the assassination the suppressed element starts into prominence, and sweeps our sympathies along with it to its triumph at the conclusion of the play.

In following the movement of the drama the action seems to divide itself into stages. In the first of these stages, which comprehends the first two scenes, the conspiracy is only forming; the sympathy with which the spectator follows the details is entirely free from emotional agitation; passion so far is indistinguishable from mere interest. The opening scene strikes appropriately the key-note of the whole action. In it we see the tribunes of the people—officers whose whole *raison d'être* is to be the mouthpiece of the commonalty—restraining their own clients from the noisy honours they are disposed to pay to Caesar. To the justification in our eyes of a conspiracy against Caesar, there could not be a better starting-point than this hint that the popular worship of Caesar, which has made him what he is, is itself reaching its reaction-point. Such a suggestion moreover makes the whole play one complete wave of popular fickleness from crest to crest.

The second is the scene upon which the dramatist mainly relies for the *crescendo* in the justification of the conspirators. It is a long scene, elaborately contrived so as to keep the conspirators and their cause before us at their very best, and the victim at his very worst. Cassius is the life and spirit of this scene, as he is of the whole republican movement. Cassius is excellent soil for republican principles. The 'rash humour' his mother gave him would predispose him to impatience of those social inequalities and conventional distinctions against which republicanism sets itself. Again he is a hard-thinking man, to whom the perfect realisation of an ideal theory would be as palpable an aim as the more practical purposes of other men. He is a Roman moreover, at once proud of his nation as the greatest in the world, and aware that this national greatness had been through all history bound up with the maintenance of a republican constitution. His republicanism gives to Cassius the dignity that is always given to a character by a grand passion, whether for a cause, a woman, or an idea—the unification of a whole life in a single aim, by which the separate strings of a man's nature are, as it were, tuned into harmony. In the present scene Cassius is expounding the cause which is his life-object. Nor is this all. Cassius was politician enough to adapt himself to his hearers, and could hold up the lower motives to those who would be influenced by them; but in the present case it is the 'honourable metal' of a Brutus that he has to work upon, and his exposition of republicanism must be adapted to the highest possible standard. Accordingly, in the language of the scene we find the idea of human equality expressed in its most ideal form. Without it Cassius thinks life not worth living.

> I had as lief not be as live to be
> In awe of such a thing as I myself.
> I was born free as Caesar; so were you;
> We both have fed as well, and we can both
> Endure the winter's cold as well as he.

The examples follow of the flood and fever incidents, which show how the majesty of Caesar vanished before the violence of natural forces and the prostration of disease.

> And this man
> Is now become a god, and Cassius is
> A wretched creature and must bend his body,
> If Caesar carelessly but nod on him.

In the eye of the state, individuals are so many members of a class, in precisely the way that their names are so many examples of the proper noun.

Brutus and Caesar: what should be in that 'Caesar'!?
Why should that name be sounded more than yours?
Write them together, yours is as fair a name;
Sound them, it doth become the mouth as well;
Weigh them, it is as heavy; conjure with them,
Brutus will start a spirit as soon as Caesar.
Now, in the names of all the gods at once,
Upon what meat doth this our Caesar feed,
That he is grown so great?

And this exposition of the conspirators' cause in its highest form is at the same time thrown into yet higher relief by a background to the scene, in which the victim is presented at his worst. All through the conversation between Brutus and Cassius, the shouting of the mob reminds of the scene which is at the moment going on in the Capitol, while the conversation is interrupted for a time by the returning procession of Caesar. In this action behind the scenes which thus mingles with the main incident Caesar is committing the one fault of his life: this is the fault of 'treason,' which can be justified only by being successful and so becoming 'revolution,' whereas Caesar is failing, and deserving to fail from the vacillating hesitation with which he sins. Moreover, unfavourable as such incidents would be in themselves to our sympathy with Caesar, yet it is not the actual facts that we are permitted to see, but they are further distorted by the medium through which they reach us—the cynicism of Casca which belittles and disparages all he relates.

    Bru. Tell us the manner of it, gentle Casca.
    Casca. I can as well be hanged as tell the manner of it: it was mere
foolery; I did not mark it. I saw Mark Antony offer him a crown;—yet
'twas not a crown neither, 'twas one of these coronets:—and, as I told
you, he put it by once: but, for all that, to my thinking, he would fain
have had it. Then he offered it to him again; then he put it by again:
but, to my thinking, he was very loath to lay his fingers off it. And
then he offered it the third time; he put it the third time by: and still
as he refused it, the rabblement hooted and clapped their chapped
hands and threw up their sweaty night-caps and uttered such a deal
of stinking breath because Caesar had refused the crown that it had
almost choked Caesar; for he swounded and fell down at it: and, for
mine own part, I durst not laugh, for fear of opening my lips and
receiving the bad air. . . . When he came to himself again, he said, If
he had done or said anything amiss, he desired their worships to think
it was his infirmity. Three or four wenches, where I stood, cried, 'Alas,
good soul!' and forgave him with all their hearts; but there's no heed to

be taken of them; if Caesar had stabbed their mothers they would have done no less.

At the end of the scene Brutus is won, and we pass immediately into the second stage of the action: the conspiracy is now formed and developing, and the emotional strain begins. The adhesion of Brutus has given us confidence that the conspiracy will be effective, and we have only to wait for the issue. This mere notion of *waiting* is itself enough to introduce an element of agitation into the passion sufficient to mark off this stage of the action from the preceding. How powerful suspense is for this purpose we have expressed in the words of the play itself:

> Between the acting of a dreadful thing
> And the first motion, all the interim is
> Like a phantasma, or a hideous dream:
> The Genius and the mortal instruments
> Are then in council; and the state of man,
> Like to a little kingdom, suffers then
> The nature of an insurrection.

But besides the suspense there is a special device for securing the agitation proper to this stage of the passion throughout there is maintained a Dramatic Background of night, storm, and supernatural portents.

The conception of nature as exhibiting sympathy with sudden turns in human affairs is one of the most fundamental instincts of poetry. To cite notable instances it is this which accompanies with storm and whirlwind the climax to the *Book of Job*, and which leads Milton to make the whole universe sensible of Adam's transgression:

> Earth trembl'd from her entrails, as again
> In pangs, and Nature gave a second groan;
> Sky lowr'd, and muttering thunder, some sad drops
> Wept at completing of the mortal sin
> Original.

So too the other end of the world's history has its appropriate accompaniments: 'the sun shall be darkened and the moon shall not give her light, and the stars shall be falling from heaven.' There is a *vagueness* of terror inseparable from these outbursts of nature, so mysterious in their causes and aims. They are actually the most mighty of forces—for human artillery is feeble beside the earthquake—yet they are invisible: the wind works its havoc without the keenest eye being able to perceive it, and the lightning is never seen till it has struck. Again, there is something weird in the feeling that the most frightful powers in the material universe are all *soft things*. The empty air becomes the irresistible wind; the fluid and yielding water wear down the hard and massive rock and determines the shape of the earth; impalpable fire that is blown about in every direction can be roused till it devours the solidest constructions of human skill; while the most powerful agencies of all, electricity and atomic force, are imperceptible to any of the senses and are known only by their results. This uncanny terror attaching to the union between force and softness is the inspiration of one of Homer's most unique episodes, in which the bewildered Achilles, struggling with the river-god, finds the strength and skill of the finished warrior vain against the ever-rising water, and bitterly feels the violation of the natural order—

> That strong might fall by strong, where now weak water's luxury
> Must make my death blush.

To the terrible in nature are added portents of the supernatural, sudden violations of the uniformity of nature, the principle upon which all science is founded. The solitary bird of night has been seen in the crowded Capitol; fire has played around a human hand without destroying it; lions, forgetting their fierceness, have mingled with men; clouds drop fire instead of rain; graves are giving up their dead; the chance shapes of clouds take distinctness to suggest tumult on the earth. Such phenomena of nature and the supernatural, agitating from their appeal at once to fear and mystery, and associated by the fancy with the terrible in human events, have made a deep impression upon primitive thought; and the impression has descended by generations of inherited tradition until, whatever may be the attitude of the intellect to the phenomena themselves, their associations in the emotional nature are of agitation. They thus become appropriate as a Dramatic Background to an agitated passion in the scenes themselves, calling out the emotional effect by a vague sympathy, much as a musical note may set in vibration a distant string that is in unison with it.

This device then is used by Shakespeare in the second stage of the present play. We see the warning terrors through the eyes of men of the time, and their force is measured by the fact that they shake the cynical Casca into eloquence.

> Are not you moved, when all the sway of earth
> Shakes like a thing unfirm? O Cicero,
> I have seen tempests, when the scolding winds
> Have rived the knotty oaks, and I have seen
> The ambitious ocean swell and rage and foam,
> To be exalted with the threatening clouds

But never till to-night, never till now,
Did I go through a tempest dropping fire.
Either there is a civil strife in heaven,
Or else the world, too saucy with the gods,
Incenses them to send destruction.

And the idea thus started at the commencement is kept before our minds throughout this stage of the drama by perpetual allusions, however slight, to the sky and external nature. Brutus reads the secret missives by the light of exhalations whizzing through the air; when some of the conspirators step aside, to occupy a few moments while the rest are conferring apart, it is to the sky their thoughts naturally seem to turn, and they with difficulty can make out the East from the West; the discussion of the conspirators includes the effect on Caesar of the night's prodigies. Later Portia remonstrates against her husband's exposure to the raw and dank morning, to the rheumy and unpurged air; even when daylight has fully returned, the conversation is of Calpurnia's dream and the terrible prodigies.

Against this background are displayed, first single figures of Cassius and other conspirators; then Brutus alone in calm deliberation: then the whole band of conspirators, their wild excitement side by side with Brutus's immovable moderation. Then the Conspiracy Scene fades in the early morning light into a display of Brutus in his softer relations; and with complete return of day changes to the house of Caesar on the fatal morning. Caesar also is displayed in contact with the supernatural, as represented by Calpurnia's terrors and repeated messages of omens that forbid his venturing upon public action for that day. Caesar faces all this with his usual loftiness of mind; yet the scene is so contrived that, as far as immediate effect is concerned, this very loftiness is made to tell against him. The unflinching courage that overrides and interprets otherwise the prodigies and warnings seems presumption to us who know the reality of the danger. It is the same with his yielding to the humour of his wife. Why should he not? his is not the conscious weakness that must be firm to show that it is not afraid. Yet when, upon Decius's explaining away the dream and satisfying Calpurnia's fears, Caesar's own attraction to danger leads him to persevere in his first intention, this change of purpose seems to us, who have heard Decius's boast that he can o'ersway Caesar with flattery, a confirmation of Caesar's weakness. So in accordance with the purpose that reigns through the first half of the play the victim is made to appear at his worst: the *passing* effect of the scene is to suggest weakness in Caesar, while it is in fact furnishing elements which, upon reflection, go to build up a character of strength. On the other hand, throughout this stage the justification of the conspirators' cause gains by their confidence and their high tone; in particular by the way in which they interpret to their own advantage the supernatural element. Cassius feels the wildness of the night as in perfect harmony with his own spirit.

> For my part, I have walk'd about the streets,
> Submitting me unto the perilous night,
> And, thus unbraced, Casca, as you see,
> Have bared my bosom to the thunder-stone;
> And when the cross blue lightning seem'd to open
> The breast of heaven, I did present myself
> Even in the aim and very flash of it.

And it needs only a word from him to communicate his confidence to his comrades.

> *Cassius.* Now could I, Casca, name to thee a man
> Most like this dreadful night,
> That thunders, lightens, opens graves, and roars
> As doth the lion in the Capitol,
> A man no mightier than thyself or me
> In personal action, yet prodigious grown
> And fearful, as these strange eruptions are
> *Casca.* 'Tis Caesar that you mean; is it not, Cassius?

The third stage of the action brings us to the climax of the passion; the strain upon our emotions now rises to a height of agitation. The exact commencement of the crisis seems to be marked by the soothsayer's words at the opening of Act III. Caesar observes on entering the Capitol the soothsayer who had warned him to beware of this very day.

> *Caesar.* The ides of March are come.
> *Sooth.* Ay, Caesar; but not gone.

Such words seem to measure out a narrow area of time in which the crisis is to work itself out. There is however no distinct break between different stages of a dramatic movement like that in the present play; and two short incidents have preceded this scene which have served as emotional devices to bring about a distinct advance in the intensification of the strain. In the first, Artemidorus appeared reading a letter of warning which he purposed to present to Caesar on his way to the fatal spot. In the Capitol Scene he presents it, while the ready Decius hastens to interpose another petition to take off Caesar's attention. Artemidorus conjures Caesar to read his first for 'it touches him nearer'; but the imperial chivalry of Caesar forbids:

What touches us ourself shall be last served.

The momentary hope of rescue is dashed. In the second incident Portia has been displayed completely unnerved by the weight of a secret to the anxiety of which she is not equal; she sends messengers to the Capitol and recalls them as she recollects that she dare give them no message; her agitation has communicated itself to us, besides suggesting the fear that it may betray to others what she is anxious to conceal. Our sympathy has thus been tossed from side to side, although in its general direction it still moves on the side of the conspirators. In the crisis itself the agitation becomes painful as the entrance of Popilius Lena and his secret communication to Caesar cause a panic that threatens to wreck the whole plot on the verge of its success. Brutus's nerve sustains even this trial, and the way for the accomplishment of the deed is again clear. Emotional devices like these have carried the passion up to a climax of agitation; and the conspirators now advance to present their pretended suit and achieve the bloody deed. To the last the double effect of Caesar's demeanour continues. Considered in itself, his unrelenting firmness of principle exhibits the highest model of a ruler; yet to us, who know the purpose lurking behind the hypocritical intercession of the conspirators, Caesar's self-confidence resembles the infatuation that goes before Nemesis. He scorns the fickle politicians before him as mere wandering sparks of heavenly fire, while he is left alone as a pole-star of true-fixed and resting quality:—and in answer to his presumptuous boast that he can never be moved come the blows of the assassins which strike him down; while there is a flash of irony as he is seen to have fallen beside the statue of Pompey, and the marble seems to gleam in cold triumph over the rival at last lying bleeding at its feet. The assassination is accomplished, the cause of the conspirators is won: pity notwithstanding we are swept along with the current of their enthusiasm; and the justification that has been steadily rising from the commencement reaches its climax as, their adversaries dispersing in terror, the conspirators dip their hands in their victim's blood, and make their triumphant appeal to the whole world and all time.

> *Cassius.* Stoop, then, and wash. How many ages hence
> Shall this our lofty scene be acted over
> In states unborn and accents yet unknown!
>   *Brutus.* How many times shall Caesar bleed is sport,
> That now on Pompey's basis lies along,
> No worthier than the dust!
>   *Cassius.* So oft as that shall be,
> So often shall the knot of us be call'd
> The men that gave their country LIBERTY!

Enter a servant: this simple stage-direction is the 'catastrophe,' the turning-round of the whole action; the arch has reached its apex and the Reaction has begun. So instantaneous is the change, that though it is only the servant of Antony who speaks, yet the first words of his message ring with the peculiar tone of subtly-poised sentences which are inseparably associated with Antony's eloquence; it is like the first announcement of that which is to be a final theme in music, and from this point this tone dominates the scene to the very end.

> Thus he bade me say:
> Brutus is noble, wise, valiant, and honest,
> Caesar was mighty, bold, royal, and loving,
> Say I love Brutus, and I honour him;
> Say I fear'd Caesar, honour'd him, and lov'd him.
> If Brutus will vouchsafe that Antony
> May safely come to him, and be resolv'd
> How Caesar hath deserved to lie in death,
> Mark Antony shall not love Caesar dead
> So well as Brutus living.

In the whole Shakespearean Drama there is nowhere such a swift swinging round of a dramatic action as is here marked by this sudden up-springing of the suppressed individuality in Antony's character, hitherto so colourless that he has been spared by the conspirators as a mere limb of Caesar. The tone of exultant triumph in the conspirators has in an instant given place to Cassius's 'misgiving' as Brutus grants Antony an audience; and when Antony enters, Brutus's first words to him fall into the form of apology. The quick subtlety of Antony's intellect has grasped the whole situation, and with irresistible force he slowly feels his way towards using the conspirators' aid for crushing themselves and avenging their victim. The bewilderment of the conspirators in the presence of this unlooked-for force is seen in Cassius's unavailing attempt to bring Antony to the point, as to what compact he will make with them. Antony, on the contrary, reads his men with such nicety that he can indulge himself in sailing close to the wind, and grasps fervently the hands of the assassins while he pours out a flood of bitter grief over the corpse. It is not hypocrisy, nor a trick to gain time, this conciliation of his enemies. Steeped in the political spirit of the age, Antony knows, as no other man, the mob which governs Rome, and is conscious of the mighty engine he possesses in his oratory to sway that mob in what direction he pleases; when his bold plan has succeeded, and his adversaries have consented to meet him in contest of oratory, then ironical conciliation becomes the natural relief to his pent-up passion.

Friends am I with you all and love you all,
Upon this hope, that you shall give me reasons
Why and wherein Caesar was dangerous.

It is as he feels the sense of innate oratorical power and of the opportunity
his enemies have given to that power, that he exaggerates his temporary amity
with the men he is about to crush: it is the executioner arranging his victim
comfortably on the rack before he proceeds to apply the levers. Already the
passion of the drama has fallen under the guidance of Antony. The view of
Caesar as an innocent victim is now allowed full play upon our sympathies
when Antony, left alone with the corpse, can drop the artificial mask and give
vent to his love and vengeance. The success of the conspiracy had begun to
decline as we marked Brutus's ill-timed generosity to Antony in granting him
the funeral oration; it crumbles away through the cold unnatural euphuism
of Brutus's speech in its defence; it is hurried to its ruin when Antony at last
exercises his spell upon the Roman people and upon the reader. The speech
of Antony, with its mastery of every phase of feeling, is a perfect sonata upon
the instrument of the human emotions. Its opening theme is sympathy with
bereavement, against which are working as if in conflict anticipations of future
themes, doubt and compunction. A distinct change of movement comes
with the first introduction of what is to be the final subject, the mention
of the will. But when this new movement has worked up from curiosity to
impatience, there is a diversion: the mention of the victory over the Nervii
turns the emotions in the direction of historic pride, which harmonises well
with the opposite emotions roused as the orator fingers hole after hole in
Caesar's mantle made by the daggers of his false friends, and so leads up to a
sudden shock when he uncovers the body itself and displays the popular idol
and its bloody defacement. Then the finale begins: the forgotten theme of the
will is again started, and from a burst of gratitude the passion quickens and
intensifies to rage, to fury, to mutiny. The mob is won to the Reaction; and
the curtain that falls upon the third Act rises for a moment to display the
populace tearing a man to pieces simply because he bears the same name as
one of the conspirators.

The final stage of the action works out the development of an inevitable
fate. The emotional strain now ceases, and, as in the first stage, the passion is
of the calmer order, the calmness in this case of pity balanced by a sense of
justice. From the opening of the fourth Act the decline in the justification of
the conspirators is intimated by the logic of events. The first scene exhibits to
us the triumvirate that now governs Rome, and shows that in this triumvirate
Antony is supreme: with the man who is the embodiment of the Reaction
thus appearing at the head of the world, the fall of the conspirators is seen
to be inevitable. The decline of our sympathy with them continues in the

following scenes. The Quarrel Scene shows how low the tone of Cassius has fallen since he has dealt with assassination as a political weapon; and even Brutus's moderation has hardened into unpleasing harshness. There is at this point plenty of relief to such unpleasing effects: there is the exhibition of the tender side of Brutus's character as shown in his relations with his page, and the display of friendship maintained between Brutus and Cassius amid falling fortunes. But such incidents as these have a different effect upon us from that which they would have had at an earlier period; the justification of the conspirators has so far declined that now attractive touches in them serve only to increase the pathos of a fate which, however, our sympathy no longer seeks to resist. We get a supernatural foreshadowing of the end in the appearance to Brutus of Caesar's Ghost, and the omen Cassius sees of the eagles that had consorted his army to Philippi giving place to ravens, crows, and kites on the morning of battle: this lends the authority of the invisible world to our sense that the conspirators' cause is doomed. And judicial blindness overtakes them as Brutus's authority in council overweighs in point after point the shrewder advice of Cassius. Through the scenes of the fifth Act we see the republican leaders fighting on without hope. The last remnant of justification for their cause ceases as the conspirators themselves seem to acknowledge their error and fate. Cassius as he feels his death-blow recognises the very weapon with which he had committed the crime:

> Caesar, thou art revenged,
> Even with the sword that kill'd thee.

And at last even the firm spirit of Brutus yields

> O Julius Caesar, thou art mighty yet!
> Thy spirit walks abroad, and turns our swords
> In our own proper entrails.

1894—Oscar Fay Adams and Frank A. Marshall.
"Julius Caesar: Critical Remarks," from
The Works of William Shakespeare

Oscar Fay Adams wrote *A Dictionary of American Authors, The Story of Jane Austen's Life,* and other works. F.A. Marshall was a Shakespearean scholar who wrote *A Study of Hamlet.*

Julius Caesar has been condemned, from a dramatic point of view, for its lack of unity. It is like two plays in one, the former being concerned with the death of Caesar, the latter with the revenge of that deed. The nominal hero disappears at the end of the third act, and only his ghost is seen thereafter. But the ghost is a connecting link between the two parts of the drama. "Julius Caesar, thou art mighty yet!" exclaims Brutus, when he comes upon the dead bodies of Cassius and Titinius; and Cassius, as he killed himself, had cried:

> Caesar, thou art reveng'd,
> Even with the sword that kill'd thee. (v. 3. 45, 46.)

It is not without purpose that the dramatist introduces these significant utterances. Caesar is dead, indeed, but we must not forget that his

> spirit ranging for revenge,
> With Até by his side come hot from hell, (iii. 1. 271, 272.)

has "let slip the dogs of war" against his butchers. The eloquent prophecy of Antony over his bleeding corpse is fulfilled.

The treatment of the living Caesar by the poet, however, has been a puzzle to many of the critics. It is evident from the many allusions to the great Roman in the other plays, that his character and history had made a deep impression on Shakespeare. Craik, after quoting the references to Caesar in *As You Like It*, II. *Henry IV.*, *Henry V.*, the three parts of *Henry VI.*, *Richard III.*, *Hamlet*, *Antony and Cleopatra*, and *Cymbeline*, remarks that these passages "will probably be thought to afford a considerably more comprehensive representation of the mighty Julius than the play which bears his name." "We have," he adds, "a distinct exhibition of little else beyond his vanity and arrogance, relieved and set off by his good-nature or affability. . . . It might almost be suspected that the complete and full-length Caesar had been carefully reserved for another drama." Hazlitt remarks that the hero of the play "makes several vapouring and rather pedantic speeches, and does nothing; indeed, he has nothing to do." Hudson says: "Caesar is far from being himself in these scenes; hardly one of the speeches put into his mouth can be regarded as historically characteristic; taken all together they are little short of a downright caricature." He is in doubt whether to explain this by supposing that Caesar was too great for the hero of a drama, "since his greatness, if brought forward in full measure, would leave no room for anything else," or whether it was not the poet's plan "to represent Caesar, not as he was indeed, but as he must have appeared to the conspirators; to make us see him as they saw him; in order that they too might have fair and equal judgment at our hands." He is disposed to rest on the latter explanation, but to me it seems very clearly a wrong one. What the conspirators thought of Caesar is evident enough from what they themselves say of him. It was not necessary to distort or belittle the character to make us see *how* they saw him; and to have done it to make us see him as they saw him would have been a gross injustice to the foremost man of all this world of which we cannot imagine Shakespeare guilty. As to its being necessary in order that we may do justice to the conspirators, if it leads us to justify their course in killing him, does it not make the fate that afterwards befalls them appear most undeserved? Does it not enlist our sympathies too exclusively on their side?

On the whole I am disposed to think that the poet meant to represent Caesar as Plutarch represents him—as having become ambitious for kingly power, somewhat spoiled by victory, jealous and fearful of his enemies in the state, and superstitious withal, yet hiding his fears and misgivings under an arrogant and haughty demeanour. He is shown, moreover, by the dramatist at a critical point in his career, hesitating between his ambition for the crown (which we need not suppose to have been of a merely selfish sort, for he may well have believed that as king he could do more for his country's good than in any other capacity) and his doubt whether the time had come for him to accept the crown. It may be a question whether even Caesar could be truly himself just then; whether even he might not, at such a crisis in his fortunes, show something of the weakness of inferior natures.

It must be remembered, too, that, as Hazlitt has said, Caesar *does* nothing in the play, *has* nothing to do, except to play the part of the victim in the assassination. So far as any opportunities of showing what he really *is* are concerned, he is at much the same disadvantage as "the man in the coffin" at a funeral—a very essential character in the performance, though in no sense an actor in it. If he is to impress us as verily "great Caesar," it must be by what he says, not by what be does, and by what he says when there is no occasion for grand and heroic utterance. Under the circumstances a little boasting and bravado appear to be necessary to his being recognized as the Roman Dictator.

After all, there is not so very much of this boastful language put into the mouth of Caesar; and, as Knight reminds us, some of it is evidently uttered to disguise his fear. When he says:

The gods do this in shame of cowardice;
Caesar should be a beast without a heart,
If he should stay at home to-day for fear, (ii. 2. 41–43.)

he is speaking to the servant who has brought the message from the augurers. "Before *him* he could show no fear;" but, the moment the servant has gone (he is doubtless intended to leave the stage), he tells Calpurnia that "for her humour he will stay at home." proving plainly enough that he *does* fear. His reply afterwards to Decius beginning

Cowards die many times before their deaths, (ii. 2. 32.)

is directly suggested by Plutarch, who says that when his friends "did counsel him to have a guard for the safety of his person," he would not consent to it, "but said it was better to die once than always to be afraid of death." His last speech—

> I do know but one
> That unassailable holds on his rank,
> Unshak'd of motion: and that I am he,
> Let me a little show it, (iii. 1. 68–71.)

though boastful, is not unnatural in the connection, being drawn from him by the persistent importunities of the friends of Cimber. The fact that Caesar has so little to say has, I think, led the critics to exaggerate this characteristic of the speeches.

With regard to Brutus also the critics have had their doubts. Coleridge asks, "What character did Shakespeare mean his Brutus to be?" He is perplexed that Brutus, the stern Roman republican, should say that he would have no objection to a king, or to Caesar as king, if he would only be as good a monarch as he now seems disposed to be; and also that, in view of all Caesar had done—crossing the Rubicon, entering Rome as a conqueror, placing Gauls in the senate, &c.—he finds no personal cause to complain of him. He resolves to kill his friend and benefactor, not for what he has been or what he is, but for what he may become. He is no serpent, but a serpent's egg; therefore crush him in the shell.

It is curious that Coleridge should not have seen that by "personal cause," so distinctly opposed to "the general," Brutus refers to his private relations with Caesar as a man and as a friend, not to public acts or those affecting the common weal. All those enumerated by Coleridge belong to the latter class.

That Brutus should be influenced by his speculations as to what Caesar might become, is in thorough keeping with the character. Brutus is a scholar, a philosopher, and a patriot; but he is not a statesman. He is an idealist, and strangely wanting in practical wisdom. It is significant that Shakespeare represents him again and again with a book in his hand. He is a man of books rather than a man of the world. His theories are of the noblest, his intentions of the most patriotic and philanthropic, but they are visionary and impracticable. There are such men in every age—reformers who accomplish no reform, because their lofty dreams are incapable of being made realities in this workaday world. Such men are easily misled and made tools of by those more unscrupulous than themselves; as Brutus was by Cassius and the rest. They are often inconsistent in argument, as Brutus in the speech that puzzled Coleridge. They are influenced by one-sided views of an important question, deciding it hastily, without looking at it from all sides, as they ought, and as those who are less rash and impulsive see that they ought. So Brutus sends to Cassius for money to pay his legions, because he cannot raise money by vile means; but he knows how Cassius raises the money, and has no scruples about sharing in the fruits of the "indirection." He is thinking only of paying the soldiers, and does not see that he is an accomplice after the act in what he so sharply rebukes in Cassius. He is inconsistent here as in many other cases; but the inconsistency is perfectly consistent with the character.

Cassius is a worse man, but a better statesman, or rather politician. He is shrewd and fertile in expedients, but not overburdened with principle or conscience. He is tricky, and believes that the end justifies the means. He can write anonymous letters to Brutus, "in several hands, as if they came from several citizens," and can put placards in the same vein "on old Brutus' statue." He is none too honest himself, but he understands the value of a good name to "the cause," and therefore wishes to secure the endorsement of one whose "countenance, like richest alchemy, will change to virtue and to worthiness" what, he says, "would appear offence in *us*"—the less scrupulous politicians.

We must not, however, take Cassius to be worse than he really is. As a politician he is a believer in expediency—whatever is likely to secure the end in view is right; but as a man he has many admirable traits of character. If it were not so, Brutus could not love him as he does. He has a high sense of personal honour withal. He is indignant when Brutus tells him he has "an itching palm;" but he has just told Brutus that bribery is not to be judged severely when it is necessary for political purposes. "At such a time as this it is not meet" to be overcritical of "every nice offence." There spake the politician; in the other case, the man. We must not be too hard upon him. Sundry good friends of ours in public life are his modern counterparts.

Except in the great scene in the forum, where his speech to the people is perhaps the finest piece of oratory to be found in all Shakespeare—and entirely his own, be it noted, no hint of it being given by Plutarch—Antony plays no very striking part in the drama. We see him roused by a sudden ambition from his early career of dissipation, and taking a place in the Triumvirate; and it reminds us of Prince Hal's coming to himself, like the repentant prodigal, when he comes to the throne. But Antony is, morally at least, a slighter man than Henry. His reform lacks the sincerity and depth of the latter's, and he cannot hold the higher plane to which he has temporarily risen. His fall is to be depicted in a later and greater drama, of which he is the hero and not a subordinate actor as here.

Portia is one of the noblest of Shakespeare's women. As Mrs. Jameson has said, her character "is but a softened reflection of that of her husband Brutus: in him we see an excess of natural sensibility, an almost womanish tenderness of heart, repressed by the tenets of his austere philosophy: a stoic by profession, and in reality the reverse—acting deeds against his nature by the strong force of principle and will. In Portia there is the same profound and passionate feeling, and all her sex's softness and timidity held in check by that self-discipline, that stately dignity, which she thought became a woman 'so fathered and so husbanded.' The fact of her inflicting on herself a voluntary wound to try her own fortitude is perhaps the strongest proof of this disposition. Plutarch relates that on the day on which Caesar was assassinated, Portia appeared overcome with terror, and even swooned away, but did not in her emotion utter a word which could affect the conspirators. Shakespeare has rendered this circumstance literally [in ii. 4. 1–20].

"There is another beautiful incident related by Plutarch which could not well be dramatized. When Brutus and Portia parted for the last time in the island of Nisida, she restrained all expression of grief that she might not shake *his* fortitude; but afterwards, in passing through a chamber in which there hung a picture of Hector and Andromache, she stopped, gazed upon it for a time with a settled sorrow, and at length burst into a passion of tears."

No critic or commentator, I believe, has thought Calpurnia worthy of notice, but the reader may be reminded to compare carefully the scene between her and Caesar with that between Portia and Brutus. The difference in the two women is not more remarkable than that in their husbands' bearing and tone towards them. Portia with mingled pride and affection takes her stand upon her rights as a wife—"a woman that Lord Brutus took to wife "—and he feels the appeal as a man of his noble and tender nature must:

> O ye gods,
> Render me worthy of this noble wife!

Calpurnia is a poor creature in comparison with this true daughter of Cato, as her first words to Caesar sufficiently prove:

> What mean you, Caesar! Think you to walk forth?
> You *shall not* stir out of your house to-day. (ii. 2. 8, 9.)

When a wife takes that tone, we know what the reply will be: "Caesar *shall* forth." Later, of course, she comes down to entreaty:

> Do not go forth to-day. Call it my fear
> That keeps you in the house, and not your own. (ii. 2. 50, 51.)

And Caesar, with contemptuous acquiescence in the suggestion to let Antony say he is "not well to-day," yields to her weak importunities. When Decius comes in and urges Caesar to go, the story of her dream and her forebodings is told him with a sneer (can we imagine Brutus speaking of Portia in that manner?), and her husband, falling a victim to the shrewd flattery of Decius, departs to his death with a parting fling at her foolish fears, which he is ashamed at having for the moment yielded to. Calpurnia was Caesar's fourth wife, and the marriage was one of convenience rather than of affection.

There are no portions of Roman history that seem so real to us as those which Shakespeare has made the subjects of his plays. History merely calls up the ghost of the dead past, and the impression it makes upon us is shadowy and unsubstantial; poetry makes it live again before our eyes, and we feel that we are looking upon men and women like ourselves, not their misty semblances. It might seem at first that the poet, by giving us fancies instead of facts, or fancies mingled with facts, only distorts and confuses our conceptions of historical verities; but, if he be a true poet, he sees the past with a clearer vision than other men, and reproduces it more truthfully as well as more vividly. He sees it indeed with the eye of imagination, not as it actually was; but there are truths of the imagination no less than of the senses and the reason. Two descriptions may be alike imaginative, but one may be true and the other false. The one, though not a statement of facts, is consistent with the facts and impresses us as the reality would impress us; the other is neither true nor in keeping with the truth, and can only deceive and mislead us. Ben Jonson wrote Roman plays which, in minute attention to the details of the manners and customs of the time, are far more scholarly and accurate than Shakespeare's. He accompanies them with hundreds of notes giving classical quotations to illustrate the action and the language, and showing how painstaking he has been in this respect. The work evinces genuine poetic power as well as laborious research, and yet the effect is far inferior to that of Shakespeare's less pedantic treatment of Roman subjects. The latter knows much lees of classical history and antiquities, but has a deeper insight into human nature, which is the same in all ages. Jonson has given us skilfully-modelled and admirably-sculptured statues, but Shakespeare living men and women.

1898—George Bernard Shaw. "Tappertit on Caesar," from *Our Theatres in the Nineties*

George Bernard Shaw was a playwright and a critic. He often expressed his ambivalence toward Shakespeare. Some of his greatest works include *Saint Joan*, *Pygmalion* (later adapted into the musical and film *My Fair Lady*), *Man and Superman*, and *Caesar and Cleopatra*.

JULIUS CAESAR.
Her Majesty's Theatre, 22 January 1898.

[29 January 1898]

The truce with Shakespear is over. It was only possible whilst *Hamlet* was on the stage. *Hamlet* is the tragedy of private life—nay, of individual bachelor-poet life. It belongs to a detached residence, a select library, an exclusive circle, to no occupation, to fathomless boredom, to impenitent mugwumpism, to the illusion that the futility of these things is the futility of existence, and its contemplation philosophy: in short, to the dream-fed gentlemanism of the age which Shakespear inaugurated in English literature: the age, that is, of the rising middle class bringing into power the ideas taught it by its servants in the kitchen, and its fathers in the shop—ideas now happily passing away as the onslaught of modern democracy offers to the kitchen-taught and home-bred the alternative of achieving a real superiority or going ignominiously under in the class conflict.

It is when we turn to *Julius Caesar*, the most splendidly written political melodrama we possess, that we realize the apparently immortal author of *Hamlet* as a man, not for all time, but for an age only, and that, too, in all solidly wise and heroic aspects, the most despicable of all the ages in our history. It is impossible for even the most judicially minded critic to look without a revulsion of indignant contempt at this travestying of a great man as a silly braggart, whilst the pitiful gang of mischief-makers who destroyed him are lauded as statesmen and patriots. There is not a single sentence uttered by Shakespear's Julius Caesar that is, I will not say worthy of him, but even worthy of an average Tammany boss. Brutus is nothing but a familiar type of English suburban preacher: politically he would hardly impress the Thames Conservancy Board. Cassius is a vehemently assertive nonentity. It is only when we come to Antony, unctuous voluptuary and self-seeking sentimental demagogue, that we find Shakespear in his depth; and in his depth, of course, he is superlative. Regarded as a crafty stage job, the play is a triumph: rhetoric, claptrap, effective gushes of emotion, all the devices of the popular playwright, are employed with a profusion of power that almost breaks their backs. No doubt there are slips and slovenliness of the kind that careful revisers eliminate; but they count for so little in the mass of accomplishment that it is safe to say that the dramatist's art can be carried no further on that plane. If Goethe, who understood Caesar and the significance of his death—"the most senseless of deeds" he called it—had treated the subject, his conception of it would have been as superior to Shakespear's as St John's Gospel is to the Police News; but his treatment could not have been more magnificently successful. As far as sonority, imagery, wit, humor, energy of imagination, power over language, and a whimsically keen eye for idiosyncrasies can make a dramatist, Shakespear was the king of dramatists. Unfortunately, a man may have them all, and yet conceive high affairs of state exactly as Simon Tappertit did. In one of the scenes in *Julius Caesar* a conceited poet bursts into the tent of Brutus and Cassius, and exhorts them not to quarrel with one another. If Shakespear had been able to present his play to the ghost of the great Julius, he would probably have had much the same reception. He certainly would have deserved it.

Julius Caesar IN THE Twentieth Century

In the twentieth century, many commentators built on past analyses to focus on the relationships between characters and the play's conflicts, both external and internal. G. Wilson Knight identified love as a major theme in the play; in his view, all the characters are lovers. Although their love may be the affection between friends, it is still an emotional and fiery love. Brutus, however, always gives preference to honor rather than love, which ultimately leads him to disaster.

Knight also pointed out the importance of internal divisions in the play's characters. Caesar, for example, is composed of two incompatible parts: He is a sick old man and a great spirit presiding over Rome. Brutus can separate his friend Caesar from the Caesar who is a nearly godlike figure. This allows him to become a conspirator.

The midcentury scholar Harold C. Goddard likewise found internal duality in Shakespeare's characters, and he took a psychological approach to *Julius Caesar.* Shakespeare not only gave the play's major characters a dual nature, Goddard said, but also dramatized parts of their natures in minor characters. For instance, Goddard saw Portia and Lucius as aspects of Brutus: Portia serves as Brutus's wisdom and is the mirror of his soul; Lucius is Brutus's innocence. Brutus ignores both of these aspects of himself to his great detriment.

The poet W.H. Auden took a different approach to the characters of *Julius Caesar.* In one of his lectures on Shakespeare, Auden identified Brutus as a precursor to Hamlet; unlike Hamlet, however, Brutus is unable to understand his own despair. Auden regarded Antony as a man of feeling who loves a crisis and craves excitement. Antony also knows how to excite emotions in others, as demonstrated by his funeral oration. Auden also examined the play's social landscape. He pronounced the overall society portrayed in the play "doomed" because of its "intellectual and spiritual failure of nerve." People in his own time were in a similarly dangerous predicament, he said, though not doomed.

In addition to the characters of the play, the critic Kenneth Burke turned his focus to the audience, and he wrote creatively of how the Elizabethan audience reacted to the play. Burke examined the character of Antony and invented an imaginary speech wherein Antony turns to the audience and becomes a critical commentator on the play, explaining exactly how the play has functioned to manipulate emotions. Burke compared the audience to the mob in the play, since the audience, too, is led by a "Great Demagogue"—that is, Shakespeare.

The playwright and actor Harley Granville-Barker examined the structure of the play. At first, everything in the plot leads to the assassination, and after the assassination it is Caesar's humble servant Antony who leads the play to its turning point and redirects the action completely. Granville-Barker, taking the perspective of a man of the theater, pointed out that many viewers fail to fully appreciate the last act of the play; they must remember that it was written to work on the Shakespearean stage.

Later in the century, the German professor Dieter Mehl examined the play not so much in terms of its characters, but in its place in Shakespeare's work overall. In this reckoning, the play is the first of Shakespeare's mature tragedies. In *Julius Caesar*, Mehl said, Shakespeare shows for the first time how individual choice has profound effects on the entire community. Mehl also believed that in this play Shakespeare started to use the soliloquy differently: It allows the audience to peer deeply into the thoughts of Brutus, who, like Hamlet, is a man who would never be the same after a key decision. His view is similar to that of Goddard, who thought that the play was a profoundly important bridge between Shakespeare's histories and tragedies: *Julius Caesar* is where the poet finally "crosses the Rubicon."

Other critics in the twentieth century examined the play's language and imagery. T. S. Dorsch, like Knight, found the play deeply concerned with relationships between individuals. Though the word *love* is mentioned many times, the play emphasizes many conflicts between individuals. Blood and destruction are key images, as are terms pertaining to metals, which are used to describe characters. Many of the strongest speeches in the play are clear and direct. Figurative language is most prominent when Caesar appears overly boastful and often when Brutus speaks, signifying his own inner turmoil and lack of a clear vision.

Finally, Harold Bloom, in his comments on the play, emphasized the importance of Brutus, a true tragic hero, whose identification with Rome is the cause of his destruction.

1931—G. Wilson Knight. "The Eroticism of *Julius Caesar*," from *The Imperial Theme: Further Interpretations of Shakespeare's Tragedies Including the Roman Plays*

G. Wilson Knight was professor of English at Leeds University and also taught at the University of Toronto. At both universities he produced and acted in Shakespeare plays. In addition, Knight wrote plays for the British stage and television. His books include *Shakespearean Production* and *Lord Byron: Christian Virtues*.

The human element in *Julius Caesar* is charged highly with a general eroticism. All the people are 'lovers'. This love is emotional, fiery, but not exactly sexual, not physically passionate: even Portia and Brutus love with a gentle companionship rather than any passion. Though the stage be set for an action 'most bloody, fiery, and most terrible', though the action be fine, spirited, and adventurous, and noble blood be magnificently spilt in the third act, yet the human element is often one of gentle sentiment, melting hearts, tears, and the soft fire of love. There are many major and minor love-themes. There is love expressed or suggested between Brutus and Cassius, Brutus and Caesar, and Antony and Caesar; Brutus and Portia, Brutus and Volumnius, Brutus and Lucius; Caesar and Decius, Cassius and Lucius Pella, Cassius and Titinius; Ligarius and Brutus, Artemidorus and Caesar. Probably there are other instances. The word 'lover' is amazingly frequent, sometimes meaning little more than 'friend', but always helping to build a general atmosphere of comradeship and affection. Love is here the regal, the conquering reality: the murder of Caesar is a gash in the body of Rome, and this gash is healed by love, so that the play's action emphasizes first the disjointing of 'spirit' from 'matter' which is evil, fear, anarchy; and then the remating of these two elements into the close fusion which is love, order, peace.

I will note first the personal themes of Julius Caesar and Antony, and thereafter more closely observe the contrasted importance of Brutus and Cassius. The simplicity of *Julius Caesar* is a surface simplicity only. To close analysis it reveals subtleties and complexities which render interpretation difficult. Nor can I hope to avoid altogether obscurity and indecisiveness in the attempt to render the meaning of so involved a pattern. The play has, as it were, four protagonists, each with a different view of the action.

The figure of Julius Caesar stands out, brilliant. From the start he is idealized in point of power, general respect, glory. His failings must not receive our only attention: he is endued dramatically with strength, importance, almost divinity. He is a sublime figure-head, but, the general acclamations at anytime stilled, we see him as a man, weak, egotistical, petulant. But his weakness must not prevent our recognition of power behind such words as Cassius'

> Why, man, he doth bestride the narrow world
> Like a Colossus . . . (I. ii. 135)

The Caesar-idea is accompanied by all the usual Shakespearian suggestions of world-glory and life-beauty. Here they are raised to a high pitch. The men of Rome put on their best 'attire' (I. i. 53) for his triumph, 'strew flowers in his way' (I. i. 55). His images are robed and decked, with his 'trophies' and 'ceremonies' (I. i. 69–74). Every one's attention hangs on his words:

> Peace, ho! Caesar speaks. (I. ii. 1)

His entry is accompanied with music. He is associated with images of infinity, the North Star and Olympus (III. i. 60, 74). He is, as it were, a frail man buoyed on the full flood of success. He is conscious of his own triumphant destiny:

>   . . . danger knows full well
> That Caesar is more dangerous than he:
> We are two lions litter'd in one day,
> And I the elder and more terrible. (II. ii. 44)

The idea of Caesar is ever far greater here than Caesar the man. It is so to Caesar himself. He has an almost superstitious respect for his own star, and is afraid of acting unworthily of it: thus he here persuades himself not to show fear, since he is greater than danger itself. Often he has to persuade himself in this fashion:

> Shall Caesar send a lie?
> Have I in conquest stretch'd mine arm so far,
> To be afeard to tell greybeards the truth? (II. ii. 65)

This shortly follows his words, 'Mark Antony shall say I am not well' (II. ii. 55): either because now Decius is present, or purely due to his sudden attempt to live up to the Caesar-idea. He often vacillates like this. He tells Antony that Cassius is a danger, then pulls himself up sharply with, 'Always, I am Caesar' (I. ii. 212). We are, indeed, aware of two Caesars: the ailing and petulant old man, and the giant spirit standing colossal over the Roman Empire to be. There is an insubstantial, mirage-like uncertainty about this Caesar. How are we to see him? He is two incompatibles, shifting, interchanging. As the hour of his death draws near, this induces almost a sickening feeling, like a ship's rocking. This is the uncertainty, the unreal phantasma, of Brutus' mind, and, for a while, of ours. Caesar is himself, curiously, aware of both his selves: hence his rapid changes, his admixture of fine phrases resonant of imperial glory with trivialities, platitudes, absurdities. Confronted by Metellus Cimber's petition, he is intent, not on justice, but on preserving his own constancy. The North Star alone remains constant in the skies, and Caesar must be such a star to men:

> So in the world; 'tis furnish'd well with men,
> And men are flesh and blood, and apprehensive;
> Yet in the number I do know but one
> That unassailable holds on his rank,
> Unshaked of motion: and that I am he,
> Let me a little show it, even in this,
> That I was constant Cimber should be banish'd,
> And constant do remain to keep him so. (III. i. 66)

He wants primarily to 'show' his constancy: to the world, to himself. He must prove its existence. His egotism thus knows no bounds. And yet his egotism is both compelling and ludicrous. The baling coexistence of these elements in single speeches, single phrases even, is remarkable: there is nothing quite like it in Shakespeare. He can say with finality, 'Caesar doth not wrong' (III. i. 47). Petitions may 'fire the blood of ordinary men' but not Caesar's (III. i. 37). All this may seem a little foolish yet if we see only foolishness, we are wrong. We must observe both Caesars, keep both ever in mind: one physical and weak, the other all but supernatural in spiritual power, a power blazing in the fine hyperboles of his egocentricity. Cassius notes how superstitions now affect Caesar:

> For he is superstitious grown of late,
> Quite from the main opinion he held once
> Of fantasy, of dreams, and ceremonies. (II. i. 195)

This is not surprising: it is a normal correlative to his superstitious respect for his idealized self. Nor, in this world, is superstition a fault: it is fully justified. Moreover Cassius himself (V. i. 77–9) and Calpurnia (II. ii. 13–14) express elsewhere an exactly similar change towards superstition. The Soothsayer's prophecy comes true. Dreams and auguries are justified by the event; portents are ever faithful harbingers of destruction. Caesar's ghost appears twice to Brutus, and he knows his hour has come (V. v. 17–20). We are vividly conscious of the supernatural. Thus Caesar's superstition and almost superstitious respect for his own importance are, in this universe, not irrational. Again, we are pointed to the root ideas here: physical weakness, spiritual energy, the supernatural. And this spiritual element burns fierce in the almost divine glory to which

Caesar tries pathetically to adjust himself. Whatever it be, this Caesar-idea, it is more powerful than Caesar the man. It controls him while he lives, survives and avenges him after his death. 'The spirit of Caesar' is not reached by slaying Caesar's body: it rather gains strength thereafter. Therefore, whatever we may think of Caesar as a man, we must see him also as a symbol of something of vast import, resplendent majesty, and starry purpose.

Antony recognizes this fully. He loves Caesar. That is, he sees him as man and as hero and does not, like Brutus, distinguish between the two. Cassius despises him as a man, and therefore will not believe in him at all as a hero; Brutus loves him as a man but believes in him only too powerfully as a hero, and thinks him therefore dangerous. To Antony the two aspects are indistinguishable. This is equivalent to saying that Antony ardently, almost passionately, loves Caesar: for in such love—and only then—the spiritual and personal elements are blended. That is ever the function of love: in creation or recognition, it mates the spiritual with the material. Antony, the lover, can thus unify our difficulties: in his words—and in his only, not in Caesar's—do we feel the dualism of Caesar's 'spirit' and physical being perfectly unified. In his words only we see the Caesar of history:

> O mighty Caesar! dost thou lie so low?
> Are all thy conquests, glories, triumphs, spoils,
> Shrunk to this little measure? (III. i. 148)

We are suddenly at home here strangely: this is how we want to see Caesar, how we expect to see him, how we are never allowed to see him till he is dead. The conspirators' swords are 'rich with the most noble blood of all this, world' (III. i. 155). Again,

> Thou art the ruins of the noblest man
> That ever lived in the tide of times.
> Woe to the hand that shed this costly blood! (III. i. 256)

He sees him as a man he loved; also as a supremely noble man; and, still further, as a symbol of government and peace. Now that he is rashly slain, forces of disorder will rage unchecked:

> Domestic fury and fierce civil strife
> Shall cumber all the parts of Italy. (III. i. 263)

Caesar's 'spirit' will have its revenge. In his oration he again stresses both Caesar's lovable personality and his importance as victor and national hero. His personal and national goodness are here entwined: to Antony Caesar is Rome's lover.

Caesar hath 'wept' (III. ii. 96) for the poor of Rome, his captives' ransoms filled Rome's 'general coffers' (III. ii. 94). He is thus a national friend or lover over and beyond his love for Antony:

> He was my friend, faithful and just to me: (III. ii. 90)

or his love for Brutus:

> For Brutus, as you know, was Caesar's angel:
> Judge, O you gods, how dearly Caesar loved him. (III. ii. 185)

So the people of Rome should 'mourn for him' (III. ii. 108) as for a dear friend. Caesar is now shown as a general lover. The common people, if they heard his will, would

> go and kiss dead Caesar's wounds,
> And dip their napkins in his sacred blood,
> Yea, beg a hair of him for memory,
> And, dying, mention it within their wills,
> Bequeathing it as a rich legacy
> Unto their issue. (III. ii. 137)

Notice the strongly erotic emotion here. Throughout Antony's speech, love—whether of Caesar for Brutus, Antony or Rome, or of Antony or Rome for Caesar—is stressed in contrast to the ever more sarcastically pronounced suggestion of 'honour': 'honourable men whose daggers have stabbed Caesar' (III. ii. 156). 'Love' is pitted against 'honour'. Even Caesar's mantle is suffused with emotion, almost sentimentality:

> If you have tears, prepare to shed them now.
> You all do know this mantle: I remember
> The first time ever Caesar put it on;
> 'Twas on a summer's evening, in his tent,
> That day he overcame the Nervii. (III. ii. 173)

So personal can be Antony's appeal. At the other extreme he sees Caesar's murder as a treason which plunges Rome in disaster. When 'great Caesar fell', Rome fell too:

> O! what a fall was there, my countrymen;
> Then I, and you, and all of us fell down,
> Whilst bloody treason flourish'd over us. (III. ii. 194)

Then Antony shows them Caesar's body itself:

> Kind souls, what! weep you when you but behold
> Our Caesar's vesture wounded? Look you here,
> Here is himself, marr'd, as you see, with traitors. (III. ii. 199)

Antony emphasizes the personal element throughout. But he is also aware of the political aspect. The idea of Caesar as an abstract principle of order is not, in his mind, divided from Caesar his friend, the lover of Rome, now a stricken lifeless body. He thinks of the wounds, the torn mantle that was Caesar's. Elsewhere he refers to Caesar's 'spirit' here, and usually, he sees Caesar as a lovable, noble, and great man whose murder is a senseless and wicked act. So close are the personal and public elements twined in his thoughts that he readily suggests that personal reasons must have urged the conspirators to their deed:

> What private griefs they have, alas, I know not,
> That made them do it ... (III. ii. 217)

Although Antony is, of course, ready to stress all that may suit his purpose, yet his attitude throughout his oration is exactly in line with his other thoughts and acts. He only has to be sincere to win over the citizens to his side:

> I am no orator, as Brutus is;
> But, as you know me all, a plain blunt man,
> That love my friend. (III. ii. 221)

It is true: he does not need to act. He reads the will, Caesar's bequests to the Roman people. The citizens recognize Caesar now as 'royal'. He is 'most noble Caesar', and 'royal Caesar' (III. ii. 248, 249). The final effect is clinched in Antony's

> Here was a Caesar! When comes such another? (III. ii. 257)

Through making a division between Caesar the man and Caesar the national hero and dictator, Brutus, Cassius, and indeed Caesar himself, have all plunged Rome and themselves in disaster. We thus find ever at the heart of this play the thought of 'spirit' dissociated from 'body'. 'We all stand up against the spirit of Caesar' (II. i. 167). This disjointing is at the root of the fiery portents, naked spirit unbodied in temporal and physical forms; the queer acts of beasts and men, bodies derelict of controlling, infusing 'spirit'. It is this division of thought that makes both Brutus and Cassius see Caesar as dangerous, though Cassius himself suffers no inward division, since he does not see

Caesar as powerfully evil, but rather as trivial, and blames not Caesar but Rome for the worship it accords him. He distinguishes only between Caesar the man—whom he sees singly—and the absurd idolatry of Rome. Thus, as I shall show, the disjointing of elements in man or state is to be related rather to Brutus than Cassius. Caesar, too, makes implicit distinction between himself as man and ruler. Now the central act, Caesar's assassination, is shown as a rough breaking of 'spirit' from 'body', whether of Caesar or Rome. Antony's love alone heals the dualism. Throughout he avoids this distinction. He unifies the dualism created by the poet in presenting Caesar as almost a dualized personality. It is the way of love. It unifies both the mind or soul of the subject, and the thing, person, or world that is loved, blending 'spirit' in 'body', seeing the physical afire with spirit-essence. So Antony alone knows the one Caesar better than Brutus and Cassius, better than Caesar himself, better than we who faithfully react to the impressions of the early scenes. Because he loves and is moved by love he sees things simplified, unified. His acts tend likewise to heal the gaping dualism of 'spirit' and 'matter' that has resulted from the gashing of Rome's civic body. Portents have blazed their terrors over Rome, the spirit of Rome being torn from its body; and supernatural portents; omens, ghosts continue after Caesar's death. Fierce civil chaos is threatened now, as Antony prophesies: the body of Rome disorganized, disjointed by lack of any controlling spirit. Antony speaks, acts, fights to heal Rome. The wounds of Rome, the separation of 'spirit' from 'body', are thus healed by a lover and his love. Caesar's 'spirit' is then at peace.

Caesar we must therefore be ready to regard as Antony sees him; and yet, as I have elsewhere shown, we are forced by the play's symbolic effects to see the action largely through the eyes of Brutus. That we may do this Caesar is also shown to us as he appears to Brutus: he is both man and demi-god curiously interwoven. But it will be clear that Brutus' failure to unify his knowledge of Caesar is a failure properly to love him, love being the unifying principle in all things, regularly opposed in Shakespeare to disorder, treachery, evils of all kinds: this is the continual 'music'–'tempest' contrast throughout the plays. Now Brutus' failure to love his friend, Caesar, is one with his worship of abstract 'honour'. Therein we have the key to his acts: he serves 'honour' always in preference to love. Both his 'love' for Caesar and his 'honour' are given exact expression. Cassius asks Brutus if he would not have Caesar made king:

> I would not, Cassius; yet I love him well.
> But wherefore do you hold me here so long?
> What is it that you would impart to me?
> If it be aught toward the general good,
> Set honour in one eye and death i' the other,
> And I will look on both indifferently:

For let the gods so speed me as I love
The name of honour more than I fear death. (I. ii. 82)

This love Brutus sacrifices to his 'honour'.

The rest of the play illustrates his attitude. Honour first, love second. His anxieties have made him forget 'the shows of love to other men' being 'himself at war' (i. ii. 46–7). Portia is distressed at his lack of kindliness. He has risen 'ungently' from their bed; last night he 'suddenly arose' at supper, and paced the room 'musing and sighing'. Questioned, he stared at her 'with ungentle looks', stamped 'impatiently', and dismissed her 'with an angry wafture' of his hand (II. i. 237–51). So she pits the strength of love against his schemes of honour:

                    . . . and, upon my knees,
I charm you, by my once-commended beauty,
By all your vows of love and that great vow
Which did incorporate and make us one,
That you unfold to me, yourself, your half,
Why are you heavy, and what men to-night
Have had resort to you . . . (II. i. 270)

She wins her fight—for the moment—and draws from him the deep emotion of:

You are my true and honourable wife,
As dear to me as are the ruddy drops
That visit my sad heart. (II. i. 288)

And she herself knows the meaning of honour and courage. She has given herself a 'voluntary wound' to prove her constancy. Brutus, hearing this, prays the gods to make him worthy of 'this noble wife' (II. i. 302). The Brutus–Portia relation is exquisitely drawn. It reminds us of Hotspur and Lady Percy. But Hotspur was stronger, more single in purpose, and, in a sense, more wary than Brutus: he gave away no secrets, whereas Brutus' surrender to Portia came near ruining the conspiracy. It is to be noted that 'honour' is so strong in Brutus that Portia knows she must play up to it, show herself courageous, possessing a sense of 'honour' like his. Brutus' obsession, almost to absurdity, with this thought is further evident from his long speech, prolixly expanding the idea that an oath is unnecessary to bind Romans to a noble enterprise:

                    . . . what other bond
Than secret Romans, that have spoke the word,
And will not palter? and what other oath

Than honesty to honesty engaged,
That this shall be, or we will fall for it? (II. i. 124)

Again, he nearly ruins his own cause: we may relate to this 'oath' speech the fact
that some one has given away details of the conspiracy to Popilius Lena and
Artemidorus. Brutus is ever out of touch with practical affairs, which is natural
in a man so devoted to an ethical abstraction. He unwisely refuses to let Antony
be slain; perhaps also unwisely objects to the inclusion of Cicero among the
conspirators. He is, in fact, a disintegrating force in the conspiracy, just as he
is a disintegrating force to Rome: without him, the conspiracy might well have
been successful, and we should then give final sanction to Cassius' rather than
Antony's view of Caesar. Here we see the profound poetic necessity of Caesar's
apparent weakness: it justifies Cassius' whole-hearted hostility. Cassius and
Antony are both order-forces, love-forces in the play: Cassius' hate of Caesar
is one with his love of his excellently arranged conspiracy, and his love of the
conspiracy is a practical, efficient thing, as efficient as Antony's love of Caesar.
Brutus loves primarily nothing but 'honour', but many things with secondary
affection: Cassius, Portia, Caesar, the conspiracy. Brutus is thus divided in mind,
in outlook. He is 'with himself at war' (I. ii. 46); in him

> the state of man,
> Like to a little kingdom, suffers then
> The nature of an insurrection. (II. i. 67)

All the disorder-symbols in the play, all our ideas of disorder and disruption in
reading it, our two-fold and indecisive vision of two Caesars—demi-god and
dolt—are to be related closely to Brutus, rather than to Cassius or Antony. They
enjoy a oneness of vision, a singularity of purpose: Brutus does not.

Brutus throughout continues his honourable course. He is aptly praised by
Ligarius:

> Soul of Rome!
> Brave son, derived from honourable loins! (II. i. 321)

All the conspirators respect him for his 'honour'. He slays Caesar boldly, without
wavering, in the cause of honour. Antony sends a message, asking to interview
the conspirators:

> Brutus is noble, wise, valiant and honest,
> Caesar was mighty, bold, royal and loving:
> Say I love Brutus and I honour him;
> Say I fear'd Caesar, honour'd him and loved him. (III. i. 126)

Brutus promises him safety by his 'honour' (III. i. 141); then assures him he
can give him ample 'reasons' for Caesar's death. He thinks ever in terms of
cold abstract processes of reason, and, unlike Antony and Cassius, ever fails
in contact with the rich warm life of reality. Thus he ever misjudges men:
he lets Antony speak at Caesar's funeral. He is half-hearted: neither a good
conspirator like Cassius nor a good lover like Antony. Next Brutus gives his
'public reasons' (III. ii. 7) for Caesar's death in his speech to the citizens. Again,
he emphasizes 'honour':

> Romans, countrymen, and lovers! hear me for my cause, and be silent,
> that you may hear: believe me for mine honour, and have respect to
> mine honour, that you may believe: censure me in your wisdom, and
> awake your senses, that you may the better judge. If there be any in this
> assembly, any dear friend of Caesar's, to him I say, that Brutus' love to
> Caesar was no less than his. If then that friend demand why Brutus rose
> against Caesar, this is my answer:—Not that I loved Caesar less, but that
> I loved Rome more . . . (III. ii. 13)

This speech exactly exposes the love–honour dualism in Brutus' experience.
Both before and after Caesar's death, we find Brutus' 'honour' conflicting with
his loves: and always this failure to unify his experiences results in disorder,
failure. He trusts to his abstractions pitifully: here he expects the citizens to
be convinced by cold reasoning. One breath of Antony's passion, one sight of
Caesar's mutilated body, will dispel that effect. So Antony's speech drives Brutus
and Cassius from Rome.

Brutus shows himself cold in his quarrel with Cassius. The rights and
wrongs of the matter are hard to decide and not important. Both appear
faulty: Brutus has 'condemned' a friend of Cassius on a paltry charge, Cassius
has refused money to Brutus, or so it seems. Brutus, however, can scarcely with
any justice both blame Cassius for accepting bribes and for refusing himself
money. His want is due to his own refusal to raise money 'by vile means' (IV.
iii. 71). Thus to desire a loan from Cassius is clearly to justify Cassius' use
of bribery. However, the issue is vague. But a general truth emerges. Brutus
is still hampering success by continued regard for his 'honour'. Cassius, less
scrupulous, shows, as always, more warmness of heart. Cassius is always in
touch with realities—of love, of conspiracy, of war: Brutus is ever most at
home with his ethical abstractions. He treasures to his heart the 'justice' of
his cause:

> Remember March, the Ides of March remember:
> Did not great Julius bleed for justice' sake?
> What villain touch'd his body, that did stab,
> And not for justice? What, shall one of us,

That struck the foremost man of all this world
But for supporting robbers, shall we now
Contaminate our fingers with base bribes,
And sell the mighty space of our large honours
For so much trash as may be grasped thus?
I had rather be a dog, and bay the moon,
Than such a Roman. (IV. iii. 18)

The quarrel is exquisitely human and pathetic. As their cause fails, these two 'noble' Romans—the word 'noble' is frequent in the play—begin to wrangle over money. Brutus starts by his noble apostrophe to 'justice': but soon we feel his primary anxiety is a very practical one—lack of gold:

> *Brutus.* . . . I did send
> To you for gold to pay my legions,
> Which you denied me: was that done like Cassius?,
> Should I have answer'd Caius Cassius so?
> When Marcus Brutus grows so covetous,
> To lock such rascal counters from his friends,
> Be ready, gods, with all your thunderbolts;
> Dash him to pieces!
>   *Cassius.* I denied you not.
>   *Brutus.* You did.
>   *Cassius.* I did not: he was but a fool
> That brought my answer back . . . (IV. iii. 75)

We may observe, with reference to Brutus' self-idealisation here, that, if he did not deny Cassius gold, he certainly ignored his letters on behalf of Lucius Pella. This quarrel marks the failure of Brutus and Cassius. Their impending joint failure is forecast in this inner dissension. Also it suggests the failure of ideals unrelated to practical expediency: Brutus' ship of 'honour' dashes on the hard rocks of finance. It is pathetic, human, and exactly true. At last their dissension is healed by Cassius' love. Brutus' coldness thaws. As with his wife earlier, a deeper loyalty replaces his frigid abstractions:

Do what you will, dishonour shall be humour. (IV. iii. 109)

Next Brutus again reverts to abstractions: this time his prided stoic philosophy:

> *Cassius.* I did not think you could have been so angry.
> *Brutus.* O Cassius, I am sick of many griefs.
> *Cassius.* Of your philosophy you make no use,

If you give place to accidental evils.
> *Brutus.* No man bears sorrow better. Portia is dead. (IV. iii. 143)

Cassius is to 'speak no more of her' (IV. iii. 158). The news is corroborated by Messala. Brutus hears it a second time: there is no possibility of mistake. Again, he receives it dispassionately, to Cassius' wonder:

> I have as much of this in art as you,
> But yet my nature could not bear it so. (IV. iii. 194)

'Art.' Brutus makes life a long process of 'art', almost 'fiction'. He aspires to impossibilities and unrealities, carries a great burden of 'honour' and 'nobility' through life: which honour is continually troubled by the deeps of emotion which he shares with Antony and Cassius. He is only outwardly cold. Throughout his story love is intermittent with the iron calls of honour. Caesar, Portia, Cassius (whose conspiracy he ruins, whose soldiership he hampers)—his love for all has been sacrificed to honour in one way or another. But that love itself need not be questioned. It is deep; its organ notes are pure:

> *Brutus.* Noble, noble Cassius,
> Good night, and good repose.
> *Cassius.* O my dear brother!
> This was an ill beginning of the night:
> Never come such division 'tween our souls!
> Let it not, Brutus.
> *Brutus.* Everything is well.
> *Cassius.* Good night, my lord.
> *Brutus.* Good night, good brother. (IV. iii. 232)

'Brother' is emphasized. Notice how Cassius is always ready to humble himself to Brutus—'my lord'. Their practical failure is here clearly heralded: but a victory has been realized in Brutus, a victory for love. Left alone, he asks Lucius to play to him. Lucius' care-free purity of youth always touches Brutus' heart to words which suggest here—both in Act II and Act IV—a more spontaneous love than any he shows to other people. He always speaks gently to him: 'Bear with me, good boy, I am much forgetful' (IV. iii. 255), and 'I trouble thee too much but thou art willing' (IV. iii. 259). Lucius is sleepy. He knows the dreamless sleep that holds no torment, unlike the 'phantasma of Brutus' divided soul. He has already 'slept':

> *Brutus.* It was well done; and thou shalt sleep again;
> I will not hold thee long: if I do live,

I will be good to thee. (IV. iii. 263)

There is 'music and a song'. So music, with Brutus' love for his boy, are blended here: music and love, healing, unifying spells casting momentary peace on Brutus' divided soul. The boy sleeps:

If thou dost nod, thou break'st thy instrument;
I'll take it from thee; and, good boy, good night. (IV. iii. 271)

That is one extreme: extreme of peace, love and music, realities Brutus has banished, repressed. He pays for his momentary heaven. Swiftly its opposing hell returns. The 'evil' in his soul accuses him:

Brutus. . . . Art thou any thing?
Art thou some god, some angel, or some devil,
That makest my blood cold and my hair to stare?
Speak to me what thou art.
Ghost. Thy evil spirit, Brutus. (IV. iii. 278)

There is no prolonged peace for Brutus. His life, in the play, has been 'like a phantasma or a hideous dream' (II. i. 65), due, like nightmare, to a divided consciousness; 'evil' none the less potent for its deriving its existence from the clash of two positive goods: 'honour' and 'love'.

Brutus is ever obsessed with his 'honour'. Octavius mocks Brutus and Cassius as 'traitors', saying he was not born to die on Brutus' sword. To which Brutus replies:

O, if thou wert the noblest of thy strain,
Young man, thou couldst not die more honourable. (V. i. 59)

He often refers to himself in a strain which repels by its egoism:

. . . think not, thou noble Roman,
That ever Brutus will go bound to Rome;
He bears too great a mind. (V. i. 111)

Curiously, this contradicts his words just spoken that suicide is 'cowardly'. His life is one long contradiction, one long abstraction. This boast is of the same order as his boast in the quarrel scene:

There is no terror, Cassius, in your threats,
For I am arm'd so strong in honesty

That they pass by me as the idle wind,
Which I respect not. (IV. iii. 66)

He is so enwrapped in a sense of his own honour that others can make no
headway against his will. The conspirators always give way to him. Cassius
cannot resist his self haloed personality ever. He submits to Brutus' judgement
as to coming down from the hills to meet Octavius and Antony: the event is
disaster. Even in the fight 'Brutus gave the word too early' (V. iii. 5). Brutus is a
continual hindrance, usually exactly because of his exaggerated sense of honour.
Yet he rouses our admiration by his consistency, his steadiness of purpose in
serving a figment of his own mind. Even when he finds Cassius dead, he shows
little emotion. Yet we feel deep surges unspoken:

I shall find time, Cassius, I shall find time. (V. iii. 103)

Strangely, though through his life he has banished the softer joys of love, when
at the end he knows his enterprise to be an utter failure, Caesar's spirit victorious,
he joys in the thought of friendship:

The ghost of Caesar hath appeared to me.
Two several times by night; at Sardis once,
And, this last night, here in Philippi fields:
I know my hour is come. (V. v. 17)

Therefore—

Countrymen,
My heart doth joy that yet in all my life
I found no man but he was true to me.
I shall have glory by this losing day
More than Octavius and Mark Antony
By this vile conquest shall attain unto.
So fare you well at once; for Brutus' tongue
Hath almost ended his life's history:
Night hangs upon mine eyes; my bones would rest,
That have but labour'd to attain this hour. (V. v. 33)

Into the darkness of death he takes the simple joy that his followers have been
true to him. There is resignation here, a knowledge of failure, an acceptance
of tragedy. The things he valued have played him false. He has 'dismembered'
Caesar, but has not 'come by' his 'spirit', partly because he himself from the first
made that unreal mental division of Caesar the man and Caesar the imperial

force in Rome. So Caesar's disembodied 'spirit', his ghost, Brutus' own creation, pursues Brutus to his death. And the long torment of division in Brutus' soul is closed, the wounding dualism healed in death, an easy 'rest'; and in thoughts of his friends' faith. Love, at the last, quietly takes him, honour-wearied, by the hand, into the darkness. But even in his dying he is anxious for 'honour'. 'Thy life hath had some smatch of honour in it' he says to Strato (v. v. 46), when asking him to hold his sword.

Antony speaks a noble eulogy over his body. Octavius will have it 'order'd honourably' (V. v. 79). Honour always. But Antony is right in saying Brutus slew Caesar 'in a general honest thought' (V. v. 7 1), though he may be wrong in attributing only 'envy' to the rest. Brutus is sincere throughout. He unwaveringly pursues an ethical ideal which appears somewhat bloodless in this play of imperial, glory, pulsing love, envy, ambition. Though bloodless, it yet sheds blood. Brutus lets his abstraction loose in the world of reality: he will not render Caesar what is Caesar's and offer his ideal to God. Thus he is the only force properly 'ethical' in the play: the rest act by emotion. Yet this ethical cast of thought itself creates division and disorder in his mind, in his view of Caesar under the two aspects, man and ruler:

> It must be by his death, and for my part
> I know no personal cause to spurn at him,
> But for the general. (II. i. 10)

He is himself confused in this speech—as we, too, are confused by the two Caesars, till Antony's strong love creates the Caesar we know. Like Caesar himself, he is anxious as to this tremendous power coming to the friend he loves. What change may it work? All the disorder-symbols of the play are to be related to Brutus' divided allegiances. The vision of naked spirit flaming over Rome is a projection of Brutus' own spirit-abstraction unharmonized with life. It cannot be too strongly emphasized that the conspiracy without Brutus might have been a life-force, a creating of order, not a destruction. So he ruins first Caesar, then the cause of his own party. Antony wins over the citizens by ringing the changes on his own slogan, 'honour'.

> So are they all, all honourable men. (III. ii. 89)

Love's mockery of 'honour'. Over and over again he drives it in: 'Brutus is an honourable man' (III. ii. 87 and 99), 'Sure, he is an honourable man' (III. ii. 104)—and again at lines 129, 132, 216, 218. Again,

> I fear I wrong the honourable men
> Whose daggers have stabbed Caesar; I do fear it. (III. ii. 156)

Brutus' honour pains and slays Portia, drives Cassius in their quarrel almost to madness, while Brutus remains ice-cold, armed appallingly in 'honesty'. He shows little emotion at his dear ones' death. You can do nothing with him. He is so impossibly noble: and when we forget his nobility he becomes just 'impossible'. Thus when he would for once solace himself for a while with Lucius—his truest love—and Lucius' music, his 'evil spirit' denies his right to such relief. This incident corresponds exactly to the irruption of Banquo's ghost into Macbeth's feast. Macbeth especially desecrates hospitality, Brutus love. Neither may enjoy what they destroy. Brutus has put love from him. He rides roughshod over domestic happiness, like Macbeth. His acts disturb Portia, dislocate meals and sleep. So, too, Caesar and Calpurnia are roused from bed, and Caesar's hospitality desecrated. Cassius, on the contrary, invites people to dinner. The contrast is important. Such pursuit of an ethical ideal in and for itself, unrelated to the time and people around, is seen at the last to be perilous. It is a selfishness. His ethic is no ethic, rather a projection of himself. A phantasma of his own mind. Like Macbeth he projects his mental pain on his country. He alone bears the responsibility of Caesar's death, since he alone among the conspirators sees—and so creates—its wrongfulness; he alone bears the burden of the conspiracy's failure. He only has a guilty conscience— anguished by an 'evil spirit'. But Cassius, at the last, is 'fresh of spirit' (V. i. 91). And yet, Brutus has glory by his losing day. He suffers, not because he is less than those around him but because he is, in a sense, far greater. He is the noblest Roman of them all. He suffers, and makes others suffer, for his virtue: but such virtue is not enough. Virtue, to Brutus, is a quality to be rigidly distinguished from love. Love, in fact, ever conflicts with it. He denies the greatest force in life and the only hope in death. He thus fails in life and dies sadly, pathetically searching at the end for some one 'honourable' enough to slay him. He has starved his love on earth: he thinks at the last of his faithful friends, would take what crumbs he can to solace him in the darkness.

Cassius is strongly contrasted with Brutus. He is described by Caesar:

> He reads much;
> He is a great observer and he looks
> Quite through the deeds of men; he loves no plays,
> As thou dost, Antony; he hears no music;
> Seldom he smiles, and smiles in such a sort
> As if he mock'd himself and scorn'd his spirit
> That could be moved to smile at any thing.
> Such men as he be never at heart's ease
> Whiles they behold a greater than themselves,
> And therefore are they very dangerous. (I. ii. 201)

The description is not one to be ashamed of. Cassius has profound understanding, a rich personality. He is very sincere. He claims, rightly, to have nothing in him of the flatterer or scandalmonger: he is no 'common laugher' like Lucio (I. ii. 72–8). His seriousness makes him sombre, gloomy, ashamed of all trivialities. Smiles, plays, music—all are barred. Instead, we have knowledge of men, books, restlessness of temperament. He has something of the morbidity of the artistic temperament. He is a perfect artist in conspiracy. Caesar is afraid of Cassius, afraid of his insight, his depth of soul: afraid, primarily, of something he cannot understand. In point of profundity and earnestness Cassius is similar to the Duke in *Measure for Measure*. The Duke had 'ancient skill' in reading other's characters (IV. ii. 164). He contended especially 'to know himself' (III. ii. 247). As for pleasures, he was

> Rather rejoicing to see another merry, than merry at any thing which professed to make him rejoice: a gentleman of all temperance. (*Measure for Measure*, III. ii. 250)

The Duke, too, was critical of music:

> ... music oft hath such a charm
> To make bad good, and' good provoke to harm. (*Measure for Measure*, IV. i. 14)

His utter sincerity—the sincerity which is at the heart of his ethic—is apparent in his distrust of display:

> I love the people,
> But do not like to stage me to their eyes:
> Though it do well, I do not relish well
> Their loud applause and Aves vehement;
> Nor do I think the man of safe discretion
> That does affect it. (*Measure for Measure*, I. i. 68)

So, too, Cassius, seems to suffer from a certain shy inwardness, hating shows and ceremonies. Cassius does not 'profess himself in banqueting to all the rout' (I. ii. 77); but he invites Casca to a private supper, as I observe above. And it is exactly this show and ceremony and music which surrounds Caesar on his first entry: Cassius, like the Duke of Vienna, instinctively distrusts it. Both are to be contrasted with Timon or Antony (in this play or *Antony and Cleopatra*)—those more free-hearted heroes who love feasting, music, display. These are both, in vastly different ways, lovers, profound lovers, although the Duke may appear, once, to deny love's power to grip his heart: in them love is compressed, controlled, its essence not readily apparent. Love is powerful in Cassius, but does not come easily. He is too sincere to be happy. This comparison is valuable since, though Cassius is in other respects vastly different from the Duke, nevertheless, in point of this oneness yet richness of personality, the likeness is striking. For Cassius has, like the Duke a 'complete bosom' (*Measure for Measure*, I. iii. 3). He is always, as it were, safe, invulnerable to chance, his own soul is a fortress:

> I know where I will wear this dagger then;
> Cassius from bondage will deliver Cassius:
> Therein, ye gods, you make the weak most strong;
> Therein, ye gods, you tyrants do defeat:
> Nor stony tower, nor walls of beaten brass,
> Nor airless dungeon, nor strong links of iron,
> Can be retentive to the strength of spirit. (I. iii. 89)

This assurance is born of a unity of soul. He is not divided, like Brutus. It will at once be clear how Brutus stands to Cassius much as Angelo to the Duke of Vienna. Angelo, like Brutus, fails by his worship of abstract virtue: the analogy there is immediately evident, and closer than the other. Now, however much we may dislike Cassius' acts—some have done so—it is clear that he possesses singleness of purpose, and a sense of integrity which renders him fearless:

> *Casca.* . . . Cassius, what night is this!
> *Cassius.* A very pleasing night to honest men.
> *Casca.* Who ever knew the heavens menace so?
> *Cassius.* Those that have known the earth so full of faults. (I. iii, 42)

He has taken deliberate pleasure in walking the streets 'unbraced', baring his 'bosom to the thunderstone':

> And when the cross blue lightning seem'd to open
> The breast of heaven, I did present myself
> Even in the aim and very flash of it. (I. iii. 50)

So strongly is his integrity emphasized. Enduring no disorder in himself, he fears no outer disorder; knowing himself perfectly, he has no fears of the mysterious and unknown. He finds a place for these disorders. To him they reflect the terrors of Caesar's tyranny, a heaven-sent warning:

> . . . why, you shall find
> That heaven hath infused them with these spirits,
> To make them instruments of fear and warning
> Unto some monstrous state. (I. iii. 68)

Caesar is fearful as these portents, himself like 'this dreadful night':

> A man no mightier than thyself or me
> In personal action, yet prodigious grown
> And fearful, as these strange eruptions are. (I. iii. 76)

Cassius despises Caesar as a 'person'. Nor can he see him, as Brutus can, as a national hero. The adulation of Rome is absurd. He does not even blame Caesar at all. The fault is his countrymen's:

> And why should Caesar be a tyrant then?
> Poor man! I know he would not be a wolf,
> But that he sees the Romans are but sheep:
> He were no lion, were not Romans hinds. (I. iii. 103)

Rome is 'rubbish' and 'offal' whose blaze illuminates 'so vile a thing as Caesar' (I. iii. 109). Cassius has nothing but contempt for Caesar, his glory is merely a madness in his admirers. He does not, like Brutus, see two Caesars he sees only one—a frail, weak, contemptible man; and, next, the hero-worship of Rome. He, like Antony, knows his own mind. After the murder, we tend to see Caesar through Antony's eyes, but at the start of the play we often see him as Cassius sees him. In the middle action we see him with Brutus' indecisive vision. Marullus and Flavius set the note of hostility at the start. Throughout the first act we hear mainly Cassius' opinion, expressed at length to Brutus and Casca. Cassius' arguments to Brutus are clear and exact. Caesar is a weak man physically, a bad swimmer, subject to fever. Cassius is himself his equal, even his superior, if the swimming contest be admitted, and, after all, Caesar suggested it as a test of 'daring'.

> Ye gods, it doth amaze me
> A man of such a feeble temper should
> So get the start of the majestic world
> And bear the palm alone. (I. ii. 128)

This frail man 'is now become a God' (I. ii. 116). Cassius must bow to him. Cassius' motive is clearly a sort of envy: but it is a fully conscious envy, which stands the test of his own reasoning. The Roman republican ideal is strong in him: he emphasizes it often. He will strike for Rome, for reason, for common sense. He sees Caesar's sudden access of power as a dangerous, fantastic, ludicrous thing: nor do Caesar's own acts and words—his fainting fits, his indecision, his pitiful attempts to be 'Caesar'—fail to bear out his view. Cassius is thus partially justified at the start. But there are other elements to be observed in him.

It is to be noted that he has little sense of abstract honour. To him the end justifies any means. He resembles Scott's 'Burley' in *Old Mortality*. The conspiracy is necessary. He wants Brutus. Therefore he will stoop to deception in the matter of the letters quite readily to win him. Yet he can respect Brutus' 'nobility', without understanding it:

> Well, Brutus, thou art noble; yet, I see,
> Thy honourable metal may be wrought
> From that it is disposed: therefore it is meet
> That noble minds keep ever with their likes;
> For who so firm that cannot be seduced?
> Caesar doth bear me hard; but he loves Brutus:
> If I were Brutus now and he were Cassius,
> He should not humour me. (I. ii. 312)

This is a crucial and curious speech. I will attempt a coherent paraphrase. Cassius honours Brutus for his high ideals. Yet he sees that Brutus' 'honour' sense can readily be 'wrought' from honourable loyalty to honourable conspiracy. It is a risky thing to be governed by. He is baffled, as we are, and Brutus is, at the complex conflict in Brutus' mind. Cassius, single in purpose, finds Brutus' unsteadiness strange. Such noble men should therefore keep, he says, not with other noble minds, but rather with men of like opinions to their own. A man who worships abstract honour can always and easily be reasoned into pursuing almost any course in the name of that honour. To Cassius such 'honour' is therefore a deceit and such cold reasoning a dangerous thing: albeit it serves his purpose here. He himself acts by instinct: instinctive envy, a dark hatred of Caesar's absurd rise to power. He observes, moreover, that Caesar dislikes him, but loves Brutus. This is also at the root of his 'envy'. If Caesar loved him, he says, no amount of reasoning would persuade him to the conspiracy. He himself could never betray love. Cassius always follows personal emotions. This argument silhouettes Cassius' personality vividly; Cassius gives one the impression of loneliness, gloom, disillusion: he has known the world 'full of faults' (I. iii, 45). He is dark with thwarted ambition and envy. But a certain golden star burns in his heart: a great longing for love. At the start he is anxious for Brutus' love:

> Brutus, I do observe you now of late:
> I have not from your eyes that gentleness
> And show of love as I was wont to have:
> You bear too stubborn and too strange a hand
> Over your friend that loves you. (I. ii. 32)

Throughout the play Cassius' love of Brutus is emphasized. We find many emotions in him: envy, ardour, love. He possesses a certain spiritual loneliness and a sense of ultimate security, he is the captain of his soul. But he is not happy: rather given to gloom and foreboding. He is romantic, compact of poetry. Intellect is subsidiary with him, and he is more at home with realities than abstractions. He does not understand Brutus' ethical finesse. Yet respect for his friend causes him to give way to Brutus time after time, thereby ruining his own conspiracy. Frustrated through life, he appears ever to expect the worst. He fears their 'purpose is discovered' (iii. i. 17):

> Brutus, what shall be done? If this be known,
> Cassius or Caesar never shall turn back,
> For I will slay myself. (III. i. 20)

And his foreboding is often justified. Brutus thinks they will have Antony 'well to friend', and he answers:

> I wish we may: but yet have I a mind
> That fears him much; and my misgiving still
> Falls shrewdly to the purpose. (III. i. 144)

After Caesar's death he is maddened by Brutus' obsession with 'honour'. His complaint is typical. He interceded for a friend, Lucius Pella, whom Brutus subsequently punished for accepting bribes. Cassius ever champions personal emotions, personal fears and forebodings, antipathies and envies, personal love. Brutus ever upholds an intellectual ideal of 'honour'. They meet, one passionate and ardent, the other aloof, scornful, self-righteous:

> *Cassius.* Most noble brother, you have done me wrong.
> *Brutus.* Judge me, you gods! wrong I mine enemies?
> And, if not so, how should I wrong a brother?
> *Cassius.* Brutus, this sober form of yours hides wrongs;
> And when you do them— (IV. ii. 37)

Throughout the quarrel Cassius is passionate in anger, grief, or love. Brutus is cold, aureoled in self-righteousness, unreachable, remote: but beneath emotion surges, too, in him. Cassius is the first to give way, to admit fault. Typically, he fights throughout, not, like Brutus, with reason, but with emotion. He is in this the more feminine of the two. First, anger; next, grief:

> Brutus hath rived my heart;
> A friend should bear his friend's infirmities,
> But Brutus makes mine greater than they are. (IV. iii. 85)

Brutus loves him not: a 'friendly eye' would not see such faults. Brutus' ethical scorn still lacerates him unmercifully. At last, he exposes the riches of his thwarted longing, passion-soul:

> Come, Antony, and young Octavius, come,
> Revenge yourselves alone on Cassius,
> For Cassius is aweary of the world;
> Hated by one he loves; braved by his brother;
> Check'd like a bondman; all his faults observed,
> Set in a note-book, learn'd and conn'd by rote,
> To cast into my teeth. O, I could weep
> My spirit from mine eyes! There is my dagger,
> And here my naked breast; within, a heart
> Dearer than Plutus' mine, richer than gold:
> If that thou be'st a Roman, take it forth;
> I, that denied thee gold, will give my heart:
> Strike, as thou didst at Caesar; for, I know,
> When thou didst hate him worst, thou lovedst him better
> Than ever thou lovedst Cassius. (IV. iii. 93)

Here Cassius challenges the rich worth of his emotional nature against the other integrity of Brutus. But what is there in Brutus that dare so boast its spiritual 'gold'? And Cassius wins, by power of love. They celebrate their new strength with a bowl of wine. His 'heart' is thirsty, he 'cannot drink too much of Brutus' love' (IV. iii. 162). Cassius is wrung with sorrow at Portia's death, and shows more grief than Brutus. And he gives way to Brutus on points of strategy. He is, indeed, the more experienced soldier:

> I am a soldier, I,
> Older in practice, abler than yourself
> To make conditions. (IV. iii. 30)

Yet, as always, he gives way to Brutus. At this point he is, indeed, far more concerned with his and Brutus' love than any military expedients:

> O my dear brother!
> This was an ill beginning of the night:

Never come such division 'tween our souls!
Let it not, Brutus. (IV. iii. 233)

Cassius' love thus saves the conspiracy from the final disgrace of 'division', enables it to meet its end intact.

But he himself appears to have passed beyond such interests. Although his temper flares for an instant at Antony's taunts, Antony who calls him a 'flatterer', the very thing he is not and would never be—'Now, Brutus, thank yourself . . .' (V. i. 45)—he appears to have found a new strength. Something in him is unloosed, freed, in the quarrel-scene: he has a strength and purpose independent of success. This 'something' is a kind of love. He still has forebodings. He tells Messala how 'ravens, crows, and kites' form a 'canopy most fatal' (V. i. 85–8) over their army. Like the others, Calpurnia, Caesar, Brutus, Cinna, he has begun to 'credit things that do presage' (V. i. 79). Yet he has always possessed a retreat, a lonely eyry of the spirit, which renders him fearless. Now, especially, he appears new in strength:

> I but believe it partly;
> For I am fresh of spirit and resolved
> To meet all perils very constantly. (V. i. 90)

A visionary light settles on him, singles him now for the first time as protagonist. As ever, it is he who expects the worst, asks Brutus what he will do if the battle be lost:

Let's reason with the worst that may befall. (V. i. 97)

He parts from Brutus. There is no more noble parting in Shakespeare. Next we see him in the flood of battle. Failure is imminent, his men fly.

> *Pindarus.* Fly further off, my lord, fly further off;
> Mark Antony is in your tents, my lord:
> Fly, therefore, noble Cassius, fly far off.
> *Cassius.* This hill is far enough. Look, look, Titinius;
> Are those my tents where I perceive the fire?
> *Titinius.* They are, my lord.
> *Cassius.* Titinius, if thou lovest me,
> Mount thou my horse, and hide thy spurs in him,
> Till he have brought thee up to yonder troops,
> And here again; that I may rest assured
> Whether yond troops are friend or enemy. (V. iii. 9)

There is now a light-foot strength of spirit in Cassius: something fiery-strong, intangible, intractable to definition. He is yet strangely 'fresh of spirit' in disaster, in foreboding:

> Go, Pindarus, get higher on that hill;
> My sight was ever thick; regard Titinius,
> And tell me what thou notest about the field. (V. iii. 20)

Pindarus leaves him:

> This day I breathed first: time is come round,
> And where I did begin, there shall I end;
> My life is run his compass. (V. iii. 23)

Cleopatra-like, he thus celebrates his birthday under the shadow of impending tragedy. And yet, this birth-remembrance yet lights this death with a sudden expectancy, a birth—a death and birth:

> Come down, behold no more.
> O, coward that I am, to live so long,
> To see my best friend ta'en before my face! (V, iii. 33)

A breathless expectancy indeed charges this scene. It is a positive, purposeful adventure, a stepping free, a death, like Cleopatra's, into love. Cassius the envious, the passionate, the lover, is now afloat on a love—Brutus before, now Titinius. Names are but symbols through which the spirit steps naked into the air and fire of love. Cassius gives Pindarus his last charge, the air aquiver with immortality. Like Antony, he bids his bondman remember the condition by which the saving of his 'life' has bound him to obedience:

> Come now, keep thine oath;
> Now be a freeman ... (V. iii. 40)

'Life', 'freeman': what are these associations? In my reading of this scene I may be thought to tread a dangerous precipice. For only by irrationalities are my statements justified. But the associations here are powerful: the 'fire' perceived by Cassius, the love of Titinius—'if thou lovedst me'—'birth', 'shouts' of 'joy' (V. iii. 32), 'my best friend', 'saving of thy life', 'freeman': all this, together with the event which proves indeed that victory has been mistaken for failure, all stresses, not death, but life-in-death. The sight of mortality is 'ever thick'. The associations here contradict the logic: it is often the way of poetry. Cassius all but accomplishes the fiery splendour and conscious purpose of Cleopatra's death-in-love. His death is a thing of ecstasy and liberation. Pindarus will fly far 'where never Roman shall take note of him' (V. iii. 50). Safe and far, Pindarus or Cassius? Far from Rome. It is well that the purest essence of this play's poetry be spilled over his body:

> No, this was he, Messala,
> But Cassius is no more. O setting sun,
> As in thy red rays thou dost sink to-night,
> So in his red blood Cassius' day is set;
> The sun of Rome is set. (V. iii. 59)

As the blood of the lover's heart streams out, the blood of republican Rome itself is spilt on the Parthian sands: and the crimson of the great sun drops level to honour with horizontal streams of fire the spirit of man victorious. This is the Shakespearian sanction of love which has the universe at its bidding. Cassius is now crowned with a wreath of victory: our final, most vivid, association:

> *Titinius.* Why didst thou send me forth, brave Cassius?
> Did I not meet thy friends? And did not they
> Put on my brows this wreath of victory,
> And bid me give it thee? Didst thou not hear their shouts?
> Alas, thou hast misconstrued every thing!
> But, hold thee, take this garland on thy brow;
> Thy Brutus bid me give it thee, and I
> Will do his bidding. Brutus, come apace,
> And see how I regarded Caius Cassius.
> By your leave, gods:—this is a Roman's part:
> Come, Cassius' sword, and find Titinius' heart. (V. iii. 80)

'Heart' always in this play of fire and love. So Titinius crowns Cassius. 'Thy Brutus . . .'

> Shall it not grieve thee dearer than thy death
> To see thy Antony . . . (III. i. 197)

It is all one. This universe of kingly ambition, divided allegiances, envy, hostility, friendship—all is dominated and finally fused by love, the love and intimacy that beats here in imagery, incident, emotion, life, and death itself. So Titinius crowns Cassius, the lover, in death:

> Brave Titinius!
> Look, whether he have not crown'd dead Cassius! (V. iii. 96)

Like Charmian over Cleopatra, he arranges the lover's crown, then hastens to follow his master. I have compared Cassius with the Duke in *Measure for Measure*; and now I relate his death to that of Cleopatra, to whom he is close in point of a certain romantic strength which solicits our respect apparently quite independently of any ethical judgement. What quality can we say binds these three? The Duke is the prince of ethical moralizers; Cleopatra, the Queen of Courtezans. Yet all three possess a certain unique richness of soul and range of feeling: and in this they conquer.

The imperial theme of mighty Caesar is thus the hub on which revolves a theme of wider scope, imperially crowned with fire of love's radiance. Human activity in all its ardour and positive splendour is set within an ever-present atmosphere of love. Man is vivid—in act and renown—all are 'noble'; his spirit-fire burns through physical weakness; the gashed body releases streams of red life. The slaying of Caesar is a grand, an historic act:

> How many ages hence
> Shall this our lofty scene be acted over
> In states unborn and accents yet unknown! (III. i. 111)

In assassination the conspirators are yet Caesar's 'friends' (III. i. 104). The power of Caesar has come on him unprepared, he is himself embarrassed, fearful of the mighty sway of the world-empire to be trusted to his weakness. The fate of the western world trembles in the balance as he puts the crown aside, 'loath to lay his fingers off it' (I. ii. 243). He knows himself, as Cassius knows him, weak—as who would not be weak?—for such an Atlas burden; and he hates Cassius for knowing it. Till he is murdered, Cassius is right. But Brutus has offered us a dualized vision: Caesar, a man lovable, a friend—and Caesar potential, under stress of power become a danger, an enemy of Rome (II. i. 10–34). He, like Caesar himself, is uneasy. The division in his soul is, like our vision of the middle scenes, a rough tearing of 'body' from 'spirit', which dualism is at the root also of Caesar's fears—Caesar who knows himself a puny man, but must live up to a lion strength of spirit equal to Danger itself. Cassius, too, sees on the one side Caesar, the weakling, and, on the other, the adulation of Rome fit only for a god. All our early fears, doubts, insecurities of vision are related to this body–spirit dualism: hence our symbols of naked fire, spirit raging unfitted to the finite, and impossible events on earth, bodies uninfused with soul. Caesar dead, Antony's love at once—as never before—shows us Caesar as he was. Hitherto we saw him in terms of fear, in terms of what he might be; and the poet well stresses his weakness, which is, however, only weakness in comparison with the superhuman glory and power about to light upon his brows. Seeing him in terms of fear, we saw him unreal; unreal with the deathly unreality of time-thinking we meet in *Macbeth*. In Antony's vision the dualism is a unity. The Caesar of history swims into our ken in Antony's first words after the assassination. Love heals the severance of 'body' from 'spirit'. Perhaps Cassius was wrong. He was blind to Caesar's greatness. To see ahead and fear is evil and unreal: reality is now, and love. Cassius who ever looks ahead, foreboding ill, yet treasures also a spiritual fortress which has no fear, and finally falls back only on this soul-treasure in his breast. Caesar's spirit has proved his course of action wrong (V. iii. 45); but not his heart 'richer than gold'. As failure nears, his love is brighter, he steps free. Antony's victory is the conquest of love, love which saw only in Caesar a true friend and a great man, that made no 'god' comparisons nor foolishly stressed his physique, and, seeing the real Caesar, was content to trust him with Rome's fate. And Cassius' death, too, is a conquest of love. Time and again he sacrifices his conspiracy for Brutus. Brutus ruins an otherwise seaworthy plot. But Cassius drinks his fill of Brutus' love at the last, and dies 'fresh of spirit' in the cause of friendship. Brutus refuses love for honour. In incident after incident he brushes love aside. He alone is throughout wholly responsible for the dualism which wrenches 'spirit' from 'body', in Rome or in his own mind. True, I have said that Cassius' view of the Caesar problem is proved false by Antony. As the play stands, it is. But without Brutus and his 'honour' there would have been no Antony to redirect our vision. Then there would have been a straightforward assassination needing no disorder symbolism. During his life, Caesar fits Cassius' view well enough. There is nothing in him to show Cassius' fears unfounded, except in the sense, noted above, in which all 'fear' is evil. Again we see the exactitude of the poet's intuition in the variations he plays on the Caesar-idea. We realize how truly the poet has refused any one explicit statement[1] of the meaning of his symbolism:

> But men may construe things after their fashion,
> Clean from the purpose of the things themselves. (I. iii. 34)

These portents are different things to different people, and their meaning varies according to the event. But the Brutus-wavering, the Brutus-division is, in a final judgement, the only exact 'cause' of what disorder and evil there is in the play. Against him are set two lovers: the lover of the republican ideal, Cassius; the lover of Caesar, Antony. Both are positive forces. Brutus is negative, because his fine intellect sees equally with the vision of the other two.

But all these complexities are but threads woven on a cloth whose delicate texture is compact of love. All wounds are healed. Brutus and Cassius part nobly, lovers at the last. Aptly, our final words are 'this happy day' (V. v. 81). The baffling, maddening, phantasma of the two Caesars is over, and Caesar's 'spirit' is at rest. It no longer exists as a bodiless, homeless abstraction: perhaps it never did.

NOTE

1. In *Macbeth*, where the murder is so extreme an evil, its essential unnatural-ness is emphasized for us. The meaning of the symbolisms is explicitly stated. See the choric dialogue in *Macbeth*, II. iv.

⸺⟐⟐⟐⸺   ⸺⟐⟐⟐⸺   ⸺⟐⟐⟐⸺

1935—Kenneth Burke. "Antony in Behalf of the Play," from *The Southern Review*

Kenneth Burke was a literary critic and theorist of rhetoric. He taught at Bennington College. *Kenneth Burke on Shakespeare* is a collection of his writings on the playwright. His other books include *The Philosophy of Literary Form* and *Language as Symbolic Action*.

At times when the standards of criticism are set by a *receptive* class, as in the decadent stages of feudalism, the emphasis of the critic tends to be placed upon *consumption*. Matters of "appreciation" and "enjoyment" are the touchstones. Conversely, in the Art for Art's Sake movement of recent decades, we find the emphasis placed almost wholly upon *production*. Our practical inventors and business promoters of this period tended to emphasize the productive factor, assuming that in the large the matter of consumption would take care of itself—and there was a corresponding trend in aesthetics, with the essence of art being seen in the "self-expression" of the artist.

Today, in nonliterary fields, we are stressing neither production nor consumption, but the integration of the two. And in the aesthetic field, this emphasis might be paralleled by a tendency to consider literature, not as a creator's device for self-expression, nor as an audience's device for amusement or instruction, but as a communicative relationship between writer and audience, with both parties actively participating. In such an approach, the poet's "self-expression" or the audience's "appreciation" will necessarily figure, but the main emphasis will be elsewhere.

This reader–writer relationship is emphasized in the following article, which is an imaginary speech by Antony. Instead of addressing the mob, as he is pictured in the third act of *Julius Caesar*, he turns to the audience. And instead of being a dramatic character *within* the play, he is here made to speak as a critical commentator upon the play, explaining its mechanism and its virtues. Thus we have a tale from Shakespeare, retold, not as a plot but from the standpoint of the rhetorician, who is concerned with a work's processes of appeal.

Act III, Scene *ii*. *Antony has entered with the body of Caesar. Brutus has made his defense before the people, has won their sympathies to the cause of the conspirators, and has departed.*
Antony: Friends, Romans, Countrymen . . .

one—two—three syllables: hence in this progression, a magic formula. "Romans" to fit the conditions of the play; "countrymen" the better to identify the play-mob with the mob in the pit—for we are in the Renaissance, at that point when Europe's vast national integers are taking shape, and all the wisdom that comes of the body is to be obscured by our putting in place of the body the political corpus, while we try to run this bigger hulk with the instincts for the little one—the Hobbesian metaphor—and the gloomy error has exalted us, so that no word handles as much, and as quickly, and as inexpressibly, as this word "countrymen," which must really mean, if pragmatic results are the test, that there is glory solely in being outdone by those within our own borders. Anyway, consider how much better my one-two-three arrangement is than was the opining salutation in Brutus' speech: "Romans, countrymen, lovers." He is an orator—but because you of England have thought the untrustworthy Latins eloquent, and because you don't think you are nearly so clever as you'd like to be, I shall seem closer to you if I apologize for bluntness. Yet how much more competent my opening syllables are: how much *truer*, since true to the process of a spell, stressing a charm's *threeness*.

My Elizabethan audience, under the guise of facing a Roman mob I confront you at a most complicated moment. As a matter of fact, up to this point in our play you have been treated most outrageously. It can honestly be said that, in no major particular, have you been granted those clear and simple responses to which, as customers, you might feel yourselves entitled. Instead, your author has kept you in as vacillating a condition as this very Roman mob you have been watching with so little respect. I doubt if he distinguishes between the two of you. All that I as Antony do to this play-mob, as a character-recipe I do to you. He would play upon you; he would seem to know your stops; he would sound you from your lowest note to the top of your compass. He thinks you as easy to be played upon as a pipe.

Oh, there have been signs you recognize quickly, that you might feel familiar with the road upon which you have been stumbling. The conspirators have met during storms and in the "vile contagion of the night." They have pulled caps over their eyes. One plucked at another's sleeve. Such labels are easily read by anyone. The streets of Rome have bristled with bad omens. Caesar's wife has cried in sleep that they are murdering Caesar. Outlandish astronomical and biologic marvels have occurred—to point the direction of our plot and give it weight by implicating the very heavens. And finally, Caesar was struck with daggers. Yet these standard things have lured you into a region where you are not competent at all.

Consider the burden you now carry, as I step before the play-mob with the fresh-murdered body of Caesar. We have established a Caesar-principle and a Brutus-principle, though I blush to consider some of the devices whereby the two principles have been set into your minds. Realize for what slight reasons you have been willing to let Caesar die. (The conspirators would not so much as touch him until you also had been brought into their band. And when Casca shouted, "Speak, hands, for me!" stabbing great Caesar, those homicidal hands spoke for you also.) First, we had the portents, beginning with the soothsayer's admonition that Caesar beware the Ides of March. In showing how things were going, these signs prepared you somewhat to go in the same direction.

But in addition, *your sympathies have been poisoned.* Caesar a conqueror, a monarch by reason of his attainments? Yet he was deaf in one ear. He had the falling-sickness, and "swounded" from the intense strain of refusing a crown he coveted. "He had a fever when he was in Spain," cried out "like a sick girl," his feebleness amazing Cassius. Cassius was a better swimmer than Caesar—and when the two of them had leaped into the Tiber on a dare, Cassius had to pull out Caesar, to whom he must "bend his body if Caesar carelessly but nod on him." His wife is barren. For all his determination to be bold, there is a timid and superstitious trait in him. And worst, for an emperor, on a night of storm and portents he appeared on the stage in his nightgown—so let him die. For such reasons as these you are willing to put a knife through the ribs of Caesar.

Still, you are sorry for Caesar. We cannot profitably build a play around the horror of a murder if you do not care whether the murdered man lives or dies. So we had to do something for Caesar—and you would be ashamed if you stopped to consider what we did. I believe we made Caesar appealing by proxy. That is: I, Antony, am a loyal follower of Caesar; you love me for a good fellow, since I am expansive, hearty, much as you would be after not too heavy a meal; and as one given to pleasure, I am not likely to lie awake at night plotting you injury. If such a man loves Caesar, his love lifts up Caesar in your eyes.

I serve a double purpose. Not only do I let Caesar shine a bit warmly by his reflection of my glow, but when the actual *persona* of the Caesar-principle is dispatched by daggers, the principle lives on in me, who continue the function of Caesar in the play. In the next act, the fourth, the *persona* itself will reappear momentarily as a ghost in Brutus' tent—but on the whole, after Caesar's death, I am the plot-substitute for Caesar. No wonder Brutus, in his address to the play-mob but a short time ago, told them that only Caesar's vices had been slain, while his virtues lived on, still active. So they do, in me, whom you like because I am marked by so serviceable a trait as loyalty. And when this play is over, Antony alone of the major characters will live; for you like to have about you such a man as might keep guard at the door while you sleep. Given certain conceptions of danger, I become the sign of safety. A little sunshine-thought, to take home with you after these many slaughterings. Only as much of the Caesar-principle as will let you relax, is left to bid you good-night—and the Brutus-principle will have died to purchase you this handsome privilege.

I grant that on this last score I am not the perfect recipe. My author has provided purer comfort-recipes for you elsewhere. I show a little too much aptitude at deception, but you should not hold that against me. This trait was merely a by-product of my place in the story: it arose from the fact that upon me fell the burden of keeping things going, and the plottiness of our drama makes naturally for plotting. Besides, recall that I was wholly the reveler as long as Caesar lived. Once he is dead, it is no longer so necessary that I be likable in Caesar's behalf and warm him by my warmth. Henceforth I am no mere Caesar-adjunct, but the very vessel of the Caesar-principle. So, in expanding to my expanded role, I must break the former mold somewhat. Let *savants* explain the change by saying that carefree Antony was made a sober man, and a bitter one, by the death of Caesar. But it is an obvious fact that if an important cog in the plot vanishes in the very middle of our drama, something has to take its place. In deputizing for Caesar, I found it impossible to remain completely Antony. Let *savants* explain my altered psychology as they will—I know it was a playwright's necessity.

You have been made conspirators in a murder. For this transgression, there must be some expiative beast brought up for sacrifice. Such requirements guided us in the mixing of the Brutus-recipe, for it is Brutus that must die to absolve you of your stabbing an emperor who was deaf in one ear and whose wife was sterile. But let us be fair. There is also the fact that you wrested certain political prerogatives from King John, and have been taught to cherish them. Here also was a source of conviction to be tapped as an ingredient in our formula. We discredited Caesar from the very opening of the play, even before he had appeared (significant timing), by letting you see the tribunes angry with certain commoners who were too cordial in their preparations for the return of Caesar after victory. Caesar, it seems, would try to retract your *Magna Carta* from the Romans. Conversely, it is the Brutus-recipe that would prevent this threatened undoing of English political emancipation. So we make Brutus honorable in your eyes by starting his conduct primarily from this fear, which is always your fear as regards conditions in the contemporary state. He is virtuous because he does for Romans what you want your popular leaders to do for you. He takes on the nobility that comes of being good for private enterprise.

On the other hand, he is a conspirator; hence from the general censure takes corruption. For tough Casca is a Brutus-adjunct; and lean, envious Cassius; and Decius the flatterer. Here are qualities which, if lodged in any but yourselves, are not comforting to contemplate—hence are "vices." Brutus' acts, though done in a good cause, have shadiness. One cannot be stealthy as a thief without partially earning the kind of judgments that are laid against thieves. Nobleness, yes, but dirty business. And if his wife, Portia, speaks for him by her deep affection (as I obediently did for Caesar), note that she is allowed to show this affection only at those moments when he is sinisterly engaged, and answers her evasively. That is: her love is conveyed by her *misgivings*, as she worries because her once regular husband roams about at night, in "rheumy and unpurged air" sucking up "the humours of the dank morning," so that even the quality of swamps is drawn upon to discredit Brutus a little, right when Portia is loving him. All told: a fit expiative offering for our offense of murder: worthy, since he was noble and aroused affection, yet yieldable on good legalistic grounds, since he was a conspirator, like a bog. In weeping for his death, you will be sweetly absolved.

At this particular point in the play, however, as I rise to address you, accompanied by Caesar's corpse, Brutus has just confronted the play-mob, stated before them the case of the conspirators, and been exonerated. They have clamored their approval. They are convinced that Caesar would have been a tyrant. And they have shouted to the Brutus-principle, who must die for you, "Live, Brutus! live! live!" It is my task, as I stand before the play-mob, to contrive a *peripety* for my audience, reversing the arrows of your expectations. When my speech is finished, we must have set you to making the preparations for Brutus' death.

Well, a dramatist is a *professional* gambler. He prefers playing with loaded dice. And don't think that we should try to bring about this reversal without first making sure that we had furtively dealt ourselves some trumps. We have stacked the cards a little—not so shamelessly as some of our rival Shake-scenes might have done, but enough. Here, I believe, we have drawn from the well of magic. As follows:

Recall how, in the early rites of communion, whereby one man's interests were made identical with another's, the risks of competitive harms were eliminated by a partnership, a partnership established by three distinct symbolic acts: the sharing of one's wife, the exchanging of blood, the sitting down together at table. Of these, the sharing of the wife is dead, buried beneath notions of virtue that go with later concepts of ownership. Yet we give you something similar, in Caesar's dying words, "*Et tu, Brute?* Then fall, Caesar!" which suggests that in Caesar's pain there is more than the pain of knives, there is the pain of wrenched intimacy, eliciting a rebuke almost Christlike in its replacing of vengefulness with sorrow, as the victim saw that "Caesar's angel" was among his slayers. At this moment Caesar becomes great—for he must die well, at the expense of Brutus. They had shared affection; hence a promise contracted within the deep-lying terms of magic had been violated.

As for the rites at table: When the conspirators had come, to make sure that Caesar would be on hand at the Senate to be murdered, Caesar welcomed them heartily: "Good friends, go in, and taste some wine with me." And lastly, as for the blood-communion, how grimly it is vivified and mocked (in pious profanation) when the conspirators, at Brutus' word, bathe in the blood of Caesar's wounds. Three magic formulae, outraged—thus Shakespeare speaks to you in accents you had heard while not listening.

I now stand before you, assigned to the definite task of contriving our peripety, turning the arrows of your future while apparently engaged only in turning those of this unruly play-mob. I shall, by what immediately follows, proclaim myself in all thoroughness the Caesar-principle perpetuated. Here I fulfill the pledge I gave when first I came upon the stage after Caesar's murder. I came ostensibly to reassure the conspirators that I was ready to make peace with them, now that the offense was definitely beyond reparation. I shook hands with them, one after the other—but in the very act of doing so, I forgot them, and fell to musing aloud upon the destroyed magnificence of Caesar. In this way I signaled you to the effect that I was not turning against Caesar, even while "shaking the bloody fingers of his foes." (You wanted me to remain with Caesar, since that has been established as my part in this play. I have been given my label—and like children, you insist that a thing's true name is the name you first heard it called by. In your insistence that I remain allied with Caesar, repeating my number, you are grateful for the little cue I give you by my absent-minded musings over Caesar's body. In your satisfaction at receiving from me this sign, to restate my identity even as I make peace with the conspirators, you do not stop to ask why the conspirators should not interpret this sign precisely as you do. Your concern with your own aesthetic problem leads you to overlook this straining of verisimilitude, as we thought you would. We judged that, in your eagerness to receive the clue, you would not be overexacting as regard our manner of conveying it.)

Brutus, you will remember, had asked the mob to weigh what he said, and to judge his statements as critics. But, as a matter of fact, he gave them no opportunity to follow his advice. He told them to choose, then stated the issue in such a way that there was no choice. Those that love Rome, he said, must agree that Caesar should have been killed. Those that do not love Rome, should object. If there are any that do not love Rome, let them step forward in protest. No move—hence, the killing is endorsed.

And now, my countrymen, hear me ask the play-mob to lend me their ears, as I proceed to lay before you a plot in miniature. It will not be a very difficult pattern that I ask you to appreciate: a rudimentary piece of translation, by which I awaken in you the satisfactions of authorship, as you hear me say one thing and know that I mean another. "I come to bury Caesar, not to praise him"—whereat I praise him so roundly that all the vigor of the Caesar-principle is brought to life again.

> . . . if I were dispos'd to stir
> Your heart and minds to mutiny and rage,
> I should do Brutus wrong, and Cassius wrong . . .

Whereat I stir hearts and minds to mutiny and rage. And as the pattern grows clear, I can subtilize it, making Brutus and his band dishonorable by calling them all, all honorable men. And by the time I mentioned Caesar's will, saying that I would not read it because it would inflame the people, in accordance with the pattern you wait to hear me read the will. You hear them entreat me, you hear me refuse. Then you observe me stepping down, to be among them, that I may better "realize" Caesar's death from them, and make them tearful coroners while I appraise the wounds:

> If you have tears, prepare to shed them now.
> You all do know this mantle: I remember
> The first time ever Caesar put it on;
> 'Twas on a summer's evening in his tent,
> That day he overcame the Nervii.
> Look! in this place ran Cassius' dagger through:
> See what a rent the envious Casca made:
> Through this the well-beloved Brutus stabb'd;
> And, as he pluck'd his cursed steel away,
> Mark how the blood of Caesar follow'd it,
> As rushing out of doors, to be resolv'd
> If Brutus so unkindly knock'd or no;
> For Brutus, as you know, was Caesar's angel:
> Judge, O you gods! how dearly Caesar lov'd him.
> This was the most unkindest cut of all;
> For when the noble Caesar saw him stab,
> Ingratitude, more strong than traitors' arms,
> Quite vanquish'd him: then burst his mighty heart;
> And, in his mantle muffling up his face,
> Even at the base of Pompey's statua,
> Which all the while ran blood, great Caesar fell.
> O! what a fall was there, my countrymen;
> Then I, and you, and all of us fell down,
> Whilst bloody treason flourish'd over us.
> O! now you weep, and I perceive you feel
> The dint of pity; these are gracious drops.
> Kind souls, what! weep you when you but behold
> Our Caesar's vesture wounded? Look you here,
> Here is himself, marr'd, as you see, with traitors.

You see my "transference," as I turn from the mantle to the dead man that had worn the mantle. You see the play-mob grow *inflamed* under my talk of *pity* (remember our pattern). There is loud talk of mutiny; the people are about to rush away in anger—but we would "consolidate" our position. And now, rounding out the pattern, I return to the matter of the will, which I had refused to read:

> Why, friends, you go to do you know not what.
> Wherein hath Caesar thus deserv'd your loves?
> Alas! you know not: I must tell you then.
> You have forgot the will I told you of.

Whereupon I read them the will of a rich philanthropist—and their vindictiveness, against the conspirators is complete. You have been engrossed—faugh! you demons, how you do love plottings, for all your censure of plotters. Or is it machinery that delights you—and are you pleased with joining me to make a smoothly running engine of fatality?

Cassius was right in proposing that they slay me, along with Caesar. But Brutus held it was enough to slay the *persona* of the Caesar-principle, on the ground that the *adjunct* would subside through want of its source:

> Our course will seem too bloody, Caius Cassius,
> To cut the head off and then hack the limbs, . . .
> For Antony is but a limb of Caesar. . . .
> And, for Mark Antony, think not of him;
> For he can do no more than Caesar's arm
> When Caesar's head is off.

So the Brutus-principle slays half the Caesar-principle, and spares the other half that will in turn destroy it.

Recall these steps: How first, after the murder, I had sent word by a servant offering to join the cause of the conspirators, if they would guarantee me safety. How I fell to musing over the body of Caesar. How, after *exeunt all but Antony*, I had let loose my full-throated venom:

> O! pardon me, thou bleeding piece of earth,
> That I am meek and gentle with these butchers;
> Thou art the ruins of the noblest man
> That ever lived in the tide of times.
> Woe to the hand that shed this costly blood!
> Over thy wounds now do I prophesy,
> Which like dumb mouths do ope their ruby lips,
> To beg the voice and utterance of my tongue,

A curse shall light upon the limbs of men;
Domestic fury and fierce civil strife
Shall cumber all the parts of Italy;
Blood and destruction shall be so in use,
And dreadful objects so familiar,
That mothers shall but smile when they behold
Their infants quarter'd with the hands of war;
All pity chok'd with custom of fell deeds:
And Caesar's spirit, ranging for revenge,
With Ate by his side come hot from hell,
Shall in these confines with a monarch's voice
Cry "Havoc!" and let slip the dogs of war;
That this foul deed shall smell above the earth
With carrion men, groaning for burial.

Then, in my speech before the Romans, I fulfilled my promises, starting those processes by which the Brutus-principle, which killed the Caesar-*persona*, is driven to his death by the Caesar-adjunct.

Thank us for this growing thing by growing with it—and in the following scene we shall allow you to squeeze the last available sum of emotion from the mounting sequence, causing it to drip, not by still hotter pressure, but by a sudden cooling. Prominent among the conspirators, there was a certain Cinna. Now another Cinna comes upon the stage, Cinna the poet, ludicrous, the cartoon of a poet, the aesthete, such as you have long before now been taught to laugh at (our author is treading on safe ground here). He is an earnest but ineffectual wretch, who probably knows a good line when he sees it, and would doubtless have been entranced to write just such verses as Shakespeare wrote; and perhaps he might even have written them had he known, like Shakespeare, how to draw finesses from toughnesses. Yet our dramatist betrays him for the delectation of you, my stinking audience, makes him your laughing stock, ridicules one of his own Guild for your benefit, though you have no desire whatever to write like Shakespeare, would much rather eat beef than hear a play, but cannot go on eating beef forever, and so come here occasionally, demanding firm, beefy diction. The mob stumbles upon this Cinna, overwhelming him. First Citizen, Second Citizen, Third Citizen, and Fourth Citizen each ask him a different question, all at the same time, insisting imperiously that he answer without delay. It is all quite hilarious, as Cinna is in a daze, comically. And when they ask him his name, and he says with assurance, "Cinna," they start pawing at him in earnest—and when he begs them for a little accuracy, insisting that he is not Cinna the conspirator but Cinna the poet, they unanswerably answer that they abominate the name, and so will pummel him for his verses, and the act ends with the brawling group moving from the stage. You somehow know that the poetic Cinna will suffer no fundamental harm. He will merely be slain-not-slain, like a clown hit by cannon balls—yet by this let-down we have reaffirmed in another way the grim intentions of the mob. We have clinched the arrows of your expectancy, incidentally easing our obligations as regard the opening of Act IV.

You will be still more wisely handled by what follows, as our Great Demagogue continues to manipulate your minds. I think particularly of the second scene of the next act, weighted by the steadily organized pressure of events. You will witness a startling quarrel between Brutus and Cassius. After this violence and the sad reconciliation (these men are disintegrating), there will be a contrasted descent to soft tearfulness, as Brutus' drowsy servant plays him a disconsolate little tune in the dead of night (Portia is dead)—and the servant is drowsy, that he may fall asleep as Varro and Claudius have done; then with three men sleeping (and you drooping in sympathy) and Brutus alone awake, there will be, all about, a sleepiness, and a Brutus-loneliness—whereat the Caesar-*persona*, now as a ghost, may return to indicate, by a vague prophecy, that all will be ended for Brutus at Philippi.

1946—Harley Granville-Barker. "*Julius Caesar*: The Play's Structure," from *Prefaces to Shakespeare*

Harley Granville-Barker was an actor, producer, playwright, and critic. As a producer he oversaw many revivals of Shakespeare and other play-wrights, as well as the work of new dramatists. He adapted a number of plays from other languages for the English stage, and he coauthored *A Companion to Shakespeare Studies*.

There is a powerful ease in the construction of *Julius Caesar* which shows us a Shakespeare master of his means, and it is the play in which the boundaries of his art begin so markedly to widen. We find in it, therefore, a stagecraft, not of a too accustomed perfection, but bold and free. The theme calls forth all his resources and inspires their fresh and vigorous use; yet it does not strain them, as some later and, if greater, less accommodating themes are to do. We may here study Elizabethan stagecraft, as such, almost if not quite at its best; and a close analysis of the play's action, the effects in it and the way they are gained—a task for the producer in any case—will have this further interest.

Plutarch was a godsend to Shakespeare. Rome, Caesar and high heroic verse, one knows what such a mixture may amount to in the theater; though we may suppose that, with his lively mind, he would never have touched the subject had he not found that admirable historian, who, with happy familiarity, tucks an arm in ours, so to speak, and leads us his observant, anecdotic way, humanizing history, yet never diminishing its magnificence. Plutarch's genius, in fact, is closely allied to Shakespeare's own, with its power to make, by a touch or so of nature, great men and simple, present and past, the real and the mimic world, one kin. And this particular power was in the ascendant with Shakespeare now.

He redraws the outline of the story more simply, but he cannot resist crowding characters in. What wonder, when they are all so striking, and he knows he can make a living man out of a dozen lines of dialogue? The fifth act is a galaxy of such creations. And if, on the other hand, Artemidorus and the Soothsayer have little or no life of their own, while the poet of Act IV is a mere irruption into the play, a species of human ordnance shot off, their momentarily important part in the action lends them reflected life enough. But much of the play's virtue lies in the continual invention and abundant vitality of these incidental figures by which the rarer life, so to call it, of the chief characters is at intervals nourished. And as there is no formal mechanism of plot, it is largely with their aid that the action moves forward with such a varied rhythm, upon an ebb and flow of minor event that is most lifelike. The whole play is alive; it is alive in every line.

Elizabethan stagecraft, with its time-freedom and space-freedom, gives the playwright great scope for maneuvering minor character and incident. He may conjure a character into sudden prominence, and be done with it as suddenly. He has not, as in the modern "realistic" theater, to relate it to the likelihoods of hard-and-fast time and place. The modern dramatist plans his play by large divisions, even as the Greek dramatist did. Time and place must suit the need of his chief characters; if minor ones can't be accommodating they can't be accommodated, that's all. The Elizabethan dramatist has his story to tell, and the fate of the chief figures in it to determine. But, as long as the march of the story is not stayed, he may do pretty well what he likes by the way. The modern dramatist thinks of his play constructively in acts; and the scenes must accommodate themselves to the act, as the acts to the play as a whole. The Elizabethan would instinctively do the contrary. This is not to say that a play did not commonly move to some larger rhythm than the incidental. Every playwright, every sort of artist indeed, feels for the form which will best accommodate his idea, and will come to prefer the comprehensive form. But whether this rhythm with Shakespeare resolved itself into acts is another matter; and that it would resolve itself into the five acts of the editors is more than doubtful.

The larger rhythm of *Julius Caesar* can be variously interpreted. The action moves by one impetus, in a barely checked crescendo, to the end of Act III. Caesar's murder is the theme; the mob provides a recurrent chorus of confusion and ends as it has begun, this part of the story. Acts IV and V are given to the murder's retribution; this unifies them. They are martial, more ordered, and, for all the fighting at the end, consistently pitched in a lower key. The five-act division can, however, be defended dramatically; and, if it is valid, it shows us some interesting points of Elizabethan stagecraft. Act I is preparatory and leads up to the conspirators' winning of Brutus, though this itself is kept for the start of Act II. Modern practice would dictate a division after Act I, Sc. ii; for here is a time interval and a change from day to night. But to Shakespeare—or his editor—it would be more important to begin a new act upon a new note, and with the dominant figure of Brutus to impress us. And this we find: each act of the five has a significant and striking beginning, while the ends of the first four all tail away. Act III begins with the ominous

> *Caesar.* The Ides of March are come.
> *Soothsayer.* Ay, Caesar, but not gone.

Act IV with the sinister

> *Antony.* These many then shall die; their names are pricked.

Act V with the triumphant

> *Octavius.* Now, Antony, our hopes are answered. . . .

It is easy to see why the beginning of an Elizabethan "act" had to be striking.[9] There was no lowering of the lights, no music, no warning raps, while eyes "in front" concentrated upon an enigmatic curtain. The actors had to walk on and command the unprepared attention of a probably restless audience, and they needed appropriate material. Equally, to whatever crisis of emotion a scene might mount, they would have to walk off again. Therefore neither acts nor scenes, as a rule, end upon a crisis.

The play is too strenuous, if not too long, to be acted without at least one pause. It must occur, of course, at the end of Act III. This one should, I personally think, be enough; if pauses are to mean long intervals of talk and distraction, it certainly would be. But if a producer thinks more relief from the strain upon the audience is advisable (his actors do not need it), there is the breathing-space at the end of Act II—better not make more of it—and, if that will not suffice, he can pause at the end of Act I. He will be unwise, though, to divide Acts IV and V.

But the form of the play should first be studied in relation to its minor rhythms, for it is in these, in the setting of them one against the other, in their adjustment to the larger rhythm of the main theme, that the liveliness of Shakespeare's stagecraft is to be seen.

The action begins with the entry of the two Tribunes . . . *and certain commoners over the stage.* The Roman populace is to play an important part; we have now but a minute's glimpse of it, and in harmless holiday mood.

Hence! home, you idle creatures, get you home:
Is this a holiday?

The first lines spoken are a stage direction for the temper of the scene. It
may be that the Globe Theatre "crowd" was not much of a crowd, was liable
to be unrehearsed and inexact. Line after line scattered through the scene is
contrived to describe indirectly how they should look and what they should be
expressing. No audience but will accept the suggestion, though the crowd itself
be a bit behindhand. Nor need a producer, here or elsewhere, strive to provide a
realistically howling mob. The fugleman convention is a part of the convention
of the play; reason enough for abiding in it.

Note before we leave this scene how its first full-bodied speech has Pompey
for a theme, and what emphasis is given to the first sound of his name. After the
chattering prose of the cobbler comes Marullus'

Wherefore rejoice? What conquest brings he home?
What tributaries follow him to Rome
To grace in captive bonds his chariot wheels?
You blocks, you stones, you worse than senseless things!
O you hard hearts, you cruel men of Rome,
Knew you not Pompey?

For Pompey dead is to Caesar something of what Caesar dead is to be to
Brutus and the rest. And—though Shakespeare naturally does not prejudice
an important effect by anticipating it and elaborating its parallel—the name's
reiteration throughout the first part of the play has purpose.

A unity is given to these first three acts by the populace; by keeping them
constantly in our minds. They are easily persuaded now, controlled and brought
to silence:

They vanish tongue-tied in their guiltiness.

The devastation of the third act's end has this mild beginning.

Against the disorder and inconsequence, Caesar's processional entrance tells
with doubled effect. We are given but a short sight of him, our impression is
that he barely pauses on his way. His dominance is affirmed by the simplest
means. We hear the name sounded—sounded rather than spoken—seven times
in twenty-four lines. The very name is to dominate. It is the cue for Cassius' later
outburst:

Brutus and Caesar: what should be in that "Caesar"?
Why should that name be sounded more than yours?

Write them together, yours is as fair a name;
Sound them, it doth become the mouth as well;
Weigh them, it is as heavy; conjure with 'em,
"Brutus" will start a spirit as soon as "Caesar."

The procession passes. And now that these opposites, the many-headed and the one, the mob and its moment's idol, have been set in clear contrast before us, the main action may begin.

It is Cassius' passion that chiefly gives tone and color to the ensuing long duologue. He sets it a swift pace too, which is only checked by Brutus' slow responses; Brutus, lending one ear to his vehement friend, the other keen for the meaning of the distant shouts. Yet, in a sense, it is Caesar who still holds the stage; in Cassius' rhetoric, in the shouting, in Brutus' strained attention. With his re-entrance, then, there need be no impression given of a fresh beginning, for the tension created by that first passage across the stage should hardly have been relaxed. It now increases, that is all. Caesar pauses a little longer on his way, and with purpose. It is like the passing of a thundercloud; presage, in another sort, of the storm by which Nature is to mark his end. To the stately words and trumpet music the procession moves on; and we are left, with the proper shock of contrast, to Casca's acrid and irreverent prose. Now the tension does relax. Then Casca goes, and Brutus and Cassius part with but brief comment on him, without attempting to restore the broken harmony of their thoughts; and Cassius' closing soliloquy, as we have seen, is little more than a perfunctory forwarding of the story.

Thunder and lightning . . .

This, the stage empty, would emphasize well enough for the Elizabethans some break of time and place, and a few claps and flashes more might suffice to put a whole storm on record. It does not now suffice Shakespeare. He sets out upon a hundred and sixty-five lines of elaborate verbal scene-painting; in the economy of the plot they really stand for little more. It is not, of course, merely a passing pictorial effect that he is branding on his audience's imagination. Consider this passage in connection with those appeals of the Chorus in *Henry V*:

Think when we talk of horses that you see them
Printing their proud hoofs i' the receiving earth;
For 'tis your thoughts that now must deck our kings . . .

O! do but think
You stand upon the rivage and behold
A city on the inconstant billows dancing;

For so appears this fleet majestical,
Holding due course to Harfleur.

All that the listeners were to do for themselves, since the dramatist could not even attempt to do it for them. Here Shakespeare is certainly concerned to picture Rome under the portentous storm, but it is upon the personal episodes he fixes—upon the slave with his burning hand, the

hundred ghastly women,
Transformed with their fear, who swore they saw
Men all in fire walk up and down the streets . . .

upon the marvel of the lion that "glar'd upon" Casca and "went surly by." And their value to him lies chiefly in their effect upon the emotions of his characters; this is his path to an effect upon ours. He has discovered, in fact, the one dramatic use to which the picturesque can be put in his theater, and the one and only way of using it. It was not, of course, a discovery sought and made all complete for the occasion. But this is, I think, the first time he brings Nature under such serious contribution. Make another comparison, with the storm-scenes in *King Lear*. Set this scene beside those, with their perfect fusion of character and surroundings and their use to the play, and its method seems arbitrary and crude enough. It takes the plot little further. And Cicero is a walking shadow, Cinna a mere convenience; Casca, unnerved and eloquent, is unrecognizable as the Casca of the previous scene, is turned to a convenience for picturing the storm; while Cassius only repeats himself, and his rhetoric, dramatically justified before, grows rodomontade. By the end of the hundred and sixty-five lines we have learned that Cicero is cautious, Casca ripe, that things are moving fast with Cinna and the rest, that Brutus must be won. At his best Shakespeare could have achieved this in fifty lines or less and given us the storm into the bargain.

The contrasting calm of the next act's beginning is an appropriate setting for Brutus, the stoic, the man of conscience and gentle mind. The play's scheme now opens out and grows clear, for Brutus takes his allotted and fatal place among his fellows as moral dictator. To his dominance is due the scene's coldness and rigidity, though the unity of tone gives it dignity and its circumstance alone would make effective drama. Incidental things give it vitality and such color as it needs; the coming and going of the sleepy boy, the knocking without, the striking of the clock followed by those three short echoing speeches. It all stays to the end rather static than dynamic; for high-mindedly as Brutus may harangue his "gentle friends," fervently as they may admire him, there is never, now or later, the spontaneous sympathy between them that alone gives life to a cause. The ultimate as well as the immediate tragedy is in the making.

The scene with Portia is the due sequel. Even from her he holds aloof. He loves her; but the more he loves her the less he can confide in her. Even the avowal of his love is wrung from him in a sort of agony. And Portia's own tragedy is in the making here. In her spent patience with his silence we might well divine the impatience at his absence which was to be her death. We may question why, after a vibrant climax, Shakespeare so lowers the tension for the scene's end. Caius Ligarius' coming will surely thrust Portia and this more intimate Brutus to the background of our remembrance. There are two answers at least. The play's main action must not only be carried on, but it must seem now to be hurried on, and Brutus, his philosophic reserve once broken, must be shown precipitate.[10] For another answer; the Caius Ligarius episode keeps the scenes between Brutus and Portia, Caesar and Calpurnia apart. It would discount the second to bring it on the heels of the first.

Thunder and lightning herald the next scene's beginning; the purpose of its repetition is plain enough. The mood wrought in us by the storm must be restored; and in a moment comes Calpurnia's speech, which is a very echo of Casca's description of the signs and portents. Caesar, rocklike at first against the pleadings of his wife, wavers from his love for her and yields to Decius' friendliness and flattery, reinforced by the thronging-in of the rest, looking, as Brutus bid them look, so "fresh and merrily." It is good preparation for the catastrophe, the sudden livening of the scene with this group of resolute, cheerful men. Besides, might not the slim Decius, have overreached himself but for their coming? Caesar was no fool, and Calpurnia would be apt to every sort of suspicion. But the friendly faces disperse the last clouds of the ominous night. Cassius is not here. It is Brutus, the irreproachable Brutus, who gives tone to the proceeding. Does he, even at this moment, feel himself

> arm'd so strong in honesty . . .

that he can meet Caesar's magnanimity without flinching? Is it only ague that makes Caius Ligarius shake as Caesar presses his hand? And that nothing of tragic irony may be wanting—

> Good friends, go in, and taste some wine with me,
> And we, like friends, will straightway go together.

The sacrament of hospitality and trust! It is a supreme effect, economized in words, fully effective only in action. And for an instance of Shakespeare's dramatic judgment, of his sense of balance between an immediate effect and the play's continuing purpose of his power, in striking one note, to strike the ruthlessly right one, take the two lines with which Brutus, lagging back, ends the scene:

That every like is not the same, O Caesar!
The heart of Brutus yearns to think upon.

Not that a pun or a quibble upon words necessarily struck an Elizabethan as a trifling thing. But it takes a Brutus to find refuge in a quibbling thought at such a moment, and in his own grief for his victim.

Caesar is now ringed by the conspirators, the daggers are ready, and the two scenes that follow are to hold and prolong the suspense till they strike.[11] Artemidorus, with his paper and its comment, may seem unduly dry and detached. But the solitary anonymous figure comes as a relief and contrast to that significant group, and against that wrought emotion his very detachment tells. It contrasts too with Portia's tremulous intimate concern. The act's end here—if it is to mean a short empty pause while the audience stay seated and expectant, not an interval of talk and movement—will have value. The blow is about to fall, and in silence suspense is greatest. We draw breath for the two long scenes that form the center section of the play.

Trumpets sound, the stage fills. Caesar comes again as we saw him go, still circled by these friends, confident, outwardly serene. The trumpets silent, we hear another prelude, of two voices, the one ringing clear, the other pallidly echoing:

> *Caesar.* The Ides of March are come.
> *Soothsayer.* Ay, Caesar, but not gone.

Then follows a little scuffle of voices, a quick shifting and elbowing in the group round Caesar as the petitions are thrust forward and aside, and once again that fivefold iteration of the potent name. Despite the ceremony, nerves are on edge. Caesar goes forward to be greeted by the Senators and to mount his state. Now comes a passage of eighteen lines. Toneless it has to be, that the speakers betray not their feelings. In the group of them there is hardly a movement; they must measure even their glances. Popilius Lena's threading his way through them is startling in itself. Yet on this monotone the whole gamut of the conspiracy's doubts, fears and desperation is run. Its midway sentence is the steely

> Cassius, be constant. . . .

with which Brutus marks his mastery of the rest. Caesar is seated. His

> Are we all ready?

turns the whole concourse to him. Some few of them are ready indeed. And now, in terms of deliberate rhetoric, Shakespeare once more erects before us the

Colossus that is to be overthrown. Then in a flash the blow falls. Butchered by Casca, sacrificed by Brutus—these two doings of the same deed are marked and kept apart—Caesar lies dead.

Remark that we are now only a quarter of the way through the scene; further, that the play's whole action so far has been a preparation for this crisis. Yet, with dead Caesar lying there, Shakespeare will contrive to give us such fresh interest in the living that, with no belittling of the catastrophe, no damping-down nor desecration of our emotions, our minds will be turned forward still. This is a great technical achievement. He might well have shirked the full attempt and have wound up the scene with its next seventy lines or so. But then could the play ever have recovered strength and impetus? As it is, by the long scene's end our concern for Caesar is lost in our expectations of the Forum. The producer must note carefully how this is brought about, lest even the minor means to it miscarry.

The mainspring of the renewed action will lie, of course, in the creation of Antony. We may call it so; for, as we saw, he has been cunningly kept, in person and by reference, an ineffectual figure so far. But now both in person and by reference, by preparation, by contrast, Shakespeare brings him to a sudden overwhelming importance.

We have the helter-skelter of the moment after Caesar's fall; Brutus is the only figure of authority and calm. Old Publius stands trembling and dumb; Antony, that slight man, has fled, and the conspirators seem confounded by their very success. Before, then, they face the Rome they have saved from tyranny, let them make themselves one again, not in false courage—if Rome is ungrateful they must die—but in high principle that fears not death. Let them sign themselves ritual brothers—and in whose blood but Caesar's?

> Stoop, Romans, stoop,
> And let us bathe our hands in Caesar's blood
> Up to the elbows, and besmear our swords:
> Then walk we forth, even to the market place,
> And, waving our red weapons o'er our heads,
> Let's all cry, "Peace, freedom, and liberty!"

We need not doubt Brutus' deep sincerity for a moment.

> Fates, we will know your pleasures.
> That we shall die, we know; 'tis but the time
> And drawing days out, that men stand upon.

This is the man of principle at his noblest. But what else than savage mockery is Casca's

Why, he that cuts off twenty years of life
Cuts off so many years of fearing death.

And does Brutus, the rapt ideologue, perceive it? Into the sophistical trap he walks:

Grant that, and then is death a benefit:
So are we Caesar's friends, that have abridg'd
His time of fearing death.

And he anoints himself devotedly. Then Cassius, febrile, infatuate:

Stoop, then, and wash. How many ages hence
Shall this our lofty scene be acted o'er,
In states unborn and accents yet unknown!

Brutus echoes him as well. And by this last daring and doubly dramatic stroke, Shakespeare reminds us that we are ideal spectators of these men and the event, having vision and prevision too. Comment is forbidden the playwright, but here is the effect of it contrived. For as we look and listen we hear the verdict of the ages echoing. In this imperfect world, it would seem, one can be too high-minded, too patriotic, too virtuous altogether. And then the commonest thing, if it be rooted firm, may trip a man to his ruin. So these exalted gentlemen, led by their philosophic patriot, are stopped on their way—by the arrival of a servant.[12]

This is the play's turning point. And, if but pictorially, could a better be contrived? On the one side the group of triumphant and powerful men; on the other, suddenly appearing, a humble, anonymous messenger.

Thus, Brutus, did my master bid me kneel;
Thus did Mark Antony bid me fall down;
And, being prostrate, thus he bade me say . . .

And so aptly and literally does he represent his master that Brutus, with this chance to test the smooth words apart from their deviser, might, we should suppose, take warning. But it is Brutus who is infatuate now. It is not, as with Cassius, passions that blind him, but principles. He has done murder for an ideal. Not to credit his adversaries, in turn, with the highest motives would be unworthy, would seem sheer hypocrisy. And Antony's message is baited with an uncanny knowledge of the man.

Brutus is noble, wise, valiant, and honest;
Caesar was mighty, bold, royal, and loving:

Say I love Brutus, and I honour him;
Say I fear'd Caesar, honour'd him, and lov'd him.

Wisdom and honesty, valor and love, honor and again honor; Brutus will harp on the very words in his own apology. It is Cassius, with his vengeance fulfilled and his passions gratified, who now sees clear, knowing his Antony as truly as Antony knows his Brutus. His

                misgiving still
Falls shrewdly to the purpose.

But he lacks authority to lead.

Then follows the revelation of Antony, in his verbal duel with the conspirators; his devoted rhapsody over Caesar's body; and the swift foresight of the passage with Octavius' servant. It is to be noted that the beginning of the scene in the Forum tags dramatically not to the end of this but to the earlier departure of Brutus and the others. Hence, perhaps, the short opening in verse and Brutus' echoing of his last spoken line,

Prepare the body, then, and follow us.

with

Then follow me, and give me audience, friends.

Once he is in the pulpit we have a sharp change to prose. Editor after editor has condemned Brutus' speech as poor and ineffective, and most of them have then proceeded to justify Shakespeare for making it so. It is certainly not meant to be ineffective, for it attains its end in convincing the crowd. Whether it is poor oratory must be to some extent a matter of taste. Personally, accepting its form as one accepts the musical convention of a fugue, I find that it stirs me deeply. I prefer it to Antony's. It wears better. It is very noble prose. But we must, of course, consider it first as a part of the setting-out of Brutus' character. Nothing—if the speech itself does not—suggests him to us as a poor speaker; nor, at this moment of all others, would he fail himself. But we know the sort of appeal he would, deliberately if not temperamentally, avoid. Shakespeare has been accused, too, of bias against the populace. But is it so? He had no illusions about them. As a popular dramatist he faced their inconstant verdict day by day, and came to write for a better audience than he had. He allows Brutus no illusions, certainly.

Only be patient till we have appeas'd
The multitude, beside themselves with fear. . . .

This is the authentic voice of your republican aristocrat, who is at no pains, either, to disguise his disdain.

> Be patient till the last.
> Romans, countrymen and lovers! hear me for my cause; and be silent,
> that you may hear. . . .

For the tone belies the words; nor is such a rapping on the desk for "Quiet, please" the obvious way into the affections of the heady crowd. He concedes nothing to their simplicity.

> Censure me in your wisdom, and awake your senses, that you may be
> the better judge.

But the compliment, one fears, is paid less to them than to his own intellectual pride. It is wasted in any case, if we may judge by the Third and Fourth Citizens:

> Let him be Caesar.
>   Caesar's better parts
> Shall be crown'd in Brutus.

He has won them; not by what he has said, in spite of it, rather; but by what he is. The dramatic intention, and the part the crowd plays in it, is surely plain. Men in the mass do not think, they feel. They are as biddable as children, and as sensitive to suggestion. Mark Antony is to make it plainer.

Antony has entered, and stands all friendless by Caesar's bier. Brutus descends, the dialogue shifting from prose to easy verse as he shakes free of the enthusiasm, and departs alone. His austere renouncing of advantage should show us how truly alone.

Antony makes no glib beginning; he protests, indeed, that he has nothing to say. He tries this opening and that, is deprecatory, apologetic.

> The noble Brutus
> Hath told you Caesar was ambitious;
> If it were so, it was a grievous fault,
> And grievously hath Caesar answered it.

But he is deftly feeling his way by help of a few platitudes to his true opening, and alert for a first response. He senses one, possibly, upon his

> He was my friend, faithful and just to me. . . .

—for that was a human appeal. But he knows better than to presume on a success; he returns to his praise of the well-bepraised Brutus. He embellishes his tune with two grace notes, one appealing to sentiment, the other to greed. More praise of Brutus, and yet more! But the irony of this will out, and he checks himself. Irony is a tricky weapon with an audience uncertain still. Nor will too much nice talk about honor serve him; that sort of thing leaves men cold. A quick turn gives us

> I speak not to disprove what Brutus spoke,
> But here I am to speak what I do know.

and, to judge by the hammering monosyllables of the last line, he is warming to his work, and feels his hearers warming to him. One may so analyze the speech throughout and find it a triumph of effective cleverness. The cheapening of the truth, the appeals to passion, the perfect carillon of flattery, cajolery, mockery and pathos, swinging to a magnificent tune, all serve to make it a model of what popular oratory should be. In a school for demagogues its critical analysis might well be an item in every examination paper. That is one view of it. By another, there is nothing in it calculated or false. Antony feels like this; and, on these occasions, he never lets his thoughts belie his feelings, that is all. And he knows, without stopping to think, what the common thought and feeling will be, where reason and sentiment will touch bottom—and if it be a muddy bottom, what matter!—because he is himself, as we said, the common man raised to the highest power. So, once in touch with his audience, he can hardly go wrong.

How easy he makes things for them! No abstract arguments:

> But here's a parchment with the seal of Caesar;
> I found it in his closet, 'tis his will.[13]

We pass now, however, to a less ingenuous, more ingenious, phase of the achievement. Those—it is strange there should be any—who range themselves with the mob and will see in Antony no more than the plain blunt man of his own painting, have still to account for this slim manipulator of Caesar's will that Shakespeare paints. It is tempting, no doubt, to make men dance to your tune when the thing is done so easily. When they stand, open-eared and open-mouthed, how resist stuffing them with any folly that comes handy? And as there is no limit, it would seem, to their folly and credulity, greed and baseness, why not turn it all to good account—one's own account? Antony is not the man, at any rate, to turn aside from such temptation. Is he less of a demagogue that Caesar's murder is his theme, and vengeance for it his cause? Does poetic eloquence make demagogy less vicious—or, by chance, more? Shakespeare's Antony would not be complete without this juggling with Caesar's will.

What so impresses the unlearned as the sight of some document? He does not mean to read it. They are Caesar's heirs. There, he never meant to let that slip! Trick after trick of the oratorical trade follows. The provocative appeal to the seething crowd's self-control tagged to the flattery of their generous hearts, the play with the mantle, which they "all do know," that soft touch of the "summer's evening" when Caesar first put it on! Self-interest well salted with sentiment, what better bait can there be? Much may be done with a blood-stained bit of cloth!

> Through this the well-beloved Brutus stabbed;
> And as he pluck'd his cursed steel away,
> Mark how the blood of Caesar followed it,
> As rushing out of doors, to be resolved
> If Brutus so unkindly knocked, or no. . . .

If our blood were still cold the simile might sound ridiculous, but it thrills us now.

> This was the most unkindest cut of all;
> For when the noble Caesar saw him stab,
> Ingratitude, more strong than traitors' arms,
> Quite vanquished him: then burst his mighty heart;
> And, in his mantle muting up his face,
> Even at the base of Pompey's statua,
> Which all the while ran blood, great Caesar fell.

How fine it sounds! How true, therefore, by the standards of popular oratory, it is! There is poetic truth, certainly, in that ingratitude; and as for Pompey's statue, if it did not actually run blood, it might well have done.

> O! what a fall was there, my countrymen;
> Then I, and you, and all of us fell down,
> Whilst bloody treason flourished over us.
> O! now you weep, and I perceive you feel
> The dint of pity. . . .

What were Brutus' tributes to their wisdom compared to this? Antony has won their tears, and has but to seal his success by showing them the very body of Caesar, and to endorse it with

> Good friends, sweet friends, let me not stir you up
> To such a sudden flood of mutiny.

They that have done this deed are honourable. . . . for irony is a potent weapon now; and to forbid mutiny is only to encourage it, the word of itself will do so.

The peroration is masterly, a compendium of excitement. We have again the false restraint from passion, the now triumphant mockery of those honorable men, of their wisdom, their good reasons and their private grief; again, the plain blunt man's warning against such oratorical snares as the subtle Brutus set; and it is all rounded off with magnificent rhythm, the recurrent thought and word flung like a stone from a sling.

> but were I Brutus,
> And Brutus Antony, there were an Antony
> Would rule up your spirits, and put a tongue
> In every wound of Caesar that should move
> The stones of Rome to rise and mutiny.

And to what end? To the routing of the conspirators from Rome, truly. A good counterstroke. But the first victim of Antony's eloquence, as Shakespeare takes care to show us, is the wretched Cinna the poet, who has had nothing to do with Caesar's murder at all.[14] The mob tear him limb from limb, as children tear a rag doll. Nor does knowledge of his innocence hinder them.

> Truly, my name is Cinna.
> Tear him to pieces, he's a conspirator.
> I am Cinna, the poet, I am Cinna the poet.
> Tear him for his bad verses, tear him for his bad verses.
> I am not Cinna the conspirator.
> It is no matter, his name's Cinna; pluck but his name out of his heart,
> and turn him going.

Well, we have had Antony's fine oratory; and we may have been, and should have been, stirred by it. But if we have not at the same time watched him, and ourselves, with a discerning eye, and listened as well with a keener ear, the fault is none of Shakespeare's. He draws no moral, does not wordily balance the merits of this cause against that. He is content to compose for the core of his play, with an artist's enjoyment, with an artist's conscience, in getting the balance true, this ironic picture; and, finally, to set against the high tragedy of the murder of Caesar a poor poetaster's wanton slaughter.

The beginning of the fourth act sets against the calculations of the conspirators the arithmetic of the new masters of Rome.

These many then shall die; their names are pricked.

It is an admirably done scene, of but fifty lines all told, giving an actor, with just twenty-two words, material for Lepidus (the feat would seem impossible, but Shakespeare manages it; and so can an actor, rightly chosen and given scope), giving us Octavius, showing us yet another Antony, and outlining the complete gospel of political success. Brutus and Cassius, its finish informs us, are levying powers. We are shown them straightway at the next scene's beginning, and from now to the play's end its action runs a straight road.

> *Drum. Enter Brutus. . . .*

The philosopher has turned general. He is graver, more austere than ever.

> Your master, Pindarus,
> In his own change, or by ill officers,
> Hath given me some worthy cause to wish
> Things done undone. . . .

But he says it as one who would say that nothing, be it big or little, can ever be undone. We hear a *Low march within*, congruous accompaniment to the somber voice. It heralds Cassius.

> *Enter Cassius and his Powers.*
>   *Cassius.* Stand, ho!
>   *Brutus.* Stand, ho!
>   *1st Soldier.* Stand!
>   *2nd Soldier.* Stand!
>   *3rd Soldier.* Stand!

The voices echo back, the drumbeats cease, the armed men face each other, silent a moment.[15]

This long scene—the play's longest—thus begun, is dominated by Brutus and attuned in the main to his mood. Now the mood of the good man in adversity may well make for monotony and gloom; but Shakespeare is alert to avoid this, and so must producer and actors be. We have the emotional elaboration of the quarrel, the eccentric interlude of the poet as preparation for the sudden drop to the deep still note struck by the revelation of Portia's death; next comes the steady talk of fighting plans (note the smooth verse), then the little stir with which the council breaks up and the simple preparations for the night. Varro and Claudius are brought in, so that their sleep, as well as the boy's, may throw the calm, wakeful figure of Brutus into relief. The tune and its lapsing brings a hush, we can almost hear the leaves of the book rustle as they are turned. Then the ghost appears; the tense few moments of its presence have been well prepared. The scene's swift ending is good stagecraft too. Lucius' protesting treble, the deeper voices of the soldiers all confused with sleep, the dissonance and sharp interchange break and disperse the ominous spell for Brutus and for us. And the last words look forward.[16]

The last act of *Julius Caesar* has been most inconsiderately depreciated. Nothing, certainly, will make it effective upon the modern "realistic" stage, but we can hardly blame Shakespeare for that. He writes within the conventions of his own theater, and he here takes the fullest advantage of them. He begins by bringing the rival armies, led by their generals, face to face.

> *Enter Octavius, Antony and their army. . . .*
> *Drum. Enter Brutus, Cassius and their army.*
>   *Brutus.* They stand, and would have parley.
>   *Cassius.* Stand fast, Titinius; we must out and talk.
>   *Octavius.* Mark Antony, shall we give sign of battle?
>   *Antony.* No, Caesar, we will answer on their charge.
> Make forth; the generals would have some words.

This to the Elizabethans was a commonplace of stagecraft. Before scenery which paints realistically some defined locality, it must needs look absurd. But, the simpler convention accepted, Shakespeare sets for his audience a wider and more significant scene than any the scenic theater can compass. And, confronting the fighters, he states the theme, so to speak, of the play's last event, and gives it value, importance and dignity.

The whole act is constructed with great skill, each detail has its purpose and effect. But we must dismiss, even from our memories if possible, the *Scene ii, The same, the Field of Battle*; and *Scene iii, Another Part of the Field*, of the editors. What happens to begin with is this. Antony, Octavius and their powers departed, the talk between Brutus and Cassius over—it is (for us) their third and last, and a chill quiet talk; they feel they are under the shadow of defeat the stage is left empty. Then the silence is broken by the clattering *Alarum*, the symbol of a battle begun. Then back comes Brutus, but a very different Brutus.

> Ride, ride, Messala, ride, and give these bills
> Unto the legions on the other side.

Now a *Loud alarum*, which his voice must drown.

> Let them set on at once, for I perceive
> But cold demeanour in Octavius' wing,

And sudden push gives them the overthrow.
Ride, ride, Messala: let them all come down.

And he is gone as he came. In its sharp contrast it is a stirring passage, which restores to Brutus whatever dominance he may have lost. But it cannot be achieved if tension is relaxed and attention dissipated by the shifting of scenery, or by any superfluous embroidering of the action.

Remark further that to follow the course of the battle an audience must listen keenly, and they must be able to concentrate their minds on the speakers. When the defeat of Cassius is imminent, when Titinius tells him:

O Cassius! Brutus gave the word too early;
Who, having some advantage on Octavius,
Took it too eagerly: his soldiers fell to spoil,
Whilst we by Antony are all enclos'd.

the situation is made clear enough. But if we do not master it at this moment, the rest of the scene and its drama will go for next to nothing.

Now we have Cassius grasping the ensign he has seized from the coward who was running away with it (and, being Cassius, not content with that, he has killed the man), the very ensign the birds of ill omen had hovered over; and he makes as if to plant it defiantly, conspicuously in the ground.

This hill is far enough.

His death is of a piece with his whole reckless life. He kills himself because he will not wait another minute to verify the tale his bondman tells him of Titinius' capture. He ends passionately and desperately—but still grasping his standard. Even at this moment he is as harsh to Pindarus as Brutus is gentle to his boy Lucius and the bondman who serves him:

Come hither, sirrah:
In Parthia did I take thee prisoner;
And then I swore thee, saving of thy life,
That whatsoever I did bid thee do,
Thou shouldst attempt it.

His last words are as bare and ruthless.
Caesar, thou art reveng'd,
Even with the sword that kill'd thee.

Pindarus' four lines that follow may seem frigid and formal. But we need a breathing-space before we face the tragically ironic return of Titinius radiant with good news. The stagecraft of this entrance, as of others like it, belongs, we must (yet again) remember, to the Elizabethan theater, with its doors at the back, and its distance for an actor to advance, attention full on him. Entrance from the wing of a conventional scenic stage will be quite another matter.

> *Messala.* It is but change, Titinius; for Octavius
> Is overthrown by noble Brutus' power,
> As Cassius' legions are by Antony.
>   *Titinius.* These tidings will well comfort Cassius.
>   *Messala.* Where did you leave him?
>   *Titinius.* All disconsolate,
> With Pindarus his bondman, on this hill.
>   *Messala.* Is that not he that lies along the ground?
>   *Titinius.* He lies not like the living. O my heart!
>   *Messala.* Is not that he?
>   *Titinius.* No, this was he, Messala,
> But Cassius is no more.

Stage direction is embodied in dialogue. We have the decelerated arrival telling of relief from strain, the glance around the seemingly empty place; then the sudden swift single-syllabled line and its repetition, Titinius' dart forward, Messala's graver question, the dire finality of the answer.

We come to Titinius' death; and it is a legitimate query why, with two suicides to provide for, Shakespeare burdened himself with this third. The episode itself may have attracted him; the soldier crowning his dead chief with the garland of victory; then, as the innocent cause of his death, set not to survive it.[17] The death speech is fine, and the questioning sentences that begin it whip it to great poignancy. But neither here nor anywhere, we must admit, does Shakespeare show full understanding of the "Roman's part" and the strange faith that let him play it. His Romans go to their deaths stoically enough, but a little stockily too. Hamlet, later, will find the question arguable, and Macbeth will think a man a fool not to die fighting. Brutus and Cassius and Titinius, it is true, could hardly be made to argue the point here. But there is an abruptness and a sameness, and a certain emptiness, in the manner of these endings.

Another and technically a stronger reason for adding Titinius to the suicides, is that it is above all important Brutus' death should not come as an anticlimax to Cassius'. This episode helps provide against that danger, and the next scene makes escape from it sure.

The bodies are carried out in procession with due dignity, and again the effect of the empty stage keys us to expectancy. Then

Alarum. Enter Brutus, Messala, Cato, Lucilius and Flavius.
Enter soldiers and fight.

It is a noisy melee; so confused that, though we hear the voices of the leaders from its midst, Brutus disappears unnoticed. The scene has its touch of romance in young Cato's death, its dash of intrigue in Lucilius' trick. If these things are given value in performance, they knot up effectively the weakening continuity of theme, which, by its slacking, would leave the death of Brutus and the play's end a fag end instead of a full close.

Yet the effects of the last scene are in themselves most carefully elaborated. Hard upon the clattering excitement of the fight, and the flattering magnanimity of the triumphant Antony, comes into sight this little group of beaten and exhausted men, the torchlight flickering on their faces.[18]

> *Brutus.* Come, poor remains of friends, rest on this rock.
> *Clitus.* Statilius show'd the torch-light; but, my lord,
> He came not back: he is or ta'en or slain.
> *Brutus.* Sit thee down, Clitus: slaying is the word;
> It is a deed in fashion. . . .

They throw themselves down hopelessly; to wait—for what!—and to brood in a silence which Brutus hardly breaks by his whisper, first to Clitus, next to Dardanius. Then he paces apart while the two watch him and themselves whisper of the dreadful demand he made. He calls on Volumnius next, to find in him, not hope, only the instinctive human reluctance to admit an end. But his own end—and he knows and desires it—is here. Threatening low alarums vibrate beneath his calm, colorless speech. His followers cry to him to save himself, and a like cry from far off pierces that still insistent alarum, and they echo it again. Well, these men have life and purpose left in them; let them go. He praises and humors their loyalty. But, at his command, they leave him. The end is very near.

But Shakespeare himself is not yet at the end of his resources, nor of his constant care to weave the action in a living texture, to give the least of its figures life. What, till this moment, do we know about Strato? He makes his first appearance in the battle; he is Brutus' body-servant, it seems. A thick-skinned sort of fellow; while the others counted the cost of their ruin, he had fallen asleep. Twelve lines or so (he himself speaks just seven) not only make a living figure of him but keep Brutus self-enlightening to the last. For the very last note struck out of this stoic, whose high principles could not stop short of murder, is one of gentleness.

> *Brutus.* I prithee, Strato, stay thou by thy lord:
> Thou art a fellow of a good respect;
> Thy life hath had some smatch of honour in it:
> Hold then my sword, and turn away thy face,
> While I do run upon it. Wilt thou, Strato?
> > *Strato.* Give me your hand first: fare you well, my lord.
> > *Brutus.* Farewell, good Strato. . . .

The man's demand for a handshake, the master's response to it;—how much of Shakespeare's greatness lies in these little things, and in the love of his art that never found them too little for his care! Then Brutus closes his account.

> Caesar, now be still:
> I kill'd not thee with half so good a will.

In silence on both sides the thing is done. Nor does Strato stir while the loud alarum and retreat are sounded; he does not even turn at the conquerors' approach—Antony, Octavius and the already reconciled Messala and Lucilius, who only see by the light of the torches this solitary figure standing there.

Nor have we even yet reached the play's formal close, the ceremonial lifting of the body, the apostrophe to the dead, and that turning towards the living future which the conditions of the Elizabethan stage inevitably and happily prescribed. Chief place is given here, as we have noted, to Octavius, Caesar's heir and—if Shakespeare may have had it in mind—the conqueror-to-be of his fellow-conqueror. But we have first a bitter-sweet exchange between Strato and Messala. They—and they know it—are commoner clay than their master who lies here; no vain heroism for them. Next Antony speaks, and makes sportsmanlike amends to his dead enemy.

The play is a masterpiece of Elizabethan stagecraft, and the last act, from this point of view, especially remarkable; but only by close analysis can its technical virtues be made plain. Within the powerful ease of its larger rhythm, the constant, varied ebb and flow and interplay of purpose, character and event give it richness of dramatic life, and us the sense of its lifelikeness.

NOTES

9. But this might often be as true, if in another degree, of the individual scene.

10. Here, incidentally, is an instance of an effect made for its own sake and in the confidence that no awkward questions will be asked. The immediate suggestion is that Brutus and Ligarius go straight to the conspirators, thence with them to Caesar and the Senate House. It is left mere suggestion and not further defined, for Portia has to be told of the conspiracy "by and by," and, when we next see her, the suggestion—still mere suggestion—is that she has been told. But Shakespeare

knows that no questions will be asked as long as the effects are spaced out, if distractions intervene and positive contradiction is avoided.

11. Unless every clearance of the stage is to mark a division of scenes, they are, of course, but one. No particular change of location is implied. Upon the question of the act-division here, see also page 381.

12. For an excellent analysis of this passage see MacCullum's *Shakespeare's Roman Plays*, quoted by Furness. And for the effect of the servant's entrance see, as before noted, R. G. Moulton's *Shakespeare as Dramatic Artist*.

13. And later, he will propose to his colleagues Octavius and Lepidus that they all three consider "How to cut off some charge in legacies."

14. A scene which the average modern producer takes great care to cut.

15. The Chorus in *Henry V* could not apologize enough for the theater's failure to show armies in being. But by a little music, this cunning of speech and action, and a bold acceptance of convention, these "ciphers to this great account" can be made to work well enough upon the "imaginary forces" of the audience.

16. "Sleep again, Lucius," would point, if nothing else did, to the drawing-together of the curtains of the inner stage upon the scene. Where Varro and Claudius have been lying is a question. They enter, of course, upon the main stage. Brutus apparently points to the inner stage with "Lie in my tent and sleep." They offer to keep watch where they are, *i.e.* by the door. I am inclined to think that they lie down there, too. This would not only make the business with the ghost better, but it would bring the scene's final piece of action upon the center stage and give it breadth and importance.

17. Shakespeare finds this more clearly put in Plutarch than he leaves it in the play.

18. It has been held (I do not stress the point) that Elizabethan outdoor performances were timed to end near twilight. In that case the torchlight would prove doubly effective here.

⎯◦∿∘◦⎯   ⎯◦∿∘◦⎯   ⎯◦∿∘◦⎯

1947—W.H. Auden.
"Julius Caesar," from *Lectures on Shakespeare*

W.H. Auden was one of the great English poets of the twentieth century. He also wrote essays, dramas, a libretto for Igor Stravinsky, and other works. He won the Pulitzer Prize for his book-length poem *The Age of Anxiety*.

(15 January 1947)

Tonight I hope to reassure the less musical, because I'm going to talk and talk and talk. *Julius Caesar* is one of the best known and most performed of Shakespeare's plays. Like *Hamlet*, the play is a puzzle. It doesn't conform to the idea of Aristotelian tragedy in presenting a noble man with a conspicuous flaw, nor to Elizabethan melodrama in presenting a conspicuous villain. Some critics think Shakespeare combined two plays in *Julius Caesar*. Certainly he combined two plots. Shakespeare's two significant tragedies preceding *Julius Caesar*—we can forget *Titus Andronicus*—are *Richard III* and *Romeo and Juliet*.

It was natural in the thirties of this century for theatrical directors to make Caesar a Fascist dictator and the conspirators noble liberals. That's a misreading, I think, but there are things to be said for it. It draws attention to *Julius Caesar* as a historical play, and it helps us bear in mind Shakespeare's continuing interest in the genre. The last play he wrote was a historical play, *Henry VIII*, an excellent collaboration with Fletcher. In the later Roman plays, history is superficial in the sense that it could be changed without changing the characters. But time and history are essential in *Julius Caesar*. What is Shakespeare's interest in writing the play? He sets himself the problem, in depicting Roman society, of whether he can understand Roman history and society as he has English history. At that time, people in Europe grew up more with Roman history, but it is still difficult for Shakespeare. There is a poetic problem alongside the technical one: what kind of rhetoric must the characters use? How must they speak? In the English chronicle plays, characters speak romantically out of the Herod character of the miracle plays and the *miles gloriosus* of Marlowe. *Julius Caesar* is unique for a plain, direct, bleak, public style of rhetoric. The language of the characters often consists of monosyllables. Brutus, for example, at the end of his first meeting with Cassius, says,

> For this time I will leave you.
> To-morrow, if you please to speak to me,
> I will come home to you; or if you will,
> Come home to me, and I will wait for you. (I.ii.307–10)

Brutus says to his servant Lucius, "I should not urge thy duty past thy might. / I know young bloods look for a time of rest" (IV.iii.261–62). Calphurnia says, in warning Caesar not to leave his house,

> The noise of battle hurtled in the air,
> Horses did neigh, and dying men did groan,
> And ghosts did shriek and squeal about the streets. (II.ii.22–24)

Contrast this speech with its imitation in Hamlet, when Horatio says,

> In the most high and palmy state of Rome,
> A little ere the mightiest Julius fell,
> The graves stood tenantless, and the sheeted dead
> Did squeak and gibber in the Roman streets. (I.i.113–16)

Julius Caesar has great relevance to our time, though it is gloomier, because it is about a society that is doomed. Our society is not doomed, but in such immense danger that the relevance is great. Octavius only succeeded in giving Roman society a 400-year reprieve. It was a society doomed not by the evil passions of selfish individuals, because such passions always exist, but by an intellectual and spiritual failure of nerve that made the society incapable of coping with its situation, which is why the noble Brutus is even more at sea in the play than the unscrupulous and brutal Antony. The Roman-Hellenic world failed to evolve a religious pattern that was capable of grasping the world, of making sense of what was happening. The Platonic Aristotelian politics of the good life proved ineffective for the public world, and Stoic-Epicurean thought proved incapable of saving the individual. The play presents three political responses to this failure. The crowd-master, the man of destiny, Caesar. The man who temporarily rides the storm, Antony. And Caesar's real successor, the man who is to establish Roman order for a time, Octavius. Brutus, who keeps himself independent, is the detached and philosophic individual.

Julius Caesar begins with a crowd scene. First things in Shakespeare are always important. There are three types of groups of people: societies, communities, and crowds. A society is something I can belong to, a community is something I can join, a crowd is something I add to. A society is defined by its function. A string quartet, for example, is a society with a specific function, to play works of music composed for a string quartet. It has a specific size, and you cannot change its size without changing the society. An individual is irreplaceable in his function to his society.

A community is an association of people with a common love. If you get a collection of people all of whom, say, love music, they form a community of music lovers. A cello player in a string quartet, for example, who hates music but plays because he must eat and playing a cello is all he knows, is a member of a society. He is not a member of the community of music lovers. A community has no definite size. If what they love is good—for example, God—the optimum size of a community is infinite. If what they love is bad—for example, marijuana—the optimum size is zero. In a community, also, "I" precedes "we."

The third form of a plurality of people is a crowd. Its members neither belong to nor join it, but merely add to it. The members of a crowd have nothing in common except togetherness. The individual is a contradiction in a crowd. The "we" precedes the "I." In itself the crowd has no function. When does a crowd or a mass or public develop? (1) When there are an insufficient number of societies and the individual can't find a meaningful function, so that he feels like a cog in a machine, or if he cannot belong to a society—he's unemployed, for example. (2) If communities disappear, individuals cease to love anything in particular and become incapable of making a choice between loves. Why can't they choose? In order to choose, there must be a number of values in terms of which a choice becomes meaningful. Lose those values, and one becomes incapable of a choice between loves. Combine that condition with an absence of society, and individuals become members of the crowd or the public. It has nothing whatever to do with education. Knowing a lot does not make one believe in anything. Knowledge can't make people believe in a society or give them a function in it. The educated and the rich can become members of the crowd and the public.

Describing the characteristics of the public, Kierkegaard writes in *The Present Age*:

> The real moment in time and the real situation being simultaneous with real people, each of whom is something: that is what helps to sustain the individual. But the existence of a public produces neither a situation nor simultaneity. . . . The man who has no opinion of an event at the actual moment accepts the opinion of the majority, or if he is quarrelsome, of the minority. But it must be remembered that both majority and minority are real people, and that is why the individual is assisted by adhering to them. A public, on the contrary, is an abstraction. . . . A people, an assembly or a man can change to such an extent that one may say: they are no longer the same; a public on the other hand can become the very opposite and still be the same—a public. . . . A public is neither a nation, nor a generation, nor a community, nor a society, nor these particular men, for all these are only what they are through the concrete; no single person who belongs to the public makes a real commitment; for some hours of the day, perhaps, he belongs to the public—at moments when he is nothing else, since when he really is what he is he does not form part of the public. Made up of such individuals, of individuals at the moments when they are nothing, a public is a kind of gigantic something, an abstract and deserted void which is everything and nothing. But on this basis any one can arrogate to himself a public, and just as the Roman Church chimerically extended its frontiers by appointing bishops *in partibus infidelium*, so a public is something which every one can claim, and even a drunken sailor exhibiting a "peep-show" has dialectically absolutely the same right to a public as the greatest man.

Kierkegaard says that if he tried "to imagine the public as a particular person,"

> I should perhaps think of one of the Roman emperors, a large well-fed figure, suffering from boredom, looking only for the sensual intoxication of laughter, since the divine gift of wit is not earthly enough. And so for a change he wanders about, indolent rather than bad, but with a negative desire to dominate. Every one who has read the classical

authors knows how many things a Caesar could try out in order to kill time.

Kierkegaard then turns to the relationship of the public and the press, the public's "dog": "In the same way the public keeps a dog to amuse it. That dog is literary scum. If there is some one superior to the rest, perhaps even a great man, the dog is set on him and the fun begins." Eventually the public tires and says the press may stop, but "the public is unrepentant, for it is not they who own the dog—they only subscribe."

With the proper gift, a man can turn the crowd into a mob—in other words, a passionate crowd. The mob is a pseudosociety that sets out to do something, but what it wishes to do is often both negative and general. The Cinna the Poet incident in *Julius Caesar* provides a very good illustration.

> *3. Pleb*. Your name, sir, truly.
> *Cin*. Truly, my name is Cinna.
> *1. Pleb*. Tear him to pieces! He's a conspirator.
> *Cin*. I am Cinna the poet! I am Cinna the poet!
> *4. Pleb*. Tear him for his bad verses! Tear him for his bad verses!
> *Cin*. I am not Cinna the conspirator.
> *4. Pleb*. It is no matter; his name's Cinna! Pluck but his name out of his heart, and turn him going.
> *3. Pleb*. Tear him, tear him! Come, brands, ho! firebrands! To Brutus', to Cassius'! Burn all! (III.iii.28–42)

The function of the mob, to destroy, is general. It is incapable of making differentiations upon which a society depends.

The negative impulse is easier for an orator to instill in a crowd. A crowd is passive, and therefore notoriously fickle. In *Henry VI, Part Two*, during Jack Cade's rebellion, both Clifford and Jack Cade speak (IV.viii), and the crowd changes its mind with each speech. In *Julius Caesar*, Brutus speaks—the crowd approves. Antony speaks—"We'll hear him, we'll follow him, we'll die with him!" (III.ii.214). A comparison of the scenes from the two plays shows Shakespeare's dramatic development. In *Henry VI*, Clifford and Cade both speak in the same way. In *Julius Caesar*, the speeches of Brutus and Antony are differentiated, so we can see not only that the crowd is fickle, but also that Brutus doesn't understand how to move them, because he tries to allay their feelings, while Antony does understand how to move them, because he tries to excite their feelings—a successful technique. Directors should make the citizens supporting Brutus different from those supporting Antony.

In a community, defective lovers require political leaders. Shakespeare's successful leaders are Henry IV, Henry V, Richard III, Caesar, Antony. His unsuccessful leaders are Richard II, Henry VI, Brutus. A successful leader needs the theatrical gift of arousing emotions, of moving and persuading others, without appearing self-interested and moved himself. Just before the assassination, when Artemidorus tries to press his suit because it's one that "touches Caesar nearer" than the others, Caesar replies, "What touches us ourself shall be last serv'd" (III.1.7–8). Richard III first refuses a crown. Caesar, Casca tells us, twice puts back the crown Antony offers him—reluctantly though, he wants it a bit. Henry V and Antony assume a bluntness of manner. Antony tells the crowd,

> I come not, friends, to steal away your hearts.
> I am no orator, as Brutus is,
> But (as you know me all) a plain blunt man
> That love my friend. (III.ii.221–24)

President Roosevelt used his smile and cigarette holder to show his disinterest, Churchill both uses gestures and keeps his hands in his pockets. Obviously one shouldn't sneer at such devices. A good leader understands that emotion precedes effective action. A study of anthropology, for example, is not a good beginning for eradicating race prejudice—one must arouse a passion for treating one's neighbor as one's self. A teacher must be a clown and arouse in his pupils a love of knowledge—the more love there is in the pupil, the less work for the teacher—he mustn't annoy or discourage the pupil. "Disingenuous compliances," Dr. Johnson called it. The love of power in a good politician— one whom one respects—is subservient to his zeal for a just society. Power is uppermost for a bad politician, a demagogue. He is like a writer who writes because he wants to be famous, rather than because he wants to write well. A good politician and a good teacher labor to abolish their own vocations.

The Peloponnesian War created a vacuum by the end of Greek society. The Third Punic War enlarged Roman society and created classes, the *Lumpenproletariat*. As Hegel wrote, "Minerva's owl takes flight in the evening," philosophy always arrives too late to give advice. The Greek's ethical cosmology formulated by Plato and Aristotle held that God, the unmoved Mover, and Nature are co-eternal and unrelated. In Aristotle, matter, in an effort to escape from the innate disorder of its temporal flux, falls in love with the Mover. In Plato an intermediary party, the Demiurge, loves the Ideas and then imposes them on matter. Matter is the limiting cause of evil, and the first task of man is to contemplate Ideas and will the good. It was assumed that sin is ignorance and that to know the good is to will it. But what can be done about the ignorant who are sinful, or those who are sinful because, even with knowledge of the good, they do not will it? Impose order on them. But if the way of wisdom is to withdraw from the temporal flux, how can the wise impose such order and control society? The best thing is to have the philosopher get hold of the king and advise him. Plato tried that, however, and it didn't work.

Ancient political philosophy is either archaistic or futuristic. Either the philosopher has to discover a timeless order, or a Hercules-savior must step in to save society from change. Aristotle's practical observation of a small middle class as the best rulers doesn't tell how society can be kept from growing and therefore changing. The successful man of action tended to be given a demiurgic, semidivine status. With the decline of the city-state and the development of agrarian Rome, the ideal of a wise man became detachment. The ideal took two slightly different forms, the philosophy of Epicurus, which Cassius professes, and the philosophy of the Stoics, such as Zeno, with which Brutus associates himself.

The man of action in the play is Caesar, the savior on horseback who appears to have arrived. Having become a legend, Caesar has to live up to the role. "Beware the ides of March," the Soothsayer tells him. Caesar's answer, "He is a dreamer. Let us leave him. Pass." (I.ii.24–25), illustrates the necessity for confident speech in a ruler. Such speech may not necessarily be a manifestation of pride, though it may become so. A general or an assertive leader in a time of sudden financial depression, for example, must give people the impression that he has no fear, or they'll lose heart, too. Like Caesar with the Soothsayer, he must exaggerate his confidence. Great men in politics like flatterers to give them confidence, which they can then radiate back. Sometimes they lose their sense of intuition and fail, a point that Caesar has perhaps reached. It is unfortunate for a ruler to be fatalistic, to make a religion of necessity, as Caesar begins to do when he rejects all warnings, "Seeing," as he says, "that death, a necessary end, / Will come when it will come" (II.ii.36–37). The most successful know the role fortune plays, they believe in the stars.

Antony has a sanguine character and he's also politically quite skillful, though not as skillful as he thinks he is. In a crisis he's in his element. He's in politics for fun, he craves excitement. He's not good at slow, patient plotting. After he has successfully turned the plebians into a mob, he says, almost indifferently,

Now let it work. Mischief, thou art afoot,
Take thou what course thou wilt. (III.ii.265–66)

Octavius or Caesar would never make such a playboy remark. Antony's bored. Later we'll see the tragedy of a bored man and bored woman. Antony impolitically gives himself away to Octavius in revealing his feelings about Lepidus:

Octavius, I have seen more days than you;
And though we lay these honours on this man

To ease ourselves of divers sland'rous loads
He shall but bear them as the ass bears gold. (IV.i.118–21)

Octavius would never talk that way. He is far too guarded and calculating, as he demonstrates in his sudden decision to take the right wing just before the battle of Philippi:

> *Ant.* Octavius, lead your battle softly on
> Upon the left hand of the even field.
>   *Oct.* Upon the right hand I. Keep thou the left.
>   *Ant.* Why do you cross me in this exigent?'
>   *Oct.* I do not cross you; but I will do so. (V.i.16–20)

Octavius is a very cold fish.

Cassius is a choleric man—a General Patton. He is passionate, short-tempered, sentimental. He is also politically shrewd. Before the assassination, he sees that Antony will be dangerous to the conspiracy and argues that he should be killed. Later he tries to conciliate Antony—"Your voice shall be as strong as any man's / In the disposing of new dignities" (III.i.177–78)—at the same time that he warns Brutus of the danger of letting Antony speak at Caesar's funeral. He also doesn't want to fight at Philippi, "to set / Upon one battle all our liberties" (V.i.74–75), as Brutus does, and he probably has the better military knowledge. He is a follower of Epicurus, as he says explicitly at the end of the play (V.i.76–77). Epicurean thought was largely determinist and materialist, it sought to achieve the condition of imperturbability, *ataraxia*, it was moderate, and it rejected, as Lucretius especially did, the irrational and the superstitious as a destroyer of life. Its aim was to show that life was rational and that there was nothing to fear. Cassius is thus a comic character, because his emotional temperament is quite opposite to his Epicurean philosophy. Early on in the play he says that "the fault, dear Brutus, is not in our stars, / But in ourselves" (I.ii.140–41), and when Casca becomes superstitious about a thunderstorm, Cassius calmly and learnedly interprets the storm as an encouragement to the conspirators to act against Caesar (I.iii.57–99). Before the battle of Philippi, however, Cassius becomes superstitious:

> You know that I held Epicurus strong
> And his opinion. Now I change my mind
> And partly credit things that do presage. (V.i.76–78)

And his desperate suicide is based on a misinterpretation.

There are no lymphatic characters in the play, "men that are fat," as Caesar says, "Sleek-headed men, and such as sleep a-nights" (I.ii.192–93). It's too rough a time. Brutus is a melancholic. "I am not gamesome," he tells Cassius, "I do lack some part / Of that quick spirit that is in Antony" (I.ii.28–29), and he tells his wife Portia that she is as dear to him "as are the ruddy drops / That visit my sad heart" (II.i.289–90). Brutus at the same time strives for the Stoic virtue of ataraxia, of freedom from disturbance and perturbation. He says to the conspirators, to encourage and calm them,

> Good gentlemen, look fresh and merrily.
> Let not our looks put on our purposes,
> But bear it as our Roman actors do,
> With untir'd spirits and formal constancy. (II.i.224–27)

His detachment is most evident during the quarrel with Cassius, when he doesn't reveal that Portia has just died until he and Cassius have reconciled:

> *Cass.* I did not think you could have been so angry.
> *Bru.* O Cassius, I am sick of many griefs.
> *Cass.* Of your philosophy you make no use
> If you give place to accidental evils.
> *Bru.* No man bears sorrow better. Portia is dead. (IV.iii.143–47)

When Messala enters with hints of news about his wife, he pretends not to know about her death in order to serve as an example to his troops.

> *Mes.* Then like a Roman bear the truth I tell;
> For certain she is dead, and by strange manner.
> *Bru.* Why, farewell, Portia. We must die, Messala.
> With meditating that she must die once,
> I have the patience to endure it now.
> *Mes.* Even so great men great losses should endure.
> *Cass.* I have as much of this in art as you,
> But yet my nature could not bear it so. (IV.iii.187–95)

Brutus maintains the same calm in the presence of Caesar's ghost:

> *Bru.* Well; then I shall see thee again?
> *Ghost.* Ay, at Philippi.
> *Bru.* Why, I will see thee at Philippi then.
> [*Exit Ghost.*]
> Now I have taken heart thou vanishest,
> Ill spirit, I would hold more talk with thee. (IV.iii.284–88)

The one thing that can throw the detached man into perturbation, as Brutus shows, is the prospect of action:

> Since Cassius first did whet me against Caesar,
> I have not slept.
> Between the acting of a dreadful thing
> And the first motion, all the interim is
> Like a phantasma or a hideous dream. (II.i.61–65)

There is really a will in Brutus to commit suicide, and when he finally does so, he has to run on someone else's sword to establish contact with others.

Cassius is childishly envious—I swim better! The conspirators don't really have a good motive. Brutus, as a man of thought and feeling, wants to play the man of action. He is haunted by two ghosts. The invisible ghost that haunts him is his ancestor Brutus, who drove Tarquin "from the streets of Rome" (II.i.53–54)—he thinks of him just before he speaks of the "phantasma" that precedes the taking of action. The visible ghost that haunts Brutus is Caesar's. Brutus really has nothing against Caesar, "no personal cause to spurn at him" (II.i.11), and nothing has happened that he condemns. He kills a man he is fond of, a man of action whom he can never replace. Brutus and Cassius are Shakespeare's criticism of the ideal of detachment, an ideal that ends up in an absorption with the idea of death, and an ideal that is ultimately suicidal. Toynbee writes in *A Study of History* that the "logical goal" of Epicurean and Stoic *ataraxia* was "self-annihilation."

We can see in A. E. Housman's poetry a good contemporary example of the morbid outcome of the ideal of detachment. In one of the poems in *A Shropshire Lad*, he writes,

> From far, from eve and morning
>   And yon twelve-winded sky,
> The stuff of life to knit me
>   Blew hither: here am I.
>
> Now—for a breath I tarry
>   Nor yet disperse apart—
> Take my hand quick and tell me,
>   What have you in your heart.
>
> Speak now, and I will answer;
>   How shall I help you, say;
> Ere to the wind's twelve quarters
>   I take my endless way.

In another poem, which refers to Rome, Housman writes,

On Wenlock Edge the wood's in trouble,
    His forest fleece the Wrekin heaves;
The gale, it plies the saplings double,
    And thick on Severn snow the leaves.

'Twould blow like this through holt and hanger
    When Uricon the city stood:
'Tis the old wind in the old anger,
    But then it threshed another wood.

Then, 'twas before my time, the Roman
    At yonder heaving hill would stare:
The blood that warms an English yeoman,
    The thoughts that hurt him, they were there.

There, like the wind through woods in riot,
    Through him the gale of life blew high;
The tree of man was never quiet:
    Then 'twas the Roman, now 'tis I.

The gale, it plies the saplings double,
    It blows so hard, 'twill soon be gone:
To-day the Roman and his trouble
    Are ashes under Uricon.

Time is up, and what's more you're not likely to enjoy yourself if you overstay
your welcome!

Epictetus argued that the peace Caesar can bring is limited in nature, but that
philosophers can give peace in all:

Behold now, Caesar seems to provide us with profound peace, there
are no wars any longer, nor battles, no brigandage on a large scale, nor
piracy, but at any hour we may travel by land, or sail from the rising
of the sun to its setting. Can he, then, at all provide us with peace
from fever too, and from shipwreck too, and from fire, or earthquake,
or lightning? Come, can he give us peace from love? He cannot.
From sorrow? From envy? He cannot—from absolutely none of these
things. But the doctrine of the philosophers promises to give us peace
from these troubles too. And what does it say? "Men, if you heed me,
wherever you may be, whatever you may be doing, you will feel no pain,

no anger, no compulsion, no hindrance, but you will pass your lives in tranquillity and in freedom from every disturbance." When a man has this kind of peace proclaimed to him, not by Caesar—why, how could *he* possibly proclaim it?—but proclaimed by God through the reason, is he not satisfied, when he is alone?

The detachment of Stoic philosophy cannot really admit love or pity, you must never sacrifice eternal calm, though you must do your best to help your fellow man. What are the modern forms of detachment? Professionalism—keep at the job. And go to psychoanalysts for a perfect personality.

Brutus is related to Hamlet. Hamlet knows he's in despair, but Brutus and other characters in *Julius Caesar* don't know. In *The Sickness Unto Death*, Kierkegaard emphasizes that unconscious despair is the most extreme form of despair, and he sees it as a condition of paganism. He praises the great "aesthetic" achievements of pagan societies, but rejects the pagan's aesthetic definition of spirit:

> No, it is not the aesthetic definition of spiritlessness which furnishes the scale for judging what is despair and what is not; the definition which must be used is the ethico-religious: either spirit / or the negative lack of spirit, spiritlessness. Every human existence which is not conscious of itself as spirit, or conscious of itself before God as spirit, every human existence which is not thus grounded transparently in God but obscurely reposes or terminates in some abstract universality (state, nation, etc.), or in obscurity about itself takes its faculties merely as active powers, without in a deeper sense being conscious whence it has them, which regards itself as an inexplicable something which is to be understood from without—every such existence, whatever it accomplishes, though it be the most amazing exploit, whatever it explains, though it were the whole of existence, however intensely it enjoys life aesthetically—every such existence is after all despair. It was this the old theologians meant when they talked about the virtues of the pagans being splendid vices. They meant that the most inward experience of the pagan was despair, that the pagan was not conscious of himself before God as spirit.

"Hence it came about," Kierkegaard continues,

> . . . that the pagans judged self-slaughter so lightly, yea, even praised it, notwithstanding that for the spirit it is the most decisive sin, that to break out of existence in this way is rebellion against God. The pagan lacked the spirit's definition of the self, therefore he expressed such a judgment of *self*-slaughter—and this the same pagan did who condemned with moral severity theft, unchastity, etc. . . . . The point in self-slaughter, that it is a crime against God, entirely escapes the pagan.

One cannot say, therefore, that the self-slaughter was despair, which
would be a thoughtless hysteron proteron; one must say that the fact
that the pagan judged self-slaughter as he did was despair.

T. S. Eliot writes, in "Coriolan,"

Cry what shall I cry?
All flesh is grass:
. . . .
Mother mother
Here is a row of family portraits, dingy busts, all looking
    remarkably Roman,
Remarkably like each other, lit up successively by the flare
Of a sweaty torchbearer, yawning.
O hidden under the . . . Hidden under the . . . Where the
    dove's foot rested and locked for a moment,
A still moment, a repose of noon, under the upper
    branches of noon's widest tree
Under the breast feather stirred by the small wind after noon
There the cyclamen spreads its wings, there the clematis
    droops over the lintel
O mother (not among these busts, all correctly inscribed)
I a tired head among these heads
Necks strong to bear them
Noses to break the wind. . . .

⚬⚬⚬⚬⚬⚬⚬⚬⚬

1951—Harold C. Goddard.
"Julius Caesar," from *The Meaning of Shakespeare*

Harold C. Goddard was head of the Department of English Literature
at Swarthmore College. His books include *Chaucer's Legend of Good
Women* and the two-volume set *The Meaning of Shakespeare*.

I

Julius Caesar is a bridge. That it is a bridge between Shakespeare's Histories and
his Tragedies has often been pointed out. It is neither quite the one, it is said, nor
quite the other. Undoubtedly this is a suggestive way of caking the play. But held
too rigidly, this view of it rests on the assumption that *Hamlet* is Shakespeare's

first real tragedy, *Romeo and Juliet* being ruled out because of the part that accident plays in its plot, and *Julius Caesar* because its protagonist is not its titular hero. I have given what I hope are sound reasons for questioning this attitude toward *Romeo and Juliet*. To exclude *Julius Caesar* on account of its title is quite as unjustifiable. It is to subordinate its spirit and total effect to the demands of mere classification and definition. If the story of Brutus is not tragedy, it is hard to know what it is.

Nevertheless, *Julius Caesar* is a bridge—in a far deeper sense. By way of it Shakespeare finally passes from one world to another. Or, rather, he shifts the center of his universe. *Julius Caesar* is his Copernican revolution. There are plenty of premonitions in his earlier works of the coming change: in the last act of *Richard III*, in *A Midsummer-Night's Dream*, throughout *Romeo and Juliet* especially, and in scattered scenes and passages of other plays. But it is in *Julius Caesar* that the poet finally crosses the Rubicon.

For he is superstitious grown of late,

says Cassius of Caesar.

Caesar, I never stood on ceremonies,
Yet now they fright me,

says Calphurnia.

You know that I held Epicurus strong,
And his opinion; now I change my mind,
And partly credit things that do presage,

says Cassius near the end. These are not coincidences. It is not that Shakespeare was growing superstitious, or beginning to be frightened by "ceremonies." Nor on the other hand had he ever held Epicurus strong. But he too at this time was tending in a profounder sense than Cassius to give more and more credit to things that do presage.

He is a dreamer; let us leave him: pass,

says Caesar, dismissing the Soothsayer who called out to him "Beware the ides of March." The event showed that he dismissed him at his peril. Shakespeare was growing more convinced that we neglect dreams and dreamers at our peril. He was a humanist, to be sure, and remained one to the end of his days. But from *Julius Caesar* on, his greater characters and greater plays are touched with the dream-light and dream-darkness of something that as certainly transcends the merely human as do the prophets and sibyls of Michelangelo. There were presentiments and visions in *Romeo and Juliet*. But this play is fairly saturated with omens and ironies, portents and wonders. There were fairies in *A Midsummer-Night's Dream*, and ghosts in *Richard III*. But the ghost of Julius Caesar is a being of another order. Brief as are his three utterances, just sixteen words in all, he speaks with a new accent. And it is not the accent of tradition, nor of folklore however well assimilated. Nor of the theater. It is the accent, we instantly know, of something that has happened in Shakespeare's own soul. The secret of human life, it seems to say, lies beyond that life as well as within it. The ghost of Julius Caesar was as truly a part of Brutus as it was of Caesar. "The soul knows no persons." That is why a play whose protagonist is one of the two is appropriately named for the other.

In spite of this new note, *Julius Caesar* is tied to the plays that precede it—and to those that follow—as intimately as anything Shakespeare ever wrote. Which makes it a bridge in a still further sense.

Brutus is one more study of a man who undertakes a role for which nature never intended him. In this respect he is a direct descendant of Richard II, Antonio, Romeo, and, in a somewhat different sense, of Hal. Often the best summary of a play of Shakespeare's is some line or couplet in the next or a closely succeeding play that seems hidden there by the poet as if on purpose.

He would be crown'd,

says Brutus in soliloquy, of Caesar;

How that might change his nature, there's the question.

That was the crucial question about Prince Henry, which *Henry IV* was written to ask and *Henry V* to answer—the question Falstaff failed to ask himself in time. The young Henry V "killed" his old friend when he rejected him, putting what he held to be the public good above personal feeling. Brutus did precisely the same thing when he assassinated Caesar. The analogy is startling. Sir John and the mighty Julius make strange bedfellows, but their situations are so similar that it is easy to imagine Falstaff saying to himself at the moment he was rejected, in whatever would have been its Falstaffian equivalent: "Et tu, Henry!" Indeed, that is just what his silence does say.

But if Henry V at the end of *Henry IV* has an affinity with Brutus, he has a deeper one with Caesar himself in *Henry V*. (His affinity with Alexander the Great, Shakespeare himself more than hints at, as we have seen, through the mouth of Fluellen.) Far apart as the two men seem, the common theme of the two plays to which their names give the titles is imperialism. The point is that we see the imperialist at different stages of his career. A conqueror at the outset is different from a conqueror at the end.

The unflattering character of the portrait Shakespeare draws of Julius Caesar is notorious. The name and spirit of Caesar ring as imperially through the play as they do through history. But the trembling epileptic the poet depicts seems like a parody of the figure that shook the ancient world. Historical critics will say that Shakespeare is following Plutarch. He is, but what of it? He had no need of Plutarch to teach him what a "strong" man becomes in his last days or at death. He had already drawn unforgettably the final hours or moments of Cardinal Beaufort, of Warwick, of Richard III and others, to demonstrate that the nemesis of worldly strength is spiritual weakness (a truth that need not be labored in a generation that has witnessed the downfall of so many men of this type). And he was to go on doing it. "To be called into a huge sphere, and not to be seen to move in't, are the holes where eyes should be, which pitifully disaster the cheeks." That description of a weakling (Lepidus) in his prime is a good characterization of this strong man (Caesar) on the edge of death.

> Now does he feel his title
> Hang loose about him, like a giant's robe
> Upon a dwarfish thief.

Those words concerning Macbeth in his decline fit Shakespeare's Caesar in his. If the poet had given us a picture of Caesar's youth, it might have been as fascinating as that of Hal, or, of his prime, as masterful as that achieved by Bernard Shaw. But his purpose here is different, and it bears an interesting relation to the story that was cut short by the death of Henry V. If Henry had lived and held France, it is obvious in what direction he would have developed. But he died, and the chief defect of Shakespeare's story is its failure to give any account of the circumstances of his death. At his funeral, however, the poet has Bedford call upon Henry's ghost and link it specifically with Julius Caesar:

> Henry the Fifth! thy ghost I invocate:
> Prosper this realm, keep it from civil broils!
> Combat with adverse planets in the heavens!
> A far more glorious star thy soul will make,
> Than Julius Caesar, or bright—

At which moment, a messenger enters to announce the beginning of the end of Henry's conquests. It is easy to see what happened in Shakespeare's imagination. In a dream, a character will sometimes grow blurry and begin to undergo a change just as another character enters. What has happened is that the original

character has split in two. So here. It is as if after the "death" in the poet's mind
of Henry V the split indicated by the hyphenated name Hal-Henry widened still
further, and what was originally one man with a dual nature became two men,
Brutus and Caesar. So regarded, the play in which the two men figure is a sort
of metempsychosis of Henry V.

II

As in life, there are characters in Shakespeare about whom men hold
antipodal opinions. Brutus is among them. There are those who consider him
one of the most noble and lovable figures the poet ever created. Others cannot
conceal their scorn for him. He was a fool, they say, an egotist, an unconscionable
prig. If this be true, it is a bit odd that almost everyone in the play seems to think
highly of him. "This was the noblest Roman of them all," Antony declares. And
Antony was Brutus' enemy. "His life was gentle," he goes on to say, and we get
the impression that, until the idea of assassinating Caesar infected it, that life
was a pattern of domestic and civic virtue. Integrity was its keynote, a balanced
mixture of the elements. And Antony, as if bent on surpassing what he has
already said, shifts at the end from a Roman to a human standard. He imagines
Nature standing up, proud of her masterpiece, declaring to all the world, "This
was a man!"

And yet the detractors of Brutus have a case. They are merely talking about
another person. They have turned their attention from the man Nature made
to the man Brutus marred. There is little evidence that Brutus was particularly
conscious of his own virtue until he began to consider Caesar's assassination.
Then he had to exaggerate his own goodness to compensate for the evil that
he contemplated. After which, Nature's formula no longer fully characterizes
him. We are compelled to add four other words to her original four: "This was a
man"—*and Brutus knew it*. And there lies the tragedy, for a man should have no
more acquaintance with his virtue than a woman with her beauty.

The shadow on the wall, or the reflection in a distorting mirror, of the most
nearly perfect human figure ever created can be grotesque. Those who disparage
Brutus are talking of his shadow.

Tell me, good Brutus, can you see your face?

asks Cassius on the occasion when he first hints at the assassination.

> *Bru.*: No, Cassius; for the eye sees not itself
> But by reflection, by some other things.
> *Cass.*: 'Tis just;
> And it is very much lamented, Brutus,
> That you have no such mirrors as will turn

Your hidden worthiness into your eye,
That you might see your shadow.

It is a case where the speaker uses a word in one sense and Shakespeare in another. Shadow! it evokes ominous memories of Richard, the Shadow King; and certainly the envious Cassius was not the one to offer a reflecting surface serene enough for the "good Brutus" to catch his image in, whatever may be true of "that poor Brutus, with himself at war" whom Brutus himself has just mentioned. It was not for nothing that Shakespeare put "good Brutus" and "poor Brutus" side by side. And so the story is at once the story of a man, and, like that of Hal, of "another fall of man."

Hence, whether we attend to the contrast between Caesar and the noblest Roman of them all, or to the conflict within that Roman between his nobility and his pride, the theme is the same. It is *King John* over again with its antithesis between the real and the titular hero. *King John* remains history because John was only a king and not a "man," while Faulconbridge, who was both man and "king," did not fall. Julius Caesar becomes tragedy because Brutus both was a "man" and did fall. *Emperor and Galilean* is the title of the play Ibsen considered his masterpiece. *Emperor and Man* might have been the name of *Julius Caesar*, had Shakespeare been given to comment in his titles. He was given to it, but in a more subtle way than Ibsen. The pride of Brutus is the ghost of Caesar within him as certainly as if at the moment Caesar expired it had literally transmigrated from the dead man to the living one. And so this Tragedy of Brutus is the story of Julius Caesar's spirit after death. The title of the play is precisely the right one.

As the political theme of *Henry V* is imperialism and war, so the political theme of *Julius Caesar* is imperialism and revolution. To say that Shakespeare in this play is asserting that assassination as a political instrument is always, everywhere, for any man, under any circumstances, morally unjustifiable would be asserting too much. Shakespeare is not given to defending or attacking universal propositions. Even when Camillo, asked by Leontes to kill Polixenes in *The Winter's Tale*, declares:

If I could find example
Of thousands that had struck anointed kings,
And flourish'd after, I'd not do't; but since
Nor brass nor stone nor parchment bears not one,
Let villany itself forswear't,

it is Camillo's opinion and not necessarily Shakespeare's, though the absoluteness of the statement is indeed interesting, coming from the author of *Julius Caesar*. "Shakespeare is no partisan in this tragedy," says Professor Kittredge. "He sides neither with Caesar and his avengers nor with the party of Brutus and Cassius. The verdict, if there must be a verdict, he leaves to history." It is a safe statement, if for no other reason than that Shakespeare is never a political partisan. But if ever Shakespeare left anything beyond doubt it is that this particular man Brutus should never have had anything to do with this particular deed. Practically every scene of the play contributes something toward this conclusion. So true is it indeed that *Julius Caesar*, if you care to take it so, becomes a sort of manual on the art of knowing what your soul is telling you to do, or not to do, of finding out what you think in contrast with what you think you think.

Brutus is an exceptional man. Yet Brutus is Everyman in the sense that every man is Brutus at some hour of his life. Whoever is aware of the disparity between what he would be and what the world seems bent on making him is a Brutus in a general sense. More specifically, Brutus is the man of sensitive nature who, outraged by the cruelty and tyranny around him, sadly and reluctantly concludes that there is no way to oppose the world but with the world's weapons, that fire must drive out fire and force force.

The lofty character of the end intended, the preservation of the liberties of Rome, blinds Brutus to the low character of the means proposed. He represses, but he cannot eradicate, that abhorrence of force which, by definition, must be inherent in every lover of liberty. The result is war in that psychological realm where all war begins.

> Since Cassius first did whet me against Caesar,
> I have not slept.
> Between the acting of a dreadful thing
> And the first motion, all the interim is
> Like a phantasma or a hideous dream.
> The genius and the mortal instruments
> Are then in council; and the state of man,
> Like to a little kingdom, suffers then
> The nature of an insurrection.

Dreadful, hideous, mortal! His own words ought to have been warning enough. But reason does not understand the language of the imagination. In the conflict of instincts let loose within Brutus, Lucius and Portia are his good angels, Caesar and Cassius his evil ones. With or without knowing it, they strive for the possession of his soul.

III

Portia is one of the first of a number of Shakespearean heroines who have brief roles of supreme importance. Speaking to Brutus, she refers to herself as "your self, your half." The phrase "better half" as applied to a wife has been so prostituted to jocosity that it is scarcely possible to use it seriously. Yet it describes precisely Portia's relation to Brutus. She is all that is fine in his unconscious nature, and their conjugal partnership is as lovely as any Shakespeare ever pictured, even including that between Coriolanus and Virgilia. The point is underlined by the fact that Calphurnia bears somewhat the same relation to Caesar. These women through their dreams and intuitions draw from deeper springs of wisdom than any to which their husbands have access. And Caesar because of his vanity and ambition, Brutus because of a strain of cold rationalism that runs through his nature, are in peculiar need of the insight of their wives.

If Portia is Brutus' wisdom, the boy Lucius is his original innocence. "Become what thou art," says Pindar. Brutus was well on his way toward obeying that injunction when this business of Caesar's assassination intervened. Lucius is Brutus before he was contaminated, and in him his master can see himself as he came from the hand of God. Innocence does not mean unsophistication. It means the state of being unpoisoned.

Lucius, naturally, does not know the role he is playing in Brutus' life. Portia is only partly conscious of her participation in his fate. Nor can Caesar suspect the evil he has unloosed within him. But it is quite otherwise with Cassius. He is cynically aware of every step he takes. He is the Seducer. He proceeds to lay siege to Brutus' integrity exactly as a seducer in a commoner sense does to a woman's chastity. Cassius looks up to Brutus, even loves him. Why, then, does he not let him alone and find someone more fit for the business he has in hand? Because the conspiracy needs the moral prestige that only Brutus can lend it.

> Into what dangers would you lead me, Cassius,
> That you would have me seek into myself
> For that which is not in me?

Like the woman who thinks it is not in her, he thinks it is not in him, but proves that it is by remaining to hear more—just as Ivan Karamazov once remained to hear more from Smerdyakov.

Cassius knows his brother will entertain no proposal save for the general good. So he attacks him where virtue and its opposite are forever getting confused, in his pride, pride in his ancestors' dedication to republicanism:

> O, you and I have heard our fathers say,
> There was a Brutus once that would have brook'd
> Th' eternal devil to keep his state in Rome
> As easily as a king.

The fathers once more! It is the clinching argument. Like Romeo and Hal, Brutus capitulates to the past, or rather to Cassius' subtle perversion of it (the earlier Brutus did not kill the tyrant). "I sense what you are driving at," Brutus confesses in effect. "Indeed, I have been meditating on these very things myself, and will confer about them—later."

> What you have said
> I will consider; what you have to say
> I will with patience hear, and find a time
> Both meet to hear and answer such high things.

The lines have a familiar ring.

> Yet when we can entreat an hour to serve,
> We would spend it in some words upon that business,
> If you would grant the time.

Macbeth to Banquo! a sinister parallel.

Caesar with his train enters, and when he has retired, Casca tells how he was three times offered the crown and three times refused it. As Casca goes out, Brutus changes his appointment with Cassius from some indefinite time in the future to a definite one on the morrow at his home. Cassius has won. He soliloquizes:

> Well, Brutus, thou art noble; yet, I see,
> Thy honourable metal may be wrought
> From that it is dispos'd. Therefore it is meet
> That noble minds keep ever with their likes:
> For who so firm that cannot be seduc'd?

Seduced: he is honest enough to use the very word. With cynical frankness he admits that he has corrupted his friend, that his own conduct has been ignoble, that, if the roles had been reversed, Brutus would never have done to him what he has done to Brutus. And yet, in the face of all this from the arch-conspirator, men have argued whether Brutus did right or wrong to enter the conspiracy!

IV

His evil angels have had their way with Brutus in the first act. As the second act opens, we find him invoking his good angel. But he does not know it: he thinks he is just a sleepless man arousing a sleeping child.

> What, Lucius, ho!
> I cannot, by the progress of the stars,
> Give guess how near to day. Lucius, I say!

> I would it were my fault to sleep so soundly.
> When, Lucius, when! Awake, I say! What, Lucius!

Here the metaphor of daybreak that figures so significantly through the play is beautifully introduced. The daybreak of the fatal day of Caesar's death is but an hour or so away. Following close upon it will be the daybreak of new liberty for Rome, or so Brutus believes. Finally, there is the daybreak of life itself incarnated in the child. Brutus cannot estimate by the stars how near day is. But he looks in the wrong place. The dawn that might save him is as near as the next room, as near as the child, as near as himself, and when he cries "Awake!" he is beseeching the child within to awaken before it is too late. The boy enters, and his master sends him to light a taper in another room, not realizing that the child himself is the best light. From end to end the role of Lucius is permeated with this symbolism. Caesar, just before his fall, announces that he is the Northern Star that alone holds a fixed place in the moving firmament. Lucius is that star. It is not by chance that the moment the boy is gone Brutus begins to lose his way, to strike the note of darkness: "It must be by his death."

Presently Lucius comes back with a paper that was thrown in at the window of Brutus' study:

> "Brutus, thou sleep'st; awake, and see thyself!"

How different that "Awake" from the one that opened the scene, and what ironical words to address to a victim of insomnia who has been awake all night! Lucius, whom Brutus has sent out for a calendar, re-enters, and the Janus-like stage direction is *"Knocking within."* The boy goes to the gate and reports that Cassius has come with others he cannot identify because their hats are plucked about their ears and half their faces buried in their cloaks. "O conspiracy!" cries Brutus, and the speech that follows shows how his soul abhors the enterprise he is nevertheless bent on undertaking. Dangerous, dark, monstrous; night, cavern, evil; shame, mask, hide: adjectives, nouns, and verbs conspire fairly to shout the truth in his ears. But he is deaf. And this lover of truth stoops to the abjectest hypocrisy when he bids the conspiracy hide itself in smiles and affability.

> To beguile the time,
> Look like the time; bear welcome in your eye,
> Your hand, your tongue: look like the innocent flower,
> But be the serpent under't.

These lines are Lady Macbeth's. Except perhaps for the touch about the serpent, where she goes a bit beyond him, they might pass unchallenged if assigned to Brutus at this point.

As Brutus and Cassius whisper together, several of the other conspirators take up, as if the scene were music, the theme of daybreak with which it opened:

> *Decius*. Here lies the east. Doth not the day break here?
> *Casca*: No.
> *Cinna*: O, pardon, sir, it doth; and yon grey lines
> That fret the clouds are messengers of day.
> *Casca*: You shall confess that you are both deceiv'd.
> Here, as I point my sword, the sun arises,
> Which is a great way growing on the south,
> Weighing the youthful season of the year.
> Some two months hence, up higher toward the north
> He first presents his fire; and the high east
> Stands as the Capitol, directly here.

"While Brutus and Cassius confer," says Kittredge, "the others courteously occupy themselves with casual talk about indifferent matters." It may have seemed casual and indifferent to the speakers. But it was not to their imaginations, nor to Shakespeare's. If there is a passage in the play that lets us into the secret of what the author thought of the conspiracy it is this. (This, and possibly two others yet to be mentioned.) As we have seen, Shakespeare is forever using such apparent parentheses for uttering his own convictions under the protection of a metaphor. These men think they are about to bring a new day to Rome when they cannot even agree as to where the geographical east lies. They promise a new spiritual morning before they have even learned where the material sun comes up! And when Casca cries:

> Here, as I point my sword, the sun arises,

we feel the presumption of expecting a new day to break at the command of a sword. Casca has surpassed Chaunticleer in egotism. Thus is the political message of the play condensed into a metaphor, its whole point suspended, as it were, on the point of a sword.

Cassius suggests in succession that the conspirators bind themselves to one another by an oath, sound out Cicero, and mark Antony to fall with Caesar. Brutus negatives each of these proposals, revealing in each instance how unfitted he is for the business he is undertaking. In the case of Cicero, the reason he gives,

> For he will never follow anything
> That other men begin,

strongly implies that he does not want to share his prestige as moral head of the conspiracy. In the other two cases he is unconsciously attempting to compensate for an ignoble major decision by minor nobler ones.

If there were no other evidence whatever, the speech in which Brutus seeks to justify the sparing of Antony would be enough in itself to show how completely the true Brutus recognizes in advance the futility of the course on which the false Brutus is embarking. Without knowing it, he puts his finger on the precise reason why the conspiracy was bound to fail. As in Richard II's tribute to Peace, or Henry V's argument with Williams about the king's responsibility for the consciences of his soldiers, the imagination of the man tells the truth over his head. He thinks he is saying one thing when actually he is saying just the opposite.

> Our course will seem too bloody, Caius Cassius,
> To cut the head off and then hack the limbs,
> Like wrath in death and envy afterwards;
> For Antony is but a limb of Caesar. I
> Let us be sacrificers, but not butchers, Caius.
> We all stand up against the spirit of Caesar,
> And in the spirit of men there is no blood;
> O, that we then could come by Caesar's spirit,
> And not dismember Caesar! But, alas,
> Caesar must bleed for it! And, gentle friends,
> Let's kill him boldly, but not wrathfully;
> Let's carve him as a dish fit for the gods,
> Not hew, him as a carcass fit for hounds;
> And let our hearts, as subtle masters do,
> Stir up their servants to an act of rage,
> And after seem to chide 'em. This shall make
> Our purpose necessary and not envious;
> Which so appearing to the common eyes,
> We shall be call'd purgers, not murderers.
> And for Mark Antony, think not of him;
> For he can do no more than Caesar's arm
> When Caesar's head is off.

Disentangle the syllogism underlying the verbiage in the first part of this speech and this is what we have: (1) The spirit of men contains no blood. (2) We wish to destroy the spirit of Caesar. Therefore (3) we must spill Caesar's blood. No one will question that major premise. All lovers of liberty will second the minor one. The tragedy is dedicated to demonstrating the absurdity of the conclusion.

The true inference from the premises is obviously: Therefore it is useless to spill Caesar's blood. Moral pride prevents Brutus from seeing it.

The logic is false, but the metaphors, as usual, slip in the truth.

> Let us be sacrificers, but not butchers, Caius . . .
> Let's carve him as a dish fit for the gods.

Dropping out the six lines that intervene between those two reveals the tricks his mind is playing upon Brutus—for who ever carved what had not previously been butchered? And the figure of the master and servants betrays him even more ignominiously. The conspirators seek the end of the man who would make himself master of Rome. Brutus tells them they must imitate the subtle master who stirs up his servants to a violent act and then appears to chide them for committing it. Thus the assassination will be received as a deed of necessity rather than envy:

> We shall be call'd purgers, not murderers.
> Purgers! the very word that in our day has been used so often to
> camouflage murder. The example establishes the point it is supposed to
> refute and stamps the act it is used to justify as murder.

Brutus' opinion prevails, Antony is spared, and to an ominous striking of the clock, anticipating the ringing of the bell that summoned Macbeth "to heaven or to hell," the conspirators disperse as Cassius cries, "The morning comes upon's," and Brutus warns,

> Let not our looks put on our purposes,
> But bear it as our Roman actors do.

He is indeed, himself, playing a part. And when he turns to the child, it is as if he were bidding a final farewell to his true but discarded self:

> Boy! Lucius! Fast asleep? It is no matter.

No matter that his innocence slumbers? He did not think so when the scene opened.

But if one of Brutus' good angels is asleep, the other is not. Portia enters to inquire why her lord has left her bed at this unwonted hour. And with a skill that would do credit to a twentieth-century psychiatrist she lists the symptoms she has noted of his mental perturbation, signs of a nervous irritability that has altered him almost past recognition. He protests that he is merely physically unwell. She will have nothing of that explanation, and piercing directly to the truth, she cries:

> No, my Brutus,
> You have some sick offence within your mind.

She kneels to him, begging him to reveal his secret.

> There is a tide in the affairs of men . . .

It was at this moment, not when, too late, he uttered those famous lines to Cassius, that Brutus should have recognized that his last chance to save himself from becoming an assassin had come.

> O ye gods!
> Render me worthy of this noble wife!

If ever a prayer was sincere, it is this. If ever a man had a chance to help answer his own prayer, this is he. Again, the stage direction registers the spiritual crisis with a "*Knocking within.*" It is as ominous a knocking as the more famous one in *Macbeth.*

And what does Brutus say and do?

> Hark, hark! one knocks. *Portia, go in awhile,*
> And *by and by* thy bosom shall partake
> The secrets of my heart.
> All my engagements I will construe to thee,
> All the charactery of my sad brows.
> *Leave me with haste.* (*Exit Portia*)
>   Lucius, who's that knocks?
> (*Re-enter Lucius with Ligarius*)
>   *Luc.*: Here is a sick man that would speak with you.
>   *Bru.*: Caius Ligarius, that Metellus spake of.
> *Boy, stand aside.* Caius Ligarius! how?

If the poet had had Brutus say, "My Wisdom, go in awhile! My Innocence, stand aside! Sickness, let me embrace you!" he could hardly have made his point clearer. There are few stage directions in his plays more pathetic than those two words: *Exit Portia.* It might have been: *Exit the Soul of Brutus.*

Brutus tells Ligarius that great things are afoot, and, summoning his failing forces, the latter inquires, "What's to do?"

A piece of work that will make sick men whole,

replies Brutus.

But are not some whole that we must make sick?

asks Ligarius, suspecting the truth. He does not know that his words fit the man to whom he is speaking better than they do the intended victim, who in an hour or two will be beyond both sickness and wholeness. "That must we also," replies Brutus, equally ignorant of the application of the words to himself. "Set on your foot," says Ligarius,

> And with a heart new-fir'd I follow you,
> To do I know not what: but it sufficeth
> That Brutus leads me on.
>   Follow me then,

says Brutus, and he too might well have added, "to do I know not what." It is tragic when a nobility that might have led only follows, when it consents to be used by envious men for their base purposes. It adds to the tragedy when weak men, trusting that nobility, follow it blindly into that baseness.

V

Brutus is not the only one whose sleep is interrupted the night before the assassination and who will not let his wife save him. The same is true of Caesar. Three times Calphurnia dreams that her husband is murdered, that his statue runs blood in which many Romans bathe their hands. And the augurers confirm her fear. Caesar decides not to go to the Capitol. But Decius Brutus, by a strained reinterpretation of the dream and by dangling the hope of a crown before him, gets him to change his mind. Brutus leads him to Brutus. The crown he is to receive is death.

Even at the last moment he might have been saved if he had regarded the Soothsayer or had received the petition of Artemidorus, the philosopher, who in some unexplained way—possibly because the conspirators had not bound themselves to secrecy by an oath—had got a hint of the conspiracy.

What touches us ourself shall be last serv'd,

he cries, brushing Artemidorus aside. What looks like magnanimity is inverted pride.

Metellus Cimber kneels before Caesar begging the repeal of his brother's banishment. If Caesar's decision had been made a genuine test of his fitness to live, the spectator might feel more sympathy with the conspirators. But his death is ordained regardless of how he decides. Brutus, with a kiss that reminds us more of Judas than of the Brutus who expelled Tarquin from Rome, seconds the petition of Metellus Cimber. Caesar, refusing, justifies his unwillingness to change his mind by comparing himself to the Northern Star and to Olympus. It is assumption of divinity. The man is infatuated. The moment has come. Casca stabs him from behind, the others follow, Brutus, significantly, striking last. "*Et tu, Brute?* Then fall, Caesar!" How much deeper into Brutus' heart those words must have sunk than did the dagger that made "the most unkindest cut of all" into Caesar's flesh. It was Caesar who stabbed Brutus.

VI

Liberty! Freedom! Tyranny is dead!

cries Cinna.

Liberty, freedom, and enfranchisement!

cries Casca.

Peace, freedom, and liberty!

cries Brutus, and unconsciously fulfilling Calphurnia's dream, he bids his fellows bathe their hands to the elbows in Caesar's blood. (Is this the man we saw bending over a sleeping child but a few hours before?)

> How many ages hence
> Shall this our lofty scene be acted over
> In states unborn and accents yet unknown!

cries Cassius as he complies with Brutus' bloody suggestion.

> How many times shall Caesar bleed in sport,
> That now on Pompey's basis lies along
> No worthier than the dust!

cries Brutus, echoing Cassius. It is significant that while the first prophecy is political, the second is theatrical. How many times since then both have been fulfilled. "So oft as that shall be," Cassius concludes,

> So often shall the knot of us be call'd
> The men that gave their country liberty.

What they did give it is best seen by turning over a few pages of the text to the opening of Act IV, where Antony, Octavius, and Lepidus, the new rulers of Rome, sit around a table pricking off the names of those who must die that their own regime may base itself in safety. So soon can tyranny succeed violent revolution. And if the immediate fruits of the assassination as depicted in this play are insufficient, the reader may turn to *Antony and Cleopatra* to behold its remoter harvest.

But this is anticipating.

Antony, whom Brutus spared, begs leave to speak over Caesar's body at his funeral, and, in the face of Cassius' protest, Brutus consents. In a speech that will precede Antony's he will placate the people. The two orations, or rather Brutus' oration and Antony's speech, have been declaimed and dissected in innumerable classrooms. Yet the contrast between them remains a better treatise on the relation of sincerity to style than a shelf of textbooks.

Though everybody sees that the wily Antony puts his speech over, as we say, while Brutus does not, just as a speech Brutus' effort has usually been declared a good one by academic authority. It was merely too good for the mob, it is said. On the contrary it is one of the worst speeches ever made by an able and intelligent man. Its symmetrical structure, its balanced sentences, its ordered procedure, its rhetorical questions, its painfully conscious and ornamental style, its hopelessly abstract subject matter, all stamp it as the utterance of a man whose heart is not in his words. It is a dishonest speech.

The cry of the Third Citizen, "Let him be Caesar," measures its practical effectiveness. Those four words have often been pointed out as one of the most crushing ironies in the play. They are, and with the other comments of the populace show how hopeless the cause of the conspirators was. These people did not deserve liberty. They were ready for slavery.

Antony's speech, on the other hand, for all its playing on the passions of the people, and for all its lies, is at bottom an honest speech, because Antony loved Caesar. Because to that extent he has the truth on his side, he is as concrete as Brutus was abstract. A sincere harangue by a demagogue is better than the most "classic" oration from a man who speaks only with his lips. It is like Henry IV and Falstaff. The good form is on one side, the veracity on the other.

Now let it work,

cries Antony in an accent with which our own day has made us well acquainted,

Mischief, thou art afoot,
Take thou what course thou wilt!

And Shakespeare devotes a little scene to Cinna, the poet, whom the mob mistakes for Cinna the conspirator. What if they do have hold of the wrong man! They go ahead anyway—on sound lynching principles. It is the Jack Cade motif over again. Mythology is wrong. It is not love, it is passion that is blind.

Meanwhile, before this, word has come to Antony that Brutus and Cassius

Are rid like madmen through the gates of Rome.

Instead of liberating Rome, Rome has "liberated" them. But a few hours before they were crying "Tyranny is dead!" and so soon it all seems like a dream.

VII

After the proscription, at which we took a glance in advance, the scene shifts to Sardis. Assassination and revolution have eventuated in war, and already the two brother-generals are blaming each other for their predicament.

Thou hast describ'd
A hot friend cooling. Ever note, Lucilius,

says Brutus to his servant who has just come from Cassius,

When love begins to sicken and decay,
It useth an enforced ceremony.
There are no tricks in plain and simple faith.

If only Brutus had remembered that truth when, at its inception, he bade the conspiracy hide itself in smiles and affability!

Cassius enters with the salutation,

Most noble brother, you have done me wrong,

and, the two beginning to wrangle, Brutus draws his friend into his own tent that their dissension may not be overheard.

A guilty conscience invariably finds in others the evil it will not admit to itself. The quarrel scene is Brutus' specific confession that the conspiracy and assassination were terrible errors.

As usual, he takes a high idealistic line. He charges Cassius with protecting bribery. "In such a time," Cassius answers, one cannot be meticulous. Brutus implies that Cassius has "an itching palm" and has sold offices for gold. Cassius declares that if he were not Brutus that speech would be his last.

Remember March, the ides of March remember,

cries Brutus in a tone that reminds us of the very dog he mentions:

> Did not great Julius bleed for justice' sake?
> What villain touch'd his body, that did stab
> And not for justice? What, shall one of us,
> That struck the foremost man of all this world
> But for supporting robbers, shall we now
> Contaminate our fingers with base bribes,
> And sell the mighty space of our large honours
> For so much trash as may be grasped thus?
> I had rather be a dog, and bay the moon,
> Than such a Roman.

Shall we who made away with the great Injustice, the great Robber, stoop to little injustices and petty thefts? But in that case, we feel like asking, how about imitating the great Apostle of Force by practicing a little assassination? Brutus is not pushing analogy that far.

> Brutus, bait not me;
> I'll not endure it,

Cassius exclaims, and the quarrel descends to common scolding with Brutus immeasurably the worse offender.

> There is no terror, Cassius, in your threats,

he declares, when Cassius warns him not to go too far,

> For I am arm'd so strong in honesty
> That they pass by me as the idle wind,
> Which I respect not.

It is the perfect echo of an earlier speech in the play. The arrogation of moral infallibility is but a step below the affectation of divinity. Brutus has become like Caesar! His victim has infected him with his own disease. It is the special nemesis of the revolutionist. He comes to resemble what he once abhorred.

And the irony goes even further. "I did send to you," Brutus goes on,

> For certain sums of gold, which you denied me;
> For I can raise no money by vile means.

By heaven, I had rather coin my heart
And drop my blood for drachmas than to wring
From the hard hands of peasants their vile trash
By any indirection. I did send
To you for gold to pay my legions,
Which you denied me. Was that done like Cassius?

He will not wring gold from the peasants by any indirection. But he will take it, even demand it, of Cassius, who, of course, has no other ultimate source from which to obtain it than just those peasants. Brutus is doing what in the same breath he declares that he would rather die than do. "I won't rob myself, but I will rob by way of you, for I can do nothing indirectly." That is what his astounding argument reduces to. "Indirection": Pandulph's word, Polonius' word. Brutus thinks he is angry with Cassius for his countenance of petty thefts and bribes. Actually he is angry with himself for robbing Rome, for robbing Portia, for robbing himself.

Cassius, stung to the quick, does just what Caesar once did to the mob: presents his bosom to Brutus' dagger—and instantly Brutus relents. But when so huge a fire is suddenly quenched some sparks are bound to escape. A Poet, overhearing and sensing something wrong between the generals, breaks boldly in in an attempt to reconcile them. In ejecting him, Brutus vents what is left of his anger. But in doing so he speaks and behaves more like Hotspur than like Brutus.

Alone again with Cassius, Brutus chooses the moment to reveal the hidden tension he has been under during their quarrel. Portia is dead—by her own hand.

In keeping this secret from his audience as well as from Cassius, Shakespeare violates a fundamental rule of stagecraft. It is one of the clearest of many indications in his plays that he cared for something more than the first impressions of a theater audience. Reread, or seen a second time on the stage, the quarrel scene sounds harmonics that the ear misses completely the first time the scene is encountered.

Brutus attributes Portia's suicide to his absence and to the successes of Octavius and Antony. We can guess, only too easily, the deeper reason why

she fell distract
And, her attendants absent, swallow'd fire.

As fact, Portia's death by swallowing fire is perhaps incredible. As truth, it rises to an order beyond the invention possibly even of a Plutarch or a Shakespeare, to the level of myth itself. But the poet has at least made the most of what he inherited. As he uses it, this incident becomes the second of his three main comments on his own play (the first being the passage on the location of the East). He has made plain in the one scene where we see them together that Portia is Brutus' other "half." As the mirror of his soul, she is bound to reflect so tremendous an event as his spiritual death in accepting the code of violence. And that is exactly what her death does. On entering the conspiracy Brutus metaphorically swallowed fire. Portia swallows it literally as an allegory of his act. It is both a picture of his dereliction and a measure of the agony she underwent because of it. The whole meaning of the drama seems somehow concentrated in this symbol.

VIII

The boy brings wine and Brutus and Cassius pledge each other and "bury all unkindness" in the cup. But Brutus will never by swallowing the fire of wine bury the memory of how Portia died. At the very moment indeed he is to be reminded of her end. Messala enters bringing news from Rome. Not knowing whether Brutus has heard of his wife's suicide, he sounds him out, and, on Brutus' insistence that he reveal what he is hinting at, tells the truth. Brutus pretends he has not heard and receives the word with stoic calm. The double report of Portia's death has often been held an error in the text, a sign of unfinished revision. But surely it is just one more bit of evidence that Brutus is acting a part. The unnatural restraint he puts himself under in this personal matter may have more than a little to do too with the rash plan of battle we find him advocating a few minutes later. He turns to it with an abruptness that would have been cruel, had the situation been what Messala supposed.

Shall Brutus and Cassius march down to the enemy and give battle at Philippi or await him where they are on the heights? Brutus is for the former course, Cassius for the latter. The decision is motivated by unseen forces. The quarrel and reconciliation, with the news of Portia's death, have left Cassius melancholy and in no mood to cross Brutus again, The unnatural restraint that Brutus has imposed upon himself with regard to Portia's death helps perhaps to make him impulsive. At any rate he argues—in words the world knows by heart—that they are now at their high tide and should strike immediately. But whatever may be true of the military situation, Brutus' moral tide is at its ebb, and the strategy he favors is ultimately dictated by that fact. Whatever the immediate reasons for it, it conforms finally to nothing less than the pattern of his whole life. His is the story of a man who instead of keeping to "the hills and upper regions" has by the assassination come down to "the enemy." Had he still had hope in his heart, his unconscious might have tried to compensate for his moral decline by insisting that his forces keep to the heights. But with the death of Portia a dark fatalism begins to possess him. He is the victim of a desperation he does not yet realize. And so the plan of battle becomes a symbolic picture of his life. He has gone down before and led other men down. He will do it for the last time. As when he entered the conspiracy, his willingness to descend to their level suits "the enemy" exactly. Reluctantly Cassius consents. He who had once led Brutus lower now follows him. "Time is come round." The nemesis is inevitable. Thus, Shakespeare seems to be saying, our particular decisions, which appear to be made freely and on the merits of the occasion, are overruled by the total pattern of our lives. Cause and effect may reign in the physical world, but likeness and unlikeness are sovereign in the realm of the imagination. In our day the man who has plunged too heavily in the stock market leaps from the twentieth story of a skyscraper to his death. The type of suicide he chooses is not chance. It was not chance that Caesar had the "falling" sickness. Nor that the man who killed him becomes a victim of that sickness in another form.

Brutus is left alone with the boy Lucius, and, as usual in his presence, his true self comes to the surface. He is all tenderness. This man who could kill Caesar cannot ask a tired child to watch one hour more. He calls in Claudius and Varro, but bids them lie on cushions rather than stay awake, so sensitive is he to their feelings. It is compensation, of course. He finds the book for which he has searched—revealing touch—in the pocket of his gown, but before beginning to read—another revealing touch—he begs for a strain or two of music from Lucius. The drowsy boy complies, but after a note or two falls asleep over his instrument, and we have Henry IV's soliloquy on sleep dramatized before us. The scholar-assassin finds the leaf turned down where he left reading and composes himself to go on. But noting something strange about the taper, he looks up, and beholds a "monstrous apparition" coming toward him. It is the Ghost of Julius Caesar!

Is the specter a creature of his own fantasy, nothing at all, or, if some-thing, angel or devil? "Speak to me what thou art."

Thy evil spirit, Brutus.

The Delphic answer leaves open the question whether it is from within or from without. But it leaves no doubt, in either case, of its infernal origin. With a promise to meet Brutus again at Philippi, it vanishes.

O, that we then could come by Caesar's spirit,
And not dismember Caesar!

Too late Brutus discovers that when his dagger entered Caesar's body it released a power as towering and uncontrollable as the genie freed by the fisherman in the Arabian tale. Julius Caesar is dead. But his spirit has volatilized into something as invulnerable as the air. "In the spirit of men there is no blood."

"Some angel, or some devil?" Brutus had asked. And promptly on the disappearance of the devil, the angel appears—as if the one had exorcised the other. Coming suddenly to himself on the exit of the Ghost, Brutus cries out:

> Boy, Lucius! Varro! Claudius! Sirs! Awake!
> Claudius!

> The strings, my lord, are false,

murmurs Lucius. The child is dreaming, and out of some divine confusion in his mind between his instrument and the trouble he has read on his master's brow his unconsciousness frames this inspired answer. (It is Shakespeare's third supreme comment on his own play.) If up to this point anyone has doubted what Lucius symbolizes, this should convince him. Brutus' slumbering innocence, awakening, gives him a last warning. On the lips of a child, from out of that borderland between sleeping and waking where it so often resides, the truth speaks. "The strings, my lord, are false." Brutus is out of tune. But a musical instrument that is out of tune is not a musical instrument. Brutus is not Brutus.

And because he is not himself, he cannot read the oracle. Victim of an auditory hallucination, he mistakes the cry of his own soul for the nightmare of one of his companions. He projects his inner conflict into the outer world and sends to Cassius to "set on his powers."

IX

Things draw to a close and the tragedy is finished at the Battle of Philippi fought on Cassius' birthday, a coincidence he turns to fatal effect:

> This day I breathed first; time is come round,
> And where I did begin, there shall I end.

The pathos of the parting predicts the outcome:

> For ever, and for ever, farewell, Cassius!
> For ever, and for ever, farewell, Brutus!

The battle has been fought and decided in the bottom of their hearts before it is even begun. It is more the conviction of certain defeat than the forces arrayed against them that determines the issue.

> . . . men may construe things after their fashion,
> Clean from the purpose of the things themselves.

So Cassius does in mistaking the shouts of joy of friends at the arrival of his messenger for the exultation of enemies at his capture. Not even waiting to confirm his conjecture, he covers his face and bids a servant run him through with the very sword with which he had assassinated Caesar—

> Caesar, thou art reveng'd,
> Even with the sword that kill'd thee.

The advantage the impulsive Brutus had gained over Octavius on the other wing of the battle is thrown away.

> O Julius Caesar, thou art mighty yet!

cries Brutus when he gazes down at his dead friend,

> Thy spirit walks abroad, and turns our swords
> In our own proper entrails.

The Ghost promised to meet Brutus again at Philippi. He has kept his word. What Brutus did not reckon on was what the Other World would say to his deed. He realizes at last that he has brought down on Rome in hundred-fold measure the very spirit to exorcise which he sold his soul to the conspiracy. Alive, Julius Caesar was a feeble epileptic. Dead, he has become an annihilating tide.

> O hateful error, melancholy's child,
> Why dost thou show to the apt thoughts of men
> The things that are not? O error, soon conceiv'd,
> Thou never com'st unto a happy birth,
> But kill'st the mother that engender'd thee!

The whole plot against Caesar had been such an error. Brutus returns to the field, but he is soon convinced that there is nothing left him but to follow Cassius. "Caesar, now be still," he cries as he runs on his sword held by a servant (after three others have refused that office):

> I kill'd not thee with half so good a will.

Those ten words are the Last Judgment of Brutus on a conspiracy the morality of which other men, strangely, have long debated.

From the level of practical affairs, of politics, of drama, imperialism and a violent hatred of imperialism look like opposites. But from the level of poetry, of those high pastures of the soul where, as Thoreau once remarked on a famous occasion, the state is nowhere to be seen, the two can have a curious resemblance. If anything was needed after *Henry V* to make plain what Shakespeare thought of imperialism, this play supplies it. Readers of William Blake will remember his habit of using names like Locke, Newton, and Voltaire as symbols for ideas and attitudes of mind that he disapproved of, quite without reference to the men themselves or the details of their thinking. Caesar and Alexander apparently came to stand for Imperialism in Shakespeare's mind in a somewhat similar fashion, Falstaff speaks of Caesar as "the hook-nosed fellow of Rome." Rosalind refers to his "thrasonical brag." Hamlet has him turned to clay and stopping a hole in the wall along with Alexander who performs the same office for a beer barrel. And we remember Alexander the Pig. Fluellen, Falstaff, Rosalind, and Hamlet. Can anyone imagine Shakespeare having sympathy for what those four scorned?

After the indictment of imperialism in *Henry V*, *Julius Caesar* is just the combined confirmation of that indictment and compensation for it that might have been expected. It makes plain that those who oppose imperialism with force run the risk of being no better than the imperialists themselves. Bernard Shaw once remarked that *Julius Caesar* glorifies a murder which Goethe described as "the most senseless of deeds." A queer way of glorifying it: to demonstrate that it brought on its perpetrators precisely what they committed it to avert. No, Shakespeare agreed with Goethe. The path of violence and the path of the violent opposition to violence can easily be the same.

> And 'mid this tumult Kubla heard from far
> Ancestral voices prophesying war!

The real opposition, Shakespeare seems to say, is not between the state and the enemies of the state. It is between those ancestral voices and the voice of the soul.

1955—T.S. Dorsch. "Introduction: Language and Imagery," from *Julius Caesar*

T.S. Dorsch oversaw publication of editions of *Julius Caesar* and *The Comedy of Errors*. He also edited and translated books of literary criticism, such as *English Tragedy Before Shakespeare*.

I have already in passing drawn attention to some of the most impressive passages in *Julius Caesar*. Cassius's tirade against Caesar, Caesar's appraisal of Cassius, the descriptions of portents, Brutus's tormented self-questioning and his Forum speech, Portia's appeal to Brutus, Antony's hoodwinking of the conspirators, his Forum speech, and his eulogy of Brutus: all these, and many other passages, are remarkable whether for their exposition of character and background or for their fine poetic or rhetorical qualities. One does not have to seek far to find speeches as memorable in their own way as any that Shakespeare wrote. In their own way: Shakespeare seems to have been trying in this play to fashion an atmosphere and a diction in keeping with the gravity and dignity traditionally associated with the Roman character. He avoided the lyricism and the humour that we find in, for instance, *Antony and Cleopatra*, and wrote probably less purely descriptive poetry than in any other of his mature plays. The strength of the most noteworthy speeches lies in their clarity, directness, and simplicity. This is seen in, for example, Cassius's speech which begins

Why; man, he doth bestride the narrow world
Like a Colossus; (I. ii. 133–59)

or in Caesar's analysis of Cassius (I. ii. 195–211); or in Brutus's farewell to Cassius (V. i. 111–19); or in a score of other fine speeches. The effectiveness of Antony's famous oration depends, not on its use of imagery or obvious rhetorical tricks, but on its structure; Antony carries the crowd with him for the most part by a series of short, direct statements, so arranged as to lead their thoughts and their feelings in a particular direction. Brutus's oration is more obviously rhetorical, perhaps, with its studied parallelism and antithesis and its carefully wrought climaxes, but its diction is simple and bare, and the total effect is that of the most lucid simplicity. Of this oration Granville-Barker writes:[1] "I prefer it to Antony's. It wears better. It is very noble prose."

As in all his mature plays, Shakespeare varies his language according to the personality and cast of mind of the speakers. I cannot agree with Dr Ifor Evans when he says:[2] "For, unlike *Hamlet*, where the diction varies with character and mood, and from soliloquy to public speech, here from public oration to the secret thoughts of the lonely meditating mind all is gathered into one cumulative surge of ordered and formal narration." There is a considerable difference between the twisted thought and comparatively complex imagery of Brutus's meditations in his orchard and the clarity and bareness to which I have drawn attention in his prepared speech in the Forum. And neither passage can reasonably be described as narration.

Brutus speaks a more metaphorical and rhetorical language than any one else in the play. This is apparent already in some of his earliest speeches:

> Nor construe any further my neglect,
> Than that poor Brutus, with himself at war,
> Forgets the shows of love to other men.

> Set honour in one eye, and death i' th' other,
> And I will look on both indifferently.

His habit of thinking in metaphors is strikingly illustrated in his soliloquies in his orchard: not only by the serpent and the ladder images of his first long speech, but also by the even more complicated imagery of the later lines beginning, "Between the acting of a dreadful thing . . ." (II. i. 63–9). In the meeting of the conspirators that follows, while his associates make their proposals in simple and straightforward terms, Brutus delivers his opinions and decisions in an inflated and rhetorical manner. His wordiness reflects his inner conflict, and emphasizes what we are to learn from his conduct, that he is an unpractical and far from clear-headed man; and it seems also to distract the minds of the other conspirators from seeing the essentials of whatever problem they are discussing.

Throughout the play Brutus tends to talk in this way. After the assassination of Caesar, not having thought of the future, he can only call upon the Fates to know their pleasures (III. i. 98), and in a theatrical fashion suggest the ritual washing of hands in Caesar's blood. In his quarrel with Cassius his resentment and self-righteousness find expression in high-flown metaphors; and the only extended image in the later acts comes from his lips when he is in one of his dictatorial moods—that of the "tide in the affairs of men" (IV. iii. 217–23). This and the previous speech of Brutus are in marked contrast with those of Cassius in this episode.

At times Caesar too speaks in figurative language, but as a rule only when Shakespeare is developing the thrasonical side of his nature. When he feels that his courage may be in question he is ready with an elaborate boast:

> Danger knows full well
> That Caesar is more dangerous than he.
> We are two lions litter'd in one day,
> And I the elder and more terrible.

In the speeches he utters just before he is stabbed he is intended to lose some of our sympathy, and Shakespeare again gives him an inflated and boastful manner of speech. In long-drawn similes he likens the suppliants to fawning curs, and himself to the unassailably constant northern star.

However, Caesar has a more forceful character than Brutus, and for the most part he speaks directly and decisively. In his description of Cassius every word is to the point. When the Soothsayer bids him beware the ides of March, he says, "Set him before me; let me see his face" (I. ii. 50); and, when the warning is repeated, "He is a dreamer. Let us leave him. Pass." Similarly, when Artemidorus importunes him to read his schedule, he brushes him aside. "What, is the fellow mad?" he says (III. i. 10), and moves on to the Senate House. And though the portents of the storm bring out some boastfulness, he speaks simply and authoritatively when he calms Calphurnia's fears and declares his resolution to go to the Capitol.

The instability and irritability of Cassius are reflected in his manner of speech. As he begins to lose control of his feelings in his denunciation of Caesar, his utterance becomes more and more disjointed and exclamatory:

> And when the fit was on him, I did mark
> How he did shake; 'tis true, this god did shake;
> His coward lips did from their colour fly,
> And that same eye whose bend doth awe the world
> Did lose his lustre; I did hear him groan;
> Ay, and that tongue of his, that bade the Romans
> Mark him and write his speeches in their books,
> Alas, it cried, "Give me some drink, Titinius,"
> As a sick girl. Ye gods, it doth amaze me. . .
> . . . Now in the names of all the gods at once,
> Upon what meat doth this our Caesar feed,
> That he is grown so great? Age, thou art sham'd! (I. ii. 119–48)

Similarly, in the quarrel scene, the difficulty with which he keeps his temper is reflected in his exclamatory manner: "Is't possible?" "O ye gods, ye gods! Must I endure all this?" "Is it come to this?" "What? durst not tempt him?"

But apart from these two episodes, the speeches in which he is sounding Casca (I. iii. 57–115), and one or two to which he is prompted by Brutus's exaltation after the death of Caesar, Cassius is in full control of his tongue. He has the second largest part in the play, and most of the time his speeches are straightforward and uncomplicated by imagery. When practical measures are to be considered he speaks concisely and sensibly. In the meeting of the conspirators, the negotiations with Antony over Caesar's funeral, and the council of the generals at Sardis, his directness and common sense reveal a grasp of practical realities such as Brutus never possessed.

Some of Antony's speeches have already been considered. He has every nuance of speech at his command. With a few subtle phrases he can at the same time bring out the greatness of Caesar and whip Brutus with his scorn. In four beautifully balanced lines he both flatters Brutus and asserts the superiority of Caesar:

Brutus is noble, wise, valiant, and honest;
Caesar was mighty, bold, royal, and loving:
Say I love Brutus, and I honour him;
Say I fear'd Caesar, honour'd him, and lov'd him. (III. i. 126–9)

In this scene, apart from the permission to speak in Caesar's funeral, he asks for nothing from his enemies—neither mercy nor concessions; he manipulates them into a position where they are only too anxious to show him good will, and he presses home every advantage he gains. Brutus thinks more highly of him with every word he utters. When at last the long fight with the conspirators is won, Shakespeare puts into his mouth, in his epitaph on Brutus, a speech of the most noble simplicity.

Caroline Spurgeon, whose investigation of Shakespeare's imagery has led to many interesting conclusions, finds little to hold her in *Julius Caesar*. After drawing attention to the relative scarcity of extended images, she goes on to say:[3]

> There is no leading or floating image in the play; one feels it was not
> written under the particular stress of emotion or excitement which gives
> rise to a dominating image. There is, however, a certain persistence in
> the comparison of the characters to animals: Caesar is a wolf, a lion, a
> falcon, a serpent's egg, an adder, a stricken deer; the Romans are sheep
> and hinds and bees; the conspirators are apes and hounds; Brutus is a
> lamb; Lepidus is an ass, a horse; Metellus and Casca are curs; Cassius
> is a showy, mettlesome steed which fails at the moment of trial; and
> Octavius and Antony are bears tied to the stake. But this animal
> imagery is not nearly so marked as in either *King Lear* or *Othello*, and
> entirely lacks consistency of character, so that it fails to produce the
> cumulative effect so strongly felt in both those plays.

Now it is true that there is no single dominating image, such as Professor Spurgeon found in *Romeo and Juliet*, for example, or *Othello*; but there are several that recur often enough to be worthy of remark.

Up to the assassination of Caesar the play is to a large degree concerned with conflicts within and between individuals: Brutus's tormented communings with himself, Cassius's notion of himself as a rival to Caesar, Portia's and Calphurnia's struggles to wrest secrets or concessions from their husbands. After the assassination there is outward, physical conflict, which develops into actual war: Antony pits himself against the conspirators, first as an individual, and then in association with Octavius as a leader of great armies at war with the armies of Brutus and Cassius. In the first half a persistent image of civil warfare, in the mind of Brutus and in the heavens, reflects the discord represented by the plot against Caesar, and prefigures the "domestic fury and fierce civil strife" which form the background of the second half of the play.

When Cassius shows concern at Brutus's recent lack of friendliness, Brutus admits that he has been vexed "with passions of some difference"; the reason for his apparent coldness, he says, is that

> poor Brutus, with himself at war,
> Forgets the shows of love to other men. (I. ii. 45–6)

Later, when he is meditating alone in his garden, he again likens the turbulence in his soul, the hideous nightmare of doubt that comes "between the acting of a dreadful thing and the first motion", to a civil uprising:

> the state of man,
> Like to a little kingdom, suffers then
> The nature of an insurrection. (II. i. 67–9)

Like other Elizabethans, Shakespeare often draws a correspondence between man and the state.

But there is also a correspondence between the microcosm, man, and the macrocosm, the universe; and the civil war metaphor is given much greater force when it is extended to the storm, that great upheaval of the elements which gives a forewarning of Caesar's death, and at the same time symbolizes what is going on in the minds of the human figures of the play—reflects on the universal scale the conflicts at the human level. To Casca the storm means either that "there is a civil strife in heaven," or that the angry gods are punishing their disobedient subjects on the earth (I. iii. 11–13). Caesar declares that "nor heaven nor earth have been at peace to-night" (II. ii. I); and Calphurnia reports that, among the "most horrid sights" seen during the night,

> Fierce fiery warriors fight upon the clouds
> In ranks and squadrons and right form of war,
> . . . The noise of battle hurtled in the air. (II. ii. 19–22)

Allied with this imagery of civil warfare is Cassius's way of looking on Caesar and himself as contestants for some kind of supremacy. He describes how he and Caesar strove, "with hearts of controversy" to outswim each other in the swollen Tiber; and it infuriates him that Caesar should have outstripped him and all other competitors in the struggle for power in the state:

> Ye gods, it doth amaze me
> A man of such a feeble temper should

So get the start of the majestic world,
And bear the palm alone. (I. ii. 127–30)

It is Cassius's rankling sense of inferiority, his knowledge that Caesar will beat him in any contest for power, that makes him organize the conspiracy. If he had really had patriotic motives for doing so, he would have thought about what was to replace Caesar's rule. He was too intelligent to have forgotten this consideration, except under the stress of his obsessing hatred.

The image of strife is used once more. Portia, in her violent agitation of mind after Brutus has gone to the Capitol, imagines that she hears "a bustling rumour, like a fray", though Lucius can hear nothing.

After Antony's speech to the citizens there is actual mutiny in Rome, and Italy is plunged into the bloody discord which he foretold over Caesar's murdered body. There is no longer any need for Shakespeare to use as an image what is one of the principal themes of the play.

Mr John Crow has drawn my attention to another, recurrent image in which the characters are seen in terms of metal; in which contrasts are brought out or implied between the sharpness and bluntness of metal objects, between liveliness and dullness, between preciousness and baseness. In his first full speech in the play Brutus says,

I am not gamesome: I do lack some part
Of that quick spirit that is in Antony. (I. ii. 27–8)

Thus Brutus himself brings to our notice a contrast which is to be most glaringly exemplified in Act III, Scene i, where the nimble-witted Antony leads him by the nose, and makes him look a very dullard. When Brutus and Cassius part after their first interview, Cassius declares that Brutus's "honourable mettle may be wrought from that it is dispos'd". There is a play here on the two meanings of the word *mettle*, "disposition" and "metal" (as it is nowadays spelt when used in this sense). Cassius, amongst other feelings about Brutus, regards him as a piece of precious metal which he can fashion into a tool that will suit his own purposes; there is also the implication that he will turn him into base metal by "seducing" him. The same metaphor occurs at the end of the following scene, when Casca says that the "countenance" of Brutus, "like richest alchemy", will make the baseness of the other conspirators appear to be worthiness.

The image of a tool that has been edged by a craftsman is put into the mouth of Brutus when, soliloquizing in his garden, he says,

Since Cassius first did *whet* me against Caesar,
I have not slept. (II. i. 61–2)

It is present again in Antony's words:

> I am no orator, as Brutus is,
> But (as you know me all) a plain *blunt* man. (III. ii. 219–20)

The ironical implication is that Brutus is "a sharp fellow", who has stolen away the hearts of the citizens by the glib arts of the practised orator.

This line of imagery would, of course, gain extra point if we could be sure that Shakespeare was consciously punning on Brutus's name in using it. It is improbable that Shakespeare would not know the meaning of the Latin word *brutus*, which in Lewis and Short's dictionary is given thus: "I. Lit., *heavy, unwieldy, immovable.* II. Trop., *dull, stupid, insensible, unreasonable.*" He would perhaps also know Livy's or Ovid's account of how the word *brutus* became the cognomen of the family from which Marcus Brutus claimed descent; and Plutarch refers briefly to the legend. According to Livy,[4] Lucius Junius Brutus, the great liberator who "did from the streets of Rome the Tarquin drive", feigned stupidity to save himself when Tarquinius Superbus was massacring all potential rivals. He "kept up the appearance and conduct of an idiot", and "did not even protest against his nickname of 'Brutus'". Now Shakespeare's Brutus has, over and above the fine qualities that he derives from his model in Plutarch, others which give us some justification for regarding him as dull and unreasonable; and it is tempting to think that Shakespeare, unable to believe that a man as wise and virtuous as Plutarch's Brutus could associate himself with the wicked and senseless murder of Caesar, took a hint from Brutus's name in providing him with less estimable traits.

The same imagery is once or twice applied to Casca. Brutus says of him

> What a blunt fellow is this grown to be!
> He was quick mettle when he went to school. (I. ii. 292–3)

Cassius defends him on this occasion, and explains that this "tardy form" is a pose; but in the next scene, wishing to whet him too against Caesar, he tells him that he is "dull", and wanting in "those sparks of life that should be in a Roman" (I. iii. 57–8).

There are other less obvious instances of the use of this and kindred metaphors: where, for example, Brutus undertakes to "fashion" Ligarius (II. i. 220); or where Flavius speaks of the "basest mettle" (in a double sense) of the citizens (I. i. 61). And when Brutus says, "To you our swords have leaden points, Mark Antony" (III. i. 173), it is possible to see an implied contrast between the leaden dullness of Brutus in this scene and the quicksilver brilliance of Antony.

Professor Spurgeon has perhaps done less than justice to the consistency and interest of the imagery in *Julius Caesar*. As in his other mature plays,

Shakespeare has used the imagery to reinforce the impressions that characters give of themselves by their speech and conduct. He has also used it to heighten atmosphere. I must content myself with citing two instances of this. Blood and destruction play an important part in the action of the play; blood plays an important part in the imagery as well. Then on three occasions a certain theatricality, whether in character or incident, is emphasized by imagery connected with the theatre: when Caesar has a fit while he is being offered the crown, when Brutus gives his final exhortation to the conspirators in the garden, and when Brutus and Cassius are swept away by their exalted but purposeless enthusiasm after they have stabbed Caesar.

Finally, Professor Price has drawn attention[5] to the importance of the word *love* as a key-word of the play. "There is this love of Brutus for Caesar and of Caesar for Brutus, the love of Brutus and Cassius, Brutus and Portia, the mutual love between Brutus and Lucius and all his servants. Brutus is a center of love wherever he goes. There is the love of Antony for Caesar, which drives him to destroy the conspirators. There is the ominous absence of love around Octavius. Love violated and betrayed, the man who lives for love violating himself, these are among the most moving *motifs* of the play."[6]

NOTES

1. *Prefaces to Shakespeare: First Series*, p. 105.
2. B. Ifor Evans, *The Language of Shakespeare's Plays*, p. 164.
3. Caroline F. E. Spurgeon, *Shakespeare's Imagery*, pp. 346–7.
4. I. i. 56ff.
5. *Julius Caesar*, ed. Hereward T. Price, Introduction, p. xii.
6. For a perceptive study of the place of *Julius Caesar* in the development of Shakespeare's style and dramatic technique, see Granville-Barker, *From Henry V to Hamlet* (British Academy Shakespeare Lecture, 1925).

1986—Dieter Mehl. "Julius Caesar," from
Shakespeare's Tragedies: An Introduction

Dieter Mehl, a professor at the University of Bonn, wrote or edited many books on literature, including *English Literature in the Age of Chaucer* and *Elizabethan Dumb Show: The History of a Dramatic Convention*.

It is not only the setting which *Julius Caesar* and the other two Roman tragedies have in common, but also their chief source, Plutarch's parallel *Lives* of famous Greeks and Romans. By its date, however, the play belongs rather to a period just before the 'great' tragedies. Although one must be careful not to reconstruct in one's mind the fiction of an ideal artistic development, it still seems clear that *Julius Caesar* has a certain transitional quality, linking the history plays with the group of tragedies beginning with *Hamlet* and ending with *Antony and Cleopatra* or *Coriolanus*.

At the time of writing *Julius Caesar* (about 1599), Shakespeare had just finished the two historical tetralogies on the reigns of the English Kings from Richard II to the first Tudor, Henry VII, using Raphael Holinshed's *Chronicles of England, Scotland, and Ireland* (2nd edn 1587) as his main source. In Sir Thomas North's translation of *Plutarch's Lives of the Noble Grecians and Romans* (1579) he found a very successful work of vivid historiography that presents the historical events with more consummate literary art, bringing back to life an epoch familiar to Shakespeare's contemporaries from several other accounts, historical and fictional. Plutarch's biographies create a memorable impression of the fascinating interplay between dynamic personalities and political change, more consistently than the English historians and without their obvious didactic application to the present. There is no divine providence governing and patterning the events, and no national interest, like the 'Tudor-myth', serves as a general focus. On the other hand, a number of political issues are touched on that are also among the central themes of the histories, so that the transition from one period to another hardly meant a completely new beginning for the dramatist nor even a radical change of genre.[8]

As in the histories, the action of *Julius Caesar* is practically all concerned with public events and affairs of state. The characters have to make political decisions, and the republican state, represented by the most respected citizens, but also by the less individualized plebeians, is the life-giving organism whose welfare and stability are as important as the fate of the individual. The same might be said of *Hamlet*, but in its persistent emphasis on the close connection between personal action and the health of the community *Julius Caesar* is closer to the histories than to *Hamlet*, *Othello*, or even *King Lear*, whereas there are striking similarities to *Macbeth*.

The close affinity between *Julius Caesar* and the histories could be demonstrated by a study of the battle scenes, the presentation of the populace and the function of foreboding, but this still does not make this Roman tragedy a history play. It might be more helpful to approach it as the first of the mature tragedies. Several themes and human situations we find in *Hamlet* and the other 'great' tragedies can already be found in *Julius Caesar*, in particular the hero's tragic dilemma which, in the last resort, claims more of our attention and sympathy than the political fate of Rome, even though the two can hardly be separated. Indeed, it is the inescapable interrelationship between individual choice of action and its consequences for the whole community that is brought out so forcefully here for the first time in Shakespearian tragedy.[9]

When Shakespeare decided to write a tragedy about Julius Caesar, Brutus and Mark Antony he chose three characters who had been the subject of controversy for centuries. Earlier critics were divided into those who thought that Shakespeare shared the republican admiration for Brutus and those who felt that he was on the side of the monarchists and Caesar-worshippers, while more recent criticism tends to see the play as perhaps the most influential contribution to a long debate that was not concerned so much with party spirit or clear evaluation as with an argumentative assessment of complex, contradictory, and seemingly incompatible characters. There were, to be sure, some definite traditions, such as the image of Caesar as an overweening tyrant who was rightly assassinated, or the cautionary picture of the sacrilegious regicide Brutus, tormented, along with Judas Ischariot, in Dante's Inferno, but the more important aspect of the whole tradition of Caesar's murder was the idea of memorable and controversial men in whom admirable greatness and fatal error were so inextricably mixed that a conflict of historical dimensions was inevitable. 'The reassessment and reconsideration of such famous historical figures was a common literary activity in the Renaissance, not merely in poetry and drama (where licence is acceptable), but in plain prose, the writing of history.'[10] This, I think, is more helpful for an understanding of Shakespeare's characters than a minutely detailed comparison of the play with every possible source. In view of the highly sophisticated efforts of so many classical or Renaissance authors to weigh all the personal and political aspects of Caesar's murder it is altogether unlikely that Shakespeare should have been content with simple glorification or indictment. The two central characters in particular, Caesar and Brutus, are dramatically presented in such a way that the spectator is not encouraged to pass confident judgement or to take sides. Rather he is confronted with conflicting impressions, suggesting agonizing uncertainty and tragic tension, not a morality in which Good and Evil are opposed.

Shakespeare's Caesar is even less simple and predictable than Plutarch's, largely due to the form of the tragedy and the dramatist's techniques of characterization. From the very first scene, Julius Caesar is powerfully present, even though he does not enter the stage before the second scene. The way the other characters speak about him is as important for his overall portrait as his personal appearances.

The first scene, contrasting the relaxed holiday mood of the opportunist plebeians with the republican zeal and indignation of the Tribunes of the People, presents the demonstrative personality cult of Caesar side by side with the political fears and apprehensions it arouses, thus introducing the crucial phenomenon that Caesar's impact, throughout the play, is more powerful, indeed more real, than his physical presence. At first, when he himself enters the stage, he seems little more than a monarch surrounded by fawning courtiers and flatterers, who commands respect. His authority is taken for granted and does not have to be demonstrated by impressive rhetoric or despotic gestures. The dramatic structure of the long second scene is worth noticing as an effective means of characterization: Caesar himself only makes two comparatively brief appearances, closely observed by Brutus and Cassius, but it is especially during his absence that the dialogue is concerned with him. His personal presence seems comparatively undramatic. We can hardly tell from his short assertions of majestic self-confidence whether arrogant pride or natural dignity is the more characteristic trait. At any rate, he hardly strikes us as a dangerous tyrant or a villain consumed by ambition. His very precise estimate of the threat posed by the cramped Cassius is proved absolutely correct by the development of the action; by the same token, there is a strong element of tragic irony in his claim to be above fear and caution. His real personality comes out much more impressively through Cassius' attempts to influence Brutus and Brutus' tragic dilemma, as well as Casca's satirical account of what happened off stage. The fact that he is deaf in one ear—a handicap added by Shakespeare—and troubled with the 'falling sickness' does not mean that the dramatist deliberately reduced his heroic stature, but rather underlines the extraordinary force of his presence which is not even impaired by these physical defects. Nor will Cassius' tales about Caesar's weakness convince us that his authority is mere sham because they are so obviously dictated by hatred and envy and say more about the speaker himself than about the man he wants to belittle. It rather confirms the impression suggested by Plutarch's account that Caesar succeeded in overcoming such corporal odds. His public image of unmatched glory is not affected by it and will, of course, survive his assassination.

As the play proceeds Caesar still remains a figure seen from the distance rather than in close-up and we learn more about his impact on others than about the actual individual. Whenever he appears in person he seems more anxious to create an impression of superhuman stature and commanding presence than to allow us any revealing insight into his real thoughts and emotions. Even in his own home he talks like a public orator. The rhetorical device of speaking about oneself in the third person, used with particular frequency in this tragedy, contributes to this distancing effect, as if the speaker himself were of much less importance than the part he is playing and the legend attached to his name:

> Caesar should be a beast without a heart
> If he should stay at home today for fear.
> No, Caesar shall not. Danger knows full well
> That Caesar is more dangerous than he.
> We are two lions littered in one day,
> And I the elder and more terrible,
> And Caesar shall go forth. (II.2.42–8)[11]

There is a hint here of the overweening pride of someone who will presently fall from the height of his power and prosperity, and Calpurnia's retort, 'Your wisdom is consumed in confidence' (II.2.49) is amply justified in view of what follows. More important in the context of the whole play is the way this sort of rhetoric turns our attention from the individual character in order to establish a personal myth. The name of Caesar and his power over other people is more interesting for the reader and spectator than the personal fate of the man behind the name, and this is how we have to understand the play's title. In spite of some more individual traits, made even more prominent by Shakespeare as compared with Plutarch, Julius Caesar is not really a tragic hero in a more than formal sense. His fall is, of course, quite in accordance with the classical pattern of tragedy, but it does not move us like the death of King Lear or even the murder of Duncan.

The real tragic conflict, to which all the audience's sympathy is directed, concerns Brutus and his decision to join the conspiracy. This rather unusual dramatic constellation is partly due to the story material and the sources, but even more to Shakespeare's evident intention to present Caesar's fall and his revenge from the murderer's point of view.

In Plutarch, the events that constitute the play's action form the basis of three different biographies: Julius Caesar, Brutus and Mark Antony. For each of the three eminent Romans the Ides of March means something different and each of them might well have been the hero of a separate tragedy, depending on the choice of episodes and of the dramatic perspective. It was obviously in the person of Brutus that the dramatist saw the most promising elements of the kind of tragic dilemma that recurs, with variations, in the later tragedies. In *Othello* as well as in *Macbeth*, a man highly esteemed as 'noble' by all around him is corrupted and becomes a brutal murderer. Like Othello, Brutus falls victim to the illusion that a bestial killing may be stylized into a ritual act of higher justice or even a necessary sacrifice, and like Macbeth he finds that the blood shed by the murderer cannot be buried together with the corpse, but poisons all the hoped-for achievement.

As in *Othello*, the actual instigation to the murder is the work of skilful and calculated persuasion, yet even more the work of the murderer's own imagination which produces arguments and motives for the final decision where genuine justification is lacking. Cassius makes unscrupulous use of Brutus' momentary melancholic mood and of his not in all respects discriminating idealism to make him an accomplice in a scheme that is clearly foreign to Brutus' noble nature, as Cassius knows well enough. He is not, to be sure, the diabolic tempter of the moralities, nor is he, like Iago, presented as a villainous intriguer, but his part in the tragedy as a most fatal influence on the protagonist is not so different from the traditional motif of temptation. Shakespeare's evident desire to suggest a characteristically Roman climate is presumably the main reason why, in contrast to the later tragedies, moral categories or Christian ethical concepts play only a very minor part in *Julius Caesar*. 'Good' and 'Evil' bear the names of 'virtue', 'honor', 'nobility' and their opposites. Cassius appeals to

Brutus' sense of honor and to his patriotism, and it is clear from the reaction of his partner that his words coincide with a process of reflection that had already begun before their meeting. Brutus himself feels that he is about to be pushed into a very dangerous decision and he is unwilling to commit himself on the spot.

The dramatic technique in this first temptation scene (I.2) is quite similar to that employed in *Othello* and reads almost like a preparation for it: the temptation is briefly interrupted by the entrance of the victim, followed here by Casca's scornful account, but in fact it is, indirectly, continued all the time because Brutus' view of the events has been profoundly influenced by Cassius' insinuations and he is likely to interpret everything in a new light. There is another possible link with Iago in Cassius' concluding soliloquy in which he reflects on his success and clearly implies that what is at issue is the perversion of a noble mind, a mind which Cassius deliberately intends to turn into a direction quite uncongenial to it.[12] Cassius does not by any means hate Brutus, but he is prepared to sacrifice him to his own hatred of Caesar and to drag him down to his own level to this purpose. As in the case of Othello, it is Brutus' very nobleness that makes the corruption possible:

Well, Brutus, thou art noble, yet I see
Thy honourable mettle may be wrought
From that it is disposed. Therefore it is meet
That noble minds keep ever with their likes;
For who so firm that cannot be seduced? (I.2.305–9)

This is clearly in the tradition of the villain's soliloquy by which the audience is informed about the schemer's designs and is, at the same time, presented with a particularly complimentary characterization of the hero which strikes us as especially reliable coming from the mouth of his opponent. Of course the situation is rather more complex here because of the political context. After what we have seen, the fear of tyranny does not seem to be entirely unfounded even though there are no very substantial grounds for assuming that a cruel reign of terror is imminent. Nor would an Elizabethan audience feel—as many twentieth-century spectators would—that the defence of a republican constitution was really a matter of life and death. Cassius' whole argumentation seems largely motivated by envious hatred of a man whom he cannot admit to be superior to himself and he insists on an abstract concept of honor which is not necessarily identical with the good of the whole community. On the other hand, the text does not rule out the possibility that, as suggested by Plutarch, there is some genuine political conviction behind his violent opposition to tyranny.[13] Cassius is considerably more than an envious hypocrite, as the rest of the tragedy will show.

As in some of the later tragedies, the threat to human order and harmony is accompanied by an uproar of nature. Destructive thunderstorms, often followed by supernatural apparitions, announce some monstrous crime or underscore the outbreak of uncontrolled human passions. The storm in the third scene, following immediately on Cassius' soliloquy, is in the tradition of theatrical foreboding and mirrors the character of the conspiracy and its fatal consequences. It is, however, explained in a variety of ways within the play itself and it is only in retrospect that we can really be sure of its ominous significance. Cicero rightly points out that interpretations of such phenomena are often quite subjective and thus touches on a theme that will return in *Macbeth*:

> But men may construe things after their fashion,
> Clean from the purpose of the things themselves. (I.3.34–5)

Cassius provides a good example when he relates nature's upheaval to Caesar's tyrannical behavior, which is hardly supported by the play itself, whereas Casca is shaken by natural fear until Cassius succeeds in securing his support, more quickly and more thoroughly than in the case of Brutus. Later, however, Cassius himself equates the thunderstorm with the deed they are about to plan and thus casts some doubt on his own earlier interpretation:

> And the complexion of the element
> In favour's like the work we have in hand,
> Most bloody-fiery, and most terrible. (I.3.128–30)

Cassius' choice of words already prepares the reader for Brutus' view of the conspiracy which more and more impresses itself on him during his nocturnal vigil. The first part of this impressive scene (II.1) can be seen as one long soliloquy, interrupted three times by Lucius' brief appearances. It is through this monologue that Brutus' central position as the real tragic protagonist of the play is established.[14] Shakespeare's most inventive adaptation of traditional forms of soliloquy can already be studied in *Romeo and Juliet* and in the histories, but it is only in the mature tragedies that we find the agony of a personality torn by conflicting impulses portrayed with such dramatic intensity as it is here. Outward impressions and deep reflection go hand in hand. Two aspects are worth singling out: soliloquy is no longer used as a kind of solo performance or aria, a recital of emotions or an unfolding of intentions for the benefit of the audience, but tries to render a continuous process of reflection, uncontrolled associations and worrying uncertainty. Equally significant for Shakespeare's interpretation of his material is the fact that Brutus experiences the whole problem of his part in the conspiracy as a moral conflict. Though his thoughts, banishing sleep, are concerned mainly with the political aspects of Caesar's ambition and the reasons that finally persuade him to join the conspirators have more to do with the well-being of the whole community than with individual morals, the intensity of the conflict sets Brutus apart from all the other enemies of Caesar and convinces the audience that this is not a decision arrived at by rational weighing of arguments, but a fundamental choice, involving the whole personality and determining all his future life. Brutus will never be the same again as he was before he had to face this agonizing decision. In this sense, though the whole context is quite different, Brutus is in a similar situation to Macbeth or, indeed, Hamlet.

The language of the soliloquy also points towards Hamlet and his lonely reflections, in particular his 'To-be-or-not-to-be' soliloquy whose syntax and occasionally even exact wording are anticipated here.[15] A number of particular considerations and fears seem to occur to the speaker and he tries to weigh their implications and consequences against each other. This is not addressed to the audience nor are we presented with a carefully considered statement, but rather with a mental process. Like Hamlet, Brutus appears to be thinking aloud:

> Crown him that,
> And then, I grant, we put a sting in him
> That at his will he may do danger with.
> Th' abuse of greatness is when it disjoins
> Remorse from power, (II.1.15–19)

This form of arguing with oneself, not by consistent reasoning but rather by unpredictable association, makes it difficult to decide at what precise point Brutus actually makes up his mind, if there is such a point.[16] More important for our impression of him is the fact that Cassius' insinuations have robbed him of his sleep and have changed his whole personality. Like Hamlet, he finds himself confronted with a moral demand whose implications fill him with terror, but whose hold on him is inescapable. Cassius' additional device of sending anonymous letters of admonition strengthens Brutus' conviction that the Roman people expect him to liberate them from oppressive tyranny; at the same time it casts a somewhat dubious light on the whole enterprise and makes it look like a sinister intrigue that has need of such dishonest means.

Once conspiracy and murder are faced as a reality, the future begins to look like a horrifying nightmare, just as it does for Macbeth before the murder of Duncan. The tone of Brutus' imaginings is very like that of Macbeth's visions when he is haunted by the prospect of the deed:

> Between the acting of a dreadful thing
> And the first motion, all the interim is
> Like a phantasma or a hideous dream.
> The genius and the mortal instruments

Are then in council, and the state of man,
Like to a little kingdom, suffers then
The nature of an insurrection. (II.1.63–9)

The way crucial moral experiences are dramatized is very similar to that in the
'great' tragedies, especially in the corruption of a potentially noble character
by influences whose nature he but dimly recognizes. Brutus is not deceived by
any illusion about the gravity of the crime he is envisaging, for which even the
night is not dark enough (II.1.77–81). 'Conspiracy' is seen as something wicked,
whose 'monstrous visage' must be disguised by a mask. The arrival of the fellow-
conspirators is certainly not greeted with joyful conviction, but with a grim and
sinister determination.[17]

It is also worth noting that Shakespeare has not made use of the best
arguments for Caesar's removal he might have found in his sources, and Brutus
himself seems unable to quote any actual tyrannical deeds committed by Caesar;
he only talks himself into a righteous indignation about the likelihood of future
acts of despotism. There is nothing really incriminating that can be said about
Caesar as he is at present. Brutus even gives one of the most complimentary
accounts of him to be found in the whole play, which again must raise grave
doubts about the justification of the murder:

and, to speak truth of Caesar,
I have not known when his affections swayed
More than his reason. (II.1.19–21)

This is a very different Caesar from the one Cassius describes as an overweening
demi-god who must be removed in the common interest. More important
than the question whether Brutus here gives a true account of the hero is the
observation that he admits Caesar's admirable qualities and his essential integrity
at the very moment when he has decided to kill him. Shakespeare evidently
wants to make clear that Brutus does not act from any personal animosity, but is
moved by genuine political concern, though it is equally clear that this concern is
largely an illusion with very little foundation in reality. Brutus is about to commit
a crime horrifying to himself and, like Othello, he is ruled by motives that arouse
respect as well as revulsion. 'Noble Roman' and 'noble moor' are in a very similar
manner characteristic of Shakespeare's concept of a tragic hero.

In his discussions with the conspirators, too, criminal intentions and
gestures of genuine human greatness are presented side by side and their basic
incompatibility seems to be apparent to the spectator alone. Brutus is led into
grave tactical mistakes and into demonstrative declamation by his almost
pathetic determination to turn the assassination into a disinterested sacrifice. The
authority of his person makes him carry all before him even where he is palpably

in the wrong. Thus, the decision to spare Mark Antony soon proves to be a fatal blunder. Even more disastrous is the erroneous notion that Caesar's spirit can be extinguished by the removal of the man. The whole play demonstrates that Brutus is unconsciously describing his own tragedy when he proclaims his illusion of a righteous and unbloody murder:

> Let us be sacrificers, but not butchers, Caius.
> We all stand up against the spirit of Caesar,
> And in the spirit of men there is no blood.
> O that we then could come by Caesar's spirit
> And not dismember Caesar! (II.1.167–71)

This separation of body and spirit soon turns out to be a fond illusion, sharply refuted by the political realities. Caesar's spirit, on the contrary, is untouched by the murder and in the end triumphs over the conspirators. Brutus' pose is discredited even by the fulsomeness of his rhetoric as well as by his complete isolation among the conspirators. None of them shares his heroic idealism, and the contradictions between the actual business of the conspiracy whose outcome the majority of the audience must know or are able to guess, and Brutus' euphoric enthusiasm—'Let's carve him as a dish fit for the gods' (II.1.174)—are so obvious as to make him a lonely and tragic figure. In addition, his dialogue with Portia, following immediately on the departure of the conspirators suggests very strongly that Brutus himself is not really convinced of the worthiness and integrity of his purpose. To his wife, at least, he appears to be deeply disturbed and their marriage union is gravely affected by his mental struggle. The drama shows the effects of his heroic pose on the most intimate personal relationship and this brings us much closer to him because we see him not only as the domineering idealist, but as a man shaken and suddenly stripped of all familiar ties, a man, moreover, who has by no means lightly made up his mind to the murder and expects neither the gratification of personal ambition nor certain fame. The last part of the scene, too, the 'healing' of Ligarius, directs our sympathy more towards Brutus whose integrity inspires such unlimited confidence and whose heroic view of the murderous project no longer stands quite alone.

The whole exposition puts Brutus and his confrontation with Caesar's spirit firmly in the centre of the action. He is presented on his own as well as in conversation with a variety of characters, from Cassius to his boy Lucius whose innocent sleep appears to him as the image of a mind untroubled by any conflict or worrying reflections, making him all the more conscious of his own dilemma. Like the King in *Henry IV, Part II*, or like Macbeth, Brutus finds that loss of sleep is perhaps the most disturbing consequence of the utter isolation produced by the agonizing moral decision he has to face.[18] His almost fatherly regard for the boy and his natural need for sleep—repeated before the final

battle (IV.2.289–322)—is an important aspect of Shakespeare's characterization
of him. His fatal blindness in matters of state by no means excludes admirable
tenderness in his relations with others and this is obviously meant to secure him
some of our sympathy in a situation where he might otherwise appear completely
misguided and repulsive. The weight and pressure of the task he considers a
political duty have indeed changed his personality, yet they have not perverted
his selfless sensibility for the individual needs of those near to him. This clearly
distinguishes him from some of the later tragic heroes who often seem to lose
sight of this unheroic human context.[19]

In deliberate contrast to Brutus, Julius Caesar is presented without such
personal ties. The interventions of the two wives, for instance, following almost
immediately upon each other, are quite different in style and dramatic impact.
Calpurnia's apprehensions are more general and far less personal than Portia's,
caused by external forebodings and warnings rather than by her own observation
of her husband, and Caesar's tone towards her is hardly different from his usual
public manner, showing little personal concern or genuine affection. In view of
what follows, his demonstrative equanimity appears rather like arrogant blindness,
not true stoic courage. Whereas Brutus thinks of the outward impression made
by his actions, if at all, only for tactical reasons, everything Caesar says seems
calculated to produce a particular effect for the benefit of his public image. His
rhetoric hardly ever gives to his replies the touch of a spontaneous reaction. Even
where there are clear signs of wavering uncertainty, as in his first refusal to go to
the Senate, it is quickly covered by high-sounding gestures.

In this case, however, the conspirators have included Caesar's excessive
concern for his reputation in their plans, which is why Decius' not very subtle
strategy succeeds in swaying his resolution. All this clearly contributes to a
certain detachment in our attitude towards Caesar and Brutus, preventing any
too personal involvement in the murder, since we have never actually seen Caesar
without his public mask. It is 'the spirit of Caesar' that determines all the action
of the play, not the inner life of an individual with whom we are asked to identify
and of which the dramatist allows us barely a glimpse.

The assassination itself is staged as a pantomimic pageant rather than a scene
of dialogue. Apart from Caesar's brief exclamation, '*Et tu, Brute?*' (III.1.77), taken
straight from the source and made to sound like an impersonal quotation by
the language alone, the victim is not given an opportunity for a dying speech or
some last words to the murderers. He dies at the moment of supreme belief in his
own power, proudly claiming invulnerability. The proclamation of an exceptional,
super-human status is rhetorically impressive, but it is swiftly and visibly refuted
by his downfall, which makes the scene almost an exemplary morality, showing
us the punishment due to the sin of *superbia*, though the remainder of the action
shows that this only applies to Caesar the man, not to his fame or his political
impact. His far-reaching influence as well as the whole idea of glamorous

monarchy associated with his name make his confident comparison of himself to the northern star that is above petty change in retrospect seem much less presumptious and absurd than it might do at first. In contrast to Duncan or old Hamlet, Caesar is not buried quietly and soon replaced. Not even the conspirators appear to count on an easy success because they immediately see themselves as defendants and victims of imminent persecution before they have time to make concrete plans for a better government. Shakespeare emphasizes the unrealistic euphoria of the murderers who are intoxicated with the historic magnitude of the moment and completely misjudge the actual political situation; Brutus even more than the rest. The fame of their deed, outliving many generations, is impressed on the audience by the prophetic glimpse of theatrical performances, such as the one we are witnessing while hearing these lines spoken. Like other Shakespearian characters, Brutus and Cassius know they will live on, immortalized by poetry:

> *Cassius.* How many ages hence
> Shall this our lofty scene be acted over
> In states unborn and accents yet unknown!
> *Brutus.* How many times shall Caesar bleed in sport,
> That now on Pompey's basis lies along,
> No worthier than the dust! (III.I.111–16)

These lines state the claim of Shakespeare's stage to contribute to the handing down and to the glorification of great human achievements, but they are also to be understood as an indirect commentary on the action because all poetic transmission is at the same time something of an illusion and has its share of the unpredictable nature of all human fate.[20] The audience is reminded of this by Cassius' continuation of the prophetic account:

> So oft as that shall be,
> So often shall the knot of us be called
> The men that gave their country liberty. (III.1.116–18)

This confident hope is justified neither by the historical events nor by the literary tradition, and even within the play itself it is soon disappointed. The entrance of Mark Antony's servant, following almost immediately upon these lines, already marks a first turning-point in the action because his ambiguous profession of loyalty to the conspirators gives us a hint of the tactical superiority and the pragmatic calculation that are more than a match for Brutus. His sense of honor is as unrealistic as it is inappropriate on that political level to which he has now descended. Caesar's assassination, celebrated by Brutus as a glorious theatrical moment, is at the same time a very ugly political fact whose consequences cannot be glossed over by idealizing rhetoric. The ritual of bathing the conspirators' arms in the blood of the victim, staged by Brutus, remains a showy gesture, a last and ineffective attempt at presenting the murder as something of a religious ceremony. Antony's reaction, however, soon makes plain enough that Caesar's friends are not to be convinced by this kind of language. Brutus is outwitted in one decisive matter and Antony's soliloquy over Caesar's body draws a very different picture of the situation, one that, in the context of the whole play, appears no more biased or distorted than Brutus' idealizing image of a disinterested sacrifice:

> O, pardon me, thou bleeding piece of earth,
> That I am meek and gentle with these butchers!
> Thou art the ruins of the noblest man
> That ever lived in the tide of times.
> Woe to the hand that shed this costly blood! (III.1.154–8)

After the calculated diplomacy of the dialogue, the soliloquy shows us the undisguised emotions of the speaker. His personal grief and his unqualified praise of the dead are a pointed means of manipulating our sympathy. Brutus' noble motives are neither known to Antony nor are they explicitly cast in doubt; in view of the bloody corpse, however, they seem rather irrelevant and Antony is not prepared to make any distinction between the individual murderers. For him they are all 'butchers' and this, to the spectator, must appear as a clear repudiation of Brutus' high-minded claim: 'Let us be sacrificers, but not butchers' (II.1.167).[21] Antony's own prophecy of internecine civil war turns out to be much more accurate and his metaphor of a revenge tragedy describes at least one important aspect of the following acts:

> And Caesar's spirit, ranging for revenge,
> With Ate by his side, come hot from hell,
> Shall in these confines, with a monarch's voice,
> Cry 'Havoc!' and let slip the dogs of war, (III.1.270–3)

The terminology associates the following events with revenge plays in the Senecan manner, where personified revenge or classical revenge deities introduce and observe the action.[22] The parallels are quite unmistakable, in the inevitability of retribution and its fateful course and even more striking in the apparition of Caesar's Ghost. The whole action demonstrates that Caesar's spirit, of all things, was not destroyed by the assassins, but survives them all and is fearfully avenged.

To be sure, the revenge is not as straightforward as in many pre-Shakespearian tragedies. The complex historical background prevents an impression of personal vendetta and the contrasted characters of Brutus and Antony make it difficult if not impossible to take sides without qualification. If, immediately after the murder, Brutus appears as a rather blind idealist, who is unable to see the criminality of the deed, the following scenes continually emphasize his disinterested sincerity, his inspiring impact on others and his courageous readiness to face the consequences of his decisions while, on the other side, we are soon made to doubt whether his opponents are really above all concerned with avenging the murder and re-establishing a stable political order or whether there are less admirable motives at work as well.

The famous Forum scene is a good instance of the close interrelation of personal tragedy and political intrigue. The contrast between Brutus and Antony makes this particularly clear; both of them have to translate personal emotions and considerations into political action. Brutus can justify the murder to himself as well as to the state only if the people are prepared to go along with him and if the stability of the republic is not upset. His speech to this purpose is finally made ineffectual by Antony's brilliant performance, but it would be wrong to call it naive or to say that Brutus does not know how to handle an audience.[23] The change from verse to prose and the skillful use of syntactic symmetry emphasize the complete contrast to the rest of the scene. The speech is a consummate demonstration of mass-manipulation by an ostensible appeal to reason and a sense of public responsibility. The spectator in the theatre knows that Brutus is really unable to produce rationally convincing grounds for his action because for him the murder was only a preventive measure, though his speech pretends to a logic that almost compels the listener to admit the inevitability of the assassination if he does not want to appear as a friend of tyranny. Yet, since Brutus has not so much his own personal advantage at heart as the preservation of the liberty won by Caesar's death, his speech, in spite of all tactical shrewdness, gives an impression of sincerity and integrity. Paradoxically, the fact that it fails to achieve its object also makes us admire the speaker's honesty more than blame his lack of political judgement.

Brutus' crucial blunder lies in his failure to see Antony's supreme talent as a demagogue and its possible effect on the Roman plebeians. His own apparent (and very short-lived) success, above all the citizens' cry, 'Let him be Caesar' (III.2.50), make clear that the people have not understood the true political motives behind the assassination and are hardly able to follow a rational argument, but he is obviously unable to recognize the thoroughly unreliable nature of public opinion, and the play leaves us in no doubt that he commits a fatal error when he leaves Antony alone with his audience. The fact that Antony turns out to be a much more effective virtuoso in manipulating the masses does not make Brutus an inept rhetorician, but it does show his limited political foresight. Though the romantic notion of a Hamlet-like Brutus, too reflective and bookish for the harsh world of political realities, was plainly mistaken,[24] it is quite obvious that his illusion of a ritual sacrifice, a disinterested murder for the sake of Rome's liberty, is inadequate when it comes to dealing with the

political situation after Caesar's death and this is the reason why the possible
fruits of the crime are soon handed over to the enemy. It is Brutus' heroic pose
as his country's liberator more than anything that makes him vulnerable against
the unscrupulously plotted revenge of his opponents, much as it commands our
respect for its noble sincerity.

Apart from Plutarch's brief hint to the effect that Brutus had a more Spartan,
Mark Antony a more Asiatic and emotional rhetorical style there is nothing
in the sources that could have given Shakespeare the idea of the two Forum
speeches. The rhetorical contrast and the dramatic tension produced by these
two efforts to sway an unpredictable audience are among the most brilliant
and memorable moments in the entire canon. It is not a case of an inferior
speaker being succeeded by a good one, but rather of two completely different
temperaments and, accordingly, two different forms of demagogism presented
side by side. Antony's triumph is by no means a victory for the better cause or
for the more substantial arguments; it throws light on the irresponsibility of the
people who are so easily betrayed into a complete dissolution of public order
and are evidently in need of judicious and disinterested political guidance. It
is not, however, critical satire of the unreliable and fickle mob that is the point
of the scene, but the question of political stability and those responsible for it.
As in the history plays, Shakespeare here seems particularly interested in the
necessary qualities of true authority and leadership. In this respect, Antony is
hardly superior to Brutus, as is brought home to the spectator in the subsequent
scene where the utterly harmless and innocent poet Cinna is butchered in the
street by the excited and totally irrational plebeians only because he happens to
have the same name as one of the conspirators. Nothing illustrates better the
threat of political chaos than his desperate and unsuccessful attempt to save his
skin by explaining the mistake. The aimless rage of the mob, especially its blind
hatred of civilized values, is strongly reminiscent of Jack Cade's popular rebellion
in *Henry VI, Part II*: there the popular cry is 'Away with him! away with him!
he speaks Latin!' (IV.7.55); here it is 'Tear him for his bad verses, tear him for
his bad verses!' (III.3.30–1), which is hardly meant as an expression of practical
literary criticism, but as a frightening outburst of inhuman brutality and political
disorder of the kind most feared by the Elizabethans.

The destructive rage of the mob is the direct result of Antony's celebrated
speech whose brilliant rhetoric, supported by well-timed gestures, pauses and
visual effects, deliberately plays on the audience's emotions and stirs up the
popular fury to an uncontrollable pitch. Brutus' point of view is ironically
deflated rather than refuted by any argument and Antony's own grief, which is
genuine enough and not merely put on, is made part of his rhetoric. Next to the
deftly manipulated about-face in the reaction of the popular audience, the most
important achievement of the speech consists in the impressive glorification of
the dead, in the creation of a larger-than-life, idealized image of Caesar. It takes

over Caesar's own idea of himself, continuing it beyond death. It is the first major demonstration of this great person's immortality and its power to direct all the following events. The scene also shows that the murder has unleashed forces not anticipated by the conspirators and certainly beyond their control.

The last part of the play presents the inexorable course of retribution, but it adds little that is new to our assessment of the characters. Brutus accepts his defeat and destruction with heroic dignity, but he also hastens them by tactical blunders and lack of self-criticism. As before with the conspirators, he now takes over, as a matter of course, the part of the authoritative leader and, here again, the catastrophe is an immediate consequence of his arrogant dismissal of Cassius' acute objections.

The long confrontation between Brutus and Cassius (IV.3) once more juxtaposes Brutus' integrity and his lack of superior foresight. His just wrath at the discrediting of the common cause by the soldier's iniquities is an expression of the tragic experience he has to undergo: he finds that the moral justification of the murder becomes more and more questionable. More shattering for him than outward defeat is the inescapable recognition that the effect to wipe out injustice has only produced new injustice. Once again he tries to present his own version of the events as actual fact:

Remember March, the Ides of March remember.
Did not great Julius bleed for justice' sake?
What villain touched his body, that did stab
And not for justice? What, shall one of us,
That struck the foremost man of all this world
But for supporting robbers, shall we now
Contaminate our fingers with base bribes, (IV.2.70–6)

This desperate clinging to an illusion, which the play has already exposed as hollow, throws light on Brutus' tragedy but also on his admirable sincerity, and this seems to be more important to the dramatist than the arrogance felt so deeply by Cassius. In principle, Brutus is in the right, and when we learn afterwards that all the time he must have been suffering under the fresh knowledge of his wife's death, it is again evident that the text wants to emphasize Brutus' essential nobility.[25] The whole scene presents the clash between two powerful and very different temperaments without putting all the blame on one of the two opponents. The quarrel and the reconciliation underline the importance of true friendship and affection in politics as well as in personal intercourse, just as Brutus' fatherly concern for the over-tired boy Lucius introduces an element of personal warmth and loyalty which makes us feel closer to the heroic Roman. On the enemy's side, the bartering about human lives and the open contempt of the triumvir Lepidus shown by his partners are a demonstration of a cynical

attitude towards humane values (IV.1) that greatly diminishes our sympathy for
the avengers. Brutus is loved by Portia, by Cassius and by Lucius, and this is in
the last resort more important for our final assessment of him than his rather
high-handed rhetoric, which is rather to be seen as Shakespeare's means of
characterizing him as the representative of aristocratic Romanness. In contrast,
Antony and Octavius seem only united by transitory common interest. Just as
Antony plans to rid himself of Lepidus as soon as he has served his purpose,
he himself will, not long afterwards, be thrown over by Octavius, as many of
Shakespeare's early spectators would surely have known. Both of them are shown
to be without that sense of human loyalty and integrity that is so characteristic
of Brutus.

Though Brutus is the chief tragic protagonist in this play, he somewhat
recedes into the background during the last scenes and we are not given much
insight into his deepest thoughts and feelings. There is a certain distancing even
in the last scene of the fourth act when the Ghost of Caesar appears to Brutus
while he is watching out the night. The brief conversation with Lucius underlines
the impression of an approaching crisis because it is made to sound like a final
parting. The boy is unable to stay awake with his master who is then left on his
own, just like Marlowe's Doctor Faustus during his last night alive or Christ in
his agony in the Garden of Gethsemane. These associations are not explicitly
suggested by the text, but they will be present for many readers familiar with the
literary tradition, if only as a vague atmospheric reminiscence. In this situation,
the apparition, which Shakespeare found in his source, could have been presented
as the moment of tragic recognition, either by a sudden pang of conscience or
a final hardening of heart. The dramatist, however, does not intensify the scene
in this way. Brutus' surprise and terror seem to last only a very short while and
the disturbed sleep of his attendants remains a rather vague gesture of dramatic
foreboding without any deeper moral significance.

In some of Shakespeare's histories, too, the last night before the decisive
battle is the time when the hero receives a last warning or encouragement, but
Brutus is neither the murderous tyrant visited by his victims, like Richard III,
nor God's own soldier who stands for justice and victory, like Richmond and
Henry V. As an 'Elizabethan Roman' he is not particularly susceptible to spiritual
impressions and he faces his impending fate with stoical equanimity:

Why, I will see thee at Philippi then. (IV.2.336)

Shakespeare neither makes him conscious of his own guilt and defeat nor does
he give him any opportunity for a final justification of his course of action. This
may, perhaps, be explained by the dramatist's idea of the spirit of Rome or by
his not completely developed concept of the tragic hero. There is, at any rate, no
doubt that in the last act the dramatic tension appears to relax and the external

action becomes predominant. To some extent, though, the same might be said of some later tragedies, such as *Hamlet* and *Macbeth*.

The battle that occupies all the fifth act, is presented mainly in terms of revenge for Caesar, whose spirit appears as the true victor at the end, not so much as a duel between two opposing moral principles or political concepts. The verbal sparring before the fight once more recapitulates the conflicting views of Caesar's assassination, though Brutus is not given the time for a reasoned account of his view. The whole sequence of scenes underlines the impression of an inescapable fate met by Brutus and Cassius with Roman fortitude. Brutus himself describes his philosophy in terms of 'patience' and 'providence', concepts which any Christian audience would be familiar with and which return in the later tragedies:

> —arming myself with patience
> To stay the providence of some high powers
> That govern us below. (V.1.106–8)

Up to the very end, Brutus insists on the dignity and integrity of his life and he never views himself, as Othello does, as one who is guilty and has deserved his destruction, but as a Roman who proves his virtue even in death. His dying words, like those of Cassius, are concerned with Caesar and his death, but his own fame means more to him than outward success:

> I shall have glory by this losing day
> More than Octavius and Mark Antony
> By this vile conquest shall attain unto. (V.5.36–8)

This verdict is largely confirmed by the play and it certainly deserves our respect. The audience will hardly take it as the author's last word, though, since the total impression of the tragedy and its chief actors is more complex than that.

There is hardly another Shakespearian tragedy in which right and wrong seem to be so evenly distributed among the two opposing parties. At least, the dramatist's manipulation of our sympathies is less clear and more ambivalent than in the 'great' tragedies that follow *Julius Caesar*?[26] Brutus' self-confidence is not often quite free from arrogance and self-righteousness and the whole play, as well as the historical facts, can be said to refute his illusion that the assassination of Caesar was a necessary and beneficial act. On the other hand, neither are his enemies guided by nobler motives nor is their final victory presented as a moment of liberation or a triumph of justice. Though the concluding couplet has a more cheerful and confident ring than the last words of *Hamlet*, *Othello* or *King Lear*, the impression of great human loss, more definite than in *Macbeth*, detracts from the glory of the victory and even those spectators who are less familiar with the further course of Roman history, will hardly fail to notice the threat of future conflict in Octavius' appeal:

> So call the field to rest, and let's away
> To part the glories of this happy day. (V.5.81–2)

More significant and decisive for our assessment of the victors and the defeated is the unqualified tribute paid by Antony and Octavius to the dead Brutus. Dramatic convention lends an authority to Antony's last words, as a kind of final appreciation for posterity, which is clearly intended to put less favorable aspects in perspective and leaves us with an impression of heroic nobility:

> This was the noblest Roman of them all.
> All the conspirators save only he
> Did that they did in envy of great Caesar.
> He only, in a general honest thought
> And common good to all, made one of them.
> His life was gentle, and the elements
> So mixed in him that Nature might stand up
> And say to all the world 'This was a man!' (V.5.69–76)

It may be difficult to reconcile this ideal portrait with all that has gone before, but, as in the case of Othello, we are not asked to admire a criminal or to forget right and wrong, but to pay respect to human sincerity, greatness and tragic suffering. This last gesture, celebrating the dead with an obituary that seems to cast a glance at future historians and poets, links *Julius Caesar* with the 'great' tragedies and it also makes clear that it is Brutus who is the tragic protagonist.

Even in the last act the play has continually suggested contradictory views and has presented the hero as well as his opponents in turn as the champions of a just cause and as self-centred criminals, but this does not mean that we are offered no more than mutually exclusive alternatives that leave us alone to make our choice. The tragedy of *Julius Caesar* is not a 'problem play' in the sense that the dramatist deliberately withholds a solution to present the audience with an open question,[27] but a classical story is retold in such a way as to make again plausible why so many generations were fascinated by it and were provoked into a fundamental debate on political and human values, complex characters and controversial decisions. The audience is clearly invited to join in this debate, not just to accept a ready-made version of the events. The fact that the text does not allow a simple interpretation or a comfortable identification with one particular point of view does not make *Julius Caesar* radically different from the other tragedies, because in hardly any of them is it possible to divide the characters into good and evil according to unmistakable authorial signals. It seems clear, on the other hand, that for Shakespeare the world of the Romans, in contrast to the early history of Denmark, Britain, or Scotland, was not ruled and ordered by Christian values and the individual character is left with a secular morality as his standard of behavior, guided at best by a tradition of Roman virtues, unprotected and unrestrained by an ethical code shared with the audience. This may well be the reason why the Roman tragedies have often provoked particularly controversial interpretations.[28]

NOTES

8. North's translation of Plutarch, at least the most relevant portions of it, is most conveniently studied in Geoffrey Bullough, *Narrative and Dramatic Sources of Shakespeare*, vol. v (London, 1964), under each Roman play, or in the useful edition by T. J. B. Spencer, *Shakespeare's Plutarch* (Harmondsworth, 1964), where the relevant passages from the plays are quoted as well. See also J. Barroll, 'Shakespeare and Roman History', *MLR*, 52 (1958), 327–43.

9. I quote from the excellent edition by Arthur Humphreys, *The Oxford Shakespeare* (Oxford, 1984); see also the very useful editions by Norman Sanders, *New Penguin Shakespeare* (Harmondsworth, 1967) and T. S. Dorsch, *The Arden Shakespeare* (London, 1955); the anthology Peter Ure, ed., *Shakespeare, 'Julius Caesar'. A Casebook* (London, 1969), provides a helpful introduction into some of the most important issues.

10. Spencer, 'Shakespeare and the Elizabethan Romans', 33. On the changing reputation of the two chief characters see the excellent chapter on the play in Ernest Schanzer, *The Problem Plays of Shakespeare: A Study of 'Julius Caesar', 'Measure for Measure', 'Antony and Cleopatra'* (London, 1963), pp. 10–70, Bullough's introduction, *Narrative and Dramatic Sources*, v, 3–57, and Virgil K. Whitaker, *Shakespeare's Use of Learning: An Inquiry in the Growth of his Mind and Art* (San Marino, 1953), pp. 224–50; excerpts from Schanzer and Whitaker are reprinted in Ure, *A Casebook*.

11. Velz speaks of 'illeism' in the play; see Velz, 'The Ancient World in Shakespeare', 9–10. On the dramatic technique of preparation, see Wolfgang Clemen, *Shakespeare's Dramatic Art* (London, 1972), pp. 49–59.

12. See Schanzer, *The Problem Plays*, pp. 38–40; on Cassius' soliloquy see Sanders' edition, p. 24 and commentary, p. 165.

13. In his commentary on 1.2.95–6 and 1.3.89–90, Sanders quotes relevant passages from Plutarch.

14. On Brutus as a tragic hero see, for instance, the chapter 'Marcus Brutus' in John Palmer, *Political and Comic Characters of Shakespeare* (London, 1962), and Moody E. Prior, 'The Search for a Hero in *Julius Caesar*', *RenD*, NS, 2 (1969), 81–101. There is a good survey of scholarship, with a useful bibliography by T. J. B. Spencer in Stanley Wells, ed., *Shakespeare: Select Bibliographical Guides* (London, 1973), pp. 203–15.

15. Cf. 'there's the question' (II.1.13) with *Hamlet* III.1.56: 'that is the question'.

16. See Kenneth Muir, *Shakespeare's Tragic Sequence* (London, 1972), p. 47, and Schanzer, *The Problem Plays*, pp. 49–51, with reference to *Hamlet*.

17. See the chapter 'Brutus and Macbeth' in G. Wilson Knight, *The Wheel of Fire. Interpretations of Shakespearian Tragedy with Three New Essays* (London, 1930) pp. 120–39.

18. In *Othello*, too, sleep is an experience of a peaceful mind (see III.3.331–4).

19. In the case of *King Lear*, however, the hero only discovers this in the course of tragic suffering.

20. See Anne Righter, *Shakespeare and the Idea of the Play* (London, 1962), p. 141; for an early poetic treatment of the vagaries of literary and historical transmission see Chaucer's *House of Fame*, and Piero Boitani, *Chaucer and the Imaginary World of Fame*, Chaucer Studies, 10 (Cambridge, 1984).

21. In *Macbeth*, too, the hero is referred to as 'butcher' (V.6.108).

22. In the anonymous tragedy *Locrine* (1591) Ate appears between the acts as a sinister prophet of coming disaster (Malone Society Reprints, 1908). The relationship between *Julius Caesar* and revenge tragedy is discussed in Norman Rabkin, *Shakespeare and the Common Understanding* (New York, 1967), pp. 105–19.

23. See Schanzer, *The Problem Plays*, pp. 47–9; similarly, Muir, *Shakespeare's Tragic Sequence*, pp. 52–3. Most interpretations of *Julius Caesar* comment on the two speeches. On the rhetoric of the play, see Gayle Greene, '"The Power of Speech/To Stir Men's Blood": The Language of Tragedy in Shakespeare's *Julius Caesar*', *RenD*, NS, 11 (1980), 67–93, and John W. Velz, '*Orator* and *Imperator* in *Julius Caesar*: Style and the Process of History', *ShakS*, 15 (1982), 55–75. On the play's language in general see the two chapters in G. Wilson Knight, *The Imperial Theme: Further Interpretations of Shakespeare's Tragedies including the Roman Plays* (London, 1931), pp. 32–95, Charney, *Shakespeare's Roman Plays*, pp. 41–78, and Traversi, *Shakespeare: The Roman Plays*, pp. 21–75.

24. See Schanzer, *The Problem Plays*, pp. 16–17, and *Hamlet*, ed. Philip Edwards, pp. 5–6.

25. See Schanzer, *The Problem Plays*, pp. 63–5; Muir is more critical of Brutus, pp. 51–3. It is in the controversial assessment of Brutus that interpretations of the play differ most markedly. See also the very balanced account of Adrien Bonjour, *The Structure of 'Julius Caesar'* (Liverpool, 1958), and the works referred to in n. 14 and 26 to this chapter.

26. See the good chapter on *Julius Caesar* in E. A. J. Honigmann, *Shakespeare: Seven Tragedies* (London, 1976), pp. 30–53, and the provocative study by J. I. M. Stewart, *Character and Motive in Shakespeare* (London, 1949), pp. 46–55. On the religious dimension of the play see David Kaula, '"Let Us Be Sacrificers": Religious Motifs in *Julius Caesar*', *ShakS*, 14 (1981), 197–214.

27. This is how Schanzer sees the play. I think he exaggerates the differences between *Julius Caesar* and the other tragedies, but his very perceptive interpretation is hardly dependent on the validity of his general thesis.

28. The play's stage history is also an important guide to its meaning and its reception. See the detailed account by John Ripley, *'Julius Caesar' on stage in England and America, 1599–1973* (Cambridge, 1980).

1994—Harold Bloom.
"Introduction," from *Julius Caesar*

Harold Bloom is Sterling Professor of the Humanities at Yale University. He has edited many anthologies of literature and literary criticism and is the author of more than 30 books, including *The Western Canon* and *Shakespeare: The Invention of the Human.*

George Bernard Shaw was not a literary critic, as Eric Bentley sensibly indicates. The Shavian polemic against Shakespeare is partly an inevitable anxiety in regard to Shakespeare's eminence, partly an overreaction against Edwardian, bardolatry. In 1898, Shaw began the year by reviewing a performance of Shakespeare's *Julius Caesar*, which he called "the most splendidly written political melodrama we possess" but which nevertheless he judged to be a disaster:

> It is impossible for even the most judicially minded critic to look without a revulsion of indignant contempt at this travestying of a great man as a silly braggart, whilst the pitiful gang of mischief-makers who destroyed him are lauded as statesmen and patriots. There is not a single sentence uttered by Shakespeare's *Julius Caesar* that is, I will not say worthy of him, but even worthy of an average Tammany boss.

How are we to reconcile this with the judgment that Shaw goes on to make?

> As far as sensitivity, imagery, wit, humor, energy of imagination, power over language, and a whimsically keen eye for idiosyncrasies can make a dramatist, Shakespeare was the king of dramatists.

Shaw presumably was clearing a space for his own *Caesar and Cleopatra*, composed later in 1898. Aside from a charming portrait of Oscar Wilde as Apollodorus the Sicilian aesthete and swordsman, there is little in Shaw's play that can compete with Shakespeare's Roman tragedies. Shaw's sixteen-year-old Cleopatra could never grow into Shakespeare's middle-aged serpent of the Nile, and Shaw's Caesar never was, on land or sea. It is a considerable puzzle just why this Caesar wants power; nothing in his character suggests the ruler or the warrior, rather than the radical journalist or the problem-playwright and social educator. We are given Julius Caesar as a will, a life-force, striving to produce something higher, but how this is properly expressed by the conquest of Gaul, or of Britain, or of Egypt, is not very clear. But this is very early Shaw, and he was learning his way, while the Shakespeare of *Julius Caesar* (1599) is on the threshold of writing *Hamlet*, probably less than a year later. *Julius Caesar* is the tragedy of Marcus Brutus, and not of Caesar, which may have inspired Shaw's protest. Shakespeare's skill in characterization is marvelously manifest in his Caesar, who is a far subtler representation than Shaw cared to understand. Set upon the verge of becoming emperor, Caesar holds back, yet he already apprehends himself as almost a god. He is intensely sympathetic, a little silly, potentially very dangerous, and distinctly past his stronger phases. Frank Kermode speaks of Caesar's "self-infatuation and dynastic longings," and adds pungently that "Caesar was beginning to forget his mortality." Perhaps because of political anxieties, Shakespeare is extraordinarily balanced and subtle in his representation of Caesar. Brutus is the tragic hero: noble, disinterested, trapped in a dilemma between wrong and wrong, rather than between a Hegelian right and right. It is wrong to murder Caesar, who has a particular affection for Brutus, and wrong (Brutus's perspective) for Caesar to rule over the Senate and establish himself as monarch-god. No one can be quite certain how these wrongs are to weigh, each against the other, and Shakespeare evades any judgment even though him Caesarism must win.

That Caesar, his bodily power failing, yet retains great shrewdness of observation, Shakespeare indicates from the start. The analysis of Cassius, made to Antony by Caesar, is accurate and prophetic. There is an extraordinary blend of uncanniness and vainglory in Shakespeare's Caesar but the uncanniness or sublimity seems to me the stronger element. Despite Shaw's contention that Shakespeare's Caesar said nothing worthy of the historical conqueror, there are affirmations not merely eloquent but actually persuasively definitive of a knowing courage that constitutes its own virtue:

> Cowards die many times before their deaths,
> The valiant never taste of death but once.
> Of all the wonders that I yet have heard,
> It seems to me most strange that men should fear,
> Seeing that death, a necessary end,
> Will come when it will come.

This is as famous as anything in Shakespeare, as memorable as Hamlet or Lear or Macbeth at their most eloquent, and one sees why: how could it be better expressed, and how can we not admire the speaker? The monosyllabic fourth and sixth lines establish the grave authority of a Caesar who is still Caesar, and the word "wonders," which alone keeps the third line from also being monosyllabic, serves to remind us that the speaker himself is one of the wonders of universal history. Nowhere else in Shakespeare are we presented with a strictly historical figure who outranks Caesar; the only rivals are figures of myth, literature, and pre-history. If this Caesar suffers from self-fixation, he still knows what he was, and declines to be less. Shakespeare is careful however to permit his waning Caesar to follow thus apotheosis with an outburst of inflated rhetoric, hyperbolical to the extreme:

> Danger knows full well
> That Caesar is more dangerous than he.
> We are two lions litter'd in one day,
> And I the elder and more terrible;
> And Caesar shall go forth.

That is deliberate bombast, and makes Caesar into an allegorical or abstract quality equal to Danger, and so dehumanizes him. Shakespeare's art is at the shrewdest when bombast and courage are so fused together that no one could hope to disentangle them:

> But I am constant as the northern star,
> Of whose true-fix'd and resting quality
> There is no fellow in the firmament
> The skies are painted with unnumb'red sparks.
> They are all fire, and everyone doth shine;
> But there's but one in all doth hold his place.

It is both pathetic and sublime; an effect not often matched in literature. Brutus, as everyone agrees, is a study for Hamlet, but Caesar is no anticipation of Claudius. There are other ambiguous portrayals in Shakespeare, but no one else at all like his Julius Caesar, neither before nor after. We do not know who acted Caesar when the play first was performed, but I like to think it was Shakespeare himself, a "character actor" (as we now call it) who evidently preferred to play the older parts. In relation to Brutus-as-Hamlet Caesar only can be the Ghost of Hamlet's father, a role Shakespeare did play. I do not think, in opposition to Freud, that there is anything Oedipal about Hamlet's tragedy, but Brutus pragmatically is a kind of Oedipus who has slain the king his father, just as Macbeth is also such a figure. Entering as the Ghost of Caesar, Shakespeare would have had the pleasure of identifying himself as: "Thy evil spirit, Brutus." It is a lovely touch, whoever first played it, and it hints at the true relation between Caesar and Brutus, father and son, king and regicide.

———

1996—Harold Bloom. "Introduction," from
Bloom's Notes: William Shakespeare's Julius Caesar

Harold Bloom is a professor at Yale University. He has edited dozens
of anthologies of literature and literary criticism and is the author of
more than 30 books, including *The Western Canon* and *Shakespeare: The
Invention of the Human*.

Shakespeare's *Julius Caesar*, though in some respects it is almost the model
of a "well-made play," is nevertheless a remarkably ambiguous work. Julius
Caesar himself is at the center of the ambiguity: how does Shakespeare's drama
wish us to regard Caesar? By the time he composed *Antony and Cleopatra*,
Shakespeare's mastery of perspectivism had so increased that we tend hardly
to notice that the ambiguities also had vastly heightened. Whether you regard
Cleopatra as a protogoddess, a whore, or something in between, is likely to
say more about you than about the role that Shakespeare created. But in
Julius Caesar, your attitude towards Caesar might only indicate your politics,
since everything in Shakespeare's representation of the Roman hero (even
that word is problematical) is capable of multiple interpretations. Beyond
question, Caesar is Shakespeare's only historical character of worldwide
importance (unless you count the Octavius of *Antony and Cleopatra*, who has
not yet become the first emperor of Rome, Augustus Caesar). Shakespeare
wrote no play about Alexander the Great; Julius Caesar is a comparable figure,
which makes Shakespeare's treatment of him all the more surprising, even
disconcerting.

Despite the play's title, Caesar's is only a supporting role in what should be
called *The Tragedy of Marcus Brutus*. Caesar, after all, is on stage for only three
scenes, is dead before the halfway point, and speaks perhaps one hundred and
forty lines. And yet he is the atmosphere of the play, its world, almost its nature
despite the uneven quality of his speeches, which vary from an egotistic inanity
to a noble, virtually godlike intensity of being. Some critics have suggested
that the Julius Caesar of Shakespeare is cunningly less interested in an earthly
crown than he is in his metamorphosis into a god. He already rules Rome;
all that he can gain by provoking the conspirators is a martyr's death that
ensures his status as a god and that guarantees the Roman Empire that will be
inaugurated by his nephew Octavius Caesar. In a strange sense, Caesar seems
to have chosen the risk of being slain as a sacrifice to his own greatness. Brutus,
who has enjoyed a son's relationship to Caesar, urges his fellow assassins to
carve up the dictator as a sacrifice fit for the gods, a sentiment by which the
Stoic Brutus intends no irony, though Shakespeare's own irony is evident, as it
is throughout much of the play.

Brutus, as the drama's protagonist, is himself presented with considerable ambiguity, perhaps because he is an anticipation of Hamlet, prince of ambiguities. Self-righteous and morally rather vain, Brutus takes for granted his own disinterestedness, a dangerous assumption in this most political of Shakespeare's plays, with the possible exception of the later *Coriolanus*. I think, *contra* Freud, that there is Oedipal conflict in Hamlet, but there certainly is one in Brutus, as there will be in Macbeth. Brutus cannot understand his own ambivalences towards Caesar and is thus unable to ward off the influence of Cassius, who knows very well why he resents Caesar. The relation between Brutus and Cassius seems to me the subtlest in the play and the most dramatic. Cassius's love for Brutus is a veneration that he denies to Caesar and that Brutus scarcely reciprocates, because Brutus is indeed so powerfully self-centered. That Brutus is noble and stoical is not to be denied, but Shakespeare has endowed this Roman hero with considerable narcissism. As a Stoic, Brutus is able to divide his reason and his passions from one another, yet Shakespeare may have made Brutus too much of a Stoic to be able to move us as profoundly as we are moved by the protagonists of the other tragedies. Since Brutus demonstrates a constant, highly conscious self-control, we have some difficulty at seeing into the abyss of his self. Yet Shakespeare provides us with enough representation of division in Brutus's soul so as to render him a tragic figure, flawed in judgment and hemmed in by his absolute conviction of his own virtue. He is so identified with his own vision of Rome that he simply does not know where he ends and where Rome begins. Though Cassius draws him into the plot to murder Caesar, he offers virtually no resistance and sees himself as fated to sacrifice Caesar to the gods. As leader of the assassins, Brutus is not less than a disaster. Cassius urges, sensibly, that Mark Antony be slain with Caesar; Brutus refuses, and yet events prove Cassius to have been correct. Again, Cassius shrewdly seeks to deny Antony the chance of a funeral oration for Caesar; Brutus overrules Cassius, with dark results for the conspirators. Finally, Brutus insists upon marching to Philippi for the final battle, and again Cassius yields out of affection and so forfeits his better judgment.

In his death speech, Brutus moves us when he rejoices that "in all my life / I found no man but he was true to me." But then we reflect that Brutus, of all the conspirators, was most untrue to Caesar, who loved him. This irony, to which Brutus is blind, marks his limits once more. And yet, there is indeed a premonition of Hamlet's greatness in Brutus: the Roman hero's meditations presage the grand speculations of Shakespeare's principal intellectual. Against the charismatic consciousness of Brutus, Shakespeare sets the nature of the political failure, perhaps even political crime: to murder Julius Caesar is to strike against the entire tradition of kingship that descends from Caesar, a tradition that includes, however remotely, Queen Elizabeth I herself. Shakespeare is both subtle and careful in the balance of this tragedy: Brutus is the tragic hero, but his identification with Rome is more flaw than virtue, and it destroys him.

JULIUS CAESAR
IN THE TWENTY-FIRST CENTURY
ชิ๛

The twenty-first century has brought new perspectives to *Julius Caesar*. The distinguished critic Frank Kermode identified the failure to see oneself clearly as an important issue in the play. While a number of critics have written about Brutus's confused speeches, Kermode saw them as the beginning of a trend in Shakespeare's work that also appears, for instance, in *Richard II* and *Troilus and Cressida*. Kermode commented that Brutus's deliberations on whether to join the conspiracy draw attention to a tense experience: the time between the making of some horrific decision and its execution. Shakespeare explores this issue further in *Macbeth*.

Like prior critics, Kermode also explained the relevance of *Julius Caesar* to audiences of Shakespeare's time. Elizabethans would have great interest in what happens in *Julius Caesar* since its situation was similar to that of their own day. Although Shakespeare does not espouse a certain political view in the play, Kermode pointed out, most Elizabethans were against republicanism and believed a monarchy was best. Furthermore, Roman history was important to Elizabethans since England had once been under imperial Roman rule.

Another commentator, Andrew Hadfield, also wrote of the play's applicability to the people of Shakespeare's time. He emphasized its focus on the death of republicanism and emerging tyranny. In the Rome dramatized in the play, republicanism can no longer function. This is a Rome where the classes are out of harmony; where the spirit of cooperation has been abandoned; where punishment can be meted out without a trial, one of the key aspects of a republic; and where superstition rather than reason predominates. Consequently, a government that more closely suits the needs of the people must eventually replace it. In watching the play, Hadfield said, Elizabethans could see how Rome changed and what the consequences were.

E. A. J. Honigmann focused not on the play's political revelations, but on Shakespeare's craft in revealing his characters to the audience. According to Honigmann, Shakespeare presents a certain perspective of each character that shifts as the play progresses; this progression is designed to elicit a sequence of different reactions from the audience. Antony, for instance, has a relatively small part in Acts I and II, and he then appears frivolous and subservient to Caesar. Thus his funeral speech in Act III appears even stronger than it otherwise might, and as the play progresses his skill and his ruthlessness become evident. In a similar way, Shakespeare shapes the audience's varying response to Cassius. In the beginning Cassius comes across as merely a cunning manipulator, whereas by the end of the play his character seems more nuanced and admirable.

Honigmann closely examined Brutus, whose flaws, though they surface only a little at a time, eventually turn the audience's sympathies against him. Shakespeare accomplishes this by having Brutus do things that make the audience uncomfortable. For example, when Brutus washes his hands in Caesar's blood, offers his bloody hand to shake Antony's, and directs the other conspirators to do the same, his actions invite a negative response. Shakespeare also keeps the audience at an emotional distance from Brutus: Unlike other Shakespearean tragic heroes, whom viewers might almost identify with, Brutus suppresses his emotions. In Honigmann's view, then, Shakespeare is not so much concerned with historical accuracy but with creating specific dramatic effects and carefully guiding the audience's reaction.

2000—Frank Kermode.
"Julius Caesar," from *Shakespeare's Language*

Frank Kermode is one of the most respected English critics of his time. He is the author of many books, including *The Age of Shakespeare* and *Shakespeare's Language*.

So far as is known, the first tragedy played in the new Globe Theatre was *Julius Caesar*. It is one of the few plays of which we have a contemporary report of a Globe performance. Thomas Platter of Basle happened to record in his diary that on 21 September 1599 (probably by the Continental calendar; the date would have been nine days earlier by the English count), he crossed the Thames and saw at a theatre that was obviously the Globe the tragedy of "the first emperor Julius Caesar with nearly fifteen characters very well acted." The performance ended with the customary dance or jig.

Platter notes that he went to the theatre around two o'clock, the usual time. *Julius Caesar* is one of the shorter tragedies, perhaps not much longer in performance than the "two hours' traffic of our stage" mentioned in the Prologue to *Romeo and Juliet*.[1] This relative terseness is echoed in the economical construction of the play and in what might be called its dialect. With the experience of nine English history plays behind him, Shakespeare deftly selects and incorporates the narratives of Plutarch in North's translation, compressing, omitting, focussing, adjusting the relationships of the main characters, and occasionally adding material from other sources, or of his own invention.

For example, he seems to have invented the scene where Calpurnia is touched by the runners in the Lupercalian ritual, and the scene of the murder of the poet Cinna, mistaken for a politician, is taken from a hint in the historian Suetonius writing about a later epoch. Perhaps this little insertion was meant as an ironic denial that poets, except by unhappy chance, have anything to do with politics; yet this is an intensely political play, a fact that has a controlling influence over its language. The rule of Julius Caesar effectively marked the end of the Roman republic and the troubled beginning of the empire. The Elizabethans were in general anti-republican, believing monarchy to be the best system of government, and propaganda claimed that Elizabeth's right descended ultimately from the Emperor Constantine, who was the son of the Englishwoman Helen and the first Christian emperor. So there was, it was believed, a direct line to Rome in the period of Caesar's assassination and the accession of Octavius Caesar as Augustus.

Plutarch had republican sentiments but admitted that Rome, having at the time suffered a century of civil war, needed the firm single rule of Caesar. In the sixteenth century some thought of Caesar as a tyrant, and some, arguing against the official view that obedience was required whatever the character of the monarch, thought tyrants ought to be killed. Others, perhaps, like Brutus, believed that Caesar was not a tyrant so long as he did not accept the crown, that despite his virtually absolute power he had shown no disposition to use it absolutely. And Plutarch himself raises the issue of whether Caesar was a tyrant or "a merciful physician." What is certain is that to the first audience this was a play about a world-historical event, still politically relevant. The conspirators, after the death of Caesar, make the point clear enough:

> How many ages hence
> Shall this our lofty scene be acted over
> In states unborn and accents yet unknown! (III.i.111–13)

Cassius goes on to predict that when Caesar will be seen to "bleed in sport," the conspirators will be revered for having given their country liberty (114–18). There must be irony here; the audience, or most of them, knew better.

The main purpose of Shakespeare's brilliant and daring opening scene, whose principal characters disappear from the play immediately, is to set up an opposition between fickle public sentiment, now favoring Julius Caesar, and the higher class represented by the tribunes, who support the defeated Pompey. We are shown a vigorous reaction to Caesar's ambition and his triumphal entry into Rome, the latter not being customary when the defeated enemy was another Roman. The opening scene, like others, and notably that of *Hamlet*, tells us much about the kind of dramatic poet Shakespeare was. He may begin obliquely, as here, or enigmatically, as in *Macbeth*; but, as in his verse, he is always putting the simple sense into question. His plays contain other scenes that sometimes puzzle the reader or (if they are not cut by some director) the audience. Another example in *Julius Caesar* is the curious little conversation among Decius Brutus, Cinna, and Casca during the meeting of the conspirators (II.i.101–11). These men, about to pledge themselves to murder, quietly disagree as to which way is east and where the sun rises in March: a small puzzle in the midst of greater ones.

Elizabethan interest in the fate of Julius would be intense and also divided. Caesar was a monarch in all but name, and Shakespeare, who had written of many monarchs, stresses his human failings (deafness, pride, perhaps sterility). On the other hand, he omits material that would darken the portrait of Brutus, who, in the thought of the period, could be either a heroic tyrannicide or a republican hero. No simple political position can be detected in the play. Whatever view one took, these Romans had immediate importance as ancient imperial ancestors, and whatever side they were on, they must be supposed to have spoken with a sort of constrained dignity. The dialect of the tragedy is quite unlike that of its predecessor *Romeo and Juliet* or of its successor *Hamlet*. The characters, apart from the crowd, speak like Romans, conscious of the honour of being Romans, contemporaries, after all, of Cicero, a principal model of Renaissance style.

This is not to say that the work is absolutely free of the rhetorical obscurities we shall encounter in the later tragedies, but it is relatively so. The play begins with the good-humoured prose of the populace, which gives way at once to the florid scolding of the tribunes; the people are to weep into the Tiber till it overflows. The jokes of "naughty knaves" and the rant of the anti-Caesarian tribunes are at the two remote ends of the rhetorical scale. In the second scene we find the middle way, something close to the register of the remainder of the play: economical dialogue followed by a more expansive discussion between Brutus and Cassius. There is no attempt to generate high poetry; the tone is thoughtful, though never lacking in force:

> *Cas.* Tell me, good Brutus, can you see your face?
> *Brut.* No, Cassius; for the eye sees not itself
> But by reflection, by some other things.
> *Cas.* 'Tis just,
> And it is very much lamented, Brutus,
> That you have no such mirrors as will turn
> Your hidden worthiness into your eye,
> That you might see your shadow. (I.ii.51–58)

Cassius is beginning his campaign to recruit Brutus for his conspiracy, but he starts from a long way off, introducing this notion of the eye's inability to see itself, its dependence on reflections or shadows. As we have already seen, the idea of the reflection as the shadow of a substance was precious to Shakespeare, and it always called forth fine contemplative verse. "How soon my sorrow hath destroy'd my face," says Richard II after smashing the looking-glass. "The shadow of your sorrow hath destroy'd / The shadow of your face," replies Bolingbroke (IV.1.291–93). And Richard develops the theme:

> The shadow of my sorrow! Ha, let's see.
> 'Tis very true, my grief lies all within,
> And these external manners of laments
> Are merely shadows to the unseen grief
> That swells with silence in the tortur'd soul.
> There lies the substance . . . (294–99)

As Peter Ure has remarked, Bolingbroke and Richard are giving different senses to the word "shadow": to Bolingbroke the broken mirror bore only the shadow, not the substance; Richard speaks of the *darkness* cast by his sorrow, and Ure adds, "My sorrow—these external ways of lamenting—are simply shadows [= unreal images] of the grief within. Richard thus uses Bolingbroke's own quibble to prove, not, as Bolingbroke had wished to, that the image in the glass is unreal, but that Richard's lamentation reflects a real substance, just as the image in the glass, though itself unreal, as Bolingbroke claims, none the less reflects a real face. A shadow is unreal compared with the substance that it is a shadow of; this fact can be used either, as by Bolingbroke, to insist on the unreality of the shadow, or, as by Richard, to insist on the reality of the substance."[2] It may be that since, as Brutus remarks, "the eye sees not itself / But by reflection," all attempts to examine what Hamlet calls "that within that passes show" (I.ii.85) must be unreliable, for in the language of the time reflections are shadows, and shadows are not only areas of darkness but unreal and possibly false representations of substance.

Shakespeare again presents the insoluble difficulty of actually seeing what is "within" in *Troilus and Cressida*, when Ulysses and Achilles have the following discussion:

> *Ulyss.* A strange fellow here
> Writes me that man, however dearly ever parted
> How much in having, or without or in,
> Cannot make boast to have that which he hath,
> Nor feels not what he owes, but by reflection;

As when his virtues, aiming upon others,
Heat them, and they retort that heat again
To the first giver.
    Achil. This is not strange, Ulysses.
The beauty that is borne here in the face
The bearer knows not, but commends itself
To others' eyes; nor doth the eye itself,
That most pure spirit of sense, behold itself,
Not going from itself; but eye to eye opposed,
Salutes each other with each other's form;
For speculation turns not to itself,
Till it hath travell'd and is mirror'd there
Where it may see itself. This is not strange at all. (III.iii.95–111)

Ulysses wants to make the point that honour and reputation lie not "within" but in the applause of others, a kind of reflection, to be represented either as reflected heat or as noise. The context, and the language or dialect, is very different from that of *Julius Caesar* or of *Richard II*, far more studied and laborious, but the figure is still virtually the same, and, as we shall see, it is recurrent and must have real, not shadow, importance to the poetry. For actors are also shadows, as Macbeth remarked—"Life's but a walking shadow, a poor player, / That struts and frets his hour upon the stage, / And then is heard no more" (V.v.24–26). And the notion that the substance, the life "within," is inaccessible except by such treacherous mediation tells us something important about an author whose business it was to present character in all its inaccessibility, in language at least as opaque as necessary.

An instance of his doing that is the soliloquy of Brutus in II.i. The first act has the long temptation of Brutus by Cassius, brilliantly set against the shouts of the crowd. Cassius is mocking Caesar's weakness, remembering him in his fever whining for water: "Give me some drink, Titinius" (I.ii.127)—a savage put-down in itself, thin and querulous and the more so in that the report coincides with another shout from the mob that wants Caesar crowned. Cassius has an embittered and calculating eloquence, and his long speeches are barely punctuated by the replies of Brutus. Then we hear more of Caesar, with Casca's account of the behaviour of the rabblement, and Caesar's fit, all in blunt, rather Jonsonian prose. Cassius ends the scene with a self-satisfied soliloquy.

At once there is a storm; and the same Casca is now terrified—in verse, for he is suffering and talking about divine portents. Coleridge did not think this authentic, supposing that the part of the terrified and superstitious man was originally given to some person other than Casca. But it is just here that verse-prose contrasts can be effective, if less obvious than the contrast between Brutus's prose and Antony's verse in the funeral orations.[3] Cassius turns them to his own advantage; indeed, the control of the play so far and the tone of its verse are largely in his hands. But the second act opens with Brutus's soliloquy.

The context is designed to make Brutus gentle; the presence of the boy Lucius, fetching a taper and a book, telling his master the date, falling asleep at his instrument, all suggest a domestic calm at odds with the associations of the fatal day to come and with the "exhalations whizzing in the air" (II.i.44), though the calm is uneasy. Coleridge declares that the soliloquy belies Brutus the "Stoico-Platonic tyrannicide," because it gives him no motive to kill Caesar; if Caesar remained as good a monarch as he now seemed, there was no reason to remove him. But, says Coleridge, there were many reasons to kill him: Caesar had crossed the Rubicon and entered Rome as a conqueror (as we saw in the first scene). He wants to know why Shakespeare did not "bring these things forward"; of course he did bring the triumphal entry forward, but not very far, and obliquely.[4]

> It must be by his death; and for my part,
> I know no personal cause to spurn at him,
> But for the general. He would be crown'd:
> How that might change his nature, there's the question.
> It is the bright day that brings forth the adder,
> And that craves wary walking. Crown him that,
> And then I grant we put a sting in him
> That at his will he may do danger with.
> Th' abuse of greatness is when it disjoins
> Remorse from power; and to speak truth of Caesar,
> I have not known when his affections sway'd
> More than his reason. But 'tis a common proof
> That lowliness is young ambition's ladder,
> Whereto the climber-upward turns his face;
> But when he once attains the utmost round,
> He then unto the ladder turns his back,
> Looks in the clouds, scorning the base degrees
> By which he did ascend. So Caesar may;
> Then lest he may, prevent. And since the quarrel
> Will bear no color for the thing he is,
> Fashion it thus: that what he is, augmented,
> Would run to these and these extremities;
> And therefore think him as a serpent's egg,
> Which, hatch'd, would as his kind grow mischievous,
> And kill him in the shell. (II.i.10–34)

The truth is that the soliloquy, which has the appearance of being spoken by a man who has already virtually made up his mind, proves, on examination, to be more opaque than one at first supposes. "No personal cause": that is, no cause that relates to Caesar as a person rather than as an official of the state. He has not abused his power by failing to show mercy ("remorse"). He has not (as tyrants do) allowed his passions to evade the control of his reason. The sole positive reason Brutus gives for wanting Caesar dead is that "He would be crown'd" (12). It is the rite of coronation that might "change his nature."

The other reasons proposed are implausible: when men become great they kick away the ladder; but Caesar has shown no signs of doing so. Only the prospect of kingship, his desire for it, and the complicity of the mob make him dangerous. We are reminded that Brutus's ancestor and namesake helped to drive out the kings long ago; Romans were suspicious of kings. We are also obliged to reflect that ceremonies mean a lot to almost everybody concerned, not least Brutus, who wants the murder to be a sacrificial, ritual act, a demonic opposite of coronation. We remember that coronation and crowns were not mere empty shows to Shakespeare's contemporaries. He himself had dramatised coronations, and said much about crowns.[5] Coleridge was right to find the passage more difficult than it looked, but his explanation was wrong; he seemed to have hoped for a more explicit expression of Brutus's state of mind. But that cannot have been what Shakespeare wanted to provide.

We come to understand, as we approach the plays of the great period, that simple clarity was less and less Shakespeare's way. Even when the point seems simple, there is often a kind of aura of obscurity, enough strain on the language to tax the reader's mind. When Brutus has committed himself, and before the conspirators arrive, he suddenly says something more remarkable than the famous soliloquy:

> Since Cassius first did whet me against Caesar,
> I have not slept.
> Between the acting of a dreadful thing
> And the first motion, all the interim is
> Like a phantasma or a hideous dream.
> The Genius and the mortal instruments
> Are then in council; and the state of a man,
> Like to a little kingdom, suffers then
> The nature of an insurrection. (II.i.61–69)

This is wonderful writing: think of the propriety of "whet," with its hint of daggers to come, and the effectiveness of the short line that follows. The rest of the speech is worthy of Hamlet, for it generalises a local situation: Brutus moves away from his broodings over Caesar and contemplates the interim between any first intention to commit "a dreadful thing" (not specified as a killing or even as a crime) and the performance that follows; the moment of deep anxiety that comes between. A phantasma is specifically a bad or evil dream, glossed as "hideous." The second figure, the interior council, makes the character of the interim clearer: the man who has taken the decision is a microcosmic version of a state disturbed by insurrection: his spirit is beset, as in an angry cabinet meeting, by his lower powers, whose protests are perhaps founded in an apprehension of danger to themselves. The scene is one of deep disturbance, as the mortal instruments rebel against the decisions of the higher soul. That Brutus should, in his metaphor, think of the state as a kingdom is a way of relating the generalisation to the more specific theme: Rome as a potential kingdom.

A few years later, in *Macbeth*, Shakespeare was to give a full representation of this fraught interim in his treatment of all that passed between the decision to murder Duncan and the actual commission of the deed. We may now think we understand the disturbances that lie under the official calm of Brutus:

No, not an oath! If not the face of men,
The sufferance of our souls, the time's abuse
If these be motives weak, break off betimes . . . (114–16)

where the breaking off of the sentence enacts the breaking off it suggests and rejects. Later "the sufferance of our souls" is accidentally remembered—"such suffering souls / That welcome wrongs" (131–32), and used in a different sense, not as a confession of spiritual suffering, but as a reproach to all who hesitate to join the conspirators simply as honourable Romans, who need no oath, as a coward might.

After that speech, the characters, and the language, once again get down to business. Here again Brutus, with his desire for a bloodless murder and his trust of Antony, proves his incompetence as a leader; he lacks the cunning of Decius Brutus, whose trickery about omens will bring Caesar to the Senate, despite Calpurnia's dream. A clock strikes, and the day dawns; and now we see that the earlier conversation about the sun rising had its dramatic purpose. We are reminded repeatedly of the time, which is, as they say, of the essence. The Ides of March has come.

Portia's entrance reaffirms the excessive humanity of Brutus. She is celebrated for her stoical strength. "Dwell I but in the suburbs / Of your good pleasure?" (285–86). Whores dwell in the suburbs; she, Cato's daughter, is indignant at the thought of being so reduced. To express that sentiment thus is itself an indication of her dignity and mental power. Brutus gives in and will tell her all. Only a brief scene with a belated conspirator separates the Brutus–Portia dialogue from that between Caesar and Calpurnia; again male folly prevails, inducing Caesar to defy the "ceremonies" or omens in which he believes.

Shakespeare, as I've suggested, often uses a special kind of "lighting scene"—
an episode a little aside from the main movement of the story that is meant
to illustrate a particular aspect of it, like, for instance, the argument between
Peter and the musicians in *Romeo and Juliet*, or the dispute between Shylock
and Antonio concerning Laban's ewes in *The Merchant of Venice*, just the kind of
scene an incautious director, worried about the pace of the performance, might
be tempted to cut but must not. We see the conspirators gather at Caesar's house,
meaning to escort him to the Senate; then there occurs the passage in which
Portia, profoundly agitated, sends Lucius there, for no reason she can provide.
She meets the polite but darkly ominous soothsayer, who immediately encounters
Caesar and again warns him. These details intensify the very sense of interim that
Brutus has defined. That interim seems to end with Caesar's death, a scene carried
out with the utmost efficiency, Caesar bragging to the last. But we discover that
this is a false end. Indeed, the true end of the story has to wait until Octavian
stands over the body of Cleopatra in the next Roman play.

There are famous moments to come: the rival funeral orations in prose and
verse (during Antony's performance even the plebeians use verse, until, moved
to destructive action at the end of the scene, they return to prose: "Pluck down
forms, windows, any thing" [III.ii.259]). Although Antony speaks at some
length, the economy of the scene is extraordinary. It is followed by another
brilliant "lighting" scene, recounting the fate of the poet Cinna, beset by prosy
rioters: "Tear him for his bad verses" (III.iii.30); and then we are with Antony
and Octavius in the quarrelsome and Machiavellian mood that, alternating with
a sort of masculine Roman tenderness, dominates most of the last two acts of
the play.

The quarrel and reconciliation between Brutus and Cassius at Philippi (IV.
ii) is a famous set piece, first angry, then surprisingly sentimental; Brutus is
angry with an obtrusive poet (again a sly comment on the redundancy of poets
in political crises), but Lucius is again at hand to preserve the sentimental mood
with broken music. An evil spirit appears to Brutus, perhaps the spirit he had
wanted to free from Caesar's body without shedding blood. Before the battle
comes a quick and angry parley; Brutus and Cassius know as well as we do that
they are bound to lose.

Julius Caesar is a rather more enigmatic play than it looks at first sight. I think
of it as a study in the first motion and the ultimate acting of a dreadful thing,
worthy to be so called because of its millennial repercussions. Shakespeare had
enacted regicide before, but here was one the consequences of which were greater
and so permanent that they could be felt sixteen hundred years later in London,
a city once within the *limes*, a city of the Roman Empire built by Caesar and his
imperial successors.

The political import of Caesar's death is such that only poets, poets of
something like Virgilian stature, could deal with it. Yet, the two poets in

this play are so unequal to the occasion that one is murdered in mistake for a politician and the other turned out when he interrupts politicians in conference. This later poet and playwright can hope to suggest to his audience the vast significance of what they are seeing, while at the same time ironically disclaiming all authority.

NOTES

1. Clearly this is not applicable to *Hamlet*, which is a great deal longer, as is *Othello*. The variations in length of the plays remains something of a puzzle. One should not take the *Romeo and Juliet* formula too literally; Andrew Gurr calls it "a bit of a fiction." The Lord Chamberlain laid it down in 1594 that plays should begin at two o'clock and end "between four and five," but plays got longer as time went on, and some were over 4,000 lines (*Hamlet*, Jonson's *Bartholomew Fair*), and even allowing for rapid delivery, they cannot have been performed in under three hours. See Andrew Gurr, *The Shakespearean Stage, 1574–1642*, 3rd ed. (1992), pp. 178–79.

2. Arden edition, pp. 141–42.

3. Brian Vickers demonstrates the rhetorical rigour and symmetry of Brutus's speech, which was nevertheless so ineffective. Brutus speaks verse immediately before and after the oration; it seems his more natural manner. *The Artistry of Shakespeare's Prose* (1968; rev ed., 1979), pp. 241–45. Vickers reminds us that Brutus had forgotten the prime rule of rhetoric, that "a speech must be adapted to the nature of the audience." It is a rule that Shakespeare never forgot, although as the audience grew more clever he allowed himself to grow more clever also.

4. Samuel Taylor Coleridge, *Shakespearean Criticism* (2 vols., 1960), Vol. 1, p. 14.

5. There are about 380 uses of the word in the canon, counting plurals and verb forms; about ten per play. Admittedly about sixty of these usages occur in *3 Henry VI*, when the word stands for what the main action is all about; but *Julius Caesar* has fifteen, in a context where coronation should, historically speaking, be less important.

2002—E. A. J. Honigmann. "Sympathy for Brutus," from *Shakespeare: Seven Tragedies Revisited: The Dramatist's Manipulation of Response*

E. A. J. Honigmann taught English literature at the Shakespeare Institute at the University of Birmingham. He is the author or editor of many titles, many of which are about or by Shakespeare. His books include *The Stability of Shakespeare's Text* and *Shakespearian Tragedy and the Mixed Response*.

When Shakespeare began to write *Julius Caesar*, in 1598 or 1599, he had not attempted a tragedy for several years. He could have looked back complacently to one of his earlier successes, *Titus Andronicus* or *Romeo and Juliet*, *Richard III* or *Richard II*, and simply repeated a formula that had already proved its worth.[1] But Shakespeare was not in the habit of looking back complacently: in *Julius Caesar* he moved decisively forward, and nowhere more so than in planning the audience-response to the tragic hero. Titus and Romeo had been presented largely as victims of malice or circumstance and, in their central scenes, appealed to the spectator's pity; Richard III and Richard II had both elicited first one response and then another, corresponding to the upward and downward thrust of Fortune's Wheel. Brutus, however, affects us differently. Whereas the early tragedies direct response firmly, so that we know exactly where we are (even in the Richard plays, where we move easily from one defined attitude to another, without losing our bearings), Shakespeare, as I have argued,[2] sought for a more intricately mixed response in his mature tragedies, and, if we may find fault with a great play by comparing it with the greater ones that succeeded it, seems to have got the mixture wrong in *Julius Caesar*, or very slightly wrong, thus weakening the tragic effect. 'Somewhat cold and unaffecting, compared with some other of Shakespeare's plays' was Johnson's verdict, with which few will disagree.[3]

Making a fresh start on tragedy, Shakespeare wished the audience to respond in an entirely new way to his hero. If this is correct it should be possible to trace some signs of his thinking in his remodelling of Plutarch's Brutus. I think it can be done; but first I have to confess that M. W. MacCallum, in his indispensable book on *Shakespeare's Roman Plays* (1910), interpreted the dramatist's intentions quite differently. According to MacCallum the play 'screens from view whatever in the career of Brutus might prejudice his claims to affection and respect; and carries much further a process of idealization that Plutarch had already begun. For to Plutarch Brutus is, so to speak, the model republican, the paragon of private and civic virtue.' Shakespeare, he went on, purified Plutarch's idealised Brutus, allowing 'nothing to mar the graciousness and dignity of the picture': the tragedy gave prominence to Brutus's 'winning courtesy', his 'affectionate nature', his 'humble-mindedness', and 'his amiable and attractive virtues are saved from all taint of weakness by an heroic strain'.[4]

Fortunately this one-sided view of the remodelling of Brutus has been challenged. T. S. Dorsch has shown conclusively that, far from 'purifying' Plutarch's idealised portrait, Shakespeare introduced 'a number of faults for which there is little or no warrant in Plutarch'.

> Shakespeare's Brutus is, with all his estimable qualities, pompous, opinionated and self-righteous. His judgement is not to be trusted. He is led by the nose by Cassius and gulled by Antony. At almost every crisis in his fortunes he makes decisions, against the advice of

experienced men of the world, that contribute materially to the failure of his cause. He seems completely blind to reality, an ineffectual idealist whose idealism cannot prevent him from committing a senseless and terrible crime.[5]

At the same time Dorsch also recognised that in the play 'the virtue and nobility of Plutarch's Brutus are brought out.' Though not specifically concerned with the spectator's response, Dorsch therefore anticipated my first point—that in refashioning Plutarch's Brutus Shakespeare made him both more and less attractive.

* * *

Comparing Plutarch's Marcus Brutus and Shakespeare's Brutus (hereafter Marcus Brutus and Brutus) one's first impression is that they have much in common. Plutarch saw Marcus Brutus as one who 'framed his manners of life by the rules of vertue and studie of Philosophie', and repeatedly returned to his love of philosophy and learning in general. His own uncle, Cato the philosopher, was the Roman whom Marcus Brutus 'studied most to follow'. 'Touching the Graecian Philosophers, there was no sect nor Philosopher of them, but he heard and liked it: but above all the rest, he loved Platoes sect best.'[6] When he joined Pompey's army Marcus Brutus 'did nothing but studie all day long'; at Athens, after the murder of Caesar, 'he went daily to heare the lectures of Theomnestus Academick Philosopher, and of Cratippus the Peripatetick', so that 'it seemed he left all other matters, and gave him selfe onely unto studye'; and before the Battle of Philippi 'he would read some booke till the third watche of the night'.[7]

Although Shakespeare could not make room for all of Plutarch's character-revealing anecdotes he gives a similar general impression of Brutus as an intellectual. The dramatic Brutus talks of Cato's philosophy and is himself told by Cassius—

Of your philosophy you make no use
If you give place to accidental evils.[8]

Brutus looks back twice to his school,[9] works late in his study (II. 1. 7), and reads at night before the Battle of Philippi. He is *homo praeoccupatus*, not only in mislaying his book and discovering it in the pocket of his gown (IV. 3. 250) but in everyday demeanour, especially in his first scenes with Cassius and Portia. Yet while the general impression is similar, Shakespeare changed many details, the effect of which is that Brutus becomes an intellectual who makes mistakes—far too many mistakes—until we question not merely his judgement but his motives. Dorsch felt that 'we may respect the motives for which he spares Antony's life, and later allows him to speak in Caesar's funeral . . . but on both occasions his decisions are foolish blunders'.[10] If we follow Brutus from one mistake to the

next, however, his motives will strike us as less than respectable. Shakespeare
leads up to his first and second fault (as Plutarch described them)—his opposing
the killing of Antony, and his permitting Antony to speak at Caesar's funeral—
by introducing two minor issues, which are changed from the source.

> they durst not acquaint Cicero with their conspiracie, although he
> was a man whome they loved dearlie, and trusted best: for they were
> affrayed that he being a coward . . . woulde quite turne and alter all
> their purpose . . .

> having never taken othes together, nor taken or geven any caution or
> assuraunce, nor binding them selves one to an other by any religious
> othes: they all kept the matter so secret to them selves . . .[11]

In the play we watch the conspirators reaching their decisions (II. i. 114ff.):
Cassius makes a proposal and Brutus, each time, immediately speaks against
it, thrice imposing his will on his fellow-conspirators—so that before long we
suspect that his declared motives are only half the story. It is tempting to think
that his 'secret motive' betrays itself in his objection to Cicero—

> O, name him not! Let us not break with him;
> For he will never follow any thing
> That other men begin. (II. 1. 150–2)

—but, though there is unconscious irony here, the truth lies deeper. After all,
Cassius began the conspiracy and Brutus followed him, and the play assumes that
he also followed Julius Caesar happily, at least for a while. Quite as disturbing
at Brutus' relationship with the conspirators is his relationship with himself, his
conviction that he speaks for the beautiful lofty things of the world, knows them,
is one of them. This, the prior motive, makes it difficult for us to respect his stated
motives when he opposes the killing of Antony. He saves Antony, as he murders
Caesar, thinking too much of Brutus—his own reputation, his own style—and
this distracts his judgement and corrupts it.

* * *

Shakespeare turned Brutus into an intellectual hideously corrupted by high-
mindedness. The play reveals his corruption so gradually that it is easy to accept
Brutus' own view of himself, yet there comes a point when spectators who have
sympathised with him must draw back, and must repudiate his idealism—after
the murder of Caesar, when he again imposes his 'style' on the conspirators.

> Stoop, Romans, stoop,
> And let us bathe our hands in Caesar's blood
> Up to the elbows, and besmear our swords. (III. i. 106–8)

Shakespeare added this episode[12] to put the finishing touch to his conception of Brutus, who, presumably, wishes to enforce his idea that they are 'sacrificers but not butchers' (II. 1. 166). Cassius agrees to humour Brutus once again, yet his reply ('Stoop then, and wash') suggests that the thought would never have occurred to him:[13] the insane logic of it belongs to Brutus alone, and the action that follows makes visible the inner corruption of one man—of 'gentle Brutus', who had said, not long before, 'Our course will seem too bloody, Caius Cassius' (II. 1. 162). And, just in case the audience gets carried away by the idealist's exaltation, and fails to feel the full horror of his action, Shakespeare added another twist that dispels all doubts. When Antony brings himself to grasp Brutus' hand, dripping with 'the most noble blood of all this world'

> Let each man render me his bloody hand.
> First, Marcus Brutus, will I shake with you (III. 1. 184–5)

the audience in effect touches blood with him and shares his physical revulsion.

Three series of impressions deal with the intellectual's corruption. His mistakes as a conspirator, his muddled thinking in general, and his dangerously high conceit of himself—all have a serial arrangement, leading by imperceptible stages to their appointed climaxes, and all work together to influence response, more and more unfavourably.

1. *Brutus' mistakes*. Plutarch had noted Brutus' two most serious mistakes or 'faults' as leader of the conspiracy,[14] and Shakespeare decided to add to them: he made Brutus personally responsible for excluding Cicero,[15] and his Brutus even begs the Romans to listen to Antony's funeral-speech (III. 2. 60–1: not so in Plutarch). Of Brutus' many mistakes, however, the one that works most insidiously against him is the first, his being duped by the papers thrown in at his windows.[16] Whereas Plutarch's hero receives 'many bills' (or letters) from 'his frendes and contrie men', faked letters 'in several hands' finally push Shakespeare's Brutus from self-questioning to a firm resolve:

> O Rome, I make thee promise,
> If the redress will follow, thou receivest
> Thy full petition at the hand of Brutus! (II. I. 56–8)

As Brutus' later mistakes all result from the ill-founded conviction that 'Rome' supports him, the audience, having seen how he was tricked into thinking this, can never trust his judgement thereafter.

As well as multiplying Brutus' mistakes, Shakespeare devised an appropriate stage-response for each one, to cue the audience and to harden its attitude. The first ('Well, Brutus, thou art noble', I. 2. 307ff.) immediately deflates Brutus as a man who has been 'seduc'd'. In Act II the serial arrangement has a delayed-action effect: when Cassius wants the conspirators to swear their resolution and Brutus protests (II. 1. 113), the proposal sounds like a mere whim, and is dropped without another word. Cassius next suggests, a little more positively, that Cicero should be sounded, Casca and Metellus agree, but Brutus objects and the others give way deferentially, though he has scarcely met their arguments. ('Cassius Then leave him out. Casca Indeed, he is not fit.') Cassius presses even more strongly for the murder of Mark Antony, Brutus again objects, and this time Cassius is definitely not convinced ('Yet I fear him . . .'). The stage-response rises to a muted climax, and thus prepares for Cassius' much more alarmed response to Brutus' next, more fateful mistake:

> You know not what you do. Do not consent
> That Antony speak in his funeral. (III. i. 233–4)

As Cassius reacted with admirable restraint before, when he disagreed with Brutus, we are bound to take him seriously now. The serial arrangement therefore helps to drive home the folly of the idealist's reply:

> By your pardon—
> I will myself into the pulpit first
> And show the reason of our Caesar's death.

2. *Brutus' muddles.* There is also progression in Brutus' muddles—by which I mean several longer speeches that go through the motions of reasoning and yet fail to hang together. The earlier ones get by, at least in the theatre, without impressing us as manifest fumbling; the later ones sound very odd indeed. I shall comment on two of each kind.

(i) 'It must be by his death' (II. i. 10ff.). Here, said MacCallum, Brutus 'seeks to find something that will satisfy his reason'.[17] Yet the soliloquy has also been called confused and 'a marvel of fanatical self-deception'.[18] The argument, starting with a foregone conclusion ('his death'), heaves and wrenches itself to reach that conclusion ('kill him in the shell'), and contrasts strikingly with Brutus' controlled utterance a little earlier ('That you do love me, I am nothing jealous . . .', I. 2. 162ff.). But as Brutus communes with himself alone his disjointed sentences affect us as stream-of-consciousness rather than as argument, and fail to destroy (though they modify) our earlier impression of Brutus as a dependable truth-seeker.

(ii) 'Romans, countrymen, and lovers!' (III. 2. 13ff.). Brutus' Forum speech makes a pretence of being reasonable, and turns out to be largely emotional. 'Rome before everything!' is a message calculated to please, and the stage-response of Third Plebeian ('Let him be Caesar!') suggests that for him the emotion succeeds, the argument fails. Antony, thereafter, has no difficulty in showing that the argument consists of mere assertion, in so far as Brutus had not proved that Caesar was ambitious. But listening to Brutus we may miss this point, if only because we remember that when offered a crown Caesar 'put it by thrice, every time gentler than other' (I. 2. 227–8). It takes an Antony to exploit the opening: we waver with the Plebeians, and our confidence in Brutus' reasoning is undermined.

(iii) 'I did send to you / For certain sums of gold' IV. 3. 69ff. Even MacCallum, who held that Shakespeare idealised Brutus, found his self-righteousness here 'a little absurd': 'What does all this come to? That the superfine Brutus will not be guilty of extortion, but that Cassius may: and then Brutus will demand to share in the proceeds.'[19] Though this reading has been challenged the weight of opinion is on MacCallum's side, except that Brutus strikes others as astounding, not just a little absurd.[20] For the first time in the play Brutus' reasoning seems wrong-headed as he speaks and, significantly, his self-admiration offends us in the same speech.[21]

(iv) 'Even by the rule of that philosophy' (V. 1. 100–12). Asked by Cassius what he will do 'if we do lose this battle', Brutus first answers that he will not commit suicide, then adds that he will not 'go bound to Rome', implying that he would sooner kill himself. Shakespeare follows Plutarch closely, making one important change. Marcus Brutus explains that he once disapproved of suicide, 'but being nowe in the middest of the daunger, I am of a contrary mind'.[22] Instead of seeing the light himself, Shakespeare's Brutus has to have his eyes opened by Cassius ('You are contented to be led in triumph . . .?'), which leads to his volte-face. Introducing Cassius' question, Shakespeare intimates an intellectual failure in Brutus, and again this coincides with an unpleasing, self-admiring tone:

> No, Cassius, no. Think not, thou noble Roman,
> That ever Brutus will go bound to Rome;
> He bears too great a mind.

3. *Brutus' opinion of himself.* It has been said, in defence of Brutus' high opinion of himself, that

> one of Shakespeare's simplest—and habitual—methods of telling us what a person is really like is to let that person himself tell us. We must be on our guard against judging, Brutus's estimate of himself according to modern notions of how people should speak about themselves, and saying that . . . he is merely 'talking big'. Nevertheless, his manner at various points in the play does not give us as favourable an impression of him as his friends entertain.[23]

If we check up on those 'various points', using 'modern notions of how people should speak about themselves', we observe that they are all in the last two acts—which suggests that Brutus' self-explanations also contribute to our sense of the intellectual's gradual corruption.

Initially Brutus' 'honour' and 'honesty' speeches scarcely jar the spectator, being cushioned by the situation.

> (i)   If it be aught toward the general good
> Set honour in one eye and death i' th' other ... (I. 2. 85ff.)

Taken to the brink and asked to declare himself, Brutus has to give a clear signal: his turn of phrase, though it may seem extravagant, thus reflects on the situation as much as on the man. (Potentially boastful speeches are neutralised by the situation in other tragedies. Compare *Macbeth* III. 4. 99: 'What man dare, I dare ...')

> (ii)   What other bond
> Than secret Romans that have spoke the word
> And will not palter? And what other oath
> Than honesty to honesty engag'd ... (II. 1. 124ff.)

>   O ye gods,
> Render me worthy of this noble wife! (II. 1. 302–3)

Shakespeare resorts to such indirect self-description to remind us in passing of Brutus' high opinion of *himself*, yet we cannot convict the speaker of boastfulness when he seems less concerned to praise himself than to praise others.

> (iii)   Believe me for mine honour, and have respect to mine honour, that
> you may believe. (III. 2. 15–16)

An orator normally reminds his listeners of what he stands for: in the special circumstances of the Forum Scene Brutus' self-description is entirely acceptable.

Before the end of Act III Brutus' high opinion of himself never irritates our sympathy; after it, it does so repeatedly. Either self-praise coincides with an intellectual muddle, so that he vaunts his 'honesty' as he rebukes Cassius for not sharing his corruptly acquired gold, and his 'great mind' just after Cassius has had to put him right on a fairly simple point of self-knowledge;[24] or he praises himself to scold others, thus introducing a note of lofty contemptuousness:

Judge me, you gods! wrong I mine enemies?
And, if not so, how should I wrong a brother? (IV. 2. 38–9)

O, if thou went the noblest of thy strain,
Young man, thou couldst not die more honourable. (V. 1. 59–60)

* * *

Brutus differs from Plutarch's Marcus Brutus in making many more political mistakes, in muddling his arguments and in thinking too well of himself. The more we learn to distrust his judgement the more confidently he speaks of his reasons, the masterstroke being his proposal to hasten to Philippi—'Good reasons must, of force, give place to better.'[25] Whatever the intellectual's virtues, we cannot respect his thinking. And Shakespeare increased the play's anti-intellectual bias by surrounding his philosophical hero with men of learning, far more than he put into any other tragedy, and this also conditions our response to Brutus. The intellectuals wish to intervene in high affairs, all of them are cut off or ridiculed—and the ridicule was usually added by Shakespeare. 'A certaine Soothsayer . . . had geven Caesar warning long time affore, to take heede of the day of the Ides of Marche . . .'[26] Shakespeare added Caesar's dismissive 'He is a dreamer; let us leave him: pass' (I. 2. 24). Artemidorus, a doctor of rhetoric, tried to warn Caesar of his danger, as in the play, and pressed a 'memorial' upon him. 'Caesar tooke it of him, but coulde never read it, though he many times attempted it, for the number of people that did salute him . . .'[27] Plutarch continued that, according to some, another man gave Caesar the memorial, since, Artemidorus 'was always repulsed by the people.' Neither version satisfied Shakespeare, whose Caesar snaps contemptuously—'What, is the fellow mad?' (III. 1. 10). In Act IV the poet is treated as unceremoniously ('saucy fellow, hence', IV. 3. 132), whilst Cinna the poet, though he makes no attempt to influence state affairs, illustrates the intellectual's ineffectiveness even more frighteningly. Shakespeare also introduced Casca's sneer that, when Caesar was offered the crown, Cicero, the most distinguished intellectual of the play, rose to the occasion like an intellectual, by speaking Greek.

> *Cassius.* To what effect?
> *Casca.* Nay, and I tell you that, I'll ne'er look you i' th' face again. But those that understood him smiled . . . (I. 2. 279ff.)

As Shakespeare could not have failed to read in Plutarch that Casca, after stabbing Caesar, 'cried in Graeke, and called his brother to helpe him', it has been suggested that his Casca 'pretended not to know Greek'.[28] Surely not: Casca, more probably, was deprived of Greek because all the play's intellectuals (including Cicero) are ineffective and he, the man of action who strikes the first blow against Caesar, was meant to contrast with them.

* * *

As the play proceeds we respond more and more unsympathetically to Brutus' intellectual pretensions. Comparing it with Plutarch's *Life* we can see how Shakespeare tried to channel our response—how Brutus' high-minded reflectiveness gradually shades off into self-righteousness, even arrogance, and how inevitably everything leads on to the quarrel-scene. Lacking in charm and entirely humourless, the would-be intellectual may seem sufficiently handicapped, yet Shakespeare thought of still more ways of enforcing a hostile response, one of the best being the short, sharp visual effect. I have already mentioned the blood-bathing episode and the bloody hand-shake,[29] two moments of physical horror. They are preceded in the murder-scene by two other visual effects of quite exceptional power.

(i) Brutus, ready to strike the fatal blow, kisses Caesar's hand—a most un-Roman gesture in the year 44 B.C. ('I kiss thy hand, but not in flattery, Caesar'). Are we to take this as an insignificant anachronism, like the striking clock (II. 1. 191)? I think not. And the usual alternatives, that Brutus offers either the kiss of Judas or 'a last tender farewell',[30] also fail to explain the peculiar effect of his kiss. But if we recall that Brutus believes that Caesar 'would be crown'd' (II. 1. 12), and that kings graciously allow their inferiors to kiss their hands, we may interpret the gesture as ironical—somewhat like that of the Roman soldiers who plaited a crown of thorns for a 'king' in the year A.D. 33. Shakespeare had dramatised such a mock coronation in *3 Henry VI*, where the Duke of York's enemies honour his royal aspirations with a paper crown, then stab him to death (I. 4. 95ff.). The extravagant servility of Metellus Cimber and Cassius, throwing themselves at Caesar's feet before they stab him, acts out a similar victim-jeering ritual, less openly but quite as unpleasantly, which implicates Brutus as well, even though his tone and gesture are more gravely ironical.

(ii) The Folio has no stage direction that helps us to visualise the killing of Caesar, but the dialogue shows that Shakespeare followed Plutarch in several points: Casca strikes the first blow, Caesar muffles his face and falls at the base of Pompey's statue. That being so, it seems reasonable to suppose that he may have followed Plutarch in other details.

> [The conspirators] compassed him on everie side with their swordes
> drawn in their handes, that Caesar turned him no where, but he was
> striken at by some, and still had naked swords in his face, and was
> hacked and mangeled amonge them, as a wilde beaste taken of hunters.
> For it was agreed among them, that every man should geve him a

wound, bicause all their partes should be in this murther: and then Brutus him selfe gave him one woude about his privities. Men reporte also, that Caesar did still defende him selfe . . . but when he sawe Brutus with his sworde drawen in his hande, then he pulled his gowne over his heade, and made no more resistaunce, and was driven . . . against the base whereupon Pompeys image stoode . . .[31]

Although the conspirators sometimes screen the killing from the audience in modern productions, Plutarch's visual detail suits the play and we can hardly improve on it, in the absence of authorial directions. Editors, however—even those who recognise that our best course is to follow Plutarch—do not care to spell out in so many words that Brutus stabs a defenceless man who has muffled his face, and wounds Caesar 'about his privities', though some of them print the direction that Brutus strikes 'the last blow', for which there is even less authority.[32] Is it because they think that such shocking actions would discredit Brutus? If so, let us repeat that Shakespeare added Brutus' kiss, the blood-bathing and the bloody handshake to this very scene—all actions designed to shock and antagonise the audience.

* * *

So, much for the unattractiveness of Brutus, compared with Plutarch's original. Shakespeare, however, aiming at a complex response, also went to some trouble to drive the audience in the other direction—by heightening the attractiveness of his hero. He achieved a great deal in the simplest possible way, by mere assertion. Others refer to 'gentle Brutus', 'gentle' is one of Brutus' own favourite words, and in the end the word sticks. 'His life was gentle' says Antony, summing up, and the audience normally agrees, even though Brutus had butchered his benefactor and precipitated a civil war. True, when used by Brutus himself the word sometimes sounds inappropriate, and this reflects back on his own reputation for gentleness:

Tell us the manner of it, gentle Casca (I. 2. 233)

And, *gentle friends*,
Let's kill him boldly but not wrathfully (II. 1. 171–2)

But whereas other assertions in the play have a rough passage ('For Brutus is an honourable man'), the gentleness of Brutus survives as a general impression.

Something can be accomplished by sheer assertion. But unlike modern salesmen, suckled on the comfortable doctrine that the more often you tell a lie the more certainly it will be believed, a dramatist must back the assertion that Brutus is gentle with other kinds of evidence. As Maurice Morgann explained,

Shakespeare steals impressions upon us, and these may act more effectively than assertions: heard melodies are sweet, but those unheard are sweeter.

A minor figure, the boy Lucius, serves as supporting evidence. Very nearly all the persons in the play except Lucius come from Plutarch: this fact, once observed, immediately raises a question—what special purpose could Shakespeare have had when he added a slave-boy or servant-boy to the story?[33] Comparing the two scenes in which Lucius appears with his master (II. i and iv. 3) we find the common factor to be that Brutus has to waken him from sleep in both: his little life is rounded with a sleep. Brutus, both times, treats him considerately, in the second scene with an almost paternal solicitude, and can thus demonstrate his own gentleness at the very time when his humanity seems about to desert him. For the first Lucius episode acts as a frame for that terrifyingly depersonalised meditation, 'It must be by his death', and the second follows Brutus' willed emotional aridity in the quarrel-scene. Lucius was added, it appears, to remind us of the hero's inner self just when we are in most danger of forgetting it. And for once Shakespeare resisted the temptation to create a 'pathetic boy', his stage stereotype, making something more genuinely affecting out of Lucius' uncomplaining service and assured relationship with his master.

Lucius sleeps soundly in Brutus' presence, as do Varro and Claudius, the two guards specially summoned to sleep on cushions in his tent (IV. 3. 241). There's meaning in their snores, and in the stage-tableau of the general surrounded by sleepers. Elsewhere in the tragedies to be caught napping by the hero can have fatal consequences—witness Duncan and Desdemona, Rosencrantz and Guildenstern—for the hero feels hemmed in and threatened as each story unfolds and becomes increasingly dangerous, a wounded beast that may suddenly lash out, at Polonius, at Cordelia's executioner, or turn in fury on innocent bystanders. 'I'd strike the sun if it insulted me!' cried Captain Ahab, speaking for the beast at bay, the tragic will that spends itself against the world at large. There are signs in the quarrel-scene (IV. 3) that Brutus can rage inwardly like the other tragic heroes, yet Shakespeare conceived him as essentially different—a man to be trusted, incapable of casual destructiveness, in whose company others may sleep. The most extraordinary glimpse of the trust inspired by gentle Brutus comes in the final scene, where one of his men sleeps on the battlefield while their enemies close in. 'A thick-skinned sort of fellow' commented Granville-Barker, which is no doubt true; but Shakespeare had a motive for adding a fourth sleeper to his story—and presumably a motive less concerned with the life-likeness of a minor character than with the audience's attitude to his tragic hero.

A dramatist, it goes without saying, can call upon more eloquent instruments than sleeping bodies strewn about the stage: he can always switch on the stage-response, if he thinks that his audience needs firm guidance. In *Julius Caesar* almost everyone loves or admires Brutus:

O, he sits high in all the people's hearts;
And that which would appear offence in us
His countenance, like richest alchemy,
Will change to virtue and to worthiness. (I. 3. 157–60)

Several characters express such feelings much more positively than in Plutarch's original, carrying the audience with them. Caius Ligarius, for example, has only a single admiring sentence in Plutarch ('Brutus, sayed he, if thou hast any great enterprise in hande worthie of thy selfe, I am whole'),[34] and Shakespeare blows it up as follows:

By all the gods that Romans bow before
I here discard my sickness. Soul of Rome!
Brave son, deriv'd from honorable loins!
Thou, like an exorcist, hast conjur'd up
My mortified spirit . . . I follow you
To do I know not what; but it sufficeth
That Brutus leads me on. (II. 1. 320ff.)

The hundred lines in which Portia and Ligarius express their love and admiration are quite indispensable, enacting emotions that were merely described by Cassius and others. Later, in the quarrel-scene, Cassius' more purified and personal feeling for his 'dear brother' reconciles us to Brutus when he has been shown at his most unendearing; and in the last scene of all, the continuing loyalty of his defeated soldiers releases a wave of feeling that cannot leave an audience unmoved. These are some of the peaks, but there is also a never-ending stream of casual information to remind us that everyone loves and trusts the hero. Even Antony contributes to it, albeit with hostile intent, in the Forum scene. Giving the play's most explicit account of Caesar's love of Brutus he magically brings it to life, a love so powerfully felt that it seems more real than Brutus' treachery.

Through this the well-beloved Brutus stabb'd,
And as he pluck'd his cursed steel away
Mark how the blood of Caesar follow'd it,
As rushing out of doors, to be resolv'd
If Brutus so unkindly knock'd or no;
For Brutus, as you know, was Caesar's angel.
Judge, O you gods, how dearly Caesar lov'd him!
This was the most unkindest cut of all;
For when the noble Caesar saw him stab,
Ingratitude, more strong than traitors' arms,
Quite vanquish'd him. Then burst his mighty heart . . . (III. 2. 176ff.)

* * *

In these and other ways Shakespeare rehabilitates Brutus in our esteem. Yet it would be wrong to pretend that an audience feels strongly drawn to him: there are times when we very nearly identify ourselves with the other tragic heroes, but Brutus keeps us at a distance, and we enter into him less completely. This is not because he lacks an emotional nature that could buoy up our sympathy and float us past the barriers of murderous words and deeds, for there are signs enough of emotional depth:

> O ye gods
> Render me worthy of this noble wife! (II. 1. 302)

> That every like is not the same, O Caesar,
> The heart of Brutus earns to think upon! (II. 2. 128–9)

> I shall find time, Cassius, I shall find time! (V. 3. 103)

No: the stoical Brutus suppresses his emotions, as far as he can, and thus keeps everyone at arm's length, including Portia and Cassius—and the theatre-audience. His inner nature reveals itself in an aside about Caesar, in his farewell to the dead Cassius, in his words to sleeping boy, and only very rarely in an exchange of mutual feeling. Only Portia breaks through his reserve in the first three acts, after the most intense pressure; and as soon as he gives way Shakespeare interrupts ('Hark, hark! one knocks. Portia, go in awhile', II. i. 304), as if unwilling to over-expose his hero in an emotional situation.

The audience is also kept at a distance by the intellectual hero's preoccupation. At the very start, Brutus ('I am not gamesome') refuses to join the crowd when Caesar goes to the 'holy chase' of Lupercal (not so in Plutarch). And Brutus withdraws not only from the throng but from his friends. Cassius complains—

> I have not from your eyes that gentleness
> And show of love as I was wont to have (I. 2. 32–3)

In Plutarch the two men had been rivals for the chief praetorship, and had to make up their 'grudge' before joining together as conspirators. Shakespeare dropped this motive, so that Brutus' aloofness can only mean withdrawal into himself. Portia, too, complains of neglect, in a scene closely modelled upon Plutarch—except that Shakespeare changed Portia's general discovery 'that there was some marvelous great matter that troubled his minde'[35] to more pointed charges of impatience and anger.

And when I ask'd you what the matter was
You star'd upon me with ungentle looks.
I urg'd you further; then you scratch'd your head
And too impatiently stamp'd with your foot... (II. 1. 241ff.)

Like Hamlet in his first scene, Brutus shrinks from human contact; but whilst Hamlet welcomes Horatio and the Players and even Rosencrantz and Guildenstern, Brutus, unless he is cornered, never expresses warmth of feeling when face to face with others.

Two unusual technical features support the impression of a preoccupied Brutus. At the beginning of Act II he has five soliloquies, interrupted by brief exchanges with Lucius, at least four of which continue the same thread of thought. Why so, rather than a single soliloquy covering much the same ground? Four times Lucius no sooner enters than he is sent out again, a human yo-yo, to see to practical necessities ('Get me a taper', 'Look in the calendar', 'Go to the gate', 'Let 'em enter'). Brutus relapses into thoughtfulness after each interruption as if into his natural element, like some creature of the deep that rises to the surface of practical affairs only to sink below again, back into himself. Between the five soliloquies he comes up for air, as it were, then retires from the practical to the reflective sphere—and this prepares for his mistakes in practical politics, three of which follow within the next hundred lines.

The other technical feature is the play's generalised mood. Like Hamlet, where doubt and uncertainty flow in all directions, *Julius Caesar* creates a mood of its own, one closely related to the hero's state of mind. Scene after scene presents characters anxiously straining to hear or see off-stage events. Brutus only half-listens to Cassius (I. 2), preoccupied by the shouts he hears and by thoughts of 'new honours that are heap'd on Caesar.' Strange noises and flashes threaten during the storm-scenes (I. 3ff.), and Casca, sword in hand, evidently expects some sudden danger. (Shakespeare expanded Plutarch's list of portents, inventing the escaped lion (I. 20) as an immediate motive for Casca's unsheathed sword.) Straining to catch sounds from the far-away Capitol, and imagining that she hears a 'bustling rumour' (II. 4. 18), Portia adds to the play's anxious expectancy. When Antony's servant arrives and so exactly repeats his master's words and gestures (III. 1. 124ff.), he conducts the mind directly to Antony; present though absent, the shadowy Antony for the first time in the play comes to life in those measured sentences, a genie issuing from his bottle, a threat that alarms Cassius—and the conspirators thereupon look forward to Antony's personal arrival as a momentous turning-point. Towards the play's end Pindarus watches the capture of Titinius, as he thinks (V. 3), and Brutus hears 'low alarums' (V. 5. 23) that grow louder as his enemies approach. These are a few of the threatening off-stage events that carry the mind into a world beyond immediate reach, a world that cannot be controlled, and create a generalised mood of expectant anxiety.

Of course mood and atmosphere play an even larger part in the later tragedies. But in Julius Caesar off-stage events sometimes contribute more than readers will observe—as in the quarrel-scene (IV. 3), where Brutus and Cassius retire into a tent, not wishing their two armies to witness their wrangling. The scene's usual heading ('*The Camp near Sardis. Within the tent of Brutus. Enter Brutus and Cassius*') allows us to forget that the tent is guarded, a fact of which Brutus and Cassius must remain at least half-aware, however the scene is staged.[36] 'Speak your griefs softly' Brutus had warned, before they begin; and during the quarrel they still cannot afford to raise their voices, although they may do so involuntarily, for the listening guards, though invisible to Brutus and Cassius, bring the pressures of an outside world into the tent.

* * *

The quarrel-scene (IV. 3), the longest and perhaps the most wonderful in the whole play, 'can hardly be defended on strictly dramatic grounds', thought Bradley, except in so far as it indicates 'inward changes'.[37] Others have disagreed, either because the scene 'lays bare the significance of the story' or because in it Brutus' 'tragic disillusion is most fully revealed'.[38] It could also be defended as the very heart of the play—as the natural culmination of its central relationship and conflict, that of Brutus and Cassius, the only relationship that continues through the five acts, the only one that steadily deepens. (*Julius Caesar* differs from the later tragedies in lacking fully developed secondary relationships: Brutus–Caesar, Brutus–Portia, Brutus–Lucius are shadowy affairs, partly because Shakespeare conceived them as relationships *in absentia*.) The quarrel-scene, where mighty opposites violently collide and claw at one another, tearing off masks and coming as near to self-knowledge as the play permits, can be defended 'on strictly dramatic grounds' as the climax of its inner action, and as no less exciting than the climactic events of the outer, political action of Act III. It also redefines and intensifies the audience's response to Brutus.

We cannot side with Brutus, it is commonly said, in the scene's opening clash with Cassius. 'No one who reads with care the first hundred lines of Act IV, Scene iii, could feel that Shakespeare meant us to have any sympathy with Brutus during this exchange'.[39] So Granville-Barker:

> But which of us might not side with [Cassius] against [Brutus], who
> . . . with things going desperately for his side, must needs stiffen his
> stiff conscience against some petty case of bribery? Is this a time for
> pride in one's principles? . . . is it a time to depreciate and dispirit your
> best friends, to refuse their apologies . . .? Brutus tries many of us as
> high as he tries Cassius . . . Supercilious, unforgiving, and in the right!
> And when anger does rise in him, it is such a cold, deadly anger that

poor passionate Cassius only breaks himself against it. Yet there is a
compelling power in the man, in his integrity of mind, his truth to
himself, in his perfect simplicity.[40]

Without wishing to deny Brutus' pride, I believe that Shakespeare prevents us
from siding against him, and attains his purpose in other ways. Who, for example,
starts the quarrel? Cassius, crying out four times that he has been wronged, insists
on quarrelling and at last strikes fire from Brutus. We must remember, too, that
Cassius threatens physical violence, and that Brutus' most contemptuous remarks
are flung back at a man whose hand is on his dagger, a choleric man who may
forget himself and stab. Taunts such as 'Away, slight man!' or 'For your life you
durst not!' can affect us as either admirable or hateful, depending on the distance
between Brutus' throat and the point of Cassius' dagger.

Brutus' disillusion with his fellow-conspirators also acts in his favour. When
he refers to the ideals with which the conspiracy started ('Remember March,
the ides of March remember!', IV. 3. 18) Shakespeare reactivates the audience's
awareness that Cassius kept quiet about his less creditable motives and tricked
Brutus with forged letters (I. 2. 306ff.): the audience must respond favourably,
knowing that Brutus has even stronger grounds for indignation than he suspects.
It is also quickly apparent, from the untypical way in which he overreacts to
Cassius, that exceptional pressures have brought him close to breaking-point,
and so we respond more leniently to what would otherwise be unpardonable
speeches, as with other tragic heroes when the heat is on.

To side with Brutus in the quarrel-scene is nevertheless impossible.
Analysing the scene we must beware of isolating it from the rest of the play:
Shakespeare prepared for it in the minor Brutus–Cassius collisions of Acts II
and III, in suggesting that Cassius will stoop to bribery (III. I. 178–9), and so
on. The short bartering-scene of the triumvirs (IV. i) also influences response
to the quarrel-scene, by placing the issues in a larger perspective. Plutarch's
view, that 'there was never a more horrible, unnatural, and crueller' exchange of
'murther for murther', perfectly expresses the effect of IV. 1. 1–6, when Antony
and Lepidus haggle a nephew for a brother, except that Shakespeare made it
even more unnatural by omitting all signs of reluctance in the triumvirs. ('But
yet', Plutarch wrote, 'they could hardly agree whom they would put to death:
for every one of them would kill their enemies, and save their kinsmen and
friends'.)[41] Wishing to suggest that another view of the scene was permissible,
T. S. Dorsch said that 'it is possible to interpret [Antony's] conduct [in IV. 1]
as just and unsentimental . . . [for] Antony shows that he will not be swayed
by family ties', and, again, that Antony's proposal to misappropriate the money
bequeathed by Caesar 'appears to have the full concurrence of his colleagues, and
there is no suggestion that he is to gain personally from the affair'.[42] But when
was a proscription ever just? And is a thief any less a thief because he shares

the loot? And who will benefit from the legacy fiddle, if not the triumvirs? The scene demonstrates how power corrupts—and prepares for the quarrel-scene by exhibiting an opportunism so degraded that it inoculates us against taking Cassius' 'itching palm' (IV. 3. 10) too seriously.

After we have seen the triumvirs, Cassius' 'corruption' seems understandable, a necessary evil 'in such a time as this' (IV. 3. 7), and Brutus' anger strikes us as excessive; and after witnessing Brutus' high-minded anger we find it all the more strange that he asks for his share of the takings. Each episode conditions a response against Brutus in the one that follows; and his condescension to Cassius also affects us disagreeably ('I will give you *audience*', 'chastisement doth therefore hide his head', 'What villain touch'd his body . . .?'),[43] since previously he had treated all the conspirators as *brothers* (III. I. 176). Worst of all, whereas 'a general honest thought' had impelled him before, we cease to respect him as well-meaning during the quarrel, his unmistakable purpose being to wound Cassius. Even when Cassius begins to break down Brutus continues to plunge verbal daggers into him, so that Cassius, like Caesar in the assassination-scene, stares incredulously and reels from blow after blow: Brutus is merciless, and in some obscure way enjoys Cassius' pain and humiliation.

In the opening clash, with Cassius, as elsewhere in the play, we simultaneously admire and dislike Brutus; he exacts a mixed response, but nowhere else are we so intensely concerned for him and so hostile. The same is true of our response to Cassius. We regret his corruption (he more or less concedes it, IV. 3. 7–8), we are disappointed by his bluster and his threats of violence; on the other hand, he seems more frank than Brutus, with whose slowly-burning anger his darting impetuousness contrasts not unfavourably, and, most important, he still loves Brutus, he accepts his rebukes, he feels all the pain of the quarrel. Unlike its immediate descendant in the line of quarrel-scenes, Hamlet's interview with Gertrude (where an idealist, whose high expectations have been let down, again lashes one who loves him and drives her to breaking-point), the quarrel in Julius Caesar by no means prompts us to take sides: the rights and wrongs are too evenly balanced, the participants are both shown at their best and worst.

Towards the end of the quarrel a poet intrudes, as in Plutarch, and unsettles the emotional temperature. If the play leaves us in any doubt about it, Plutarch helps to explain his function: the poet, something of a clown, on more than one occasion pushed in where he was not wanted and, with a 'frantick motion' of counterfeit scoffing and mocking 'made all the companye laugh at him'.[44] Shakespeare, groping for an effect like that of the Porter in Macbeth, inserted him between two emotional climaxes, not to arrest or bisect the scene with comic relief but, quite the contrary, to make it gather itself together and spring forward the more vigorously. The poet may seem to dispel the mood of the quarrel, yet really serves, like an electric conductor, to carry that mood into the next episode, confirming our impression of Brutus' irritability just before the secret motive for it is allowed to emerge. We hear a distant after-vibration of the earlier thunder—

> *Cassius.* I did not think you could have been so angry.
> *Brutus.* O Cassius, I am sick of many griefs.

—and then, very quietly, the news of Portia's death, three words that are so effective partly because they signify that Brutus has buried the quarrel.

Placed at this point by Shakespeare (not so in Plutarch) the news about Portia retroactively colours our impression of the quarrel and is undoubtedly 'the scene's great stroke', as Granville-Barker described it. I am not so sure, however, that it is also 'the winning stroke in Brutus' own cause with us',[45] for the simple reason that Brutus' self-concerned attitude is immediately dwarfed by Cassius' outgoing, more expansive emotion.

> *Brutus.* No man bears sorrow better. Portia is dead.
> *Cassius.* Ha! Portia?
> *Brutus.* She is dead.
> *Cassius.* How scap'd I killing when I cross'd you so?
> O insupportable and touching loss!

If, as some believe, Shakespeare wanted Portia's death to be reported twice (IV. 3. 141–57, IV. 3. 179–93), Brutus' concern for his public image almost insults the 'holiness of the heart's affections'; but even if Shakespeare deleted the second report and it was printed in error, as others have argued,[46] the undeleted remark that 'no man bears sorrow better' wins less than total sympathy, focusing as it does upon the loser not the loss. The scene's winning stroke comes later, when Lucius has fallen asleep:

> Gentle knave, good night.
> I will not do thee so much wrong to wake thee.
> If thou dost nod, thou break'st thy instrument;
> I'll take it from thee; and, good boy, good night.

* * *

Intertwined with the response to Brutus in the quarrel-scene and throughout the play, the response to Cassius appears to improve steadily. He begins as a malcontent or tempter, the technical 'villain' who tricks Brutus into joining the conspiracy, but Shakespeare softens and ennobles him, and by the time he dies he may well be thought the play's most attractive character.[47] Though there is some truth in such a reading, it unfairly simplifies the Cassius of Act I.

To believe, with MacCallum, that 'resentment of pre-eminence' makes Cassius a malcontent we have to trust Caesar's judgement:

Such men as he be never at heart's ease.
Whiles they behold a greater than themselves,
And therefore are they very dangerous. (I. 2. 208–10)

Shakespeare, however, had already undermined our confidence in Caesar's judgement of men; Caesar had gazed intently at the Soothsayer ('Set him before me; *let me see his face*'), and had erred disastrously in weighing him up, as even the semi-educated spectator could not fail to know:

Soothsayer. Beware the ides of March.
Caesar. He is a dreamer; let us leave him. Pass. (I. 2. 23–4)

And Caesar also errs about Cassius who, far from resenting preeminence, needs someone greater than himself to lean upon, as he candidly admits:

Him and his worth and our great need of him
You have right well conceited. (I. 3. 161–2)

In scene after scene he abases himself before Brutus and all but says to him what Peter Verkhovensky tells Stavrogin in Dostoyevsky's more sensationalised handling of a similar relationship: 'You're the boss. You're a force. I shall only be at your side . . .', 'I, especially, need a man like you . . . You're my leader, you're my sun, and I am your worm.'[48] Cassius envies not pre-eminence in general, but only one man's; and that one man, Julius Caesar, offends him not just because as an 'envious malcontent [he] is obsessed with a sense of his inferiority'[49] but for more admirable reasons as well—because he loves freedom, he loves the glory that was Rome. There may be an ulterior motive when he addresses Brutus and Casca, but there is genuine feeling as well:

Age, thou art sham'd!
Rome, thou hast lost the breed of noble bloods! . . . (I. 2. 150–1)

Nor stony tower, nor walls of beaten brass,
Nor airless dungeon, nor strong links of iron,
Can be retentive to the strength of spirit . . . (I. 3. 93–5)

Exalted feelings coexist with lower ones in Cassius. Caesar polarises one side of him, the envious malcontent, and Brutus the other ('The last of all the Romans, fare thee well!', V. 3. 99), the audience, from he beginning, responds to both.

In the first act we must resist the temptation to simplify Cassius; in the last, Shakespeare himself seems to simplify him, especially in his suicide. Such an efficient way to go, after all his big talk of suicide and fine flourishes!—

[I] thus unbraced, Casca, as you see,
Have bar'd my bosom to the thunderstone,
And when the cross blue lightning seem'd to open
The breast of heaven, I did present myself
Even in the aim and very flash of it! (I. 3. 48–52)

I know where I will wear this dagger then;
Cassius from bondage will deliver Cassius. (I. 3.89–90)

Thinking that the conspirators are betrayed he may, mean it when he says, less melodramatically, that he will slay himself (III. 1. 21–2); he then descends to his most improbable gesture in the quarrel-scene, one strangely reminiscent of Caesar (who 'pluckt me open his doublet, and offered them his throat to cut', I. 2. 265):

There is my dagger,
And here my naked breast; within, a heart
Dearer than Plutus' mine, richer than gold;
If that thou be'st a Roman, take it forth. (IV. 3. 99–102)

When it comes to the point, however, he swiftly makes his decision, presses his sword upon Pindarus, covers his face (like Caesar again)—and all is over. In the fifth act a complicated man shrinks into 'the last of all the Romans', a mere husk of himself, perhaps because the whole act falls away, and the play itself contracts.

* * *

Most modern theatre-goers learn their Roman history from Shakespeare (and there are worse teachers). Educated Elizabethans knew the age of Cicero and Caesar from other sources, and Shakespeare must have taken their expectations into account, especially in his handling of the principal historical figures. There are several surprises, some of which the modern theatre-goer may not savour as he should.

Take Cicero. Mentioned twice in I. 2, he meets Casca in I. 3 and speaks four times, merely as a 'feed', where anyone else would have done as well. Thereafter we hear of him (II. 1. 141ff., IV. 3., 176ff.) but never see him again. Why then introduce him, when he might just as well have figured as a magic name, like Pompey and Cato? Presented in person Cicero raises expectations ('great spirits now on earth are sojourning') that Shakespeare chose not to meet, and thus helps to scale down his great contemporaries, even those who show real signs of greatness in the play.

Shakespeare also teased his audience, I think, in giving a one-sided view of Mark Antony before the assassination-scene. The historical Antony had already climbed too high to impress his fellow-Romans as 'but a limb of Caesar' or, at the worst, a 'shrewd contriver' who 'may well stretch so far / As to annoy us all'.[50] He had held many important offices, including that of general of the horsemen ('the second office of dignitie, when the Dictator is in the citie: but when he is abroad . . . the chiefest man', according to Plutarch).[51] At the time of the Lupercalia Antony was Consul, together with Caesar, and 'did stowtly withstand' him on at least one issue.[52] His deferential reply when told to touch Calphurnia—

> I shall remember.
> When Caesar says 'Do this', it is perform'd. (I. 2. 9–10)

—gives a totally different impression. Before Caesar's assassination the man about to emerge as one of the triumvirs seems little more than 'a masker and a reveller' (V. 1. 62), speaks just five times, and speaks only when spoken to (thirty-five words in all, his longest speech being one of two lines). Shakespeare reduced his stature in this part of the play, which must have puzzled some spectators—and thus made his metamorphosis in Act III all the more stunning, when Antony for the first time takes the initiative and (like the Silent Woman) finds his tongue.

The biggest surprise must have been the portrait of Caesar. Can we doubt that once again Shakespeare aimed at a divided response? We marvel at the public figure, and we smile at the private man—a simpler version of the divided response than in the case of Brutus, but similar in pulling the audience in different directions at once. Introducing so many unhistorical touches (Caesar's deafness, defencelessness against flattery, self-deception, and so on) the dramatist repeated a process that we have observed throughout this chapter: he disregarded history wherever the alternative was a special dramatic effect. Here, and indeed in all of the plays, Shakespeare was much less interested in history than in audience-response.

NOTES

1. *Richard III* and *Richard II* were described as tragedies on the Quarto title-pages. Though the authorship of *Titus Andronicus* has been much debated, there is now a tendency to accept it as immature but authentic Shakespeare.

2. See pp. 26–7.

3. Raleigh (ed.), *Johnson on Shakespeare*, p. 170.

4. M. W. MacCallum, *Shakespeare's Roman Plays and their Background* (1910) pp. 233–7.

5. *Julius Caesar*, ed. T. S. Dorsch (New Arden ed., 1955) p. xxxix.

6. *Narrative and Dramatic Sources of Shakespeare*, ed. Geoffrey Bullough, 8 vols (1957–75) v, p. 90. (Hereafter cited as Bullough, *Sources*.)

7. Ibid., pp. 92, 107, 116.

8. *Julius Caesar* V. 1. 100ff., IV. 3. 143–4.

9. I. 2. 295, V. 5. 26.

10. Dorsch (ed.), *Julius Caesar*, p. xl.

11. Bullough, *Sources*, p. 97.

12. In Plutarch the conspirators 'were every man of them bloudied' as they killed Caesar (ibid., p. 102).

13. Compare Cassius' then ('Stoop then') here and elsewhere when he gives way to Brutus: 'Then leave him out' (II. 1. 152.), '*Then*, with your will, go on' V. 3. 222).

14. See p. 32.

15. See p. 33.

16. I. 2. 314–19, II. 1. 36–58.

17. MacCallum, *Shakespeare's Roman Plays*, p. 201.

18. Dorsch (ed.), *Julius Caesar*, p. 33.

19. MacCallum, *Shakespeare's Roman Plays*, p. 264.

20. See Harold C. Goddard, *The Meaning of Shakespeare* (1965) I, 325. J. Dover Wilson (ed.), *Julius Caesar* (1949) p. 176, has argued that Cassius was suspected of taking bribes (IV. 3. 10–12) but not of extorting money, 'a very different thing. Nowhere does Shakespeare say that the money Brutus asks to share had been got "by vile means"'. But this is mere hair-splitting, for Brutus knows that the money Cassius might have lent him was acquired corruptly (line 15), i.e. by vile means.

21. Compare p. 38.

22. Bullough, *Sources*, p. 120.

23. Dorsch (ed.), *Julius Caesar*, p. xl.

24. IV. 3. 67–8, V. 1. 110–12 (compare p. 36). Brutus, of course, intends great mind as 'great spirit', but Shakespeare's irony seems as unmistakable as when Caesar talks of his constancy.

25. IV. 3. 201. Compare III. 1. 225, 238, III. 2. 7.

26. Bullough, *Sources*, p. 83.

27. Ibid., p. 85.

28. See Bullough, p. 102.

29. Compare pp. 33–4. A. C. Sprague (*Shakespeare and the Actors, 1660–1905*) (Cambridge, Mass., 1945, p. 321) mentions one Brutus who shrank from touching Caesar's hand, and adds that on the stage the conspirators did not often 'stoop and wash' in Caesar's blood.

30. MacCallum, *Shakespeare's Roman Plays*, p. 240.

31. Bullough, *Sources*, p. 86 (from the *Life of Julius Caesar*).

32. Compare Dover Wilson's stage direction (*Julius Caesar*, p. 45), which is nevertheless much closer to Plutarch than that in most modern editions. Notice that there is no support in Plutarch or Shakespeare for the common stage direction that Brutus strikes 'the last blow'. Plutarch says (in the *Marcus Brutus*) that when Caesar had cast his gown over his face the conspirators, 'thronging . . . to have a cut at him', accidentally hurt each other, Brutus being wounded in the hand (Bullough, *Sources*, p. 102); Marcus Brutus seems to have struck Caesar 'about his privities' in the general melee, his one and only blow; and Shakespeare may well have intended the same.

33. Editors describe Lucius as one of Brutus' *servants*. Though the Folio gives no indication of his exact status, it is reasonable to suppose that the boy who has to serve his master at all hours, and to follow him to the wars, will be a slave, a point that could be made visually by his costume and bearing. The lower his status, the more considerate is Brutus' treatment of him.

34. Bullough, *Sources*, p. 96.

35. Ibid., p. 98.

36 How was the quarrel-scene staged at the Globe? Dover Wilson thought that the 'inner stage' served as tent (*Julius Caesar*, p. 175). But there is no certainty that an inner stage existed, and there are two other possibilities: either the main stage itself becomes the inside of a tent, or a real tent was erected on the stage (as in *Richard III* V. 3, and several other plays of the period). If a real tent or mansion was used, the guards would be clearly visible to the audience; if not, the audience could still be made aware of the physical presence of the guards, just off-stage, by anxious glances from either Brutus or Cassius as the other speaks too loudly.

37. Bradley, *Shakespearean Tragedy*, p. 60.

38. See Ernest Schanzer, *The Problem Plays of Shakespeare* (1963) p. 65.

39. Dorsch (ed.), *Julius Caesar*, p. xli.

40. Granville-Barker, *Prefaces*, I, 58–60.

41. Bullough, *Sources*, pp. 268–9.

42. Dorsch (ed), *Julius Caesar*, p. li.

43. IV. 2. 47, IV. 3. 16, 20.

44. Bullough, *Sources*, pp. 114–15.

45. Granville-Barker, *Prefaces*, I, p. 60.

46. Kenneth Muir, *Shakespeare's Tragic Sequence* (1972) p. 51, believed that 'Shakespeare intended the duplicate revelation to stand'; Dorsch (*Julius Caesar*, p. 106) took the opposite view.

47. MacCallum, *Shakespeare's Roman Plays*, pp. 275ff. Compare Dorsch (ed.), *Julius Caesar*, pp. xlivff.; Muir, *Shakespeare's Tragic Sequence*, p. 53.

48. *The Devils* (Penguin ed., 1971), part II, section 6, p. 388, section 8, p. 420.

49. Dorsch (ed.), *Julius Caesar*, p. xxx.

52. II. 1. 165, 158ff.

51. Bullough, *Sources*, p. 260.

52. Ibid., p. 263.

—⟨ɰ/ɰ⟩— —⟨ɰ/ɰ⟩— —⟨ɰ/ɰ⟩—

2005—Andrew Hadfield. "The End of the Republic: *Titus Andronicus* and *Julius Caesar*," from *Shakespeare and Republicanism*

Andrew Hadfield is Professor of English at the University of Sussex. He is the author of *Shakespeare and Renaissance Politics* and other books on Renaissance literature.

... Five years later [1598], the Chamberlain's Men, having established themselves as a major company able to attract large audiences, made their new home at the Globe Theatre near Southwark Cathedral.[57] The first play they performed was Shakespeare's *Julius Caesar*. Yet again, a work on a conspicuously republican theme marks a key moment in Shakespeare's career, indicating that such subjects clearly caught the public imagination and that he wished to be known as the playwright who explored republican history.[58] The performance was watched by the Swiss traveller Thomas Platter and his party, perhaps an indication of the significance of the event. Platter notes that he 'witnessed an excellent performance of the tragedy of the first Emperor Julius Caesar', suggesting that he realized the significance of the play as a work about the death of the republic and the rise of imperial Rome.[59] Platter makes only two other references to the theatre in his account of London, observing that a playhouse can be seen on the south bank of the Thames west of the Tower, next to 'two rings for bull and bear baiting', and that prostitutes, a huge problem in the city, 'haunt the town in the taverns and playhouses'.[60] Platter's comments suggest that he was not a habitual theatregoer—one reason why his comments on *Julius Caesar* are so limited in comparison to his comments on other aspects of London life (inns, palaces, executions)—which further emphasizes the importance of the staging of the play.

Julius Caesar has often been read as though it could be accommodated into one of the prevailing modes of tragedy, its formal classification, principally because the main characters appear more 'rounded' and have greater psychological depth than those in Shakespeare's earlier plays.[61] It has also been read as a play of studied balance, exposing the limitations of creeping tyranny and the republican argument for selective political assassination.[62] However, the play appears in a different light if we read it as a work designed to intervene in the political debates of a culture that has a keen interest in republican history, issues and questions, an ambition that its first staging clearly signals. One of the great clichés of Shakespeare criticism is that the real hero of the Roman plays is Rome itself.[63] *Julius Caesar*, like *Titus Andronicus*, depicts a dying and perverted republican Rome that has lost the ability to inspire its citizens to behave virtuously.[64] Without this basic requirement the republic cannot function as a political force and will be superseded by a more suitable form of government, one that matches the needs and desires of the people. Rome has returned to a state that resembles the last days of the monarchy under the Tarquins—not quite the bloody anarchy that characterized the dying city under threat from the barbarians—rather than the apotheosis of the republican ideal.

However, as Shakespeare was undoubtedly aware, the republic was always an ideal that was in the process of becoming or receding. Its most celebrated writings describe either the hope that came with its foundation or the need to preserve a constitution about to disappear for ever. The main republican figure from the last days of the republic was not Brutus, whose actions are a parody of those of his famous ancestor, but Cicero, one of the most influential intellectual influences on the development of sixteenth-century European thought.[65] Cicero appears in Shakespeare's play as a minor character. The fact that he does not join the conspirators shows how their actions, however they are presented, are at odds with the proper goals of the republic.

Cicero is indeed a shadowy figure in *Julius Caesar*. The conspirators are aware of his presence and importance, but they never discover what he thinks even though he is always close to the main sites of the action. As Caesar enters after the games, Brutus describes Cicero in terms that indicate his importance, as well as the anxiousness he inspires in the conspirators. He says that Cicero 'Looks with such ferret and such fiery eyes / As we have seen him in the Capitol / Being crossed in conference by some senators'.[66] The conspirators do not know which way Cicero's sympathies will turn, a significant problem for them because of his status as one of the central figures in the republic, whose goal was a culture of deliberative oratory, designed to facilitate a public forum in which citizens could debate central issues on equal terms.[67] Given his central importance in late sixteenth-century England, the audience would have registered this failure as an exposure of the limitations of the conspiracy to assassinate Caesar. Cassius decides to send Caska to sound out Cicero. That this is done in secret, while Antony and Caesar discuss the loyalties of the Senate elsewhere on stage, reveals how fragmented Roman political culture has become, and how far from the stated aims of republicans such as Cicero.[68]

It is also significant that it is Caska who is sent to discover Cicero's loyalty. Caska is one of the most edgy of the conspirators, as Cassius tells him (1.3.57–78), keen to scoff at Caesar's pretensions, and later he is the first to stab him in the Capitol with the words, 'Speak hands for me!' (3.1.76), a sign that the oratory of the republic has run its course and the new form of political argument is violence. The scene which contains Caska's encounter with Cicero further reveals Caska's nervousness, a marked contrast to the Cicero's detachment. Caska, who enters with a drawn sword, lists all the strange phenomena happening in the city: tempests, unusual tides, a slave whose hand 'did flame and burn / Like twenty torches joined' (1.3.16–17) yet who remained unscathed, a lion wandering at large, a large group of women who swear that they have seen men engulfed in fire in the streets, and an owl screeching in the marketplace at noon. Yet Cicero remains a model of calm: 'Indeed it is a strange-disposed time. / But men may construe things after their fashion / Clean from the purpose of the things themselves' (lines 33–35). Given Caska's state of mind, it is not certain that everything he claims to have seen really exists. The scene serves as a counterpart to the portents observed by the equally sensitive Calpurnia (2.2.13–31). Nevertheless, it is Cicero's point that is the most telling. There are signs available to be interpreted, but the private meanings they yield shows that political culture in Rome is rapidly disintegrating. The search for shared meanings available to everyone is an implicit goal of Cicero's major works, notably his attempts to establish a workable Roman constitution in his dialogues on the commonwealth and the laws; and his vast array of speeches defending individuals accused of crimes by the state.[69]

Two other works are of even greater relevance to *Julius Caesar*. Cicero's last philosophical treatise, *De Officis* (*Of Duties*), was one of the most influential books published in England in the sixteenth century, occupying a central place in the school curriculum, going through numerous editions and translations, and being cited whenever there were discussions of virtue, government and citizenship.[70] *De Officis* was an attempt to articulate the political and ethical values of the Roman republic, outlining the duties Roman citizens owed to the collective state that was their country. The work, however, was composed after the assassination of Julius Caesar, when it seemed to Cicero that the ideals to which he had dedicated his life were in danger of disappearing for ever. It was dedicated to his son, Marcus, in itself a sign of the loss of values held in common and of a public sphere. Cicero is sharply critical of the militarized culture that has taken over Roman society and is openly nostalgic for the community and friendship that the republic fostered.

Cicero's social vision might usefully be linked to the opening scene of *Julius Caesar* in which the tribunes, Flavius and Murellus, try to persuade the plebeians to remove scarves tied on statues to celebrate Caesar's victory over Pompey (for which they are later said to have been 'put to silence' (1.2.285)).[71] Cicero pays due respect to citizens who behave well and help the republic through amassing wealth. The highest plaudits, however, are reserved for those who promote the public culture of the republic: 'Our judgement should be that the achievements which are greatest and show the greatest spirit are those of the men who rule the republic. For their government reaches extremely widely and affects the greatest number.'[72] As public culture declined in importance, resulting in the loss of oratory as a mode of public argument, greater emphasis was placed on the significance of conversation as a means of preserving the values of the republic.[73] As a result, there was also greater stress on the republican celebration of friendship.

Cicero's dialogue on friendship, *De Amicitia*, is the other work that is of most relevance to Shakespeare's play. Like *De Officis*, it was a key plank in the intellectual culture of sixteenth-century Europe.[74] Cicero's protagonists argue that friendship helped distinguish men from beasts, and was to be valued above virtually all worldly things.[75] Friendship cannot exist unless the two men involved are virtuous—a condition the treatise reiterates several times—making it a republican goal, one that can preserve the spirit of the republic even if the constitution is absent (fos. 10, 29). Friendship 'is geeven by Nature to bee an ayde to Vertue' (fo. 36). Tarquin, significantly enough, helped friends to unite against him and found friendship when he was expelled from office (fos. 14, 24), indicating that friendship was not a virtue easy for monarchs to practise. Friendship can withstand many disputes and disagreements, but not 'dissemblinge' (fos. 13, 29, 39), another point that is repeated at regular intervals. Moreover, friendship is not at odds with a Stoic philosophy of indifference to the world, as friends make each other's lives better through their relationships, establishing examples for others to copy (fo. 14). Friends must not break the law, as this invalidates their friendship and shows that they are too attached to the world to treat it with the correct amount of Stoic detachment (fos. 18–19). Friends need to 'delighte in justice and equitie' (fo. 35).

Julius Caesar portrays a state that bears only a passing resemblance to the republican ideals established by Cicero, who, knew that he was preserving for posterity an ideal that was dying. All the main conspirators, as well as the principal characters, in the play meet their untimely deaths in the aftermath of the assassination of Julius Caesar. Brutus and Cassius perish in the civil war with the combined forces of Antony and Octavius, each committing suicide during the Battle of Philippi. Before the battle, they receive letters informing them that seventy senators have been put to death as a result of their actions, 'Cicero being one' (4.3.176). Plutarch's 'Life of Cicero' informs us that Cicero was 'not only fearful in wars, but timorous in pleading' (p. 597). Nevertheless, he uses his impressive bearing, derived from his formidable oratorical skills, to confront the murderers Antony has sent, and meets his end with dignity:

> Cicero . . . commanded his men to set down his litter, and taking
> his beard in his left hand, as his manner was, he stoutly looked the
> murderers in the faces, his head and beard being all white, and his face
> lean and wrinkled, for the extreme sorrows he had taken: divers of them
> that were by, held their hands before their eyes, whilst Herennius did
> cruelly murder him. So Cicero being three score and four years of age,
> thrust his neck out of the litter, and had his head cut off by Antonius'
> commandment, and his hands also, which wrote the orations . . . against
> him. (p. 610)

Shakespeare would have known this account.[76] The absence of Cicero's voice within the play serves only to draw attention to his writings, and the lack of importance they have at this crucial historical juncture. Cicero's thought has no role in the militarized society that was developing under Caesar, something the opening scene demonstrates, as Caesar returns to celebrate a victory over his fellow Romans. His minor part in the action of *Julius Caesar* shows that he has become a private rather than a public citizen, anxious to keep his thoughts to himself (not surprisingly, perhaps, as according to Plutarch his death results as much from his attacks on Antony in his speeches as his association with the conspirators). But neither is he able to play any role in the conspiracy, a misguided attempt to restore the values of the republic to Rome. In between the two violent extremes the republic has retreated with Cicero, although its goal of individual liberty can, of course, be revived later.[77]

Shakespeare represents Roman society as a toxic mixture of decayed republicanism and emergent tyranny. There is no shared public culture, a fact emphasized by the stage arrangements which carefully divide up the characters into small groups whispering secrets to each other (few plays make such extensive use of the aside and clandestine meeting). Trials were one of the main features of the republic—as exemplified in Cicero's wide range of speeches, words that lead to his murder—but Flavius and Murellus can be silenced, Caesar assassinated, and seventy senators put to death without any due legal process at all. Superstition rather than reason, one of the defining attributes of republican society, dominates everyday life as portents are witnessed and interpreted in different ways.[78] Far from existing as a successful 'mixed' constitution, classes are at odds with each other, the tribunes opposing the actions of the Senate and the senators eager to displace the military commander who plays an uncertain role but whom they fear will emerge as a tyrant and end the liberties they have enjoyed as citizens of the republic.[79]

The word 'liberty' is not mentioned in the first two acts. However, after the assassination of Caesar it becomes the watchword of the conspirators as a means of justifying their actions. As soon as Caesar is dead, Cinna cries, 'Liberty! Freedom! Tyranny is dead! / Run hence, proclaim, cry it about the streets' (3.1.78–79), as though producing the words themselves ensured that the reality would immediately follow. This was, of course, the case when Tarquin was deposed—although, even then, a protracted war had to be fought with the forces loyal to the Roman monarchy. Yet, when Brutus directs that they all bathe their hands 'Up to the elbows' and cover their swords in Caesar's blood, 'Then . . . walk forth even to the market-place', waving their weapons and crying '"Peace, Freedom, and Liberty"' (lines 108–10), the naivety of the conspirators' assumptions is painfully, almost comically, evident.[80]

This scene, one that Shakespeare invented, shows that the actions of the second Brutus are a parody of those of the first. We know that the attempt to restore the republic was always doomed to fail. The institutions of the republic are too feeble to be revitalized. Those who supposedly guard their spirit have either retreated into private life, like Cicero, or replaced collective action with violent conspiracy. Whereas there was strong popular support for the birth of the republic, as all historical accounts make clear, in *Julius Caesar* the conspirators have to persuade the people to follow their lead. Their isolation from the population they supposedly represent makes them acutely vulnerable to more astute populist politicians such as Antony. Liberty appears as a concept that suddenly erupts in the aftermath of a bloody act, something that almost has to be imposed on a reluctant, uncomprehending people who, like the conspirators, have lost sight of what functions their institutions—the Senate and other political offices, the law courts, the forum, and so on—actually serve. Caesar's rise to potential tyranny is not simply a result of his own efforts. Rome exists as a militarized culture weary from years of civil war, very similar to the society that Shakespeare had already represented in *Richard III* in which post–civil war England bore a striking resemblance to imperial Rome. Rome has gone too far to be saved from itself. In Plutarch's 'Life of Marcus Brutus', Faonius, a follower of Marcus Cato the Stoic, makes the telling point 'that civil war was worse than tyrannical government usurped against the law' (p. 822).

The actions and behaviour of the characters further demonstrate how much the ideals of the republic have decayed and not yet been replaced by the more austere philosophy of imperial Rome, designed as a means of living under tyranny. Brutus and Portia are shown to be an affectionate and well-matched couple in their only scene together. Yet, for all her loyalty, virtue and republican credentials, Brutus will not tell Portia the substance of his secret plans, however hard she pleads with him. Their marriage exists as a parallel to that of Caesar and Calpurnia—Caesar ignores his wife's advice not to venture out on the Ides of March (2.2)—when political logic suggests that they should be strikingly different. Portia reminds Brutus that there should be no secrets within a marriage (2.1.279–81), but he maintains his silence even though he praises her as his 'true and honourable wife' (line 287), a description that is both gender-neutral and could also be read as casting her as a loyal republican, honour being the reward of true virtue.[81] Portia's protestations show that she realizes that it is her sex that has served to exclude her from the conspiracy. Commenting on his praise of her virtue, Portia argues:

> If this were true, then I should know this secret.
> I grant that I am a woman: but withal
> A woman that Lord Brutus took to wife.
> I grant I am a woman: but withal
> A woman well reputed, Cato's daughter.
> Think you I am no stronger than my sex
> Being so fathered and so husbanded?
> Tell me your counsels. I will not disclose 'em.
> I have made strong proof of my constancy,
> Giving myself a voluntary wound,
> Here in the thigh. Can I bear that with patience
> And not my husband's secrets? (lines 191–301)

Portia asks to be treated as an equal and to be allowed to share Brutus's life in an exchange which is Shakespeare's invention and therefore a gloss on the private lives of eminent Romans in the dying republic. The culture of secrecy and spying, a situation that would have reminded many playgoers of their own times, dictates otherwise, but if Brutus were acting to save his wife pain and suffering, he evidently fails.[82] Roman philosophy was characterized by Stoicism, but we witness the rash and rather over-passionate suicide of Portia, a parody of the Stoic ideal as represented via the death of Cato, her father, one of the heroes of the Pharsalia, and later Lucan and Seneca the Younger.[83] Portia appeals to one of the central Stoic principles, 'constancy' (line 298), struggling with her weak, female nature. Her self-inflicted wound is an act that protests too much, which, in Cynthia Marshall's words, 'directs attention inward, toward the vulnerable interior of her bodily self'.[84] Furthermore, it apes the violent plot of her husband, as well as showing how debased the ideals of the republic have become, so that self-mutilation stands as a sign of honour (given what represents virtue in his marriage, it is perhaps hardly surprising that Brutus imagines that an excess of blood will symbolize liberty).[85]

Republicanism was invariably cast as a masculine phenomenon, and was established over the dead body of a woman, as the myth of the birth of the republic demonstrates. Portia's heroic struggle with herself, which reads like a parody of Elizabeth's professions of her androgynous nature, shows that the strength of the republic is ebbing away and it is returning to the effeminacy/hypermasculinity of tyranny.[86] When left alone in her last scene (2.4), Portia again appeals to 'constancy', demonstrating that women's role in late republican Rome is to suffer in isolation: 'Set a huge mountain 'tween my heart and tongue. / I have a man's mind, but a woman's might. / How hard it is for women to keep counsel' (lines 6–8). Portia is overwhelmed by fear after her discussion with the soothsayer, another sign that reason has been usurped by superstition in Rome. The broken syntax of her last words before her suicide further indicates the crisis of values in Rome:

> Ay me, how weak a thing
> The heart of woman is. O Brutus,
> The heavens speed thee in thy enterprise.
> Sure the boy heard me. Brutus hath a suit
> That Caesar will not grant. O, I grow faint:
> Run, Lucius, and commend me to my lord.
> Say I am merry. Come to me again
> And bring me word what he doth say to thee. (lines 40–47)

The lines are hardly the most memorable in the play. However, they reveal a number of points that confirm our understanding of the action. Portia is struggling to maintain an equilibrium that proves impossible, as is the rest of Rome. Her chaotic syntax and distracted thought patterns express the confusion that is endemic in Rome. She is perturbed by Brutus's enterprise yet dependent on him for direction, again, just like the rest of Rome. And she has no real sense of his plans, imagining that he has a suit to take to Caesar, a notion undoubtedly gleaned from overhearing the conversations of the conspirators. Her death, unlike that of Lucrece, which it repeats and so parodies, leads nowhere. The exhausted Brutus, on the verge of death and defeat, simply notes the causes: she was 'Impatient of my absence' and was afraid of the growing power of Octavius and Antony's army (4.3.150–52).

Marriage is not the only relationship between supposed equals which does not function properly in the play. Friendship is also shown not to work as the republican ideal of Cicero demanded it should, Cicero's own isolation within Roman society dramatically pointing up the gap between theory and practice. Friendship has become a private and furtive affair, whereas *De Amicitia* stated that it should be a relaxed and public manifestation of a healthy society. Brutus and Cassius clearly have a mutual bond of comradeship expressed in their final words to each other before the fateful Battle of Philippi (5.1.120–26). But their relationship is increasingly characterized by argument and division, most fatefully in Brutus's famous insistence that Antony be allowed to deliver Caesar's funeral oration (3.1.232–42), and then later with their dispute over tactics in the next act, which sees Brutus sweeping aside Cassius's objections to his plan that they seek an immediate confrontation with the enemy. On each occasion Cassius's commonsense is overruled by Brutus's disastrous principles: each time with the polite use of the term 'pardon' (2.2.235; 4.3.211). Cicero explicitly warns friends against this sort of behaviour. Friendship needs to preserve truth and virtue and will not work properly if the two friends involved do not allow themselves to correct each other when the occasion demands. Cicero states that 'freendes must often times bee both admonished and chidden . . . And this is to bee friendly taken, when it is done freendlye and of good will' (fo. 38). Brutus is at fault for refusing to take advice, and Cassius is to blame for not correcting his friend.

There are other flaws in their friendship. When they first meet and start to plot the overthrow of Caesar, we might imagine that Brutus and Cassius act as equals planning an enterprise together. But when Brutus departs, Cassius reveals that he is manipulating his partner, leading him towards a predetermined course of action, using what he sees as Brutus's good nature, universal popularity and high principles:

> Well, Brutus, thou art noble: yet I see
> Thy honourable mettle may be wrought
> From that it is disposed. Therefore it is meet
> That noble minds keep ever with their likes.
> For who so firm that cannot be seduced?
> Caesar doth bear me hard, but he loves Brutus.
> If I were Brutus now, and he were Cassius,
> He should not humour me. I will this night
> In several hands in at this window throw,
> As if they came from several citizens,

Writings all tending to the good opinion
That Rome holds of his name—wherein obscurely
Caesar's ambition shall be glanced at.
And after this, let Caesar seat him sure,
For we will shake him, or worse days endure. (1.2.306–21)

Although the last lines show that Cassius does have honourable motives for wanting to assassinate Caesar, we also learn that he has personal reasons for wishing to do so, having been slighted by the dictator. In Huguenot treatises that argued that tyrants could be assassinated, such as *Vindiciae, Contra Tyrannos*, magistrates who undertook such drastic actions were supposed to be pure in spirit as befitted their role as servants of God and the people.[87] Cassius is evidently not such a creature. Shakespeare is following Plutarch's hostile description of Cassius's motives: 'Cassius being a choleric man, and hating Caesar privately, *more than he did the tyranny openly*, he incensed Brutus against him' (my emphasis) ('Life of Marcus Brutus', p. 810). Cassius plans to use Brutus because he is trusted, and admits that he would not be persuaded by his own arguments, an observation that establishes an inherent imbalance in their alliance. The attempt to fake popular support by throwing stones at the window once again stresses the fragmented nature of Roman society and the isolation of the conspirators.

Cassius's behaviour further violates the rules of proper friendship as determined by Cicero. Cicero argues that dissimulation invalidates friendship: 'Dissimulation in all thinges is euill (for it taketh awaye the righte judgement of truthe and corrupteth it) yet namely to Friendshippe it is most repugnant. For it raseth out the truth, without which, the name of Frendshippe cannot endure' (fo. 39). (Republican) friendship depends on virtue and any violation of this fundamental principle renders proper friendship invalid: 'For sithens the opinion of Vertue is the breeder of frendshippe, it is harde for Frendshippe to remayn, if a man swerve from Vertue' (fo. 18). Cicero also argues that friendship is invalidated if a friend tries to persuade another to commit an unlawful act. The assassination of Caesar may or may not fall under this heading, but Cassius's impure motives reveal the dangers involved in such an enterprise.[88]

Cassius grows more passionate towards Brutus near the end of the play, petulantly demanding that Brutus kill him because Brutus loved Caesar more than him: 'Strike as thou didst at Caesar: for I know, / When thou didst hate him worst, thou lov'dst him better / Than ever thou lov'dst Cassius' (4.3.104–6). In contrast, Brutus tries to be as little affected by the mutable nature of the world as is possible. Throughout *Julius Caesar*, Brutus attempts to treat everyone with equal concern, rationally assessing how he should behave towards them. Following Stoic principles, he does not react with excessive grief to the death of his wife; he persuades himself that it is best if Caesar is killed, even though he is

Caesar's friend; he allows Antony to speak to the people in the name of fairness
and friendship, even though it is obvious to all concerned that this is a recipe
for disaster; and he maintains his friendship with Cassius on general, egalitarian,
republican principles. When they part for the last time, Cassius utters words of
affection for his friend, 'For ever and for ever farewell, Brutus: / If we do meet
again, we'll smile indeed; / If not, 'tis true parting was well made' (5.1.120–22).
Brutus sticks to more general, quasi-philosophical terms and practical matters:

> Why then, lead on. O that a man might know
> The end of this day's business ere it come:
> But it sufficeth that the day will end,
> And then the end is known. Come ho, away. (lines 123–26)

The similarity to his reaction to the death of Portia is striking. Cicero, arguing
for the central importance of friendship in men's lives, claims that 'A man void
of al affections is like a logg or a stone' (fo. 22), a perpetual danger that Stoicism
courted.[89] Brutus certainly runs the risk of appearing too detached from the
world to be properly human.

The friendship of Cassius and Brutus has to be weighed against that of
Antony with his now-dead friend, Caesar. Antony's passionate loyalty to Caesar
is more obviously appealing than Brutus's detached indifference to people and
loyalty to an ideal. Brutus's willingness to use friendship for his own ends, revenge
on the conspirators, balances Cassius's manipulation of Brutus to persuade him
to help carry out the killing of Caesar. Once again, the society of Rome appears
as a perversion of republican principles. Antony's funeral oration for Caesar is
Shakespeare's expansion of the bare details provided by Plutarch who notes that
he mingles 'his oration with lamentable words', and so moves them 'unto pity
and compassion' for the dead Caesar. When he shows the people the 'bloody
garments of the dead, thrust through in many places with their swords', Antony
puts 'the people into such a fury' that they burn Caesar's body in the market-
place and then run 'to the murderers' houses to set them afire, and to make them
come out and to fight' ('Life of Marcus Antonius', p. 689). Antony's statement
when he is left alone on stage in Shakespeare's play, 'Now let it work. Mischief,
thou art afoot: / Take thou what course thou wilt' (3.2.251–52), shows that he is
prepared to use friendship to further his personal revenge, just as Cassius was.

The central feature of the republic at its height was rhetoric, the public art
of persuasion, enabling listeners to weigh up the evidence on either side of any
argument and choose the right way forward.[90] The rights and wrongs of Brutus's
assassination of Caesar was, in fact, a historical case that was often cited as
an example of a problem that should be debated by aspiring orators eager to
persuade an audience.[91] In his dialogue *Brutus*, written in c. 55 BCE, before the
assassination (44 BCE), Cicero represents Marcus Junius Brutus as an urbane and

keen student of oratory, keenly aware of its passage from Greece to Rome and its central place within the social fabric of the republic.[92] Titus Pomponius Atticus constructs a familial and intellectual genealogy linking Brutus and his namesake and ancestor:

> Who, for example, can suppose that Lucius Brutus, the founder of your noble family, was lacking in ready wit, who interpreted so acutely and shrewdly the oracle of Apollo about kissing his mother; who concealed under the guise of stupidity great wisdom; who drove from the state a powerful king, son of a famous king, and freeing it from the domination of an absolute ruler fixed its constitution by establishing annual magistrates, laws, and courts; who abrogated the authority of his colleague so that the very memory of the regal name might be obliterated? All this certainly could not have been accomplished without the persuasion of oratory.[93]

Atticus's use of a series of rhetorical questions—a form of anaphora (repetito), 'where the same word is repeated at the beginning of a sequence of clauses or sentences'—serves to link the political and social purpose of oratory to the generations of the Brutus family.[94] Lucius Junius Brutus's oratorial skills, even though they are not immediately apparent, are instrumental in driving out the hated monarchy of the Tarquins. The keen interest shown in oratory by Marcus Junius Brutus is part of the same process. In using his own powers of persuasion, Atticus establishes the continuity of the republic.

Cassius persuades Brutus to join the conspiracy by using exactly the same parallel:

> O, you and I have heard our fathers say
> There was a Brutus once that would have brooked
> Th' eternal devil to keep his state in Rome
> As easily as a king. (1.2.157–60)[95]

However, what we witness in Julius Caesar is the paucity of republican oratory, a confirmation of the republic's drastic decline. Brutus, for all his obvious qualities as the 'noblest Roman of them all', the only one of the conspirators whom Antony acknowledges acted out of pure motives rather than 'envy of great Caesar' (5.5.68–69), is an ineffective orator. His virtue is at odds with the body politic, as his troubled personal relationships with Portia and Cassius demonstrate. Whereas Cicero's Brutus is a key figure who holds the Roman republic together, Shakespeare's is easily outmanoeuvred and defeated by Antony, a better friend and orator, whose angry passion serves him well. The Stoic ideal of the rule of reason and the control of the emotions has been superseded by fierce tribal loyalties as dictatorship and tyranny replace the republic.[96]

Brutus's soliloquy in his orchard betrays a circular reasoning that does not
follow the accepted rules of forensic oratory, established principally by Cicero:

> It must be by his death: and for my part
> I know no personal cause to spurn at him
> But for the general. He would be crowned;
> How that might change his nature, there's the question.
> It is the bright day that brings forth the adder,
> And that craves wary walking . . .
> . . . and to speak truth of Caesar
> I have not known when his, affections swayed
> More than his reason. But 'tis common proof
> That lowliness is young ambition's ladder
> Whereto the climber upward turns his face;
> But when he once attains the upmost round
> He then unto the ladder turns his back,
> Looks in the clouds, scorning the base degrees
> By which he did ascend. So Caesar may.
> Then, lest he may, prevent. (2.1.10–15, 19–27)[97]

Given that what is to be carried out is effectively a legal judgement, that Caesar
deserves to die, Brutus should adhere to the guidelines for judicial oratory in
making the case against Caesar. Instead, he decides what has to be done before
his fellow conspirators arrive, an indication of the perverse relationship that
exists between the public and the private spheres in Rome. What should be
an art of persuasion has become a personal meditation in which the answer is
already known and the reasoning follows the conclusion. The imperative ('must')
is followed by a series of conditionals ('would', 'might', 'may'), indicating that the
cart has been placed before the horse. There is, in fact, no evidence in Brutus's
speech—nor in the play—that Caesar will definitely become the tyrant that
Brutus claims he will. What is certain is that his assassination leads to tyranny—
although whether Brutus's actions are a sufficient or necessary condition of the
triumph of Augustus and the reigns of Tiberius, Caligula, Claudius and Nero is
impossible to prove.

Thomas Wilson, the author of *Arte of Rhetorique* (1560), one of the most
influential English treatises on rhetoric in the sixteenth century, follows Cicero
in dividing oratory into three distinct forms: demonstrative, deliberative and
judicial.[98] Demonstrative oratory was used 'when a man is commended or
dispraised, for any acte committed in his life'; deliberative oratory is designed
to 'perswade, or disswade, entreate, or rebuke, exhorte, or dehorte, commende,
or comforte any man'; and judicial oratory 'is an earnest debatyng in open
assemblie in some weightie matter before a judge, where the complainaunt

commenseth his action, and the defendaunt thereupon aunswereth at his peril to al suche thynges as are laied to his charge'.[99] Brutus's soliloquy could be read as a combination of all three types of oration: the speech does 'dispraise' Caesar for acts he may well commit as dictator; it is designed to persuade the speaker that he is acting in the right way; and it condemns Caesar to death. Of course, Brutus is not entirely to blame for the impure and eccentric nature of his argument. There is no public forum for him to practise his oratory, a problem Cicero experienced in his own career and which resulted in his placing greater emphasis on the virtues of friendship than the arts of public persuasion. Wilson, again following Cicero, argued that any speech should conform to a pattern, having seven parts: the entrance or beginning; the narration; the proposition; the division; the confirmation; the confutation; and the conclusion.[100] Yet Brutus's speech demonstrates no principle of organization: the argument does not develop logically; the examples are not persuasive because they are not based on any observation or evidence; there is no consideration of the contrary case, specifically in the use of proverbial wisdom (Caesar climbing the ladder of ambition), which is not balanced by an argument with an opposite case leading to a considered conclusion.

Brutus's speech is not, of course, an oration as such. However, given what is at stake, it appears to be a shadow of the proper sort of argument that ought to be made. Certainly the extensive arguments made in monarchomach literature were clear that resistance to tyrants who were oppressing the people was the only available option for would-be liberators. The questions posed centred around the issue of who could carry out the deed, not whether tyranny could be predicted and killed before it hatched, as Brutus's concluding metaphor claims (lines 31–34).[101]

The speech Brutus gives in the market-place after Caesar's death confirms our understanding of his lack of rhetorical skills, a failing that exposes the absence of republican sophistication rather than simply demonstrating his plain honesty or commitment to the ideals of Stoicism.[102] Brutus speaks in prose and makes the unconvincing case that, although he loved Caesar in many ways, he killed him because 'he was ambitious' (3.2.26), an argument that does not even reach the rhetorical level of his soliloquy. He is demonstrating his lack of interest in, even contempt for, the public institutions and spaces that used to characterize republican Rome and which his ancestor helped establish, persuading the people to take action against the Tarquins after the rape of Lucrece. Antony is able to subvert Brutus's use of the term 'honour' with ease, partly because he has only to dispute the one negative trait that Brutus has attributed to Caesar, 'ambition'. Brutus makes no mention of the disastrous effects of the civil wars, of the silencing of the tribunes, of the decline of the republic, or of the fears he and the other conspirators have for the future, allowing Antony to represent the dead Caesar, not without reason, as a populist in tune with the immediate needs of the ordinary citizens, as he reads out Caesar's will promising each citizen seventy-five drachmas and leaving his orchards and private arbours beside the Tiber for their 'common pleasures' (line 241).[103] Antony uses one of the most important cultural and political legacies of the republic, public oratory, to help destroy the republic, continuing the civil wars that signalled its decline into dictatorship. He also uses his friendship with Caesar—another chief republican virtue—to the same end as he demonstrates in his soliloquy over the dead body of Caesar:

> O pardon me, thou bleeding piece of earth,
> That I am meek and gentle with these butchers.
> Thou art the ruins of the noblest man
> That ever lived in the tide of times.
> Woe to the hand that shed this costly blood . . .
> A curse shall light upon the limbs of men:
> Domestic fury and fierce civil strife
> Shall cumber all the parts of Italy:
> Blood and destruction shall be so in use,
> And dreadful objects so familiar,
> That mothers shall but smile when they behold
> Their infants quartered with the hands of war. (3.1.254–58, 262–68)

Shakespeare's dramatic representation of Antony's speech is a significant elaboration of the brief description of his words in Plutarch's 'Life of Marcus Brutus'.[104] Antony is a war monger who does not have the good of the state at heart—unlike Brutus—and his reputation for a fatal combination of reckless cruelty and sensual indulgence is a more culpable version of Brutus's paralysing division of his life into the public and private spheres.[105]

The political charge of a staging of the story of Julius Caesar in 1599 is obvious enough, even if it is only in relatively recent times that the relationship has been recognized.[106] As Ian Donaldson has pointed out, 'it is reasonable to say that any play concerned with conspiracy, political ambition, and the assassination of a ruler was bound to be of absorbing interest to audiences in England in the late 1590s, who would no doubt have seen some broad resemblances to their own times in the political uncertainties and jockeyings for power of late Republican Rome'.[107] The connections the play makes between the two historical situations are perhaps rather more wide-ranging than even this perceptive comment suggests. *Julius Caesar* does not just chart the power struggles of an elite which clearly resembled those taking place in the last years of Elizabethan England and expose the uncertainty of the succession. Such connections were routinely made in the drama of the 1590s and would have done little on their own to distinguish the play from numerous other works competing for the attention of the theatregoing public.[108] More significantly, Shakespeare's play represents a necrotic body politic that has abandoned its healthy republican institutions and values, allowing its citizens to lapse into vice. Brutus's attempt to reestablish republican values is itself tainted by these vices—secrecy, contempt for the citizenry, the decline of the art of persuasion, and so on—and so doomed to failure, represented most eloquently in his naive faith that bathing oneself in the victim's blood will ensure the support of the populace. Republican values have become reduced to the public badge of murder. As in the early English history plays, the public sphere shrinks from the general control of the many to the concern of a few who, to adapt the words of Thersites in *Troilus and Cressida*, a play written in the wake of *Julius Caesar*, 'yoke [them] like draught-oxen and make [them] plough up the war'.[109] Shakespeare may not, of course, be alluding to a specific war, although everyone in London knew that war in Ireland was imminent in 1599, and his next play, *Henry V*, is written as an 'at war' play.[110] But the disenfranchised citizens of Rome had no stake in their collective destiny and it may have been this aspect of their lives that struck the English audience at the Globe. Certainly their political and intellectual life bore little resemblance to that outlined in the extensive writings of Cicero, which were supposedly one of the chief sources of Elizabethan culture.

NOTES

57. See Peter Thomson, *Shakespeare's Professional Career* (Cambridge: Cambridge University Press, 1992), pp. 101–3; Andrew Gurr, *The Shakespearean Stage, 1574–1642* (3d ed., Cambridge: Cambridge University Press, 1999), pp. 142–52. See also Janette Dillon, *Theatre, Court and City, 1595–1610* (Cambridge: Cambridge University Press, 2000), *passim*.

58. A very different interpretation of the pivotal importance of *Julius Caesar* is provided in Steve Sohmer's somewhat eccentric *Shakespeare's Mystery Play: The Opening of the Globe Theatre, 1599* (Manchester: Manchester University Press, 1999).

59. Thomas Platter, *Thomas Platter's Travels in England, 1599*, trans. Claire Williams (London: Cape, 1937), p. 166. See also Richard Wilson, '"Is this a holiday?": Shakespeare's Roman Carnival', in Wilson, ed., *Julius Caesar: Contemporary Critical Essays* (Basingstoke: Palgrave, 2002), pp. 55–76, at pp. 55–56.

60. Platter, *Travels*, pp. 64, 175.

61. See, for example, A. D. Nuttall, *A New Mimesis: Shakespeare and the Representation of Reality* (London: Methuen, 1983), pp. 99–114; Alan Bloom with Harry V. Jaffa, *Shakespeare's Politics* (Chicago: University of Chicago Press, 1964), ch. 4; Wells, *Wide Arch*, ch. 3.

62. See Blair Worden, 'Shakespeare and Politics', *Sh. Sur.* 44 (1991), 1–15; Robert S. Miola, '*Julius Caesar* and the Tyrannicide Debate', *RQ* 36 (1985), 271–90; Alexander Leggatt, *Shakespeare's Political Drama: The History Plays and the Roman Plays* (London: Routledge, 1988), ch. 6.

63. Wells, *Wide Arch*, p. 15; Geoffrey Miles, *Shakespeare and the Constant Romans* (Oxford: Clarendon Press, 1996), pp. 1–2.

64. Kahn, *Roman Shakespeare*, p. 90.

65. For an example of Cicero's influence on an ordinary writer, see Haly Heron, *The Kayes of Counsaile: A New Discourse of Morall Philosophie* (1579), ed. Virgil B. Heltzel (Liverpool: Liverpool University Press, 1954), p. 3, *passim*. More generally, see Howard Jones, *Master Tully: Cicero in Tudor England* (Nieuwkoop: Bibliotheca Humanistica & Reformatorica, Vol. LVII, 1981); Jennifer Richards, *Rhetoric and Courtliness in Early Modern Literature* (Cambridge: Cambridge University Press, 2003); John O. Ward, 'Cicero and Quintillian', in Glyn P. Norton, ed., *The Cambridge History of Literary Criticism: Volume III, The Renaissance* (Cambridge: Cambridge University Press, 1999), pp. 77–87; Virginia Cox, *The Renaissance Dialogue: Literary Dialogue in its Social and Political Contexts, Castiglione to Galileo* (Cambridge: Cambridge University Press, 1993), *passim*.

66. William Shakespeare, *Julius Caesar*, ed. David Daniell (London: Thomson: The Arden Shakespeare, 1998), 1.2.185–87. Subsequent references to this edition in parentheses in the text.

67. In Plutarch's 'Life of Marcus Brutus', the conspirators do not ask Cicero to join them because 'although he was a man whom they loved dearly, and trusted best: for they were afraid that he being a coward by nature, and age also having increased his fear, he would quite turn and alter all their purpose, and quench the heat of their enterprise, the which specially required hot and earnest execution': Plutarch, *Selected Lives*, ed. Judith Mossman (Ware: Wordsworth, 1998), p. 822. Subsequent references to this edition in parentheses in the text.

68. See Kahn, *Roman Shakespeare*, pp. 82–90.

69. Cicero, *On the Commonwealth and On the Laws*, ed. James E. G. Zetel (Cambridge: Cambridge University Press, 1999). For the speeches, see, for example, *The Speeches: Pro Lege Manilia, etc.*, trans. Hodge; *The Speeches: Pro Sestio, In Vatinium*, trans. R. Gardner (London: Heinemann, 1958).

70. Richards, *Rhetoric and Courtliness*, *passim*; T. W. Baldwin, *William Shakspere's Small Latine and Lesse Greeke*, 2 vols. (Urbana: University of Illinois Press, 1944), *passim*; John O. Ward, 'Renaissance Commentators on Ciceronian Rhetoric', and Paul O. Kristeller, 'Rhetoric in Medieval and Renaissance Culture', in James P. Murphy, ed., *Renaissance Rhetoric: Studies in the Theory and Practice of Renaissance Rhetoric* (Berkeley: University of California Press, 1983), pp. 126–73, and pp. 1–20, at p. 3.

71. Cicero, *On Duties*, trans. M. T. Griffin and E. M. Atkins (Cambridge: Cambridge University Press, 1991), p. 25. See also *Marcus Tullius Ciceroes three bookes of duties to Marcus his sonne, tourned out of Latine into English, by Nicolas Grimald* (London, 1583).

72. Cicero, *On Duties*, p. 36.

73. Richards, *Rhetoric and Courtliness*, p. 47.

74. Ibid., p. 3; Baldwin, *William Shakspere's Small Latine*, *passim*; William Shakespeare, *The Two Gentlemen of Verona*, ed. William C. Carroll (London: Thomson: The Arden Shakespeare, 2004), introduction, pp. 3–18.

75. Cicero, *Fowre Severall Treatises of M. Tullius Cicero: Conteyninge his most learned and eloquent discourses of Frendshippe, Oldage, Paradoxes: and Scipio his Dreame*, trans. Thomas Newton (London, 1577), fo. 8. Subsequent references to

this edition in parentheses in the text. For an image of bad friendship, see Geoffrey Whitney, *A Choice of Emblems* (1586) (ed. Henry Green [1866], rpt. New York: Verlag, 1970, p. 24.

76. Stuart Gillespie, *Shakespeare's Books: A Dictionary of Shakespeare Sources* (London: Athlone, 2001), pp. 106–12, 425–36; Robert S. Miola, *Shakespeare's Reading* (Oxford: Oxford University Press, 2000), pp. 98–109.

77. See Rebecca Bushnell, '*Julius Caesar*', in Dutton and Howard, eds., *Companion to Shakespeare's Works: Volume III, The Comedies*, pp. 339–56, at p. 348.

78. See Jonathan Scott, 'Classical Republicanism in Seventeenth-Century England and the Netherlands', in van Gelderen and Skinner, eds., *Republicanism*, I, pp. 61–81; Simone Zurbuchen, 'Republicanism and Toleration', in van Gelderen and Skinner, eds., *Republicanism*, II, pp. 47–71. More generally, see Jill Kraye, 'Philologists and Philosophers', in Kraye, ed., *The Cambridge Companion to Renaissance Humanism* (Cambridge: Cambridge University Press, 1996), pp. 142–60.

79. Kahn, *Roman Shakespeare*, p. 86.

80. For comment, see Katherine Duncan-Jones, 'Did the Boy Shakespeare Kill Calves?', *RES*, ns, 55 (2004), 183–95; Edward Berry, *Shakespeare and the Hunt: A Cultural and Social Study* (Cambridge: Cambridge University Press, 2001), pp. 186–94.

81. Peltonen, *Classical Humanism*, pp. 34–35, 113–14.

82. On secrecy and spying and its relationship to literature, see Robert Maslen, *Elizabethan Fictions: Espionage, Counter-espionage and the Duplicity of Fiction in Early Elizabethan Prose Narratives* (Oxford: Clarendon Press, 1997); Curtis C. Breight, *Surveillance, Militarism and Drama in the Elizabethan Era* (Basingstoke: Palgrave, 1996); David Riggs, *The World of Christopher Marlowe* (London: Faber, 2004), chs. 7, 12–14.

83. Lucius Annaeus Seneca, *Letters from a Stoic*, trans. Robin Campbell (Harmondsworth: Penguin, 1969); Janet Coleman, *A History of Political Thought*, 2 vols. (Oxford: Blackwell, 2000), I, chs. 5–6. On the conception of Stoicism in the Renaissance, see Jill Kraye, 'Moral Philosophy', in Charles B. Schmitt and Quentin Skinner, eds., *The Cambridge History of Renaissance Philosophy* (Cambridge: Cambridge University Press, 1988), pp. 303–86, at pp. 360–75; Miles, *Shakespeare and the Constant Romans*, ch. 7.

84. Cynthia Marshall, 'Portia's Wound, Calphurnia's Dream: Reading Character in *Julius Caesar*', in Wilson, ed., *Julius Caesar*, pp. 170–87, at p. 173.

85. See the well-known analysis in G. Wilson Knight, *The Wheel of Fire: Interpretations of Shakespearean Tragedy* (London: Routledge, 1989, rpt. of 1930), ch. 6. See also Gail Kern Paster, '"In the spirit of men there is no blood": Blood as Trope of Gender in *Julius Caesar*', in Wilson, ed., *Julius Caesar*, pp. 149–69.

86. On Elizabeth, see Carole Levin, *The Heart and Stomach of a King: Elizabeth I and the Politics of Sex and Power* (Philadelphia: University of Pennsylvania Press, 1994). On tyranny, see Rebecca Bushnell, *Tragedies of Tyrants: Political Thought and Theater in the English Renaissance* (Ithaca, N.Y.: Cornell University Press, 1990).

87. Stephanus Junius Brutus, the Celt, *Vindiciae, Contra Tyrannos, or, concerning the legitimate power of a prince over the people, and of the people over a prince* (1579), ed. George Garnett (Cambridge: Cambridge University Press, 1994), pp. 63–66.

88. For analysis of the discussion of the rights and wrongs of the killing of Caesar, see Miola, '*Julius Caesar* and the Tyrannicide Debate', 271–90; Paulina Kewes, '*Julius Caesar* in Jacobean England', *The Seventeenth Century* 17 (2002), 155–86.

89. William L. Davidson, *The Stoic Creed* (Edinburgh: T. & T. Clark, 1907), p. 156; E. Vernon Arnold, *Roman Stoicism* (Cambridge: Cambridge University Press, 1911), p. 366.

90. For analysis of this notion in the Renaissance, see Wayne C. Rebhorn, *The Emperor of Men's Minds: Literature and the Renaissance Discourse of Rhetoric* (Ithaca, N.Y.: Cornell University Press, 1995), ch. 1.

91. See Michael Wood, *In Search of Shakespeare* (London: BBC, 2003), p. 52. See also Thomas Wilson, *Arte of Rhetorique*, ed. Thomas J. Derrick (New York: Garland, 1982), p. 143.

92. The treatise on eloquence, *Orator*, was also addressed to Brutus: see Cicero, *Brutus and Orator*, trans. H. M. Hendrickson and H. M. Hubbell (London: Heinemann, 1952). Shakespeare refers to this work in *Titus Andronicus*, 4.1.14: see Gillespie, *Shakespeare's Books*, p. 109.

93. Cicero, *Brutus and Orator*, pp. 53–55.

94. Brian Vickers, *In Defence of Rhetoric* (Oxford: Clarendon Press, 1988), p. 491; Wilson, *Arte of Rhetorique*, pp. 399–400.

95. For comment, see Leggatt, *Shakespeare's Political Drama*, p. 140; Miola, *Shakespeare's Rome*, pp. 81–82.

96. Kraye, 'Moral Philosophy', in Schmitt and Skinner, eds., *Cambridge History of Renaissance Philosophy*, 1988), pp. 303–86, at pp. 365–68.

97. For analysis, see Kahn, *Roman Shakespeare*, pp. 90–91.

98. Wilson, *Arte of Rhetorique*, bk. 1; Cicero, *De Oratore*, trans. E. W. Sutton and H. Rackham, 2 vols. (London: Heinemann, 1959), I, p. 99.

99. Wilson, *Arte of Rhetorique*, pp. 54, 76, 184.

100. Ibid., pp. 33–34; Cicero, *De Oratore*, I, p. 99.

101. Brutus, *Vindiciae, Contra Tyrannos*, pp. 50–66; Buchanan, *Law of Kingship*, pp. 155–57, *passim*; Robert M. Kingdon, 'Calvinism and Resistance Theory, 1550–1580', in Burns and Goldie, eds., *Cambridge History of Political Thought*, pp. 193–218.

102. For discussion, see Miles, *Shakespeare and the Constant Romans*, ch. 7.

103. On Caesar's popularity, see Plutarch, 'Life of Julius Caesar', in *Selected Lives*, ed. Mossman, p. 519.

104. Plutarch, 'Life of Marcus Brutus', in *Selected Lives*, ed. Mossman p. 830. 105 See also Plutarch, 'Life of Marcus Antonius', in *Selected Lives*, ed. Mossman, pp. 677–756.

106. See Ian Donaldson, '"Misconstruing Everything": *Julius Caesar* and *Sejanus*', in Grace Ioppolo, ed., *Shakespeare Performed: Essays in Honour of R. A. Foakes* (Newark: University of Delaware Press, 2000), pp. 88–107, at p. 89. See also Wayne C. Rebbhorn, 'The Crisis of the Aristocracy in *Julius Caesar*', *RQ* 43 (1990), 78–109; Bushnell, '*Julius Caesar*'; Robin Headlam Wells, '*Julius Caesar*, Machiavelli, and the Uses of History', *Sh. Sur.* 55 (2002), 209–18, p. 211.

107. Donaldson, '"Misconstruing Everything"', pp. 90–91.

108. For discussion, see Axton, *The Queen's Two Bodies*; David Bevington, *Tudor Drama and Politics: A Critical Approach to Topical Meaning* (Cambridge, Mass.: Harvard University Press, 1968), chs. 17–18.

109. *Troilus and Cressida*, ed. David Bevington (London: Thomson: The Arden Shakespeare, 1998), 2.1.1003–4.

110. I owe this point to Jim Shapiro. On the Irish war, see Steven G. Ellis, *Tudor Ireland: Crown, Community and the Conflict of Cultures, 1470–1603* (London:

Longman, 1985), ch. 9. See also Nicholas de Somogyi, *Shakespeare's Theatre of War* (Aldershot: Ashgate, 1998); Nina Taunton, *1590s Drama and Militarism: Portrayals of War in Marlowe, Chapman and Shakespeare's Henry V* (Aldershot: Ashgate, 2001).

BIBLIOGRAPHY

Alexander, Catherine M. S. *Shakespeare and Politics.* Cambridge: Cambridge University Press, 2004.

Bloom, Harold. *Shakespeare's "Julius Caesar."* New York: Riverhead Books, 2005.

———. *William Shakespeare.* Modern Critical Views series. Philadelphia: Chelsea House, 2003.

Bonjour, Adrien. *The Structure of "Julius Caesar."* Liverpool: Liverpool University Press, 1958.

Brown, John Russell. *Shakespeare's Dramatic Style: "Romeo and Juliet," "As You Like It," "Julius Caesar," "Twelfth Night," "Macbeth."* New York: Barnes & Noble, 1971.

Brown, John Russell. *Shakespeare: The Tragedies.* New York: Palgrave, 2001.

Burckhardt, Sigurd. *Shakespearean Meanings.* Princeton, N.J.: Princeton University Press, 1968.

Burke, Kenneth. "Antony in Behalf of the Play." *Southern Review* 1 (1935): 308–319.

Champion, Larry S. *The Essential Shakespeare: An Annotated Bibliography of Major Modern Studies.* 2nd ed. New York: G.K. Hall, 1993.

Charney, Maurice. *Shakespeare's Roman Plays: The Function of Imagery in the Drama.* Cambridge, Mass.: Harvard University Press, 1961.

Coles, Blanche. *Shakespeare Studies: "Julius Caesar."* 1940. Reprint, New York: AMS Press, 1969.

Daiches, David. *Shakespeare: "Julius Caesar."* London: Arnold, 1976.

Dean, Leonard Fellows, ed. *Twentieth-century Interpretations of "Julius Caesar": A Collection of Critical Essays.* Englewood Cliffs, N.J.: Prentice-Hall, 1968.

Eagleton, Terry. *Shakespeare and Society: Critical Studies in Shakespearean Drama.* London: Chatto & Windus, 1967.

Evans, Bertrand. *Shakespeare's Tragic Practice.* New York: Oxford University Press, 1979.

Fairchild, Arthur Henry Rolph. *Shakespeare and the Tragic Theme.* Columbia: University of Missouri, 1944.

Garber, Marjorie B. *Shakespeare After All*. New York: Pantheon Books, 2004.

Hamer, Mary. *William Shakespeare: "Julius Caesar."* Plymouth, UK: Northcote House, 1998.

Heilman, Robert B., ed. *Shakespeare, the Tragedies: New Perspectives*. Englewood Cliffs, N.J.: Prentice-Hall, 1984.

Howard-Hill, T. H. *Shakespearian Bibliography and Textual Criticism: A Bibliography*. 2nd ed. Signal Mountain, Tenn.: Summertown, 2000.

Knowles, Ronald. *Shakespeare's Arguments with History*. Houndmills, UK: Palgrave, 2002.

Martindale, Charles, and A. B. Taylor, eds. *Shakespeare and the Classics*. Cambridge: Cambridge University Press, 2004.

Miola, Robert S. *Shakespeare's Rome*. Cambridge: Cambridge University Press, 1983.

Phillips, James Emerson. *The State in Shakespeare's Greek and Roman Plays*. New York: Columbia University Press, 1940.

Ripley, John. *"Julius Caesar" on Stage in England and America, 1599–1973*. Cambridge: Cambridge University Press, 1980.

Rosenblum, Joseph. *Shakespeare: An Annotated Bibliography*. Pasadena, Calif.: Salem Press, 1992.

Schanzer, Ernest. "The Problem of *Julius Caesar*." *Shakespeare Quarterly* 6 (1955): 297–308.

———. *The Problem Plays of Shakespeare: A Study of "Julius Caesar," "Measure for Measure," "Antony and Cleopatra."* London: Routledge & Kegan Paul, 1963.

———. "The Tragedy of Shakespeare's Brutus." *ELH: A Journal of English Literary History* 22 (1955): 1–15.

Siegel, Paul N. *Shakespeare's English and Roman History Plays: A Marxist Approach*. Rutherford, N.J.: Fairleigh Dickinson University Press, 1986.

Sohmer, Steve. *Shakespeare's Mystery Play: The Opening of the Globe Theatre 1599*. Manchester, UK: Manchester University Press, 1999.

Strindberg, August. *"Julius Caesar:* Shakespeare's Historical Drama." In *Shakespeare and Scandinavia: A Collection of Nordic Studies*, edited by Gunnar Sorelius, 19–30. Newark, Del.: University of Delaware Press, 2002.

Thomas, Vivian. *Julius Caesar*. New York: Twayne Publishers, 1992.

———. *Shakespeare's Roman Worlds*. London: Routledge, 1989.

Traversi, Derek Antona. *Shakespeare: The Roman Plays*. Stanford, Calif.: Stanford University Press, 1963.

Ure, Peter. *Shakespeare: "Julius Caesar," a Casebook*. London: Macmillan, 1969.

Van Doren, Mark. "Literature and Propaganda." *Virginia Quarterly Review* 14 (1938): 203–208.

Watson, Robert N. *Shakespeare and the Hazards of Ambition*. Cambridge, Mass.: Harvard University Press, 1984.

Wells, Stanley, ed. *Shakespeare: A Bibliographical Guide*. New York: Oxford University Press, 1990.

Wells, Stanley, and Lena Cowen Orlin, eds. *Shakespeare: An Oxford Guide*. Oxford: Oxford University Press, 2003.

Wilson, J. Dover. "Ben Jonson and *Julius Caesar*." *Shakespeare Survey* 11 (1949): 36–43.

Wilson, Richard, ed. *Julius Caesar*. New Casebooks edition. New York: Palgrave, 2002.

Zander, Horst, ed. "Julius Caesar": *New Critical Essays*. New York: Routledge, 2005.

ACKNOWLEDGMENTS

❧

Twentieth Century

Knight, G. Wilson. "The Eroticism of *Julius Caesar*." In *The Imperial Theme: Further Interpretations of Shakespeare's Tragedies Including the Roman Plays*, 63–95. London: Oxford University Press, 1931.

Burke, Kenneth. "Antony in Behalf of the Play." In *The Southern Review* 1 (1935–1936): 308–319. © 1935–1936 by Louisiana State University Press.

Granville-Barker, Harley. "The Play's Structure." In *Prefaces to Shakespeare*, Volume II, 189–213. Princeton, NJ: Princeton University Press, 1946. Reprinted by permission of the Society of Authors as literary representative of the estate of Harley Granville-Barker.

Auden, W. H. "Julius Caesar." In *Lectures on Shakespeare*, reconstructed and edited by Arthur Kirsch, 125–137. Princeton, N.J.: Princeton University Press, 2000. © 2000 by the Estate of W. H. Auden; lectures given from 1946 to 1947.

Goddard, Harold C. "Julius Caesar." In *The Meaning of Shakespeare*, pp. 307–330. Chicago: University of Chicago Press, 1951. © 1951 by the University of Chicago.

Dorsch, T. S. "Introduction: Language and Imagery." In *Julius Caesar*, edited by T. S. Dorsch, lxi–lxix. 6th ed. The Arden Edition of the Works of William Shakespeare. 1955. Reprint, Cambridge, Mass.: Harvard University Press, 1958.

Mehl, Dieter. "Julius Caesar." In *Shakespeare's Tragedies: An Introduction*, 133–152. Cambridge: Cambridge University Press, 1986. © 1986 (for the English translation) by Cambridge University Press. Reprinted with the permission of Cambridge University Press.

Bloom, Harold. "Introduction." In *William Shakespeare's* Julius Caesar, edited by Harold Bloom. Bloom's Notes series. New York: Chelsea House, 1996. © 1996 (for the Introduction) by Harold Bloom.

Twenty-first Century

Kermode, Frank. "Julius Caesar." In *Shakespeare's Language*, 85–95. New York: Farrar, Straus & Giroux, 2000. © 2000 by Frank Kermode. Reprinted by permission of the publisher.

Honigmann, E.A.J. "Sympathy for Brutus." In *Shakespeare: Seven Tragedies Revisited: The Dramatist's Manipulation of Response*, 30–53. Rev. ed. Houndmills, UK: Palgrave, 2002. © 1976, 2002 by E.A.J. Honigmann. Reprinted with permission of Palgrave Macmillan.

Hadfield, Andrew. "The End of the Republic: *Titus Andronicus* and *Julius Caesar*." In *Shakespeare and Republicanism*, 167–183. Cambridge: Cambridge Univerisity Press, 2005. © 2005 by Cambridge University Press. Reprinted with the permission of Cambridge University Press.

INDEX